Upgrade Your Life

Upgrade Your Life

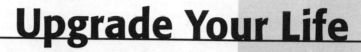

The Lifehacker Guide to Working Smarter, Faster, Better

Gina Trapani

WILEY

Wiley Publishing, Inc.

Upgrade Your Life: The Lifehacker Guide to Working Smarter, Faster, Better

Published by
Wiley Publishing, Inc.
10475 Crosspoint Boulevard
Indianapolis, IN 46256
www.wiley.com

Copyright © 2008 by Gawker Media
Published by Wiley Publishing, Inc., Indianapolis, Indiana
Published simultaneously in Canada

ISBN: 978-0-470-23836-3

Manufactured in the United States of America

10 9 8 7 6 5 4 3 2 1

Library of Congress Cataloging-in-Publication Data
Trapani, Gina, 1975-
  Upgrade your life : the Lifehacker guide to working smarter, faster, better / Gina Trapani.
    p. cm.
  Includes index.
  ISBN 978-0-470-23836-3 (pbk : web)
  1. Microcomputers. 2. Time management. 3. Computer software. 4. Internet. I. Title. II. Title: Lifehacker guide to working smarter, faster, better.
  QA76.5.T6737 2008
  004.16—dc22
                              2008001371

Dedicated to Terra, my favorite reason to finish work faster

About the Author

Gina Trapani (http://ginatrapani.org) is a web programmer and technology writer whose work has been mentioned in *Wired* magazine, *The Wall Street Journal*, *The New York Times*, *O, The Oprah Magazine*, and *TIME Magazine*. She is the founding editor of Lifehacker.com, a daily blog on software and productivity, which she and her editorial staff update up to twenty times a day. A Sun Microsystems–certified Java programmer, Gina builds web sites and Firefox extensions. When she's not surfing the Web, you can find her surfing the waves of sunny San Diego, California.

Credits

Executive Editor
Carol Long

Development Editor
Maryann Steinhart

Production Editor
Dassi Zeidel

Copy Editor
Susan Christophersen

Editorial Manager
Mary Beth Wakefield

Production Manager
Tim Tate

**Vice President and
Executive Group Publisher**
Richard Swadley

**Vice President and
Executive Publisher**
Joseph B. Wikert

Project Coordinator, Cover
Lynsey Stanford

Compositor
Kate Kaminski,
Happenstance Type-O-Rama

Proofreader
Candace English

Indexer
Robert Swanson

Cover Designer
Michael Trent

Cover Image
© Alan Sirulnikoff and
Will Knight/Jupiter Images

Contents

Acknowledgments

Second chances are a rare and special gift in this life. I am so thankful for the opportunity to put out a second edition of this book. My name may be on the cover, but many people were behind this book's latest incarnation.

First and foremost, I have to thank my mate, Terra, whose support and partnership make everything I do possible. Thanks to Lifehacker.com's publisher, Nick Denton, for funding my compulsive blogging habit. Thanks to my agent, David Fugate, at LaunchBooks and several folks at Wiley, especially Maryann Steinhart, Dassi Zeidel, and David Mayhew, for midwifing this book. Thanks to Patric and Su at House of Pretty for making my online alter ego a complete hottie, and for conceiving the killer Lifehacker logotype, which graces the cover of this book and Lifehacker.com. Countless thanks to my co-editor at Lifehacker.com, Adam Pash, not only for taking the reins at the web site while I wrote but also for being one of the most hard-working, upstanding, and thoughtful tech writers in the business. Special thanks to Danny O'Brien for hacking my life by coining the term *life hack*, as well as Merlin Mann and David Allen for their inspirational, oft-quoted work in personal productivity. Also, thanks to my mom for finally learning how to send me text messages. You can do it, Ma!

Last but not least, thanks to the community of readers at Lifehacker.com, especially samhealer and the rest of the Lifehacker book mailing-list membership. Your email messages and comments informed every page of this book and make me smile at my computer screen every day. You all are the sharpest knives in the Internet's kitchen drawer.

Introduction

"The highest-performing people I know are those who have installed the best tricks in their lives."

David Allen, productivity expert [1]

Every day, you have dozens of opportunities to get work done faster, smarter, and more efficiently — with the right shortcuts. Contrary to what some "gurus" will tell you, there's no single, life-changing secret to working less and living more. The reality is that small changes practiced over time yield big results.

There are hundreds of simple techniques and small adjustments you can make to the way you work that will help you get done and get out the door with a clear mind and a clean slate. Armed with the right know-how, you can put tech tools to work for you and be more effective, efficient, and on top of your game than ever before.

Thousands of web sites, software apps, and gadgets promise to make your life easier. I've spent the last three years hunting down, testing, and writing up each and every one of them on Lifehacker.com, a weblog that my editorial team and I update almost twenty times a day with the latest and greatest in software and productivity technology. This book highlights the cream of that crop. These tricks will fast-track you through tedious work, solve common computer problems we all face, and give you access to information anywhere you need it. Whether you're a middle manager at a huge corporation or a freelancer who works at home, a PC or Mac user, or someone just comfortable enough to get around or a power user, there's something here for you.

The most precious thing anyone has in this life is time. Spend more time *doing* things and less time fiddling with your computer. This book shows you how.

Computer Manual Meets Productivity Book

This book isn't a computer user manual, and it isn't a productivity system — it's a little bit of each. It isn't an exhaustive guide to all the features of a particular software application or gadget. You won't find seven habits or four steps to becoming a productivity powerhouse. Instead, this book takes established personal-productivity principles and outlines 116 concrete ways to apply those concepts in your everyday work. This is where the rubber hits the road, dear reader: here, you learn how to practice big-picture productivity methods on your very own computer desktop.

I don't work for a software or gadget company. As an independent software developer, I'm simply obsessed with the ways that computers can help humans get things done. In this book, you'll find information you won't get in the user manual: practical applications of the features you should actually care about, and nothing else. Alpha geeks use the tools outlined in this book. Now it's time for you to get in on the good stuff as well.

Pick Your Tricks

Think of this book as a giant buffet of shortcuts. No one person will use all of them. You're going to browse its contents and add to your plate only the ones that can help you. Instead of reading this book from cover to cover, read each chapter introduction, which describes a productivity challenge. The rest of the chapter is a collection of clever tricks — or "hacks" — that can tackle it. The best hacks for your work and life depend on your needs, your skill level, your situation, and your biggest pain points.

For example, do you get too much email and struggle to keep on top of all your incoming messages? Go directly to Chapter 1, "Control Your Email." Have you been procrastinating on checking anything off an impossibly long to-do list? Proceed to Chapter 3, "Trick Yourself into Getting Done." Are constant interruptions and distractions keeping you from getting work done? See Chapter 5, "Firewall Your Attention." Want to shave seconds or minutes off of computer chores you do every day? You want Chapter 6, "Streamline Common Tasks." Are you sick of doing the same boring, tedious jobs every day? Have a helping of hacks from Chapter 7, "Automate Repetitive Tasks."

To help you choose your best tricks, each hack appears with the platform (or operating systems) and the skill level of the user it applies to.

Your Operating System (Matters Less, But Still Matters)

Some readers of the first edition told me they'd like to see a Mac-only or a Windows-only version of this book. However, as operating systems converge and the Web matures, desktop operating systems matter less. As application software moves off our desktop and onto the Web, it takes only an Internet-connected computer with a modern web browser from any OS to get things done (more on that topic in Hack 69). Today, file and network compatibility among Mac, Windows versions, and even Linux is a nonissue. You can run Windows on your Mac (see Hack 114) or boot Linux from a CD or thumb drive on your PC (see Hack 108). More open-source software is cross-platform and free (such as Mozilla Firefox, which appears throughout this volume.) Almost all other software has an equivalent on other operating systems. In the coming years you'll use more computers with more operating systems than you ever did before. (Weren't you just considering switching to a Mac? Or was it Linux?)

Therefore, this book is as operating system-inclusive as I could make it. Whenever possible, I recommend software that runs on Windows, Mac, and Linux. Failing that, I include both Mac and Windows solutions. However, the platform listed on many of the hacks within is simply "Web," which applies to everyone.

Your Skill Level

Finally, if you're a power user worried this book will be too basic, or a beginner wondering whether it's too technical, fear not. Each hack in this book has a user skill-level rating — Easy, Medium, or Advanced:

- **Easy:** You are comfortable enough on your computer to get by, but that's it. You know how to browse the folders on your computer's hard drive to attach a document to an email message. You know there are lots of interesting tech tricks out there that you wish you knew how to do, but you don't know where to start. You want the hacks labeled "Easy."

- **Medium:** You've been using computers for some time now and you're comfortable putting together Excel formulas, downloading music, finding elusive information on Google, or helping your grandpa get his email set up. Maybe you have your own blog, and you set up a wireless Internet connection at home yourself. You should check out the hacks labeled "Medium" and "Easy."

- **Advanced:** You're the family tech-support geek, the one everyone calls when they're having a computer problem. You've survived a hard drive crash or two; maybe you administer a web site. You've delved into the deepest settings on your computer, such as the Windows registry, or you have experience at the command line — or at least feel confident that you'd be able to teach yourself those things easily. Hacks marked "Easy" will be yawners to you, but the "Advanced" and "Medium" hacks will feed your head.

What the Heck Is a "Lifehacker"?

Contrary to the popular misuse of the term to denote a computer criminal, a hacker is someone who solves a problem in a clever or nonobvious way. A life hack is a workaround or shortcut that overcomes the everyday difficulties of the modern worker. A lifehacker uses clever tech tricks to get her work done.

A Brief History of Life Hacks

In 2004, tech journalist Danny O'Brien interviewed several people he called "over-prolific alpha geeks" — skilled and highly productive technologists whose continuous output seemed unaffected by the constant disruptions of modern technology. O'Brien hoped to identify patterns in the way these productive techies managed their work processes. Commonalities did emerge, and the term *life hacks* was born.[2]

These so-called alpha geeks had developed uncommon systems and tricks for getting through their daily drudgery. They used simple, flexible tools such as text files and email. They avoided bloated, complex software. They imposed their own structures on their information and set up mechanisms that filtered and pushed the data they needed in front of their eyes at the right time automatically while keeping the rest at bay.

The life hacks concept resonated with geeks across the Internet, including the one typing these words. A movement was born. In January of 2005, I began writing Lifehacker.com, a daily weblog devoted to life hacks.

Three years later, I have the privilege of sharing the best life hacks that came out of that work with you in these pages.

Bonus Material at Lifehackerbook.com

Time flies, and technology moves fast. As I wrap up this manuscript in December of 2007, I fear that by the time it reaches you, tools I've described will have already morphed. Luckily, we have the Internet.

At this book's companion web site, `http://lifehackerbook.com`, you'll find hack updates, additional information, and even tips and tricks that didn't make the final cut. Navigate directly to a single chapter's hack list by visiting `http://lifehackerbook.com/chx/`. (Substitute the x for any chapter number you want.)

Just remember: on your deathbed, you'll never say, "I wish I'd checked my email more often!" Go forth and start using tech to spend less time working and more time living.

References

1. David Allen, *Getting Things Done* (Penguin Books, 2001), 85.
2. "Interview: father of 'life hacks' Danny O'Brien," Lifehacker.com, March 17, 2005 (`http://lifehacker.com/software/interviews/interview-father-of-life-hacks-danny-obrien-036370.php`).

Control Your Email

Do you wish you received less email? Sure you do. Do you want to live without the convenience of electronic mail? Of course you don't. The greatest double-edged sword in productivity technology, email both empowers and overwhelms its users. But the most successful professionals know how to control their email instead of letting it run their workday.

On one hand, email enables anyone with an Internet-connected device to send information great distances at the press of a button. On the other, you've got 1,762 unread messages sitting in your inbox, and you don't know when you'll have time to get through them all. *Ding!* Another one just arrived.

Before email became ubiquitous, to send a letter, a person had to commit the information to paper, stuff and address the envelope, affix postage, and drop it in the mailbox. Days or weeks later, the message arrived on the recipient's desk. Today, email offers the same type of text-based communication, just faster and easier, complete with a cute little envelope icon. But the same ways you deal with arriving postal mail don't work on electronic mail. Incoming messages are incoming messages. But email's effect on workers is vastly different from paper mail for one fundamental reason: volume. The speed, convenience, and low cost of sending email has increased the number of transmissions to levels that turn the postal service green with envy: about 150 *billion* emails are sent daily.

This virtually free and instantaneous message transmission is great for the sender but not for the recipient. The cost and inconvenience of sending postal mail acts as a filter: when that envelope appears in the recipient's mailbox, she can trust that the message is important enough to the sender to warrant the investment.

Electronic mail, however, shifts that burden. With the volume of electronic mail sent each day, the onus is on the recipient — not the sender — to sort through the avalanche of messages she's received. Email overload is such a common malady in the information age that experts estimate it costs companies billions of dollars a year in worker productivity losses.

Some companies and users resort to extreme tactics to combat email overload:

- In 2004, Stanford professor Lawrence Lessig declared "email bankruptcy" when faced with the thousands of unread messages dating back two years that had accumulated in his inbox. Instead of attempting to open them all — a task he said would have been impossible — he sent an automated apology to his contacts and asked that they resend their unanswered message only if it was still very important.[1] A web search for the term "email bankruptcy" shows that several others followed suit, publicly announcing their email bankruptcy on their web sites.

- Overwhelmed by the effort that writing lengthy responses requires, designer Mike Davidson instituted a personal policy that any message he writes will be fewer than five sentences. Recipients who wonder about the brevity can get more information about the policy, which he includes in his message signature.[2]

- One cellular company designated a weekly email-free day. Employees refrain from sending or checking email (except from customers) every Friday. Workers report that the freedom from the distraction and interruption once a week helps them accomplish a lot more.[3]

Anyone who's spent hours processing a backlog of email can understand why you'd take such tactics. It's so easy to let email take the reins of your workday. All you have to do is leave your email software open while you work. Each time it notifies you that a new message has arrived, stop what you're doing, no matter how important it is or how involved you are, and switch to your inbox. Scan the new message. If it's an emergency, deal with it right away. If not, switch back to the task at hand. Try to remember where you were before that message arrived. At the end of the day, wonder how all those read messages accumulated in your inbox, what you're supposed to do about them again, and where the day went.

This is how most people operate. But there is a better way.

You can reduce the amount of time you spend fiddling with email to less than 30 minutes per day. You can empty your inbox and enjoy the feeling that you're completely caught up every single workday. You can process your messages in bunches, in between other tasks, when your mind is free and clear. You can hear "Thanks for getting back to me so quickly" from your boss and co-workers more and more often. You can elicit the response you need in shorter exchanges. You can keep your inbox free of a festering pile of unfulfilled obligations. You can become known as responsive — and therefore responsible — engaged, and reliable around the office simply by being on top of your email. Soon, wealth, fame, and fortune will ensue.

You can control your email without declaring bankruptcy or refraining from using it just because it's a certain day of the week. Small changes and better habits practiced every day can get the constant influx of communication working *for* you instead of against you. This chapter provides practical strategies for getting your email under control and keeping it there.

NOTE For updates, links, references, and additional tips and tools regarding the hacks in this book, visit http://lifehackerbook.com/. (Append the chapter number — http://lifehackerbook.com/ch1/, for example — to go directly to a specific chapter's updates.)

Hack 1: Empty Your Inbox (and Keep It Empty)

Level....... **Easy**
Platforms ... **All**
Cost .... **Free**

When you can empty your inbox on a regular basis, you've reached the ultimate level of email control. Emptying the inbox clears away that pile of unidentified pieces of information, keeps it from stacking up higher every day, and frees your mind to worry about more important work.

Why an Empty Inbox?

Your inbox is a temporary holding pen for unprocessed messages. An unprocessed email is one you haven't made a decision about yet. When you get into the habit of deciding what to do with a new message within a day of its arrival, move it out of your inbox.

Some people enjoy keeping their inbox full so that they can glance at a list of most recent messages and see what's going on — what they should be working on, what their group is discussing, the latest funny YouTube video that's making the rounds. But just as you'd never leave a physical paper inbox full of documents whose only commonality is that they're *incoming*, so you don't want to leave your email inbox full of messages, either. An inbox full of read messages does you no favors: You have no way to prioritize what's most important, or to access the message contents in their most useful context. For example, a meeting invitation that comes in via email is much more meaningful on your calendar than in your inbox. A web site address you want to visit later would do better in your bookmarks than in your email. A project document belongs in its appropriate folder, not in your email program. Everything should have its own place, and the inbox isn't it.

Furthermore, an empty inbox lightens the psychological load of an endless list of messages staring at you every time you check your email. It creates a clear demarcation between what's incoming and what's been resolved or placed into motion.

This hack introduces a simple, three-folder system that keeps your inbox clear and ensures that every single message you receive is both findable and actionable without cluttering your inbox.

Set Up the Trusted Trio of Folders

The three folders you need to keep your inbox empty and your messages in process are Archive, Follow Up, and Hold, as shown in Figure 1-1.

NOTE Some email programs — most notably Gmail (http://gmail.com) — have a built-in message archive. In that case you don't need to create an Archive label or folder. Simply use the program's built-in archived message storage place (which you can get to by clicking on "All Mail.")

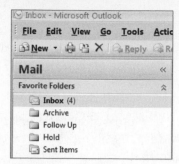

Figure 1-1 Archive, Follow Up, and Hold folders clear your inbox.

The Archive Folder

Most email you receive is stuff you don't need right now but may need to look up later. Archive these messages. The Archive is your long-term email reference library. It's where you place all the messages that contain information you may want to retrieve at some point in the long-term future, including any completed threads, completed requests, memos you've read, questions you answered, and completed project email. Basically, any email exchange that's closed but that you may want to refer to at some point in the future belongs in the Archive.

The Archive is one single folder, with no subfolders. That's a scary concept to those who enjoy organizing information into specifically named folders. However, you're not a librarian, and you don't have time to waste deciding what message should go in what folder. The archive is completely searchable. You can retrieve any message you place there later using the right search operators. For more on plucking messages out of the Archive (without a complicated folder scheme), see Hack 6, "Master Message Search."

The Follow Up Folder

Messages in your Follow Up folder represent tasks you must complete, whether that's a response that will take more than a minute to write or whether it's another type of action. Each of these messages maps to a task on your to-do list. A message from a long-lost high school friend whom you haven't spoken to in years and a request from the boss to update the quarterly report would both go into the Follow Up folder because you need to follow up with an action. It's not enough to just move this message into the `Follow Up` folder; make sure you also enter the task onto your to-do list — so that you'll actually do it.

The Hold Folder

The `Hold` folder is a temporary holding pen for important messages you'll need quick access to within the next few days. If you're waiting on someone else to get back to you with crucial information, or you're maintaining a thread about a time-sensitive topic, keep it in the `Hold` folder.

Examples of messages that would go in `Hold` are a FedEx confirmation number for a delivery that's on its way, or a message from a co-worker that says, "I'll get back to you Tuesday re: The Big Project."

Review the `Hold` folder once a week, and clear it out as the messages in it become irrelevant — such as when that FedEx package gets delivered or when your co-worker gets back to you.

Process Your Messages

Now that the three folders are in place, it's time to empty your inbox. Whether you're starting with an overstuffed inbox with months' worth of messages or the two dozen that arrived since you last checked, the method is the same. Beginning with the oldest email in your inbox, open the message and do the following:

- Delete it if you don't need it.
- Respond on the spot to quick questions or requests. Then archive or delete it.
- If it requires action that will take more than one minute to complete, move it to the `Follow Up` folder and add the task to your to-do list.
- If it's an item you're waiting on or may need within the next few days, move it to `Hold`. If it's time-sensitive (your co-worker promised you the document by Friday, for instance), add a note on your calendar to check in about the item you're waiting for.
- If it's an informational message you may want to refer to later, move it to the `Archive`.

Wash, rinse, and repeat for every message in your inbox until it is completely empty.

NOTE This exact folder scheme may not work for everyone, but it's a good start on the road to a simple, well-defined processing system. If you tweak and modify this method, just remember: the fewer folders you have, the less thought has to go into dealing with each individual message.

Keep It Empty

After you've emptied your inbox, keeping it that way is a matter of repeating the process a few times a day. Schedule regular email sessions — such as once mid-morning, once after lunch, and once in the late afternoon. Train yourself to follow the golden rule:

Never leave a read email in your inbox.

Make a decision about the fate of every message you read the first time you read it — no excuses. Be ruthless about this new practice. File information that incoming messages contain in its right place: dates in your calendar; project documents in their folder; web site addresses in your bookmarks. Respond on the spot to messages that need a quick yes or no. Never touch an email in your inbox more than once.

Technologist Mark Hurst wrote, "Consider that an incoming email has the shelf life of Chinese takeout in the refrigerator. It's best to eat it as soon as it arrives; within a day is OK, but after that it starts to get funky."[4]

Your First Time

If you're starting out with an inbox loaded with thousands of messages, emptying it the first time can be an overwhelming task. One way to get started with your new good habits *right now* is to move all your existing messages into a separate, special folder (email management expert Merlin Mann calls it the "Email DMZ"[5]).

Resolve to empty your inbox each time you check from this moment forward. Then, during each processing session, *after* you empty your inbox, take on a handful of the oldest messages in your "DMZ" folder as well. Slowly but surely, you'll catch up on the backlog *and* hone your new good habits as you go.

The Catch

Just because you have all unresolved messages filed neatly away in Follow Up and Hold doesn't mean you're free and clear. The trick to this system is to consistently review Follow Up folder messages (which should be on your to-do list) and Hold folder messages, and to complete the items stowed away there. To keep yourself from getting lulled into a total sense of completeness, you can mark all the messages in Hold and Follow Up as unread to easily monitor the number of outstanding items.

NOTE Special thanks to Merlin Mann, author of the Inbox Zero series (http://inboxzero.com) and "The Inbox Makeover," which appeared in MacWorld magazine (available at http://macworld.com/2005/04/features/tipsinbox/index.php) and which greatly influenced the methods outlined in this hack.

Hack 2: Decrease Your Response Time

Level. . . . . . . **Easy**
Platform. . . . **All**
Cost . . . . **Free**

Responding to your email in a timely manner is one of the best things you can do for your career. But no one emerges from the womb with a natural talent for parrying a constant stream of new messages vying for your attention all day long. Email responsiveness is an acquired skill — the one that just may differentiate you from everyone else in the world who's overwhelmed by an overloaded inbox.

Michael Hyatt, CEO of Thomas Nelson Publishers, agrees. He said, "The truth is, you are building your reputation — your brand — one response at a time. People are shaping their view of you by how you respond to them. If you are slow, they assume you are incompetent and over your head. If you respond quickly, they assume you are competent and on top of your work. Their perception, whether you realize it or not, will determine how fast your career advances and how high you go. You can't afford to be unresponsive. It is a career-killer."[6]

Although it's impossible to instantly respond to the dozens of new email messages you receive every day, you can increase your responsiveness rate without becoming a slave to your inbox. This hack provides strategies for responding to your email in a timely fashion without killing your entire workday.

Process Messages in Batches

Your inbox dictates the ebb and flow of your work if it interrupts you every time a new message arrives. Don't let it.

The explosion of email communication and proliferation of email-enabled PDAs has led many Americans to nonstop inbox monitoring. In fact, 41 percent of respondents in a 2005 survey said they checked their email in the morning before going to work. More than 25 percent said they had never gone more than a few days without checking email, 60 percent said they check it on vacation, and 4 percent look at email in the bathroom.[7]

The reality is that checking email adds up to a whole lot of time, much of it wasted. The world will not end if an email sits in your inbox for a few hours.

Schedule two or three "meetings" with your inbox each day at predetermined times to process email. If your job requires that you keep your email program running at all times, set it to check for new messages every hour (or two!) instead of every five minutes. (For more on protecting your sanity from the insidiousness of constant email checking, see Hack 38, "Reduce Email Interruptions.")

The One-Minute Rule

When you've begun an email processing session, start at the oldest message you received and work up. Follow the one-minute rule: if a message will take less than one minute to process and respond to, do it on the spot. One minute doesn't sound like a lot of time, but in reality a whole lot can happen in 60 seconds. Dash off quick answers to questions, follow up with questions on requests, and knock down any "Sounds good" and "Let's discuss on the phone; when's a good time?" and "Received the attachment, thanks" type of messages. If you think that a message needs a lengthy, complicated response, consider taking it offline and making a phone call instead.

Most of your new messages will fall under the "can respond in less than a minute" umbrella, so go ahead and answer them.

Respond to Task Requests — Before the Task Is Done

If someone asks you to complete a project or task, it's natural to think, "I don't have time to deal with this right now, so I'll just leave it in my inbox to handle later." There the message atrophies for weeks, and a month later, you've never gotten back to the sender and the task still isn't done. That's the quickest route to Irresponsibleville.

When asked to do something via email, respond right away with the following:

- Questions you may need answered to get started
- A request for the task completion deadline
- How busy you are and when you think you'll be able to get started
- The next time the requester can expect to hear from you regarding the task

An immediate response that says, "I'm booked solid for the next three months. What's your deadline? Drop me a note in September if you're still interested in having me work on this" — effectively, "no can do" — is much more professional and appreciated than no response at all, or a three-week delay.

Don't Leave It in Your Inbox

Touch a message once in your inbox and commit yourself to taking it to the next step, whether that's dashing off a reply or moving it into your queue for a next step. But whatever you do, don't scan messages in your inbox and just leave them there to scan again later. It's a waste of time to repeat the same action again (and again).

Hack 3: Craft Effective Messages

Level....... **Easy**
Platform.... **All**
Cost .... **Free**

The old computer-science adage, "Garbage in, garbage out" (GIGO), means that if you give a computer the wrong input, it returns useless output. Humans are much more forgiving than computers, but in many ways GIGO applies to email correspondence as well. The clearer your email messages are, the more likely you'll get the result you want quicker — whether it's a response, a completed task, or an informed recipient.

A recent survey of workers at big companies reveals that employees waste anywhere from half an hour to three hours a day processing poorly written messages.[8] In an ineffective email message, the sender's expectations aren't clear, the most important information is hard to find, and the body of the message is too long and difficult to read.

You spend at least a couple of hours a day reading and responding to email. How much of that time could be saved if all the messages you sent and received were to the point and free of any unnecessary information?

This hack covers ways to get the most out of email you send with the least amount of time, energy, and work.

Composing a New Message

Keep in mind the following simple strategies for whittling the messages you send down to their most effective state.

Determine Your Purpose

Every email message has a very specific purpose. Either you are conveying information or requesting action from the recipient. Before you click that Compose button, know what you expect to get out of the exchange. If you don't know your message's purpose, don't write it.

If you need to flesh out your thoughts by writing, send the email to *yourself*. Then follow up with anything you need to ask or tell others.

Use an Informative Subject Line

First impressions are pretty important in a world in which two dozen different things are already competing for your email recipient's eyeballs and attention. The first thing your correspondent will see is the subject line of your message. Boil that line down to a few words that convey your message's purpose. Think of yourself as a newspaper headline writer, tasked with telling the whole story in just a few words to grab the reader's attention.

Remember that your recipient will use subject lines to scan and sort her inbox, track conversations, prioritize tasks, and absorb information at a glance, so make your subject lines amenable to that.

Here are some examples of bad subject lines:

```
Subject: Hi!
Subject: Just wanted to tell you...
Subject: Can you do me a favor?
Subject: IMPORTANT!!!
```

None of those subject lines gets specific about the content of the message. Yes, this message may be IMPORTANT!!!, but what is it regarding? A "favor" might range from lending the sender your stapler to donating your kidney. One might want to "just tell you" a lot of things, from "I like your tie" to "I hear you're getting fired tomorrow."

Some examples of good subject lines include the following:

```
Subject: Tomorrow's managerial meeting agenda
Subject: Questions about Monday's presentation
Subject: QUESTION: May I quote you in an article?
Subject: FYI: Out of the office Thursday
Subject: REQUEST: Pls comment on the proposed redesign layout
Subject: IMPORTANT: Must fax contract before 3PM today
```

Notice the optional use of prefixes (FYI, REQUEST, IMPORTANT) that convey the message type before addressing the content in the rest of the line. You can even shorten them to Q: for Question, REQ: for Request, and IMPT: for Important.

If your message contains several requests for action or info related to different topics entirely, break it down into separate messages. That will help get each point addressed in specific, relevant conversation threads.

Be Succinct

The purpose of writing an email isn't to hear yourself think; it's to elicit the desired response from the recipient.

The shorter your email, the more likely it is that it will be read and your request filled. No one wants to muddle through a long, wordy missive picking out the questions, task requests, and important points. Respect your recipient's time and expect that your message will be skimmed quickly. Get right to the point and hit Send. Everyone appreciates brevity.

NOTE Lots of email-savvy folks send subject-only messages to convey very short bits of information. For example, a blank email with the subject line, FYI: Out of the office for the rest of the afternoon [EOM] (where EOM stands for End of Message) says all that it has to.

Put Your Messages on a Diet

If you're sending messages to people outside your corporate network, where download speeds and email software may differ from your environment, eliminate unnecessary attachments and HTML elements that may weigh down the message. Here are some tips:

- If you're attaching photos, be sure to rotate them to the correct orientation and resize them. (See Hack 51, "Batch Resize Photos," for a quick way to make your photos better suited for email.)

- Don't assume that everyone has HTML email enabled; many folks (including myself) disable HTML email to avoid marketing trackers and long message downloads.

- Don't assume that your message looks the same way in your recipient's software as it did in yours; all email applications format messages differently.

- In some email software, a long web site address that wraps in the message may be unclickable. Use a service such as TinyURL (http://tinyurl.com) to shorten that address before you send your message.

Facilitate a Complete Response

A few line breaks can go a long way in a message that contains a set of questions, important points, or task requests. Use line breaks and bullet points liberally to make your message easy to read and respond to.

For example, the following message intersperses information with questions in one continuous paragraph:

```
Hi, Becky,
Got your message about Tuesday, thanks! What's the conference room
number? Turns out I'm going to drive instead of take the train.
Will I need a parking pass? Also, I have the PowerPoint
presentation on my laptop. Is there a projector available I can
hook it up to, or should I bring my own?
```

It would be a lot easier for Becky to see the bits of the message that require a response if it were formatted this way:

```
Hi, Becky,
I'm all set for Tuesday's meeting. A few questions for you:
* What is the conference room number?
* If I drive, how should I get a parking pass?
* Is a projector available that will work with my laptop?
```

The second version clearly delineates what questions the sender needs answered and makes responding inline to the questions much easier on Becky.

Make It Clear Why Everyone Got the Message

Messages that have several recipients in the To: field can spread account-ability too thin across a group of people. If everything thinks, "Someone else will take care of it," nothing will get done. As a sender, include multiple recipients on a message only when you absolutely must — and then make it clear in the body of the message why everyone is receiving it, as in the following example:

```
To: Victor Downs, Lorrie Crenshaw, Kyran Deck
Subject: Staff luncheon confirmed for June 18th

We reserved a room for 40 at Lottie's for 1PM on Tuesday, June
18th.

VD: Will the shuttle be available for transportation that day?
Please let Kyran know.
KD: Please send out a staff-wide email invite with directions and
shuttle information by the 4th.
LC: FYI, we'll have to cancel our weekly meeting.
```

Don't Forget the Attachment

It's too easy to dash off a message saying "the file's attached" and then never actually attach the file. The Bells & Whistles plugin for Microsoft Outlook (free trial, $29.95 per license, available at `http://emailaddressmanager.com/outlook-bells.html`) notifies you when you try to send a message with the word "attached" or "attachment" in it and no file is attached. The Gmail Attachment Reminder Greasemonkey user script, available at `http://userscripts.org/scripts/show/2419`, does the same for Gmail users.

Replying to a Message

Nothing's worse than sending an email with three questions and getting back the answer to only one. To avoid unnecessary email back-and-forth, answer all the messages that require a response as thoroughly as possible.

Respond to Individual Points Inline

For email that includes lists of questions or response-worthy points, press the Reply button and include your comments inline — that is, interspersed within the original email — to ensure that you address every point. For example, Becky might reply to the earlier message this way:

```
Hi Rich,

Rich Jones wrote:
> * What is the conference room number?
It's room 316 in B Building.

> * If I drive, how should I get a parking pass?
Park in the west lot and give your name at the booth. The guard
will issue you a guest pass there.

> * Is there a projector available that will work with my laptop?
Yes, there is - a member of our tech team will be there to help set
you up.

See you then,
Becky
```

Task Requests

When you receive a request for action, don't delay your response until you're ready to complete the action. Instead, review the request and respond with any questions you need answered before you can get it done right away.

For example, if you receive the following email:

```
Subject: REQUEST: Please comment on the redesign layout proposal
Let us know what you think about the new font choice and background
color.
```

you might respond right away:

```
Subject: Re: REQUEST: Please comment on the redesign layout
proposal

Tamara Smith wrote:
> Let us know what you think about the new font choice and
background color.

Can you send me a link to the new proposal?

Also, when is the deadline for final comments?
```

Lead by Example

You may be a master at writing effective email, but communication is a two-way street. Lead by example when you receive poorly written messages. When you respond, edit an email's unspecific subject line so that further correspondence on the topic is easily identifiable in your inbox. Break up someone's run-on message into chunks and respond inline. If the purpose of the message is unclear to you, respond with the question, "What's my next step regarding this?" If someone sends you a rambling, five-screen description, reply briefly: "Sounds good." These strategies train others to not expect long messages from you in real time and to craft better subject lines and task requests.

Don't Respond in Real Time

Although some folks may live and die by the "Bing! You have new mail!" of their email client, email was never meant to be instant, real-time communication and shouldn't be used as such. If someone needs to engage you at this moment in time, he can call. Otherwise, create the expectation that email to you will not get answered on the spot.

Even if you are checking your email in real time (and you shouldn't be unless you don't want to get anything else done), don't respond to non-emergency messages right away, especially from co-workers. It sets an impossible expectation for the future. Settle on a reasonable maximum response-time goal; for example, commit to responding to email within four to six hours on business days, or within 24 to 48 hours at most.

Get Outside the Inbox

Tone-deafness is the biggest pitfall of textual communication — especially quick, off-the-cuff methods such as email. The sender's facial expression or tone of voice doesn't come inside her email messages, and feelings can be hurt, recipients can be offended, and messages can be taken the wrong way. In fact, the American Psychological Association published a study that shows emailers overestimate their ability to convey their tone by about 25 percent when they press the Send button, and overestimate their ability to correctly interpret the tone of messages others send to them as well.[9]

Some issues are too complex or sensitive to be communicated via email. Know when it's appropriate to just pick up the phone and call someone or visit in person to convey a message and answer questions on the spot.

Know When Not to Say a Thing

Even though email correspondence *seems* private, it's not. Copies of every message you've ever sent out were made on servers across the Internet, and business email is saved on your employer's server as well. A recent study shows that about one-third of large companies in the United States actively monitor their employees' email.[10] This number will only go up as liabilities and privacy issues related to email increase.

Keeping that in mind, never write email when you're upset, emotional, stressed, tired, hungry, drunk, or otherwise impaired. After an email is sent, there's no taking it back, and every email you send is written documentation that can be used in court or to support a case for promotion or firing. Never say something in an email that you wouldn't publish in a company newsletter, say to a newspaper reporter, or announce at a meeting.

If an email upsets you or you're feeling a rant coming on, write it in a text file, save it, and give yourself time to think things over. Later, go back and edit or start all over on a more composed note.

Hack 4: Highlight Messages Sent Directly to You

Level . . . . **Easy**
Platform . . . . **All**
Cost . . . . **Free**

When you're faced with an inbox full of new, unread email, it's nearly impossible to determine which messages need to be dealt with right away and which can be put off until later. You get CCed on memos and included on large mailing lists, or receive company- or department-wide notifications. When you're pressed for time, those types of messages are all good candidates for later reading. But what about those few messages addressed *only* to you?

Email overload expert Itzy Sabo says,[11]

Such messages are most likely to be more important than the rest of the stuff that fills up my inbox, because:

> *They have not been sent to a bunch of people, but specifically to me.*
>
> *They are therefore more likely to relate to my area of responsibility.*
>
> *They are also more likely to require action.*
>
> *If I don't answer, nobody else will.*

Microsoft Outlook: Color Me Blue

Using Microsoft Outlook, you can make those important to-me-only messages jump out of your inbox with one simple setting. Choose Tools ➪ Organize, and in the Using Colors section, click the Turn On button next to Show Messages Sent Only To Me In Blue, as shown in Figure 1-2.

Then, messages sent only to you will be a different color than the others. During your email processing sessions, you'll do well to deal with the blue messages first. (Of course, you can use the color drop-down list to select a different color for your only-to-me emails if you want.)

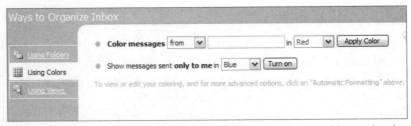

Figure 1-2 Organize your inbox by highlighting messages addressed only to you.

All Other Email Programs: Create a Not-to-Me Filter

Most modern email applications have a rule or filter feature that matches incoming messages against criteria you define and performs some action. Create a not-to-me filter that de-highlights lower priority messages or even moves them to an Inbox–Low Priority folder. See Hack 10, "Filter Low-Priority Email Messages," for more on using email filters to automatically clean out and prioritize your inbox.

> **TIP** Gmail can indicate messages sent only to your address with the right-angle quotation mark (which looks like a double greater-than sign, or >>) pointing to the message subject. Messages addressed to you and other people get a single greater-than sign (>). Messages without your address in the To: field — such as to distribution lists — have no indicator near them. In Gmail's Settings area, turn this on under Personal Level Indicators.

Hack 5: Use Disposable Email Addresses

Level. . . . . . . **Easy**
Platform. . . . **Web**
Cost . . . . **Free**

Much of the junk email you receive is from spammers who bought or scraped your email address from a web site where you registered for membership. Most registration-based web sites require that you use a legitimate email address; often, you have to retrieve an email from that address's inbox to complete registration.

If you hate the idea of giving your email address to any web site that asks for it and you want to protect your email address from junk mail and spam, use a disposable email address instead.

Web-Based Public Email Addresses

Several services, such as Mailinator (http://mailinator.com) offer free, public, disposable email addresses. Choose any email name at the mailinator.com domain — such as goaheadspammer@mailinator.com or joe@mailinator.com — and use it to register at a web site. Then, visit Mailinator.com to check the public inbox, which doesn't require a password.

> **CAUTION** Remember, anyone can check the joe@mailinator.com inbox, so make sure nothing too personal winds up there!

Dodgit (http://dodgit.com) offers a service similar to Mailinator, with the capability to check all public email accounts at dodgit.com via RSS. If you use the Bloglines (http://bloglines.com) RSS reader, you can also create an unlimited number of disposable email addresses there to receive newsletters, mailing-list messages, and other low-priority mail inside your newsreader.

For more on RSS, see Hack 82, "Subscribe to Web Sites with RSS."

Multi-Domain Email Addresses

If you host your email at your own web site domain (see more on that in Hack 7, "Future-Proof Your Email Address," later in this chapter), you have a limitless supply of email names available to you; really, anything followed by @*yourdomain*.com. Each time you sign up for a web site, use a unique name that you can block or filter later if you start receiving spam.

For example, if my real email address is `gina@example.com`, I might register at Amazon.com using the `amazon.com@example.com` email address, which also comes to me. If Amazon sells my address and I start receiving spam at `amazon.com@example.com`, I can block further email to that address and I'll know it was Amazon who sold me out. (This is just an example. In all the years I've been a registered Amazon.com user, I've never received spam at the unique address I use there.)

> **NOTE** For more on how to avoid signing up for a web site at all, see Hack 53, "Bypass Free Site Registration with BugMeNot."

Hack 6: Master Message Search

Level. . . . . . . **Easy**
Platforms . . . **All**
Cost . . . . **Free**

In an earlier hack, you created an archive of closed messages for later reference, and your `Archive` folder has no subfolders in it. That makes a lot of compulsively organized people who like to have a folder for every sender, project, and day of the week very anxious. But in contrast to paper documents, you don't need folders to find where you've stored messages. As long as you know a few key characteristics of the message you're looking for, a well-crafted query can pluck out the email you're looking for immediately — without traversing a six-folder-deep hierarchy.

In the physical world, you can't throw years' worth of letters, cards, and memos into a drawer and then pick out the one Tom sent you about that fabulous rental he got in Key West back in 2003 in seconds. However, that is absolutely possible with an email folder containing thousands of messages.

Search Criteria

Most email programs have message search built right in. Not surprisingly, Google's web-based email product Gmail has the strongest searching capabilities on the market; undoubtedly, other email software makers will follow suit in the near future.

For example, your search for Tom's message might look like Figure 1-3 in Gmail's Search Options area:

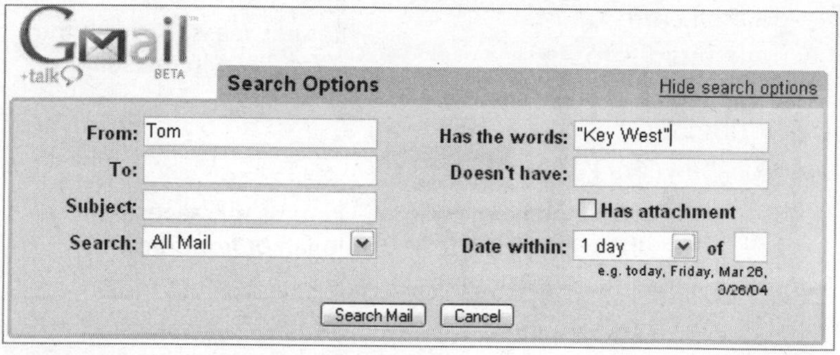

Figure 1-3 Searching for a message from Tom that contains the phrase "Key West."

You can do even more complex queries with Gmail's advanced search operators. For example, if you wanted to search for messages from Tom or Kelly that have the phrase "Key West" or the word "rental," use the OR operator (also signified with the pipe |). As with a Google web search, enclose phrases in quotation marks. The entire query can go into one search box and will look like this:

```
From:(Tom | Kelly) ("Key West" OR rental)
```

You can exclude terms as well. For instance, if you wanted to see all the messages from people except for Joe at a specific company (at the example.com domain), you could search for

```
From:(*@example.com AND -joe@example.com)
```

A summary of all Gmail's search operators is available at `http://mail .google.com/support/bin/answer.py?answer=7190`. Here's a sampling:

OPERATOR	DEFINITION	EXAMPLE
from:	Specifies the sender.	from:Amy Returns messages from Amy.
to:	Specifies the recipient.	to:Jonah Returns messages addressed to Jonah.

(continued)

(continued)

OPERATOR	DEFINITION	EXAMPLE
`Subject:`	Searches the subject line	`subject:lunch` Returns messages with the word *lunch* in the subject line.

OR	Searches for messages with either term A or term B. OR must be in all caps. A pipe (|) works in place of OR.	`from:Jonah OR`
		`from:Amy`
		Returns messages from Jonah or from Amy.

-	Excludes a term from the search.	`Java -coffee` Returns messages containing the word *Java* but not the word *coffee*.

`has:attachment`	Searches for messages with an attachment.	`from:david`
		`has:attachment`
		Returns messages from David that contain any kind of file attachment.

`filename:`	Searches for an attachment by name or type.	`filename:poem.doc`
		Returns messages with an attachment named `poem.doc`.
		
		`filename:jpg`
		Returns messages with JPEG photo attachments.

`" "`	Searches for an exact phrase (capitalization isn't considered).	`"Nice job"`
		Returns messages that contain the phrase *nice job* or *Nice job*.
		
		`subject:"dinner and a movie"`
		Returns messages containing the phrase *dinner and a movie* in the subject.

`()`	Groups words; used to specify terms that shouldn't be excluded.	`from:amy(dinner OR movie)` Returns messages from Amy that contain either the word *dinner* or the word *movie*.

OPERATOR	DEFINITION	EXAMPLE
		`subject:(dinner movie)` Returns messages in which the subject contains both the word *dinner* and the word *movie*. Note that AND is implied.
`after:`	Search for messages sent after a certain date (date must be in yyyy/mm/dd format).	`after:2001/09/11` Returns messages sent after September 11, 2001.
`before:`	Search for messages sent before a certain date (date must be in yyyy/mm/dd format).	`before:1997/05/17` Returns messages sent before May 17, 1997. `after:2007/06/01 AND before:2007/07/01` Returns messages sent after June 1, 2007, but before July 1, 2007. (Or messages sent in June, 2007.)

When you use these operators, a well-crafted query can turn up messages with specific attributes from your `Archive` folder — or entire email archive — in seconds.

NOTE To search email messages in Microsoft Outlook or Mozilla Thunderbird using operators like Gmail's, consider using the free Google Desktop Search (`http://desktop.google.com`). See also Hack 12, "Instantly Retrieve Files Stored on Your Computer," for more on using Google Desktop Search.

Saved Search Folders

Another efficient digital filing technique is to save a search as a folder. No more dragging and dropping messages by hand; you can create a virtual email folder defined by search criteria.

For example, during the writing of this book, I created a `Book` email folder that contained all the correspondence between my publishing company, Wiley, and me.

To do this in Thunderbird, execute a search from the upper-right corner search box. Then, from the drop-down list, choose Save Search as a Folder and edit your criteria. In my case, any message whose sender or recipient contained the phrase `wiley.com` or my agent's email address should be included in my `Book` folder. The query is defined in Thunderbird, as shown in Figure 1-4.

Then, the `Book` folder appears in my folder list as usual, except a small magnifying glass over the folder icon indicates that it's a saved search. When I click the folder, Thunderbird updates its contents with all the messages that match the search.

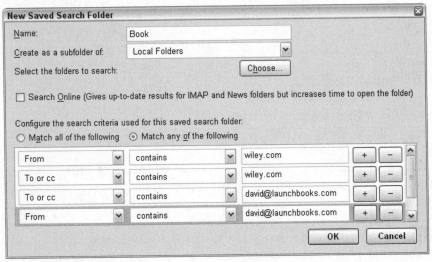

Figure 1-4 Creating a folder from saved search criteria.

Microsoft Outlook 2007 also offers saved search folders. In the Mail Folders bar, right-click Search Folders and choose New Search Folder to create one.

The advantage of saved search folders is that one email can live in any number of saved searches, as long as it fulfills the criteria. Folder deletion just removes the query — not the messages themselves.

After this book is completed, I'll delete that folder — but all the messages will remain in their original locations.

Hack 7: Future-Proof Your Email Address

Level. . . . . . . **Easy**
Platform. . . . **All**
Cost . . . . **Free**

You probably have as many email addresses as you do pairs of socks, but you don't want to change them as often. In fact, switching your primary email address can be a big inconvenience that leads to missed messages and lost relationships. You give your email address to countless friends, relatives, and web services, and publish it on mailing lists, web sites, and documents forever cached in search engine indexes. But if your email address is tied to a former ISP, the company you used to work for, the university you attended, or the embarrassing handle you chose in college, switching to a new address can become a necessity.

If you're thinking about changing your primary email address, you've got many choices. Before you commit to your next unique identifier on the Internet, check out some do's and don'ts for future-proofing your email address.

Don'ts

- **Don't use your company's or school's email address for personal use.** Someday you will graduate or leave your current company, and you don't want to leave your email messages behind, not to mention try to make sure all your contacts' address books are updated. Certainly your company or school email address is appropriate to use for company and school correspondence, but as your primary individual address, not so much.

- **Don't use the address your ISP gave you.** You upgrade to broadband and RoadRunner gives you a free name@yourstate.rr.com email account. Nice, right? Wrong! Someday you will live in another state and use another ISP, and that address won't work anymore. Pass.

Do's

- **Use an address that is accessible from anywhere.** More and more, you will use multiple computers at home, at work, and in public places. Make sure you can securely access your email from any-where, and choose an address that enables you to do so. Many popular web-based email services use SSL logins and have easy-to-use dynamic interfaces (such as Google's Gmail), so use an address at one of them or that works with one of them. You can even use email forwarding to, say, send a copy of every email you receive and send to a web-based account for online searchable archives from anywhere.

▪ **Choose an easy-to-remember name you won't regret down the road.** Remember when qtGrrl81 was an email handle that made you proud? Well, now that you're a freelancer soliciting business or applying for jobs, you want something more professional. Choose an email address that will be easy to remember and recognize, and one that won't make you cringe when you have to recite it over the phone to your mutual fund company.

Bottom Line

You want an email address that will stick with you for years to come. The most ideal (and most costly) solution is to register a domain name and set up an email address at a provider (such as `yourname@yourname.com`). Your provider goes away and you can move that domain to a new provider, no address change required.

NOTE Lifehacker.com readers make email hosting service recommenda-tions at `http://lifehackerbook.com/links/emailhosts`.

For those who don't want to plunk down the cash for their own domain and email provider, any of the popular, free, web-based mail ser-vices are a great option. Gmail and Yahoo! Mail are two free, take-it-with-you web-based email providers. Your best chance for getting the username you want is probably at Gmail, which was most recently launched.

The problem with depending on a free web-based service for your email is loss of control. If Gmail changes its domain, decides to start charging, has server problems, or goes away (all unlikely but possible scenarios), you're affected without much recourse. In a pay-for situation with your own domain name, you can change providers and only you own your data if something goes wrong.

TIP A service called Google Apps For Your Domain (`https://www`
`.google.com/a/`) **lets you use your custom domain with Google's email service, Gmail, which gives you the best of both worlds. If at some point in the future you want to move away from Gmail, you can simply remap your domain to another service without changing your address.**

Hack 8: Consolidate Multiple Email Addresses with Gmail

Level. . . . . . . **Medium**
Platform. . . . **Web**
Cost . . . . **Free**

After reading Hack 7, you've decided to move all your email online to Google's web-based service, Gmail. Great! But what about messages still going to your old email address(es)? Fear not. Gmail is not only an email host; it's an email client that can fetch mail from any number of external services and consolidate it all right there in your Gmail inbox. You can avoid having to tell all your contacts to update your email address again and you don't miss a single message in your transition to Gmail.

Receive Messages for Other Addresses in Your Gmail Inbox

You have two ways to receive email from other addresses in Gmail: use Gmail's Mail Fetcher feature or forward your other addresses' mail to Gmail automatically.

Option 1: Set Up Gmail's POP Mail Fetcher

Most likely, your former email provider offers POP (Post Office Protocol) access for retrieving messages for it. Gmail's Mail Fetcher feature can retrieve those messages via POP and display them in your inbox alongside messages that come directly to your Gmail address. You can fetch email from up to five other email addresses via POP in Gmail.

To use Gmail's Mail Fetcher, your old email account must offer POP access. Not all free addresses offer POP, but most do. Check the other account's settings or contact customer support to find out whether POP

access is available on your non-Gmail account. You'll need four settings:
the POP server address, the port, and your username and password.
Also, if you haven't already, you'll need to sign up for a free Gmail account
at http://gmail.com.

After you're logged in to your Gmail account, configure Mail Fetcher
to retrieve messages from your old account. Here's how:

1. From the top of any page within Gmail, click Settings.

2. Click Accounts.

3. In the Get Mail From Other Accounts section, click Add Another
    Mail Account.

4. Enter the full email address of the account you'd like to access,
    and click Next Step.

5. Gmail will fill in the username, POP server, and port fields when
    possible, based on the email address, as shown in Figure 1-5. Enter
    your password.

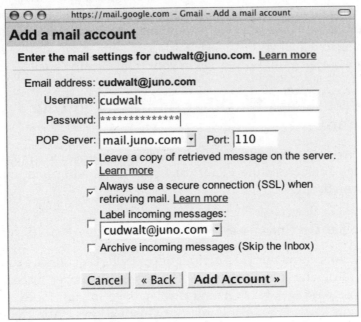

Figure 1-5 Retrieving email via POP for a non-Gmail address.

6. If Gmail will be the single place you check mail, deselect the box labeled "Leave A Copy Of Retrieved Message On The Server." If you want to access the other mail from other software (or if you're just using Gmail as a backup), do select this box. You can also set options to use SSL (a secure connection) to retrieve mail (some servers support this, others don't). And you can choose whether to label or archive incoming messages.

7. After your options are set, click Add Account. Gmail will issue an error if your username, password, or other settings are incorrect. When Gmail can fetch messages successfully, it will give you the option to set up a custom From: address. (See the section "Write Messages from Non-Gmail Addresses," later in this chapter, for more on that.)

After you set up Mail Fetcher, Google will check your other account(s) on a regular basis, and new mail will appear automatically in your Gmail account.

NOTE Gmail checks for new messages at different rates, depending on previous mail-fetch attempts. You can't customize the default frequency of mail fetches.

Option 2: Forward Messages to Gmail Automatically

If your old address doesn't offer POP access — or you have more than five addresses that you'd like to consolidate in Gmail — you can set your former address to automatically forward messages to Gmail instead. The exact way to do this differs, depending on your email account, but if your provider offers auto-forwarding, this feature will most likely be listed in your account options area.

For example, to auto-forward email from your Hotmail email account (which does not offer POP access), click your account options, and under Manage Your Account, click Forward Your Mail To Another E-Mail Address. There you can set your new Gmail account as the destination address, as shown in Figure 1-6.

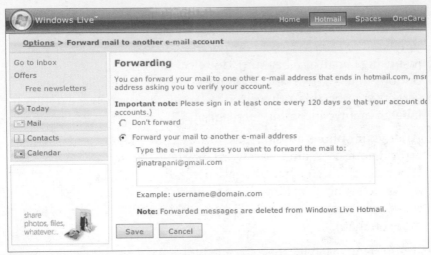

Figure 1-6 Automatically forwarding Hotmail email to Gmail.

Write Messages from Non-Gmail Addresses

Now that you have email addressed to several different accounts arriving in your single Gmail inbox, you may want to use those various From: addresses when replying to those messages. For someone who maintains several different online personas — but accesses them all in Gmail — the option to use various From: addresses when sending mail is crucial. Here's how to set up multiple From: addresses after you're logged into Gmail:

1. Click Settings along the top of any page and then select the Accounts tab.

2. Click Add Another Email Address in the Send Mail As section.

3. Enter your full name in the Name field, and enter the email address you'd like to send messages from in the Email Address field.

4. Click Next Step >> and then click Send Verification. Gmail will send a verification message to your other email address to confirm that you'd like to add it to your Gmail account. If you are already receiving this mail in Gmail, it will appear in your inbox. Click the link in that message, or enter the confirmation code in the Accounts section of your Gmail account, to complete the process.

You can add several possible From: addresses to your Gmail account, as shown in Figure 1-7.

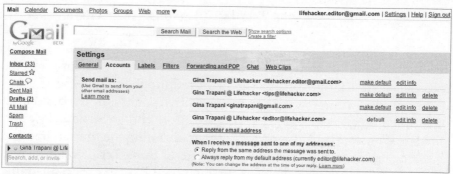

Figure 1-7 List several From: addresses for a given Gmail account.

Set one of your addresses as your default for receiving new messages. You can also set the From: name and a different reply-to address if you'd like (by clicking the Edit Info link).

After you've verified that you want to add the address to your account, you can start sending messages using your custom From: address. When you click Compose, you can choose the From: address to use from the drop-down list, as shown in Figure 1-8.

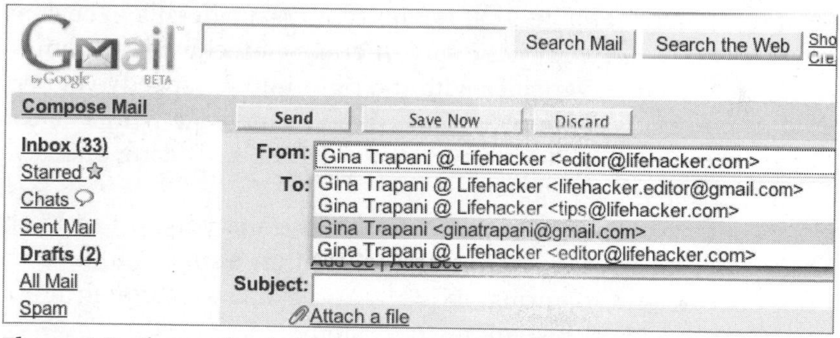

Figure 1-8 Choose the desired From: address from the drop-down list.

NOTE To help prevent your mail from being marked as spam, your Gmail address will be included in the email headers of your message in the Sender field. Most email clients do not display the Sender field, although some versions of Microsoft Outlook may display "From customaddress@ domain.com on behalf of yourusername@gmail.com."

Hack 9: Script Repetitive Responses

Level....... **Medium**
Platform.... **Windows XP and Vista, Mac OS X, Unix (Thunderbird)**
Cost .... **Free**

Is there an echo in your Sent email folder? Do you consistently receive messages that ask the same questions or require the same type of information in response? To knock down repetitive email quickly, build a set of scripted email responses that you can drop into emails quickly, personalize if necessary, and send off without spending the time composing the same information every time. With a set of trusty scripted templates, you can whip through tedious, recurring email like an expert air-traffic controller in the busy airport of your inbox.

The Quicktext Thunderbird extension saves collections of reusable text snippets that help you compose personalized replies to those tiresome email messages with a few keystrokes.

> **NOTE** For more on text substitution — especially if you don't use Thunderbird — see Hacks 48 and 49, "Reduce Repetitive Typing with Texter for Windows" and "Reduce Repetitive Typing with TextExpander for Mac."

In contrast to other text saver utilities, Quicktext is specific to email because it recognizes variables that reference message details — such as the recipient's first or last name, the subject line, or attachment filenames. Quicktext replaces these variables with the right info for speedy yet personalized responses. Easily reply to Lucy Wood's message with a "Dear Ms. Wood" or to Robin Cullen's email with "Hi, Robin" using one keyword or click. No name-typing required.

Here's an example: You have a computer for sale and you post an ad on a message board or in the local newspaper. Within a day, you have an inbox full of messages inquiring about it. You can dash through those messages with Quicktext. Just follow these steps:

1. Download Quicktext from `http://extensions.hesslow.se/quicktext`. Save the `.xpi` file to your computer.

2. From the Thunderbird Tools menu, choose Extensions. Click the Install button and browse to the `.xpi` file you saved. Click Install Now. When installation is complete, shut down Thunderbird and start it again.

3. Click the Compose button to start a new email message, and then click Tools ➪ Quicktext.

4. Click the Add button, choose Group, and enter **computer sale**.

5. Click Add again and choose Text. Call this script **lowbid**, and in the Text section on the right, enter your snippet (see Step 6). Also set the keyword to **lowbid**, as shown in Figure 1-9.

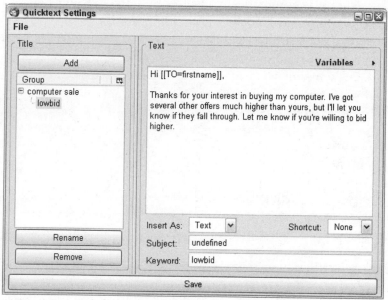

Figure 1-9 Create the lowbid script in Quicktext.

6. Set the text to the following:

```
Hi [[TO=firstname]],
Thanks for your interest in buying my computer. I've got several
other offers much higher than yours, but I'll let you know if they
fall through. Let me know if you're willing to bid higher.
```

7. Create any more Quicktexts that might apply to computer-inquiry responses. For example, create one called **more info** with the keyword **moreinfo** that reads as follows:

```
Hi [[TO=firstname]],
Thanks for your interest in buying my computer. It's a 700Mhz IBM
Thinkpad with 32MB of RAM and a 3GB hard drive. Let me know if you
need any more information.
```

8. After you've set up your scripts, go to a message about the computer. When you press the Reply button, you see a drop-down list of the Quicktext groups you set up. The computer sale and greetings Quicktexts are shown in Figure 1-10.

9. Insert the appropriate reply either by selecting it from the drop-down list or by typing the keyword — lowbid, in this example — and pressing the Tab key. Your response, complete with the recipient's first name, is automatically inserted into the message body.

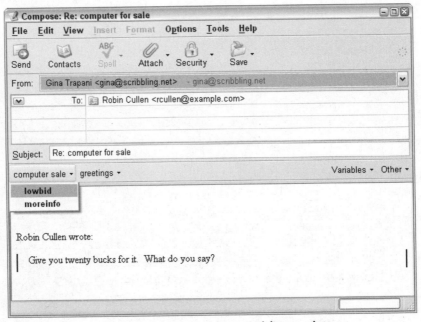

Figure 1-10 Composing a message using a Quicktext script.

Quicktext can also reference snippets within other snippets. For example, you could set up a group called **greetings** that contains two snippets:

■ **personal**, which is set to

```
Hi, [[TO=firstname]],
```

■ **business**, which is set to

```
Dear [[To=firstname]] [[To=lastname]]:
```

Then, in other snippets, you can reference one greeting by using the `[[TEXT=greetings|personal]]` variable. See the Quicktext homepage (`http://extensions.hesslow.se/text/3/All+Tags/`) for the full list of variables.

Hack 10: Filter Low-Priority Messages ("Bacn")

Level....... **Easy**
Platform.... **All**
Cost .... **Free**

You're head-down at work on that important presentation that's due in two hours. BING! An unopened envelope appears in your system tray.

"You have 1 unread message."

Maybe it's your co-worker with game-changing information about the presentation. Maybe it's your boss asking to see you right away. You switch and take a look at your inbox. Oh. Aunt Eunice forwarded you a picture of a kitten in a tutu. Again.

Millions of email messages course over the Internet per second, and a bunch of them land in your inbox. Your spam filter helps shuttle junk mail out of sight, but what about messages from CC-happy co-workers, Aunt Eunice's forwarded emails, Facebook friend notifications, Google Alerts, and mailing-list messages that clutter your inbox with low-priority noise? A group of web users coined the term "bacn" to refer to this "middle class of email" that's "better than spam but not as good as a personal email"[12]. In other words, they're messages you want to read eventually, just not right now. Clearing away the bacn automatically can help you drill down to what's important more quickly.

> **NOTE** Bacn (pronounced "bacon") is an Internet slang term cooked up by a group of web users at PodCamp Pittsburgh 2. It means email that you want to read, but not right away.

Filter Bacn

Set up rules — also called email filters — to make low-priority messages skip your inbox and file themselves away someplace less urgent. A mail filter is a list of conditions you define that trigger an action on an incoming email message. Filters can be as simple as "Delete any message from `annoying.person@example.com`" or much more complex, such as "Any message that doesn't contain any one of my five email addresses in the To: field and does not have the word URGENT in the subject line should be moved to the `Not Important` folder."

The steps for creating a mail filter or rule vary depending on your email software. The following examples use the excellent, free, cross-platform email program Thunderbird, available at `http://mozilla.org/products/thunderbird`.

To configure your email filters in Thunderbird, choose Tools ⇨ Message Filters and click the New button. Figure 1-11 displays a rule that files Aunt Eunice's forwarded messages and any messages from a mailing list to a folder called `Later`.

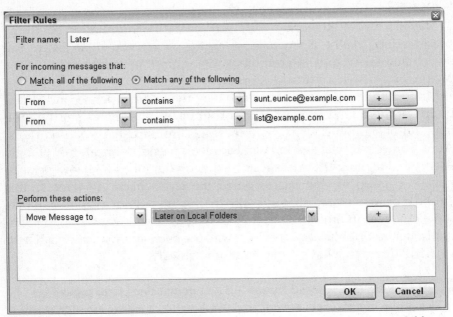

Figure 1-11 A mail filter that moves low-priority incoming messages to a folder called Later in Mozilla Thunderbird.

Filter CCed Messages

One of the most common misuses of email — especially in an office situation — is carbon copying anyone and everyone even tangentially related to the topic of a message. It's safe to assume that messages not directed to you (that is, your email address is not in the To: line) are less urgent and more informative; CCed messages most likely don't require a response or action on your part. On a day when you're firewalling your attention to include only the most important disruptors, set up a rule that shuttles email you've been CCed on out of your inbox and into a separate folder for searching and browsing later.

To do so, first create a cc folder in your email program. Then set up a rule (filter) to say, "If my email address does not appear in the To: field, file this message," as shown in Figure 1-12.

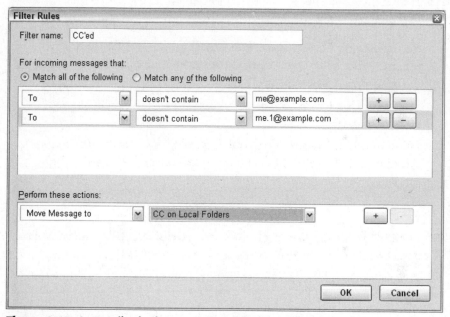

Figure 1-12 An email rule that moves messages not directed to either of two email addresses to a folder called CC.

NOTE Hack 6, "Master Message Search," provides tips for digging up messages based on specific criteria.

When the filter is enabled, all new messages that arrive without your email address in the To: field are automatically filed in the cc folder.

References

1. Michael Fitzgerald, "Call It the Dead E-Mail Office," Wired (http://www.wired.com/culture/lifestyle/news/2004/06/63733).

2. Mike Davidson, "A Lo-Fi Solution to Email Overload: Sentenc.es" (http://www.mikeindustries.com/blog/archive/2007/07/fight-email-overload-with-sentences).

3. "Companies limit email use to boost productivity," Quad-Cities Online (http://qconline.com/archives/qco/display.php?id=351875).

4. Mark Hurst, *Bit Literacy* (Good Experience Press, 2007), 24.

5. Merlin Mann, "Fresh Start: The Email DMZ," 43 Folders (http://www.43folders.com/2006/01/04/email-dmz/).

6. Michael Hyatt, "What's the Secret to Your Success?," Working Smart weblog (http://www.michaelhyatt.com/workingsmart/2006/02/whats_the_secre.html).

7. "Got Two Extra Hours For Your E-Mail?," *The New York Times*, November 2005 (http://nytimes.com/2005/11/10/fashion/thursdaystyles/10E-MAIL.html?ei=5090&en=eb222acdf706a35d&ex=1289278800&partner=rssuserland&emc=rss&pagewanted=print).

8. Center for Media Research, Research Brief (http://centerformediaresearch.com/cfmr_brief.cfm?fnl=050921).

9. American Psychological Association (http://apa.org/monitor/feb06/egos.html).

10. "Companies Read Employee E-Mail," Reuters (http://wired.com/news/wireservice/0,71071-0.html?tw=rss.index).

11. Itzy Sabo, "Small Change Makes Big Difference to Email Prioritization: How to Color-code Your Messages," Email Overloaded weblog (http://itzy.wordpress.com/2005/12/27/how-to-color-code-your-messages/).

12. Eric Weiner, "Move Over, Spam: 'Bacn' Is the E-Mail Dish Du Jour," NPR (http://www.npr.org/templates/story/story.php?storyId=14032271&ft=1&f=1006).

Organize Your Data

Never before have human beings been subject to the daily onslaught of information as they are in the age of the Internet and email. Bits and pieces of data flow into your digital life nonstop. Every day, web site addresses, usernames and passwords, appointments, memos, songs, documents, digital images, and videos gather on your computer, vying for your attention and begging the question, "Where do I go?" Chapter 1 ("Control Your Email") covered the best strategies for parrying the daily influx of electronic messages. This chapter tackles the best way to organize the data those messages and other information channels contain.

As with email overload, the only way to overcome information overload is to put everything in its place on arrival. But you're not a librarian, and you don't want to spend time arranging information in folders all over your hard drive. Although there are infinite ways to organize data into complex, multitiered systems, you're going to take the smart and lazy approach to organization: you'll arrange stuff only as much as is needed to make that data useful to you.

The better organized your personal information library is, the faster you'll be able to draw from it and act on it in the future. But better organized does not equal more folders. In fact, the fewer buckets your system has, the better.

There are three key ways in which you're going to interact with your data:

- Store it.
- Retrieve it.
- Do something wonderful with it.

When you design your data-organization system, concern yourself with storage and retrieval — that is, make those two actions as simple as possible. Next time you make a purchase online, you're not going to stop and try to remember whether you save receipts in the shopping folder, the receipts folder, or the expenditures folder. You will not ask yourself whether you should you save your password in your web browser, or add it to the passwords.doc file. (Although you might secretly wonder whether either place is secure enough anyway.)

The trick is to set up the most effective digital shelves to stow the different types of information you deal with every day. When you organize those spaces, keep the filing system simple. Create fewer destinations for quick entry. When it comes time for retrieval, you will use advanced search techniques to drill down to what you're looking for.

This chapter shows you how to create systems that make it easy to shuttle incoming bits and pieces into their right places for instant retrieval in the future. You will clear away the amorphous piles of stuff that spring up around you on your physical and digital desktops. Your parking places will have ample space to accommodate every type of item in them. Your personal "librarians" will fetch what you need when you need it with a quick keyword search. When you receive a new piece of information you may need later — such as a co-worker's change of address or a web page you may use in next month's report — where to place that new bit will be immediately obvious. Moving it into your system will be an automatic act that requires no thought or effort.

Although you may tweak the exact folder schemes and data labels outlined in this chapter for your own purposes, the principles are immutable. While you design your personal system for dealing with information, keep in mind the following:

- Every item has its place.
- Make those places big, general, and as few and simple to identify and remember as possible.
- Do *not* split up those places into complex, multiple subfolder trees that make you stop and think about what should go where or how to navigate to what you need.

- Every item is highly findable and instantly retrievable.

- You will purge unneeded information regularly. You will archive old items out of sight.

Information streams into your life all day long. You can master the art of immediate, thoughtless filing — the moment a new bit arrives at your digital doorstep. You can build a vast knowledge library each day *and* keep a clear workspace and mind in the process. You're most effective when your data is out of your face but still within reach. The psychological burden of information overload will never weigh you down if you're confident and facile at processing every incoming bit in a flash. This chapter shows you some of the best practices for doing just enough organizing to keep your information accessible without wasting your time.

Whether it's a computer desktop or a physical tabletop, clutter represents procrastination, distraction, and unprocessed information. Let's clear it away.

Hack 11: Organize Your Documents Folder

Level. . . . . . . **Easy**
Platforms. . . **All**
Cost. . . . . **Free**

Every operating system comes with a default location to save user documents. If you've had a computer for any length of time, you know that your PC's My Documents folder can get disorganized really fast. (On the Mac, it's simply called Documents.) If you frequently find yourself letting files clutter your computer's desktop, or if you spend time rearranging files in a bunch of unmanageable subfolders, it's time for a revamp. You can create a simple set of folders that will accommodate every type of file in an accessible way that keeps the files you need to work with right at your fingertips.

Over the years, I've developed a six-folder structure for My Documents that I create on every computer I use without fail. This scheme accommodates every file you will accumulate, clears the desktop, smoothly fits in with an automated backup system (see Hack 59, "Automatically Back Up Your Files to an External Hard Drive"), and makes command-line file wrangling a breeze.

In alphabetical order, the six main folders are called bak, docs, docs-archive, junkdrawer, multimedia, and scripts, as shown in Figure 2-1.

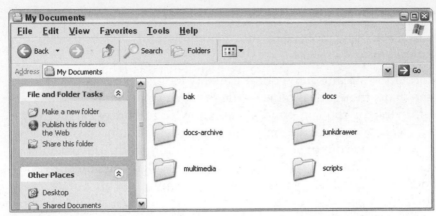

Figure 2-1 The six core folders of a My Documents organization system.

Here's a quick rundown of what each does and what it might contain:

- bak — Short for backup, this is your backup destination of first resort. Your actual data backups should reside on external disks, but bak is where you store your Quicken backup file, your address book exported to CSV, or a dump of your web site's database.

NOTE I spend a lot of time at the command line, so I prefer the short name bak, but there's no reason you can't name your folder backup — or any name you prefer.

- docs — docs is the Big Kahuna of all six folders. It's the place where all the working files for your current tasks, projects, and clients go. Its contents change frequently, and the folder should be purged often.

- You can keep subfolders in docs — finance, clients, or creative-writing, for example. The clients folder might have subfolders, too, such as acme and book-in-progress. That gets you three subfolders into the hierarchy, however, and that's as deep as you can go before your file tree gets in the way of your work.

- docs-archive — Purge your docs folder of closed working files — those for completed projects, former employers, or past tax years, for example — every few weeks. These go into your docs-archive folder. The archive exists for reference and search, but the separate folder keeps all that extra stuff from cluttering up docs, which is your working task dashboard. The files in docs-archive don't change much, if ever, so you can back them up on a different (less frequent) schedule.

- junkdrawer — The junkdrawer (or temp or tmp) is a temporary holding pen for files you're working with this moment but don't need to save long-term. Your web browser and email program should both save downloaded files and attachments to junkdrawer by default. If you're checking out a video, just testing a script, or need a place to store a software's setup.exe program, place those files into junkdrawer. junkdrawer files you want to keep should graduate into docs; otherwise, the automated hard-drive janitor (see Hack 62, "Automatically Empty Your Digital Junk Drawer") comes sweeping through and deletes anything older than a couple of weeks from junkdrawer while you sleep.

- multimedia — Here's where your music, video, and photos folders go. The benefit of having all those space-hogging files under one umbrella parent folder is backup. Chances are, your multimedia backup plan is different than your documents backup because of the sheer amount of disk space required. Drop them all in the multimedia folder and you can easily exclude them from your backup scheme. Keep in mind that sharing your media with a home web server (see Hack 74, "Run a Home Web Server") works nicely with an all-encompassing multimedia folder, too.

- scripts — Any executable script or shortcut lives in scripts. This is the place for your weight logger (described in Hack 68, "Automatically Update a Spreadsheet"), the janitor script, and any other batch scripts you use regularly.

How to Change the Windows XP Default Home Directory

Anyone who works at the command line appreciates short, to-the-point file paths. The Windows XP default user documents directory is something like this:

```
C:\Documents and Settings\username\My Documents\
```

Which makes you wonder what Microsoft was thinking at the time. (In fact, Microsoft rethought things in Windows Vista and made the users' default home directory something along the lines of C:\Users\username\, similar to the Mac OS /Users/username/ home directory path.)

You can change the Windows XP My Documents directory to C:\home\username\documents\ or something similar; a consistently lowercase path without spaces is much easier to remember, type, and script.

Here's how:

1. Right-click the My Documents icon and select Properties. The My Documents Properties dialog box opens.

2. Click the Move button and choose the new location.

3. Windows politely asks whether you'd like to move all your documents from the old location to the new one. Go ahead and confirm so that Windows can transfer your documents to the new location for you.

4. Click OK until you've exited the dialog box.

Beyond the Big Six

These may not be the only folders that live in your home directory. For example, a programmer may keep a code or dev directory as well. Just make sure that any additions don't truly belong within one of the core six. Remember, with simplicity comes effortlessness; the more folders you have, the more easily things get scattered and disorganized — so add to your system sparingly.

Hack 12: Instantly Retrieve Files Stored on Your Computer

Level. . . . . . . **Medium**
Platform. . . . **Windows XP and Vista, Mac OS X**
Cost. . . . . **Free**

There are two ways to manage documents on your computer: As an old-fashioned "filer," you can create dozens of folders to organize your data in a complicated structure; or, as a new-fangled digital "piler," you can dump data into a single or small set of folders. In your transition from filer to piler, the most important skill you must develop and learn to trust is *search*.

Paper is the paradigm that we still use to understand digital documents. Manila folder icons, for example, represent digital folders in all operating systems. Although the metaphor works well enough for new computer users, power users understand that in reality, those so-called folders are just pointers to data on a disk that never actually changes location. Digital documents have special characteristics that their paper ancestors do not: your operating system indexes them automatically, making them findable without requiring a human to store them in a big filing cabinet with carefully labeled folders.

When you first transition from a paper-based world into a digital document scenario, filing digital documents the way you would paper is a natural thing to do. But now you know that your data is already indexed and searchable without the work of dragging and dropping it into these illusory folders, so it's time to move to the next level, to use and trust that the right search will retrieve the data you need.

Built-in Desktop File Search Features

Every major operating system offers some sort of file-search feature. Windows XP's default search (available on the Start menu) is the weakest. (To its credit, Microsoft replaced it with the optional but free-to-download Windows Desktop Search, available at `http://microsoft.com/windows/desktopsearch/default.mspx`). Windows Vista's search feature is much improved over Windows XP's, with a built-in search box in every Explorer window and the Start menu itself. Mac OS X offers Spotlight search, and on the Linux desktop, tools such as Beagle are available.

However, the company that offers the best-of-class web search also offers a product that indexes and searches your computer's files just as well as it does web documents: Google Desktop Search. This hack covers the installation, configuration, and use of Google Desktop to make every file — even ones you created years ago and forgot about that contain your keyword — instantly retrievable with a query using Google's advanced search operators.

NOTE Many of the search query operators that work on Google's web search tool also work in Google Desktop, and Google Desktop can also include your Gmail email messages in its results. For these reasons, Google Desktop is my choice of local search tools. However, for users who don't want to use Google Desktop, many of the search techniques covered in this hack will work or have an equivalent in Windows Desktop Search, Vista's built-in search, and Spotlight.

Google Desktop Installation

The best time to install Google Desktop is just before you go to bed or leave the office for lunch, because it takes time for the program to index the email, files, and web pages that are already stored on your computer. The polite Google Desktop indexes your files only while you aren't using your computer so that it won't slow you down, but it may take several hours of idle computer time to build a complete index, depending on how much data you have stored. (You can search your computer before the index is complete, but you won't get full results.)

When you're ready to let Google Desktop build a complete index, download it from `http://desktop.google.com`, install as usual, and get it started.

Google Desktop Configuration

Google Desktop has several options to consider. To access them, right-click the Google Desktop icon in your system tray and select Preferences. (Mac users, in the System Preferences panel, under the Other header, should choose Google Desktop.) In the Local Indexing tab, set the drives (including network drives) and file types you want indexed, choose whether secure web pages and password-protected office documents should be included, and choose whether your index should be encrypted for increased security. If you use Gmail and want Google Desktop to index your messages, enter your Gmail login in the Google Account Features tab.

> **TIP** Mac users who don't want the Google Desktop icon taking up space on their Dock can disable the icon while still running Desktop. In the Google Desktop pane of System Preferences, under Search Results, deselect the Show Icon In Dock check box.

PC users can also turn on the controversial Search Across Computers feature, which enables you to search the documents on your home computer from, say, the office. (Before you do, please read the sidebar about security implications.)

Google Desktop offers many features, such as mini-applications called Gadgets, but this hack focuses on its most important and useful feature: search.

SECURITY IMPLICATIONS OF THE GOOGLE DESKTOP SEARCH ACROSS COMPUTERS FEATURE

Google Desktop includes a Search Across Computers feature that stores your computer's files on Google's servers so that you can search them from other computers. If you use this feature, your desktop files are searchable only by you, but storing them on Google's servers brings up a lesser-known privacy issue: The Electronic Communications Privacy Act (ECPA), enacted by Congress in 1986, states that while a search warrant is required to seize files on your home computer, a subpoena is enough to get access to files stored on the server of a service provider (like Google).

For these reasons, the Google Desktop Search Across Computers feature made privacy-advocacy groups skittish. In February 2006, the Electronic Frontier Foundation (EFF) advised consumers not to download and use Google Desktop version 3 because its default setting was to copy the files on your hard drive onto Google's servers.[1]

At the time, an EFF attorney said, "If you use the Search Across Computers feature and don't configure Google Desktop very carefully — and most people won't — Google will have copies of your tax returns, love letters, business records, financial and medical files, and whatever other text-based documents the Desktop software can index. The government could then demand these personal files with only a subpoena rather than the search warrant it would need to seize the same things from your home or business, and in many cases you wouldn't even be notified in time to challenge it. Other litigants — your spouse, your business partners or rivals, whoever — could also try to cut out the middleman (you) and subpoena Google for your files."

Version 4 of Google Desktop turned off the Search Across Computers feature by default and requires you to explicitly turn the feature on to store your files on Google's servers.

Although the Search Across Computers feature is admittedly convenient, I recommend that you keep it turned off and use your own server to keep your files accessible, private, and in your own control. (See Chapter 8, "Get Your Data to Go," for several free ways to make your documents available from anywhere without a "man in the middle" such as Google.)

Files that Google Desktop Indexes

As of version 5.1, Google Desktop Search indexes the following:

- Email from Gmail, Outlook, Outlook Express, and Thunderbird
- Files on your computer, including text, Word, Excel, PowerPoint, PDF, MP3, the contents of ZIP files, and image, audio, and video files

- Media files' metadata; for example, MP3 song files by artist name and title, not just the filename

- Web pages you've viewed using Internet Explorer 5+, Netscape 7.1+, Mozilla 1.4+, and Firefox

- Instant messenger logs from Google Talk, AOL Instant Messenger 5+, and MSN Messenger

When your file index is complete, Google Desktop provides a search box in your task bar (or floating, or in the Sidebar, depending on your choice in the Display section of the Preferences page). Now you're ready to start finding information.

Refining Your Search

As does Google web search, Google Desktop Search displays search results using your web browser. The results from your computer are included at the top of the regular Google web search results page, as shown in Figure 2-2.

Figure 2-2 Google Desktop incorporates results for files on your own computer in regular Google web searches.

TIP Press the Ctrl key twice (Command key for Mac users) to summon a Google Desktop search box; press the Ctrl key twice again to dismiss it.

Also as you can with the Google web search, you can use advanced operators when searching your file system to narrow down results by all sorts of criteria. Advanced search operators currently include those shown in the following table.

OPERATOR	DESCRIPTION
"..."	Enclose all or part of your query in quotation marks, and Desktop returns only items that contain that *exact* quoted phrase. For example, the query `"Copyright 2007"` would not return an item containing the phrasing "In 2007, I filed for copyright'" because it is not an exact match.
–	Used directly in front of a word, causes searches to not return items containing that word. For example, results for the search `bats -baseball` would include all items in the Desktop cache that contain the word *bats*, *except* for the items that also contain the word *baseball*.
Site:	Limits Desktop search to results from the web site you specify. For example, a Desktop query of `help site:www.google.com` returns only pages you've visited on `www.google.com` that contain the word *help*. Important: There can be no space between the `site:` operator and the specified web site.
filetype:	Restricts the type of files Desktop returns. The argument is either a file type extension or the full name of an Office application. For example, a search for `tax filetype:xls` or `tax filetype:excel` results in only Excel files that have the word *tax* in them. Do not put any spaces between `filetype:` and the extension or type argument.
under:	Restricts the folder from which your file search results can come. For example, results for the search `basketball under:"C:\Documents and Settings\username\My Documents"` include only files found in the `C:\Documents and Settings\username\My Documents` folder.

Email searches can be restricted to matches within email message headers. The available search operators are `Subject:, To:, From:, Cc:,` and `Bcc:`. You can combine any of these operators in a single query; you also can include either or both of the `" "` and `-` operators.

See the full list of Google Desktop advanced search operators and the details of how to use them at `http://desktop.google.com/support/bin/answer.py?answer=10111&topic=1158`.

Hack 13: Overhaul Your Filing Cabinet

Level. . . . . . . **Easy**
Platform. . . . **All**
Cost. . . . . **Free**

One of the main clutter culprits in most offices is the To File pile. Often, this heap spontaneously appears right on top of or next to the filing cabinet, which is pretty silly. Instead of adding stuff to the pile, why wouldn't you just file it? The reason is generally an unworkable, messy, overflowing file cabinet.

This hack explains how to revamp your overstuffed, underlabeled file system and turn it into a neat, breezy, and pleasurable place to organize your important paperwork.

Give Your Paperwork a Spacious Place to Live

Face it: That plastic file box or enormous binder held shut with a rubber band just isn't going to cut it. You have personal, financial, insurance, car, client, tax, and medical paperwork to track.

If you've been using an undersized filing cabinet that can't possibly accommodate your stuff — or have no filing cabinet at all — invest in a spacious, well-designed file drawer or cabinet that leaves you room to spare. Lots of room. In fact, *Getting Things Done* author David Allen says that your file drawer should be only three-quarters full: "If you want to get rid of your unconscious resistance to filing, then you must keep the drawers loose enough that you can insert and retrieve files without effort."[2]

If you're out to buy a new filing cabinet, he also advises you not to skimp on quality.

"Nothing is worse than trying to open a heavy file drawer and hearing that awful *screech!* that happens when you wrestle with the roller bearings on one of those $29.95 special-sale cabinets. You really need a file cabinet whose drawer, even when it's three-quarters full, will glide open and click shut with the smoothness and solidity of a door on a German car."

It's true. A tool that's easy and fun to use is a tool you *will* use.

Limit One File Folder per Hanging Folder

As soon as things start to get crowded inside filing-cabinet land, your first instinct is to start putting several manila folders into one hanging folder. Bad idea. Allocate one single manila folder to one single hanging folder.

This cleanly separates your folders and makes them easy to ruffle through them. (Using hanging folders at all is a matter of preference.)

Keep a supply of both manila folders and hanging folders within reach so that creating a new one is as easy as possible.

Choose a Simple, Logical Naming Scheme

You may be a plain A-to-Z–type person, but there are more ways than one to alphabetize file folders. One great method divides things into categories, such as Car, Client, Taxes, Bank Account; then you preface a folder name with that word. For example, one folder might be Car: Honda Accord and another is Client: Acme, and another Bank Account: ING Direct.

Whatever method you choose, make sure it is obvious and consistent throughout your files to make retrieving paperwork as simple and thoughtless as feasible.

Use a Label Maker

You may be tempted to save money and space and skip getting a label maker. That's understandable. But don't underestimate the value this inexpensive, small tool provides. Neatly labeled folders make a file drawer look sharp, accessible, organized, and professional. Making a new label is a lot more fun and satisfying than scribbling onto a tab with a pen and running out of room, or having to cross something out (or white it out!) and start all over. Printed labels also make your folders legible, and presentable at meetings with clients and co-workers.

The Brother P-Touch Home and Hobby Label Maker, for example, gets the job done, and it'll set you back about 20 bucks.

Purge and Archive

Over time, it's easy for your filing drawer to get out of control and filled with stuff that doesn't matter anymore or that you simply don't need on hand at all times. In fact, according to the Small Business Administration, 80 percent of filed paperwork is never referenced again. Purge your paperwork every few months — get rid of the irrelevant stuff, such as user guides you can get on the Web or for gadgets you no longer own, past project research, and former-employer paperwork.

Archive old stuff you don't want to trash but don't need immediate access to by packing it into cardboard file boxes and putting it in storage. Closed bank-account records, old credit reports, and your 1996 taxes are good candidates here.

Hack 14: Instantly Recall Any Number of Different Passwords

Level. . . . . . . **Easy**
Platform. . . . **All**
Cost. . . . . **Free**

Any computer-system administrator will tell you that the easiest and most secure place to store passwords is in your head. However, remembering the dozens of passwords you need to access networks, web sites, and computers at work and at home seems like an impossible task — unless you've got the right system.

A good password is easy for you to remember and hard for others to guess. Easy enough for one password, but everywhere you turn you have to come up with another to register for a web site or wireless network or to set a PIN. How do you choose new passwords? More important, how do you remember them?

Don't Use the Same Password for Everything

You wouldn't use the same key for your car, home, office, garage, and safety deposit box, so you shouldn't use the same password for all your virtual locks, either. The problem with using the same password for everything you do is that if it's compromised and someone finds it, the rest of your identity is at risk.

If your mutual fund company, for example, has a security breach that exposes usernames and passwords, and you use the same login details there as for your online banking and at Amazon.com, the thieves could compromise not only your mutual fund account but also your bank account and the credit card details stored at Amazon.com. If you give your roommate your wireless-network password and it's the same as your email password, it wouldn't be difficult for your roomie to snoop into your private messages.

The trick is to keep a unique password for each service you use.

Remember 100 Different Passwords with One Rule Set

Remembering a unique password for the dozens of logins you have may sound impossible, but it's not. You don't need to remember 100 passwords if you have one rule set for generating them.

Here's how it works: Create unique passwords by choosing a base password and then applying a single rule that mashes in some form of the service name with it. For example, you could use your base password plus the first three letters of a service name. If your base password were `asdf` (see how easy that is to type?), for example, then your password for Yahoo! would be `ASDFYAH`, and your password for eBay would be `ASDFEBA`.

Another example that incorporates numbers (which some services require in passwords) might involve the same letters to start (say, your initials and a favorite number) plus the first two vowels of a service name. In that case, my password for Amazon would be GMLT10AA and for Lifehacker.com GMLT10IE. (Include obscure middle initials — such as your mother's maiden name or a childhood nickname — that not many people know about for extra security.)

Before you decide on your single password-generation rule, remember that although password requirements differ for each service, a good guideline is a password that's at least eight characters long and includes both letters and numbers. To make a password even more secure — or applicable for services that require special characters — add them around or inside it, such as #GMLT10LIF# or GMLT10#LIF.

One problem with rules-based passwords is that some sites have their own rules that conflict with your own, such as no special characters. In those cases, you have to document or remember the exception to your rule for those services. The next hack explains how you can keep track of passwords that don't follow a single rule.

TIP A clever password-generator bookmarklet, available at `http://angel.net/~nic/passwd.html`, generates a random password based on a web site URL. View a video demonstration of this bookmarklet in action at `http://weblog.infoworld.com/udell/2005/05/03.html`.

CHOOSING YOUR BASE PASSWORD

Here are some options for choosing your base password:

■ The first letter of a phrase or song refrain. For example, if you wanted to use the famous Jackson 5 song "I Want You Back," your base password might be IWUB. Remembering the password is a matter of singing the song to yourself.

■ Use a pre-established keyboard pattern, such as yui or zxcv. Just look at your keyboard to remember it.

(continued)

CHOOSING YOUR BASE PASSWORD *(continued)*

■ Use your spouse's initials and your anniversary, such as TFB0602. (This one guarantees that you won't forget an anniversary card, either.)

■ For extra security, choose an easy-to-remember base, such as your spouse's initials or the word *cat*, and then shift your fingers up one row on the keyboard when you type it. In the case of cat, you get dq5.

Then combine this base with some extra information unique to the service.

Hack 15: Securely Track Your Passwords

Level. . . . . . . **Advanced**
Platform. . . . **Windows XP and Vista, Mac OS X**
Cost. . . . . **Free**

Hack 14 covers how to choose memorable passwords, but what about the passwords you already have? Or passwords that were assigned to you that you can't change? Or passwords for systems with special requirements that your usual password scheme doesn't work for?

Sometimes you just *have* to write down a password to remember it. Don't do it where others can read it, such as on a Post-It note or in an easy-to-read text file or Word document. You can keep a secure and searchable database of those hard-to-remember passwords using the free, open-source software application KeePass (http://keepass.sourceforge .net; Mac version: http://keepassx.sourceforge.net).

One Master Password to Rule All

A KeePass database stores all your passwords in an encrypted state and uses one master password (and, optionally, a special file called a key-file) to access that database. KeePass has fields for username, password, URL, and notes associated with each login, and you can create login groups — such as Windows, web sites, Wi-Fi networks — to organize your passwords. KeePass is very secure; if you keep it running, it will lock its workspace after a certain amount of idle time and require you to enter the master password again to access the database.

Here's how to set up KeePass:

1. Download KeePass from `http://keepass.sourceforge.net` and install. (Mac users, get KeePassX at `http://keepassx .sourceforge.net`.)

2. To create your KeePass database, choose File ⇨ New. The Set Master Key dialog box opens, as shown in Figure 2-3.

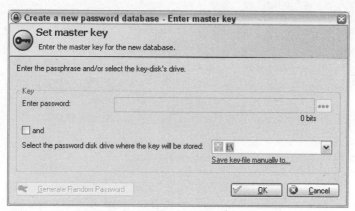

Figure 2-3 The KeePass database dialog box.

3. To use a master password to access your database, just enter one into the password field. (You'll have to enter it one more time to confirm.)

   To use a key-file stored somewhere on your computer, either choose a disk from the drop-down list or choose Save Key-File Manually To and place the key-file somewhere other than the root of the drive. (A thumb drive is a great place to store a key-file so that you can take it with you like one of your house keys.)

   For extra security, use both a key-file and a master password to secure your KeePass database. If you associate a key-file with your password, anyone who somehow gets your master password (perhaps using keylogging software) still can't access your database without the key-file.

   If you choose to use a key-file, KeePass employs random mouse movement or random keyboard input (see Figure 2-4) to generate the file. Press OK when you're done.

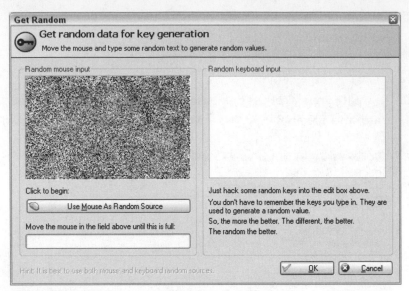

Figure 2-4 KeePass generates a secure key file.

4. KeePass creates your database, and then you add entries to it. KeePass suggests some default groupings for your passwords — Windows, Network, Internet, eMail, and Homebanking — as shown in Figure 2-5.

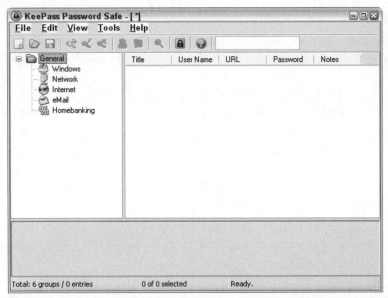

Figure 2-5 A new KeePass database comes with preinstalled groups.

5. To add an entry, right-click in the right pane and choose Add Entry. Assign your login a title (for example, Gina @ Home computer). (The title will be displayed in your list of logins inside KeePass, so make it as descriptive and unique as possible so that you can scan the list and pick it out quickly.) Enter your username, a password, and an optional URL, notes, expiration date, and file attachment to the entry, as shown in Figure 2-6, for each of your existing logins. Toggle the . . . button next to the Password field to display the contents of your password or obscure it with asterisks.

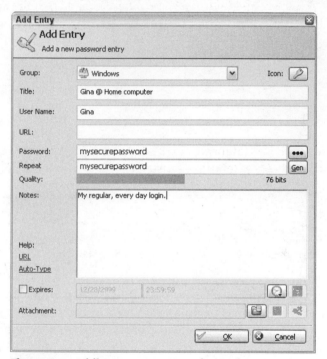

Figure 2-6 Adding a new password entry into your KeePass database.

KeePass displays how secure your password is with an as-you-type quality meter, just below the Repeat field.

6. Click OK and your login is entered into the KeePass database. Repeat the process for every login you want to track in the database.

Find and Use Your Passwords with KeePass

After you have entered all your username and password information into KeePass, you can find and use your login information whenever you need it. For example, you can set up a Wifi Networks password group that lists your logins at all the networks you use, including school, home, friends' houses, and coffee shops, as shown in Figure 2-7.

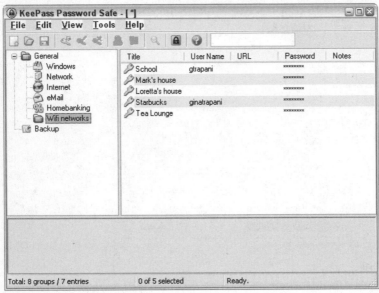

Figure 2-7 A Wifi Network group of saved passwords in KeePass.

When you're at your friend Mark's house, you can then either browse to the `Wifi Networks` folder or simply enter **Mark** in the search box on the upper right to retrieve the `Mark's house` entry. Right-click the entry, select Copy Password To Clipboard, and then drop it into Mark's Wi-Fi login prompt.

Configure other useful KeePass features for instant password retrieval in the Options panel in the File menu, including the following:

- Start KeePass with Windows automatically.
- Clear any password copied to the clipboard after a certain amount of time, or allow for only one password paste for extra security.
- Minimize KeePass to the system tray to save Windows taskbar real estate.
- Attach files to KeePass entries. This feature is useful for storing even passworded Microsoft Word documents or encrypted text

files or disk images (see Hack 19, "Create a Password-Protected Disk on Your PC," later in this chapter).

▪ Install KeePass on a thumb drive with your database for instant, secure access to your passwords from any computer with a USB port.

NOTE For web site passwords, you can securely save login information directly in Firefox. The advantage of that method is that copy and paste isn't required; Firefox autofills the login box with your details. However, this works only for web-based passwords — not Wi-Fi, network, email, or Windows login information. See Hack 55, "Securely Save Web Site Passwords," for more information.

You can encrypt a text file with your passwords saved in it, but a text file or Word document doesn't provide the structured password detail entry that a KeePass database does. In fact, because KeePass is a searchable encrypted database, you can use it to store other types of important information, such as software serial numbers, credit card numbers, and PINs. (But remember: although KeePass is very secure, the most secure place on the planet to keep a very important piece of information is in your head.)

Hack 16: Tag Your Bookmarks

Level. . . . . . . **Medium**
Platform. . . . **Web**
Cost. . . . . **Free**

The Web gets bigger every day, and so does your bookmark list. A social bookmarking service called del.icio.us (http://del.icio.us) stores your bookmarks online and associates keywords (called *tags*) to each bookmark for easy retrieval. Storing your bookmarks online also makes them accessible from every computer you use.

The bare-bones interface and peculiar URL of the del.icio.us service hides the feature-rich, highly hackable nature of this web application. Recently acquired by Yahoo!, del.icio.us is a fantastic option for any web researcher or power bookmarker who wants to quickly access and organize web content that matters to him. This hack covers just some of the ways to use del.icio.us to manage your bookmarks, create a personal index of web content, and tap into the community to find even more useful resources on the Web.

Getting Started with del.icio.us

Register for a free account at `http://del.icio.us`. When you're signed in, your del.icio.us bookmarks will be available at `http://del.icio.us/username`. A social bookmarking service means, by default, that all your bookmarks are public and viewable by other members of the del.icio.us community. You can enable private bookmark saving in the settings area of your del.icio.us account at `http://del.icio.us/settings/username/privacy`.

Add a Bookmark

The basic way to add a bookmark to del.icio.us is to use the `post` link at `http://del.icio.us/post`. But that's also the least efficient way. For faster bookmarking, go to the del.icio.us browser buttons area at `http://del.icio.us/help/buttons` and drag and drop a quick post link to your browser toolbar. Then, when you browse to a page you want to save, just click the button to add your bookmark.

Tags, Not Folders

Most web browsers organize your bookmarks in folders and subfolders. Arguably the best feature of del.icio.us is the use of tags: labels or keywords that let you view your bookmark list based on single or combined keywords.

For example, to bookmark a web page that describes a foolproof technique for slicing a ripe mango, add it to your del.icio.us bookmarks and tag it `mango`, `howto`, `kitchen`, `fruit`, `cooking`, and `summer`. One bookmark can have as many tags as you'd like.

If you also bookmarked a page with a great smoothie recipe and you tagged it `smoothie`, `fruit`, and `recipe`, the mango page and the smoothie page would both appear under the `fruit` tag listing. However, only the mango page would appear under the `howto` tag. A list of both `fruit` and `summer` tags would include only the mango page as well, because the smoothie page was not tagged `summer`.

To enter a set of tags for a bookmark in del.icio.us, you simply type a list of words separated by spaces. So, you'd enter

```
smoothie fruit summer
```

in the `tags` field for the smoothie page bookmark. The freeform nature of the tags field makes creating and assigning new tags extremely easy, but it also leaves the door wide open for misspellings and similar tags (such as `fruit` and `fruits`). After using del.icio.us for some time, you'll develop a vocabulary of tags you use often, and del.icio.us will make suggestions from your tag as you type.

In Figure 2-8, I'm bookmarking a page called "Silva Rhetoricae." I've included a description for the bookmark: "An exhaustive directory of rhetorical devices from a BYU professor."

As I type the letter w into the tags field, del.icio.us uses my preestablished tag vocabulary (under `your tags`) to suggest tags that could match (such as `writing`, `weblogs`, `work`, and `wikipedia`). In this case, I was looking for `writing`.

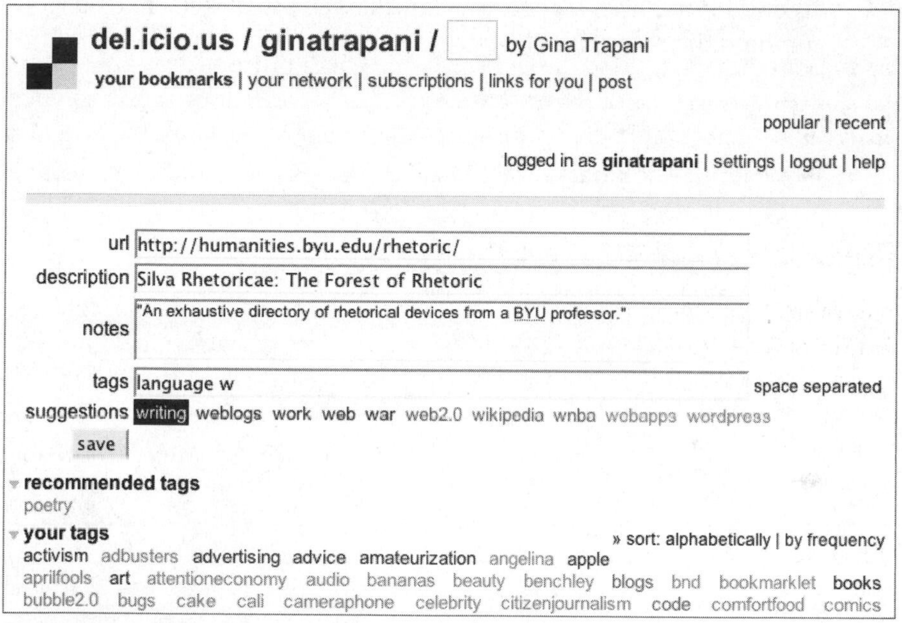

Figure 2-8 Adding tags to a bookmark in del.icio.us.

Navigating del.icio.us by URL

Getting around del.icio.us is easiest if you use its hackable URL scheme to get what you want. All you need to do is add what you're looking for to the end of the del.icio.us URL. For example, here's the base URL:

```
http://del.icio.us/
```

To find bookmarks tagged `mango` by all del.icio.us users, you simply add `tag` and `mango`, like this:

```
http://del.icio.us/tag/mango
```

To find bookmarks tagged `writing` by the user `ginatrapani`, add the username and then the tag:

```
http://del.icio.us/ginatrapani/writing
```

(Replace `ginatrapani/writing` with your own username and your tag(s) to quickly find your bookmarks.)

To find bookmarks tagged `tech` and `howto` by all del.icio.us users, combine the tags with + signs:

```
http://del.icio.us/tag/tech+howto
```

How about bookmarks tagged `tutorial`, `router`, and `linksys` by all del.icio.us users?

```
http://del.icio.us/tag/tutorial+router+linksys
```

Find all bookmarked sound files:

```
http://del.icio.us/tag/system:media:audio
```

Find all bookmarked video files:

```
http://del.icio.us/tag/system:media:video
```

Find MP3 files tagged `mashup`:

```
http://del.icio.us/tag/system:filetype:mp3+mashup
```

Other del.icio.us Features

You can import your current browser bookmarks into del.icio.us using its import feature, located at `http://del.icio.us/settings/username/import`. You can also export your del.icio.us links at `http://del.icio.us/settings/username/export`.

To keep your del.icio.us links in sync with the Firefox web browser, use the Foxylicious Firefox extension, freely available at `https://addons .mozilla.org/firefox/342`.

Hack 17: Organize Your Digital Photos

Level. . . . . . . **Easy**
Platform. . . . **Windows XP and Vista**
Cost. . . . . **Free**

The ubiquity of digital cameras and cheap storage means that even the most amateur photographers can accumulate hundreds — even thousands — of digital photos on their computers over time. After even just a few months of taking photos, it's easy to wind up with a hard drive cluttered with a bunch of folders filled with images named things like `IMG_8394.jpg`. Pictures don't mean anything unless someone sees them, and no one will see the photos buried on your computer if you can't find the best ones.

The problem with digital photos is that your computer doesn't have much information about them. To your computer, a digital picture is just a collection of different-colored dots. Minimal information is stored inside a photo when it's snapped, such as what your camera settings were and the date and time. The photo doesn't have information such as who it depicts, where, or at what event it was taken. To make your photos searchable (and therefore useful), you have to add metadata such as captions, labels, and ratings to them. Google's free photo organizer for Windows and Linux, Picasa (`http://picasa.com`), can help you organize, edit, caption, label, and star your digital photos.

Import Your Photos into Picasa

Download Picasa from `http://picasa.com` (free) and install it on your PC. The first time you launch the program, it asks whether it should scan your entire computer, or just your `My Documents` folder, for photos. Make your choice and Picasa will build its index of all the photos and videos on your computer automatically. When it's complete, you'll see a list of folders organized by year in the left panel, and you'll see a grid of images on the right side, as shown in Figure 2-9.

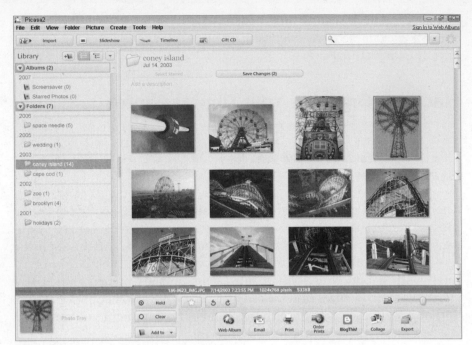

Figure 2-9 Viewing photos in Picasa.

Now you're ready to start organizing and adding meaning to your photos.

Organize and Label Your Collection

Until your computer is smart enough to recognize places and faces in your digital photos automatically, you have to provide that information so that you can retrieve pictures based on it. For example, to see all Dick and Jane's wedding photos, or just portraits of Jane, those photos would have to be labeled "Jane" or "wedding."

Captions

Click an individual photo to focus on it in Picasa. Then click the small button on the bottom left labeled Show/Hide Caption. When you show the caption, type in a descriptive phrase using words you'd search for later, such as **Joey in a tuxedo at Mom's wedding**, as shown in Figure 2-10.

Use as many keywords as you think you'll ever use to search for the photo in the future. Avoid nicknames, abbreviations, or otherwise opaque captions — they won't help you later! After you've set your caption as the example shows, a search for *wedding*, *Mom*, *Joey*, or *tuxedo* will turn up that picture.

Figure 2-10 Assign a caption to a photo in Picasa.

NOTE The best part of Picasa's caption system is that it actually saves the text *inside* the photo itself. So if you publish the photo online or decide to stop using Picasa, you don't lose your photo's caption.

Albums

When adding an individual caption to every photo is too monstrous an undertaking, use albums instead. Albums are collections of photos that don't necessarily all exist in the same folder. You can't do this with folders, but with albums, you can have one photo live in several albums.

Name your albums something descriptive (such as "Mom's Wedding") and Ctrl+click to select several photos and place them in Picasa's "tray" on the bottom-left side. Then click the Add To button to place those photos into an album.

Stars

After a frenetic photography session or event, one or two special photos often stand out from the rest. Use stars to mark your favorite photos in Picasa. To star (or un-star) a photo, select it in Picasa and click the star button on the bottom panel to toggle the star notation on and off.

Search Your Photos

After you've organized your photos into albums with captions and stars, you can search and sort pictures for easy retrieval. Use Picasa's search box on the top panel to filter your photos down to just what you need. As you type each character, Picasa will filter the list of matching photos dynamically, searching on filename, caption, album, and folder name.

Click the arrow next to the search field to expand the criteria form. Click the star to narrow your results to Starred Photos only, as shown in Figure 2-11. (There are also buttons for filtering down to just movies, or just uploaded photos, too). Using a date slider, you can narrow the list by time period as well.

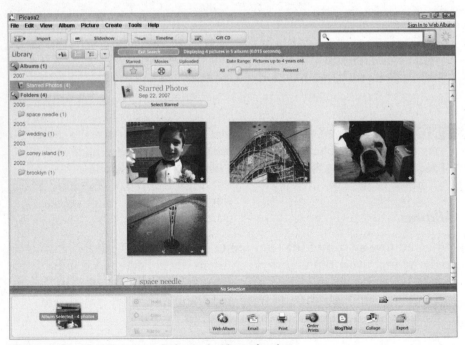

Figure 2-11 Viewing starred photos in Picasa by date.

Other Picasa Features

Picasa boasts more useful photo-management features, including these:

- Slideshows to play on your computer or burn to CD
- Password-protected albums
- Batch moving and renaming photos between folders within Picasa
- Editing tools that can fix red-eye, crop, tune, and otherwise make your pictures look better inside Picasa
- Burning of photo archive DVDs

Hack 18: Create Saved Search Folders

Level. . . . . . . **Easy**
Platform. . . . **Windows Vista, Mac OS X (10.4+)**
Cost. . . . . **Free**

As you begin to file your documents less and depend on searches more, it only makes sense to combine the folder paradigm and search capabilities with saved search folders. A saved search folder is a container for files that match certain criteria. For example, if you have several files in different folders and subfolders on your computer, each with the word *lifehacker* in the title, a search for "all files with the word lifehacker in the title" would list those files. Save that search as a folder, and you get an on-the-fly collection of documents that share the same characteristics in a virtual folder.

The main advantage of saved search folders versus regular old-fashioned folders is that a file can exist in more than one folder at the same time. A Word document named `lifehacker.doc` will appear in both the `lifehacker in title` saved search folder and the `All Word documents` saved search folder. This way of organizing your search results allows you to slice and dice your information any way you need it. Saved search folders come in most handy on a temporary basis: while you're working on a certain project, for instance. When you delete a saved search folder, the files inside it aren't deleted; they continue to live on in their respective locations. This hack shows you how to start creating saved search folders in both Windows Vista and Mac OS.

NOTE Windows XP does not feature saved search folders.

Search Folders in Windows Vista

Windows Vista includes a search box on the top-right side of every Explorer window. Run your search by entering criteria (such as the keyword *lifehacker*) there, and Vista will return its file-search results. By default, a search from Explorer's search box looks for results only in the folder you're browsing. Click the Advanced Search button to change the search location and add other criteria. When you're satisfied with the results, save the search as a folder by clicking the Save Search button, as shown in Figure 2-12.

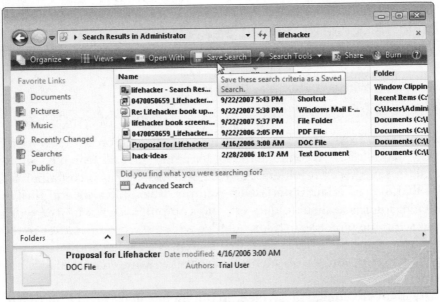

Figure 2-12 Creating a search folder in Windows Vista.

Vista comes with a few preconfigured search folders, such as Recent Documents (files that have been modified recently) and Attachments (email attachments.)

The key to creating the most useful search folder is to pinpoint its contents to exactly what you need. Several special operators used in Vista's search box can do just that. For example, searching for Jack NOT Jill will return documents that include the word Jack but not Jill (note that NOT has to be all uppercase.) A search for Jack OR Jill returns documents that mention Jack, Jill, or both Jack and Jill. A search for "Jack and Jill" (in quotation marks) will do an exact phrase match and return only documents that include the exact words *Jack and Jill*.

A complete list of all Vista's search operators is available at `http://windowsvistablog.com/blogs/windowsvista/pages/advanced-search-techniques.aspx`, including those shown in the following table.

TYPE THIS	TO FIND THIS
`Windows`	Items containing WinDOwS, windows, WINDOWS, or any other combination of uppercase and lowercase letters
`microsoft windows`	Items containing the words *microsoft* and *windows*
`microsoft NOT windows` Note: The word NOT must be in all uppercase letters	Items containing *microsoft*, but not *windows*.
microsoft OR windows Note: The word OR must be in all uppercase letters	Items containing *microsoft*, *windows*, or both.
"microsoft windows"	Items containing the exact phrase *microsoft windows*.
author:"Jane Smith"	Items created by Jane Smith.
date: > 11/05/04	Items with a date after 11/05/04

After you save your search folder, its icon will look slightly different from a traditional folder, as shown in Figure 2-13.

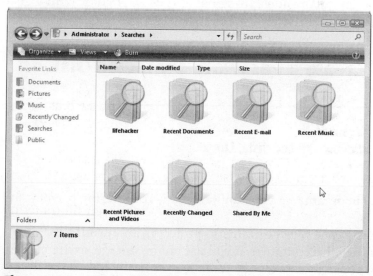

Figure 2-13 A Windows Vista saved search folder.

Saved Search Folders in Mac OS

Mac OS X's saved search feature is called Smart Folders (like iTunes' Smart Playlists). To create a Smart Folder, from any Finder window, enter your terms into the search box on the upper-right corner. To add criteria to your search, click the + button. You can add as many lines of search criteria as you please, such as the kind of file, the date last modified, the author, and contents, as shown in Figure 2-14.

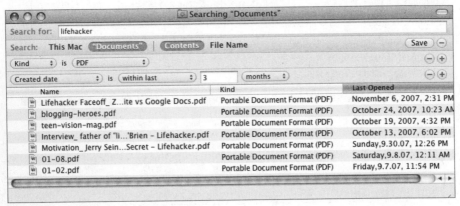

Figure 2-14 Searching within Finder.

When you're satisfied with your search, click the Save button to save your Smart Folder to a location of your choice. Smart Folders sport a different icon than regular folders; they have a lavender color with a gear image on them.

Hack 19: Create a Password-Protected Disk on Your PC

Level. . . . . . . **Advanced**
Platform. . . . **Windows XP and Vista, Linux**
Cost. . . . . **Free**

The next level in organizing your digital stuff is considering privacy and safety.

Everyone has some files he wants to protect from intruders or others who have access to his computer. If you use online storage, exchange sensitive information over email, or store data on an easily lost CD or thumb drive, you may want to encrypt that data to keep it from getting into the wrong hands.

When you encrypt data, you use a special algorithm to scramble the bits that make up that file into nonsensical information, which can be restored to its meaningful state only with the right password.

TrueCrypt is a free, open-source encryption application that works on Windows and Linux. Given the right credentials, TrueCrypt creates a virtual hard drive that reads and writes encrypted files on the fly. This hack explains how to encrypt your private files using TrueCrypt.

Set up the Encrypted Volume Location

Here's how to set up an encrypted virtual disk with TrueCrypt:

1. Download TrueCrypt from `http://truecrypt.org`. Install and launch it.

2. Click the Create Volume button to launch a wizard that prepares the encrypted drive location. Choose Create A Standard TrueCrypt Volume and click Next.

3. On the Volume Location page, click the Select File button, navigate to the location where you want to store your encrypted files, and type a name for it. I'm going with `C:\Documents and Settings\penelope\My Documents\4myeyesonly`, as shown in Figure 2-15.

Figure 2-15 Create an encrypted volume with TrueCrypt.

The name (`4myeyesonly` in this example) isn't the file you want to encrypt; it's the container that will store the files you encrypt. Click Next.

4. Choose your encryption algorithm. The curious can flip through the drop-down list and view info on each option, but you can't go wrong here; the default AES (Advanced Encryption Standard) selection will work for most purposes. (Hey, if it works for Top Secret government files[3], it should work for you.) Click Next.

5. Choose the size of the virtual drive — for example, 100MB, as shown in Figure 2-16.

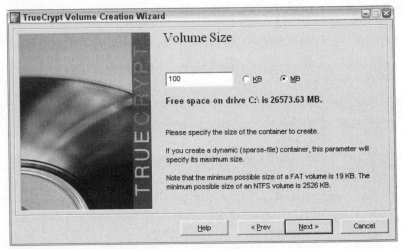

Figure 2-16 Set the size of your encrypted container.

The advantage here is that the file will always look as though it's exactly 100MB, giving no hint as to the actual size of its contents. Click Next.

6. Choose your volume password. TrueCrypt wants something hard to crack, such as 20 characters with letters and numbers mixed together. The whole point here is to keep snoopers at bay, so make your password a nondictionary word that's difficult to guess. Alternatively, you can use a key-file to lock your volume.

WARNING Keep in mind that if you forget your password or your key-file gets corrupted or lost, the files on your TrueCrypt volume will be inaccessible — forever.

7. Format the volume. This part is fun: TrueCrypt gathers random information from your system — including the location of your

mouse pointer — to format the file drive location with random data to make it impossible to read. Click the Format button to go ahead with this operation, which may slow down your computer for a few seconds. (Don't let the word *format* scare you; you're not erasing your hard drive, you're just formatting the drive location file — the 4myeyesonly file in this example — that you just created.)

When the formatting is complete, your encrypted volume location is ready for use.

Store and Retrieve Files from the Encrypted Volume

Your TrueCrypt file can hold your highly sensitive files locked up as tight as a drum. Here's how to get to it:

1. From TrueCrypt, choose Select File and navigate to the volume file you just created.

2. Select an available drive letter such as z: from the list in True-Crypt (see Figure 2-17).

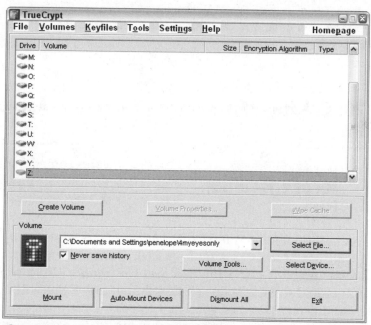

Figure 2-17 To mount a TrueCrypt drive, select the file container and an available drive letter.

3. Click the Mount button and enter your volume password. If you enter the correct password, the virtual drive z: will be mounted.

4. Go to My Computer. Listed alongside all the other drives on your computer is a new one: Local Disk Z:. Drag and drop all your sensitive data to this drive and work from it as you would any other disk.

5. When you're finished working with the data, in TrueCrypt, select the mounted drive (z: in this example) and click the Dismount button. The z: drive will no longer be available; all you'll have left is the 4myeyesonly file you created, which can be dropped onto a thumb drive, emailed to yourself, burned to CD, or placed on your iPod, totally encrypted.

If someone managed to open this file, its contents would be meaningless, indecipherable nonsense. Only a user with TrueCrypt installed and the password or key-file would be able to mount the drive and access the files on it.

TIP Using TrueCrypt you can secure an entire drive — such as a USB thumb drive. To do so, click Select Device instead of Select File and choose your thumb drive. You can also install TrueCrypt to the thumb drive itself.

Hack 20: Create a Password-Protected Disk on Your Mac

Level. . . . . . . **Medium**
Platform. . . . **Mac OS X (10.4 or later)**
Cost. . . . . **Free**

If you have files and folders you'd like to keep private and secure on your Mac, you can use Mac OS X's built-in Disk Utility to encrypt a disk image. A disk image is just a file that you can mount like a separate disk, and unmount to lock again — like a thumb drive, but without the actual physical drive. Whether you want to password-protect sensitive customer data or your spouse's surprise birthday party plans, an encrypted disk image can lock up any number of files and folders behind a password. This hack covers how to lock and unlock a disk image.

Create a New Encrypted Disk Image

Here's how to create an encrypted disk image:

1. Launch Disk Utility, located in /Applications/Utilities/.

2. From the File menu, choose New ➪ Blank Disk Image.

3. Enter a name (my-secret-files, for example) for your disk in the Save As dialog. From the Size drop-down list, choose how big you'd like the disk to be. (Make it large enough to accommodate all the data you want to store there.) From the Encryption drop-down list, select 128-Bit AES Encryption (Recommended), as shown in Figure 2-18.

Figure 2-18 Set the name, size, and encryption for your new password-protected disk image.

4. Next, you'll set a password to access the disk image. Make your password both secure and memorable. (For help choosing a password, click the button with the key icon on it to launch the Password Assistant, which can make suggestions for your password.) By default, your new password will be saved in your Keychain (see Figure 2-19) to make it harder to forget.

Disk Utility will create and mount the my-secret-files disk image. After it's created, you'll see the new disk appear on your Desktop. Move, save, or copy files onto this disk as if it were any other while using your Mac.

When you're done adding all your private files to the disk, dismount it as usual (Ctrl+click and choose Eject my-secret-files.) Now you can move the my-secret-files.dmg file onto any other disk, such as a thumb drive or CD. No one will be able to mount it without the password.

Figure 2-19 Set the password needed to mount your new encrypted disk image.

Access Your Password-Protected Disk

To access the files on your encrypted disk image, double-click it, and your Mac will attempt to mount it. If your password is saved in the keychain, the disk will mount and you'll be able to save and open files from it as usual. If not, you'll have to enter your password to mount and decrypt the file for use.

Hack 21: Design Your Own Planner

Level. . . . . . . **Easy**
Platform. . . . **All**
Cost. . . . . **Office supplies**

There are many good reasons to ditch your expensive, electronic PDA for a paper-based planner system: cost, portability, and maintenance, to name a few. Paper-based planners never run out of battery juice or memory; they never crash or refuse to work the way you expect. Lots of even the most tech-savvy are going retro with paper calendars and to-do lists.

This hack explains how to build your own custom paper planner, calendar, and project manager using your computer and your printer.

The D*I*Y Planner system (http://diyplanner.com) is an extensive library of PDF templates from which you can pick and choose. Then, print the pages you need and assemble your planner.

Why Build Your Own Planner?

You can walk into any office-supplies store and choose from a variety of prefab paper planners. But the advantages of a do-it-yourself planner are customization and scalability. Maybe you're thinking about giving up the BlackBerry and you just want to test-drive a paper solution. Maybe you don't want to have to order a new set of custom-print pages from your store-bought planner's manufacturer every time you run out. With a D*I*Y Planner, you can add, replace, and reshuffle pages very easily. Refills are a matter of printing a new set of pages.

You can also easily make D*I*Y Planners for your staff that cover custom timelines such as the duration of a particular project. Keep your D*I*Y Planner thin and portable by carrying around only the next couple of weeks' worth of information.

How to Assemble Your D*I*Y Planner

First, decide on the size and type of planner you want to create. The D*I*Y Planner site has templates available to print in several sizes:

- Classic (half pages of 8 1/2×11-inch paper, common in North America)
- Letter size (8 1/2×11-inch paper)
- A4 (the equivalent to letter size in Europe and countries outside North America)
- A5 (half of A4 size)
- Hipster PDA (index cards)

Download the template kit you need from http:// diyplanner.com/templates/official. Open and print the templates using a PDF reader such as Adobe Acrobat or Foxit (http://foxitsoftware.com). Depending on the size you choose, you may have to cut the paper in half (for Classic and A5) and punch holes in it to fit it inside a binder. The Hipster PDA index-card–sized version can be held together with a small binder clip.

D*I*Y Planner Templates and Sizes

The D*I*Y Planner system offers an extensive set of templates, including these:

> Calendar, to-do lists, and note-taking pages
>
> Stephen Covey's priority matrix
>
> David Allen's *Getting Things Done* system buckets (such as Next Actions, Waiting, Projects)
>
> Mind maps
>
> A photographer release form
>
> Book notes
>
> Storyboard
>
> Shopping lists
>
> Address book
>
> Contact logs (phone call/email/IM log of contacts)
>
> Financial ledger
>
> Meeting agenda
>
> Goals tracker
>
> Lined horizontal, lined vertical, and graph paper
>
> Project outline and notes forms

Print only as many pages of the forms as you need to assemble your custom planner. Later, if you decide to change the planner size you use, or need to add pages for certain kinds of information (such as another address-book page to accommodate contacts whose last names start with *S*, or larger daily calendar pages to write your appointments), simply print the pages and reassemble or add them to your planner.

References

1. "Google Copies Your Hard Drive — Government Smiles in Antici-pation," EFF Breaking News (http://eff.org/news/archives/2006_02.php#004400).

2. David Allen, *Getting Things Done*, (Penguin Books, 2001), 100.

3. "National Policy on the Use of the Advanced Encryption Standard (AES) to Protect National Security Systems and National Security Information" (http://cnss.gov/Assets/pdf/cnssp_15_fs.pdf).

Trick Yourself into Getting Done

Just as Mom used to grind up that bitter pill in a bowl of ice cream, you can make working on tough tasks easier for yourself to swallow. Checking an item off your to-do list — and the sense of satisfaction and completion that comes with that simple motion — is one of the best things that can happen during your workday. But there are roadblocks, both environmental and just plain mental, on the way to "done."

Part of the reason that you leave the office at night feeling so behind comes from the nature of the modern workplace. Rife with distractions and interruptions, many offices couldn't be less conducive to productivity. Noise and drop-by co-workers aside, the reality of information work is that there's always another email to open, another web site to visit, another message that's making your PDA vibrate off the desk. At any moment there are a dozen things that you *could* work on, and the choice itself is a source of distraction and paralysis. It's easy to spend the day constantly switching gears and re-evaluating what's the biggest fire to put out next — instead of making progress on important work.

Even when you're alone, with email and phone turned off, procrastination rears its ugly head. Starting in on a tough project feels like an impossible feat; suddenly you're spending the afternoon you set aside to get to work on the big presentation ripping your CD collection into iTunes instead. In a culture that says "you can do anything you want!" your to-do lists fill up with gargantuan tasks that would scare off the most functional person on earth: "Learn French. Start small business. Buy new house. Go back to school."

The self-sabotage doesn't stop there. A 2005 study[1] shows that people overestimate the amount of time they think they have in the future to get things done, leaving them with overbooked calendars and more incomplete commitments. An exaggerated sense of how much time you have — and how much time tasks can take you to complete — can cut off your best efforts at getting things done.

In his excellent book *The War of Art*, writer Steven Pressfield calls the inner force that keeps you from doing your work Resistance with a capital *R*.[2] Pressfield says a true Professional (with a capital *P*) gets her work done no matter how strong Resistance pushes against her. I'd add that the Professional arms herself adequately in the war against Resistance to make victory more likely. In short, she makes the *right* thing to do the *easy* thing to do.

You can organize your tasks and your calendar in a way that speeds you toward the finish faster, and this chapter shows you how. In contrast to other chapters in this book, the hacks here focus more on adjusting the way you work than on computer tricks. Use these hacks to cross off items on your task list more often and treat yourself to that delicious sense of completion every single day.

Hack 22: Make Your To-Do List Doable

Level. . . . . . . **Easy**
Platform. . . . **All**
Cost. . . . . **Free**

There's no better feeling than checking something off your to-do list. Done! Finished! Mission accomplished! Yet it's so easy to let a whole day or week go by without knocking one task off your list. How does that happen? Well, your to-do list can be a tool that guides you through your work, or it can be a big fat pillar of undone time bombs taunting you and your unproductive inadequacy. It all depends on how you write it.

Think of your to-do list as an instruction set your Boss self gives your Assistant self. Like a good computer program, if the instructions are clear, specific, and easily carried out, you're golden. If not, you'll get undesirable results, such as fear, procrastination, and self-loathing. Read on to take a closer look at how to write a to-do list that makes getting your stuff done dead-simple.

You Are the Boss of You

At any point during the workday, you are in one of two modes: thinking mode (that's you with the Boss hat on) and action mode (that's you with the Personal Assistant hat on). When a project or task comes up, the steps you've got to take start to form in your mind. Now you're in thinking/Boss mode — the guy/gal who gives the orders. Your to-do list is a collection of those orders, which your Assistant personality will later pick up and do.

When you're wearing your Boss hat, it's up to you to write down the instructions in such a way that your Assistant self can just do them without having to think. Taking the thinking out of the acting is one of the best ways to make your to-do list a cinch to finish off.

How to Order Yourself Around

When it's time to add something to your to-do list, think it through using the following guidelines.

Only Put Items on the List that You're Definitely Doing

Sometimes you think of tasks you're just not ready to do yet. Maybe learning a new language — while it's an eventual goal — just doesn't fit into your life right now. Maybe upgrading the web site is low priority because your business is shifting gears in a major way, and any site over-haul will look very different — or maybe won't be needed — in six months.

Instead of letting tasks you're not quite committed to loiter on your to-do list until you're sick of looking at them and remembering you're not quite there yet, move them off to a separate list, a holding area for Some-day/Maybe items. You'd tell your assistant to do something only if you absolutely, positively want it done, so only concrete actions you're committed to completing should live on your to-do list.

Break It Down

The best way to make yourself avoid working on a to-do is to make it a vague monstrosity. Put an item such as "Clean out the office" on your to-do list, and I guarantee that's the last thing you'll ever start working on. In fact, "Clean out the office" isn't a to-do at all; it's a *project*. Author of *Getting Things Done* David Allen says projects are not tasks; projects are collections of tasks. That's an important distinction. Internalize it, because your to-do list is not your project list. Don't add multiaction tasks to it, such as "Clean out the office." Break it down to smaller, easier-to-tackle subtasks such as "Purge filing cabinet," "Shred old paperwork," and "Box up unneeded books for library drive." Assistant you will ask "What do you want done?" when Boss you says "Clean out the office."

The smaller and more atomic these subtasks are, the more doable they are. Inspirational writer SARK breaks down her tasks into five-minute increments, and calls them "micromovements." She writes, "Micromovements are tiny, tiny little steps you can take toward completions in your life. I'm a recovering procrastinator and I have a short attention span, so I invented micromovements as a method of completing projects in time spans of 5 minutes or less. I always feel like I can handle almost anything for 5 minutes!"[3]

Coming up with those tiny tasks requires thinking up front, when you're putting the task on your list. The following examples show the contrast between vague to-do's that will throw up roadblocks, and their doable counterparts:

ROADBLOCK TO-DO'S	DOABLE TO-DO'S
Find a new dentist.	Email Jayne and ask what dentist she goes to.
Replace the broken glass tabletop.	Measure the table dimensions. Call San Diego Glass at 555-6789 with dimensions.
Learn Italian.	Check U of Whatever's web site (whatever.edu) for fall Italian-class offerings.
Upgrade web site.	Draft a list of five web site upgrades.

As you can see, breaking down your tasks into next actions will create more than one task for items that *look* like regular to-do's but turn out to be small projects. For example, replacing the broken glass tabletop involves measuring the table, calling and ordering a replacement, and possibly going to pick it up, which brings us to the next guideline.

Focus Only on the Next Action

When you've got yourself a multiaction task — such as replacing the glass tabletop — keep only its next sequential action on your to-do list.

When the task is complete, refer to your project list (again, separate from to-do's) and add its next action to your to-do list. At any given moment, your to-do list should contain only the next logical action for all your working projects. That's it — just one bite-sized step in each undertaking.

Imagine that you're at your desk, you have a spare 10 minutes before a meeting, and you pull out the preceding roadblock to-do list. Can you find a dentist or replace the tabletop? No. But you could get an item done from the doable list. You could email a friend about a dentist referral, or check the university web site for fall class offerings.

Use Specific, Active Verbs

When you're telling yourself to do something, make it an order. An item such as "Acme account checkup" doesn't tell you what has to be done. Make your to-do's specific actions, such as "Phone Rob at Acme re: Q2 sales." Notice I didn't use the word *Contact*; I used *Phone*. Contact could mean phone, email, or IM, but when you take out all the thinking and leave in only action, your verbs will be as specific as possible. Literally imagine yourself instructing a personal assistant on her first day on the job as to what you need done.

Include as Much Information as Possible

When formulating a to-do, the onus is on your Boss self to make it as easy as possible for your Assistant self to get the job done. For example, if you have to make a phone call, include the name or number. Instead of "Donate old furniture," assign yourself "Call Goodwill to schedule pickup, 555-9878." When you're stuck in the doctor's waiting room for 20 minutes with only your cell phone, you can't donate your old furniture, but you sure can make a phone call — if you have the number. Be a good Boss. Arm your Assistant self with all the details she needs to get your work done.

Keep Your List Short

Just as no one wants to look at an email inbox with 2,386 messages in it, no one wants to have an endless to-do list. It's overwhelming and depressing, as though there's no light at the end of the tunnel. Instead, keep your to-do list under 20 items. (This morning, mine's only 17 tasks long, and I call myself a busy person.) Does that sound like too short a list? Remember, your to-do list isn't a dumping ground for project details, or "Someday I'd like to" items. These are tasks you've committed to completing in the very near future, such as the next two weeks. Keep your projects and someday/maybe items elsewhere. Your to-do list should be short, to-the-point commitments that involve no more deciding as to whether you're really serious about doing them.

Prioritize Your Tasks

Although your to-do list might have 20 items on it, the reality is that you're going to get only a couple done per day (assuming that you're not writing down things like "get up, shower, make coffee, go to work. . ." — and you shouldn't be). So make sure those tasks are at the very top of your list. How you do this will depend on what tool or software you use to track your to-do's, but do make sure you can see at a glance what you need to get done next.

Keep Your List Moving

Although my to-do list is only 20 items or so, it's 20 items that change every single day. Every day, two to five tasks get checked off, and two to five tasks get added. Remember, your to-do list is a working document, not some showy testament to organization that quietly gathers dust because you're off doing real work that's not written down anywhere.

Purge and Update Your List Weekly

In addition to sorting by priority, you should be able to sort your list by age. What items have been on your list the longest? Chances are you've got mental blockage around the tasks that have been sitting around forever, and they've got to be reworded or broken down further. Or perhaps they don't need to get done after all. (Remember! Deleting an item from your to-do list is even *better* than checking it off, because you've saved yourself the time and effort of actually doing it.)

Just as a manager would meet with her staff members once a week, schedule a 20-minute meeting with yourself every Friday or Monday to review your to-do list, project list, and someday/maybe list. Use that time to rewrite any items that aren't broken down as much as they should be, purge irrelevant items, and move next actions from your project list to your to-do list.

This short, weekly ritual will make you feel more on top of your game than ever. It'll focus your energy and weed out any detritus that's accumulated over the past week.

Log Your Completed Tasks

As any good assistant does, you want to show the boss exactly how much you've accomplished. Make sure you stow your done items somewhere so that you can revel in your own productivity and even refer to past work activities. Your "done" list is a great indicator of whether your to-do list is working. If more than two days go by without a new done item, it's time to revamp your to-do list and get back to best practices.

Practice Makes Perfect

This may seem like a long set of guidelines for something as simple as adding to your to-do list. But 90 percent of the work in doing things that matter is the planning, and that's true for what may seem to be the most trivial tasks. As with any good habit, practice makes perfect. The more you practice the art of creating effective to-do's, the faster and easier it will come to you, and the more you'll be crossing items off your list and leaving the office with that delicious sense of completion.

NOTE Many of the concepts in this hack (especially the next action, projects, and someday/maybe lists) come from David Allen's productivity bible, *Getting Things Done*. Also, Merlin Mann's two-part feature on building a smarter to-do list[4] and his follow-up article for Macworld magazine[5] inspired and informed this hack.

Hack 23: Set up a Morning Dash

Level. . . . . . . **Easy**
Platform. . . . **All**
Cost. . . . . **Free**

You love that sense of satisfaction and accomplishment when you check off an item on your to-do list as done, completed, out the door, in the can. But so many things can keep you from getting to that moment, from unexpected emergencies to long, dragged-out meetings to getting way-laid by a conversation with a co-worker in the hallway.

Although those spontaneous gear shifts are necessary and will happen, there is one way to ensure that you'll knock at least one thing off your list: dedicate the first hour of your day to your most important task — *before* you check your email, or your paper inbox, or go to any meetings.

Get One Thing Done First

Author of *Never Check Email in the Morning* Julie Morgenstern suggests spending the first hour of your workday email-free. Choose one task — even a small one — and tackle it first thing. Accomplishing something out of the gate sets the tone for the rest of your day and guarantees that no matter how many fires you're tasked with putting out the minute you open your email client, you *still* can say that you got something done. When you're open for business and paying attention to incoming requests, it's too easy to get swept away into the craziness. So get your day started off on the right foot, with just one thing done.

Morgenstern writes, "Change the rhythm of the workday by starting out with your own drumbeat.... When you devote your first hour to concentrated work — a dash — the day starts with *you* in charge of *it* rather than the other way around. It's a bold statement to the world (and yourself) that you can take control, pull away from the frenetic pace, and create the time for quiet work when you need it. In reality, if you don't consciously create the space for the dashes, they won't get done."[6]

To work this hack, you have to set yourself up for your morning dash.

Park on a Downward Slope

The point of this technique is to remove any thought or planning from your first action of the day so that you can get rolling immediately while you're fresh and not distracted by incoming requests. That means you have to choose and gather your materials for the morning dash the evening before.

Near the end of each workday, as you straighten up your desk and get ready to leave the office, deliberately decide on the next morning's most important task. Make sure it's tiny, achievable, and important. That point is critical: to successfully set yourself up for the next morning's dash, you want to choose the smallest and most doable to-do item.

Keep in mind that much of your work may be dependent on information stored in your email inbox. (I've worked this trick in earnest, only to find that during my dash, I had to open my email to retrieve information, and that bold number of unread messages threatened my focus and concentration.) The key is to set yourself up the night before with *all* the information you need to get your dash completed the next morning. Put all the materials you'll need to complete the task in a `first thing` folder on your desktop or taskbar.

Write down your small, doable assignment and place it somewhere you will see it, even if it's a Post-It note on your keyboard. When you arrive the next morning, that's the first thing you're going to do — no matter what.

Hack 24: Map Your Time

Level. . . . . . . **Easy**
Platform. . . . **All (with a spreadsheet or calendaring program)**
Cost. . . . . **Free**

The busy person's perennial question is, "Where did the day go?" It's easy to get tossed from one thing to the next like a piece of driftwood caught in the tide of your crazy life. A thousand things compete for your time and attention and tug you here and there, but only you know how you really want to spend your time. You *can* take control, mindfully structure your days, and deliberately choose the activities — and time limits — that reflect your values and goals.

As with most things, the best way to start keeping your ideal, balanced schedule is to write it down. A personal time map will help you align the activities that fill your day with your personal goals more closely.

Your Ideal Time Map

Author of *Time Management from the Inside Out* Julie Morgenstern says that the time you have in a day, week, or month is like the space in the top of your closet: only a certain amount of stuff can fit in it.[7] Before you start running from one appointment to the next, decide how you want to fill the limited space of your day with a time map. A time map is a simple chart of your waking hours that displays how much time per day you devote to different areas of your life.

For example (and simplicity's sake), say that you've decided you want to spend about one-third of your time on work, share one-third of your time with family, and save one-third of your time for yourself. Your time map might look something like Figure 3-1.

Obviously, your ratios will vary and should reflect your life choices. If you're an entrepreneur, for example, work will take up more space. Family time will dominate for parents of young children. An entrepreneurial new parent? Well, you shouldn't expect too much "me" time. When constructing your ideal ratios, be realistic.

	Sun	Mon	Tue	Wed	Thu	Fri	Sat
5:00 AM							
6:00 AM							
7:00 AM	A	A	A	A	A	A	A
8:00 AM	A	A	A	A	A	A	A
9:00 AM	C	B	B	B	B	B	C
10:00 AM	C	B	B	B	B	B	C
11:00 AM	C	B	B	B	B	B	C
12:00 PM	C	A	A	A	A	A	C
1:00 PM	C	B	B	B	B	B	C
2:00 PM	C	B	B	B	B	B	C
3:00 PM	C	B	B	B	B	B	C
4:00 PM	C	B	B	B	B	B	C
5:00 PM	C	B	B	B	B	B	C
6:00 PM	C	A	A	A	A	A	C
7:00 PM	C	C	C	C	C	C	C
8:00 PM	C	C	C	C	C	C	C
9:00 PM	A	A	A	A	A	A	C
10:00 PM	A	A	A	A	A	A	C
11:00 PM							
12:00 PM							

		Focus	Code	Hours	%		
		Me	A	36	32%		
		Work	B	40	36%		
		Family	C	36	32%		
			D	0	0%		
				112			

Figure 3-1 A sample time map.

Put together your ideal time map using your favorite calendaring software (Microsoft Outlook, iCal, or Google Calendar, for example), or just download the Excel time map template shown in Figure 3-1. It automatically shades in your map and calculates percentages based on focus codes (A, B, C, and D) and is available at `http://lifehackerbook.com/ch3/timemap.xls`.

Here are some guidelines for your time map:

- Keep the categories broad and generic, at least for your whole life map. You can do subtime maps (such as a work time map) separately.

- Don't schedule things down to the minute. This is a guide, not an exercise in down-to-the-minute accounting.

- Keep overall ratios in mind, aligned with the things you deem most important in life right now. That is, if career is your top priority, the largest percentage of your map should reflect that.

Now that you've determined how you'd like to place your life's priorities into your days' space, you're halfway to making that a reality.

Submaps

After you've created your overall time map, submap sections of it — for example, your time at work. Schedule in blocks of time to process email, attend meetings, and write reports.

Make sure all your job responsibilities are represented — and likewise for your personal and family time.

Your Actual Time Map

Now you're ready to see how your actual schedule lines up with your ideal. Place your time map somewhere in plain view, such as at your desk or on the refrigerator. Each day for a couple of weeks, jot down how you spend your time, and then compare your vision to reality. Note how close your actual time map is to your ideal. Adjust the actual; adjust your ideal. Wash, rinse, and repeat.

The more you work with your time map, the more you'll become aware of how that extra hour spent at work — because you were feeling pressured or generous or simply lost track of time — means you'll spend an hour less with your family, doing things that you enjoy, or sleeping.

Most important, when someone asks, "Where did the day go?" you'll have the answer.

Hack 25: Quick-Log Your Workday

Level. . . . . . . **Easy**
Platform. . . . **All**
Cost. . . . . **Free**

Keeping tabs on what you actually spend your time doing is not an easy task, although keeping a daily log of your work can help and also provide other benefits.

A daily work log helps you become a better time estimator. By becoming aware of how long things actually take, you can more realistically estimate the length of future assignments, and budget your time — and in the case of people who bill by the hour, money — more accurately. A work log enables you to get a real picture of your job responsibilities and how they line up with your ideal time map; it also lets you look back at a day or week and have a concrete idea of where your time went. It can help you identify time sinks and make strategic decisions about what you can delegate, add, or simply delete from your schedule.

When you start keeping a daily work log, you might be surprised to find out what your workday really consists of.

When keeping a work log, you have several options, from paper to a plain text file to a quick-logger script.

Paper

A plain notebook or standard desk diary with dates on each page is an easy way to jot down what you've accomplished in a day.

For a more specialized work log form, designer Dave Seah created what he calls the Emergent Task Timer. This form uses rows of small boxes, each representing 15 minutes of time. You fill out the form as the day progresses, as shown in Figure 3-2.

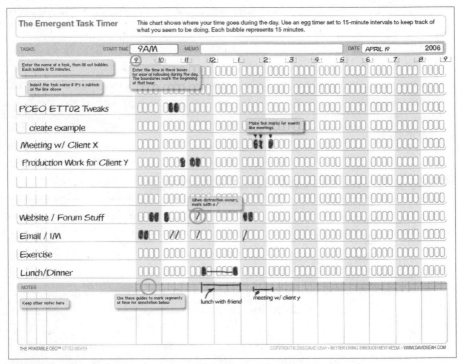

Figure 3-2 Dave Seah's Emergent Task Timer printable PDF form.

Seah's Emergent Task Timer is especially effective for those who work in 15-minute dashes. The Emergent Task Timer is available for download as a PDF file at http://davidseah.com/archives/2006/04/18/the-printable-ceo-iii-emergent-task-timing. (The Printable CEO is a trademark of David Seah.)

Notepad .LOG File (Windows Only)

Alternatively, if you want the searchability and archiving capabilities of a digital work log, a simple text file can get the job done. One of the lesser-known features in Notepad, the Windows simple text editor, is log files: text files that automatically add the current date and time when you update them.

To set up your log file:

1. Open Notepad to create a new file.

2. Enter the word `.LOG` on the first line (use all capital letters and don't forget the dot).

3. Save the file (`worklog.txt`, for example).

Now any time you open that file in Notepad, the current date and time will be added to it, and the cursor will automatically go to the next line — perfect for logging your current task or keeping any kind of journal.

Quick-Log in a Plain-Text File (Windows Only)

You switch between tasks quickly during your workday, and breaking your concentration to write in a desk diary or double-click a text file may disrupt your flow. However, the process can be streamlined by using a simple script and a keyboard shortcut.

The Quick Logger VB script displays a single input box prompt (see Figure 3-3) where you can enter text such as the description of your current task and append it to your work log.

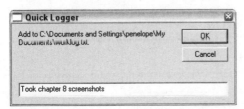

Figure 3-3 The Quick Logger input box.

When you press Enter (or click OK), the text you entered is added to your work log file with the current date and time, as shown in Figure 3-4.

```
worklog - Notepad
File   Edit   Format   View   Help
7/24/2006 9:45:11 AM Drafted Lifehacker.com feature article
7/24/2006 10:21:31 AM Processed reader email
7/24/2006 11:55:17 AM Edited Chapter 8
7/24/2006 1:15:27 PM Lunch
7/24/2006 2:06:54 PM Took chapter 8 screenshots
```

Figure 3-4 A work log generated using the Quick Logger script.

Here's how to get Quick Logger set up:

1. Using your favorite text editor, open a new text file and save it as `worklog.txt` in your `documents` folder.

2. Enter the following code into a file called `quicklogger.vbs` (or download it from `http://lifehackerbook.com/ch3/ quicklogger.vbs`):

```
'----------------------------------------------------------------
-------
' QuickLogger v.0.1
' Appends the date and a line of text to a file.
' Based on code written by Joshua Fitzgerald, 7/2005.
' Modified by Gina Trapani, 7/2006.
'----------------------------------------------------------------
-------
Option Explicit

Dim filename
filename = "C:\Documents and Settings\penelope\My
Documents\worklog.txt"

Dim text
text = InputBox("Add to "&filename&":", "Quick Logger")
WriteToFile(text)

Sub WriteToFile(text)
 Dim fso
 Dim textFile
 Set fso = CreateObject("Scripting.FileSystemObject")
 Set textFile = fso.OpenTextFile(filename, 8, True)
 textFile.WriteLine Now & " " & text
 textFile.Close
End Sub
```

Save the `.vbs` file to your `documents` (or `scripts`) folder.

3. Edit the line in `quicklogger.vbs` that reads as follows, replacing `C:\Documents and Settings\penelope\My Documents\worklog .txt` with the full path to your work log file.

```
filename = "C:\Documents and Settings\penelope\My↵
Documents\worklog.txt"
```

(Remember: the ↩ symbol is not part of the code. It merely indicates that the code line was too long to fit on one line in the book, and the code on the following line is actually a continuation of the first line.)

4. Right-click `quicklogger.vbs` and choose Send To ⇨ Desktop (Create Shortcut).

5. Right-click the `quicklogger.vbs` shortcut on your Desktop and select Properties. In the Properties panel, set the Shortcut Key to Ctrl+Alt+L by simply typing **L** (Windows fills in Ctrl+Alt for you, as shown in Figure 3-5) and clicking OK.

Figure 3-5 Assign a shortcut key to the Quick Logger script.

Now, to append an item to your work log, just press Ctrl+Alt+L, enter your current task in the text box, and press Enter.

Getting into the habit of updating your workday log takes some concentration at first, but with practice, the action becomes second nature. Use your work log to fill out time sheets, analyze your schedule, or explain to the boss what you accomplished that week.

TIP Add a special notation (such as STAR!) to the best accomplishments listed in your work log. These lines will come in handy when you're in salary negotiations, getting your performance review, revising your resume, or interviewing for your next potential career move.

QuickLogger 2 Logs Your Time in a Spreadsheet or Text File (Windows)

Inspired by Quick Logger, developer Joshua Tallent released QuickLogger 2 (available at `http://quicklogger.com`), a free, graphical application that does everything the script does and more. With QuickLogger 2, you can set up repetitive tasks that you perform often (such as "process email") for easy entry. QuickLogger 2 lists these so-called "static tasks" at the top of a list of possible tasks, as shown in Figure 3-6. (You can't see it in the black-and-white figure, but the top three static tasks are listed in blue onscreen.)

Figure 3-6 Repetitive tasks are listed at the top of the list. Double-click one to add it to your log.

QuickLogger 2 can also append your tasks to a spreadsheet as well as a plain-text file. (The spreadsheet option provides a nice way to do easy calculations on how much time you spent on certain tasks by adding formulas to the spreadsheet.) It can also automatically "rotate" — or save the previous and create a new — work log file daily, weekly, monthly, or yearly. Last, you don't have to edit a script by hand to set where your log file should be located — you can do that in QuickLogger 2's options, as shown in Figure 3-7.

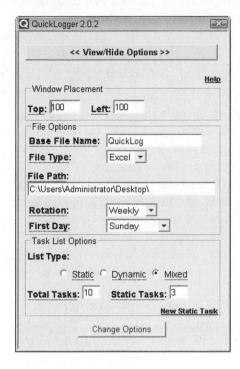

Figure 3-7 Set whether you'd like your log to be a spreadsheet or text file and many other preferences in QuickLogger 2's Options dialog.

Finally, Figure 3-8 shows what the spreadsheet that QuickLogger 2 produces looks like.

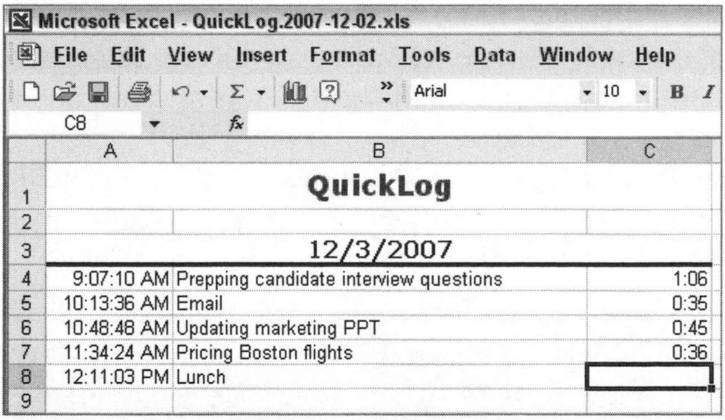

Figure 3-8 QuickLogger 2's resulting spreadsheet tallies how much time each activity takes, to easily total how much time you spend per day or week on, say, email.

Hack 26: Dash through Tasks with a Timer

Level. . . . . . . **Easy**
Platform. . . . **All**
Cost. . . . . **Free**

The only way to stop procrastinating is to simply *start* the task you've been putting off. I know what you're thinking: *Thanks a lot, Captain Obvious.* We all know that "just do it" *sounds* simple, but in reality, getting started on a dreaded to-do can feel impossible. Some tasks are just so big and awful that you can't bring yourself to start in on them because the end seems so far in the future, and the journey there torturous.

The key is to make it as easy as possible to get started. Trick yourself into getting going by deciding to work on the task for just a handful of minutes and guaranteeing yourself a break at the end of those minutes.

For example, commit to work on your task for 10 minutes. Ten minutes! That's one minute for each finger on your two hands. Anyone can work on anything for 10 minutes, and that includes you and that thing you're putting off.

Starting your novel is a daunting task, one most people put off for their entire life. But typing something — anything — for 10 minutes? No problem. This very book was written in short bursts of writing regulated by the beep of my favorite kitchen timer. This hack explains how to take timed dashes through your work.

Do Your First Dash

First, get yourself a timer — an egg timer, a digital watch, a cell phone timer, a software timer, the kitchen timer, whatever's available. Pick your biggest, scariest, most put-off task. Choose the next action, set your timer for 10 minutes, start the timer, and begin.

When the timer goes off at the end of the 10 minutes, stop. Get up, walk around, get a drink, and pat yourself on the back for what you've just done: you stopped procrastinating and got *started.*

Then, do it again.

Adjust Your Dash

Ten minutes is a good time period to start running timed dashes. After applying the dash a few times, you'll experience something amazing: when your timer beeps, you'll want to keep working.

As you become more proficient at working the dash, you can adjust the amount of time you set yourself up to work your tasks. Depending on your energy level, available time, and total stress level around a certain task, extend — or shorten — the length of your dash. The goal is to work up to 30-minute or even 60-minute dashes, but everyone has different workplace circumstances and attention spans for bursts of focused activity. Find your comfort zone, set that timer, and go. You'll be amazed at how much you can get done in short, focused bursts.

Why Time Constraints Work

What you're really doing with that timer is creating and committing to a self-imposed deadline, a constraint. Limitations are usually viewed in a negative light, as something that holds you back from achieving goals. In reality, a constraint can be a *help*, not a hindrance. Lots of people work better under pressure because the limitation puts their brains into overdrive and forces them to think quickly and creatively about the best way to spend that little time they've got. It makes you race yourself to an imaginary finish line and gets you there more efficiently than if you had all the time in the world.

Game developer and writer Kathy Sierra says that going fast can boost your creativity as well: "One of the best ways to be truly creative — *breakthrough* creative — is to be forced to go fast. Really, really, really fast. From the brain's perspective, it makes sense that extreme speed can unlock creativity. When forced to come up with something under extreme time constraints, we're forced to rely on the more intuitive, subconscious parts of our brain. The time pressure can help suppress the logical/rational/critical parts of your brain. It helps you EQ up subconscious creativity (so-called 'right brain') and EQ down conscious thought ('left brain')."[8]

Timer Software Applications

If you have a choice, use a nonsoftware-based timer (such as an egg timer, stopwatch, or kitchen timer) for your dash because it's a separate entity that won't get buried in your computer's taskbar or blocked behind another window. A physical timer forces you to look up and reset it by taking your hands off the mouse and keyboard and doing something. It breaks your work trance, gets your eyes off the screen, and encourages you to stand up, stretch, walk around, and not just immediately switch to browsing ESPN.com to check the Yankees score. If you're dashing through intense, computer-based work, a change in mode is important when the timer beeps.

However, if external timers make you feel silly or you don't have one readily available, there are quite a few software-based timers. One of the best I've seen for working dashes on your PC is a free download for Windows called Instant Boss (available at `http://appsapps.info/instantboss.php`). Instant Boss is an interval timer that can set you up for a timed dash plus a timed break for so many times. For example, you could do a 10-minute dash plus a 2-minute break (for a total of 12 minutes), 5 times an hour, as shown in Figure 3-9.

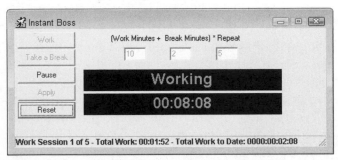

Figure 3-9 Interval timer Instant Boss for Windows counts down your work dashes and can time your breaks, too.

While Instant Boss is counting down, you can minimize it to your system tray. When it's time to work or have a break, Instant Boss pops up an alert box saying, "Get back to work!" or giving you the option to take your break or continue working.

Other software timers include the following:

- **Minuteur** — Mac OS X only; free download (donation suggested) at `http://perso.orange.fr/philippe.galmel/index_mac.html`. Minuteur's web site is in French; check its Help menu for usage instructions.

- **Stop It!** — Mac OS X 10.4 and later Dashboard Widget; free download (donation suggested) at `http://metabang.com/widgets/stop-it/stop-it.html`.

- ▪▪ **Kitchen Timer Yahoo! Widget** — Windows and Mac OS X; free download at `http://widgets.yahoo.com/gallery/view.php?widget=28040`. The free Yahoo! Widget Engine is required to run it.

You can find more timer software suggestions at `http://lifehackerbook.com/ch3`.

Hack 27: Form New Habits with Jerry Seinfeld's Chain

Level. . . . . . . **Easy**
Platform. . . . **Web**
Cost. . . . . **Free**

Once upon a time, Jerry Seinfeld gave a young comic advice. He said that to have better jokes, he had to write every day. To help himself form the habit of writing every day, Seinfeld used a simple system. He told the comedian to get a red felt-tip marker and an extra-large calendar with a whole year on the page to hang on a prominent wall in his home. The comic writes,

> *Seinfeld said that for each day that I do my task of writing, I get to put a big red X over that day on the calendar.*

> *"After a few days you'll have a chain. Just keep at it and the chain will grow longer every day. You'll like seeing that chain, especially when you get a few weeks under your belt. Your only job next is to not break the chain."*

> *"Don't break the chain," he said again for emphasis.*[9]

As anyone does who's achieved success, Seinfeld knows that reaching goals happens by accretion: ordinary everyday effort and small actions that accumulate and grow over time into extraordinary movement, like compounding interest.

You can get your chain started even without a wall calendar and felt-tip marker. At the web site Don't Break the Chain (`http://dontbreakthechain .com`), you can create any number of Seinfeldian chains, and check off your newly acquired habit as you practice it, one day at a time. Register for a free account at Don't Break the Chain, and you'll have a new calendar ready for you to start building your chain, as shown in Figure 3-10.

Click the Manage Chains link to name your chain, change the chain's color, or add additional chains. Use the links on the upper-right side to view different time periods, such as the last four weeks (default view), one month, four months, or one year. As Seinfeld said, the more days you mark off, the longer your chain becomes, and the more motivated you'll become to keep it going. After a week or two, switch to the year view and set yourself to coloring in an entire year. Seinfeld said to hang your chain on a prominent wall in your home, so make sure your online version is in a visible place in your digital space. Try making the chain your browser homepage or add it to your iGoogle start page (a widget is available).

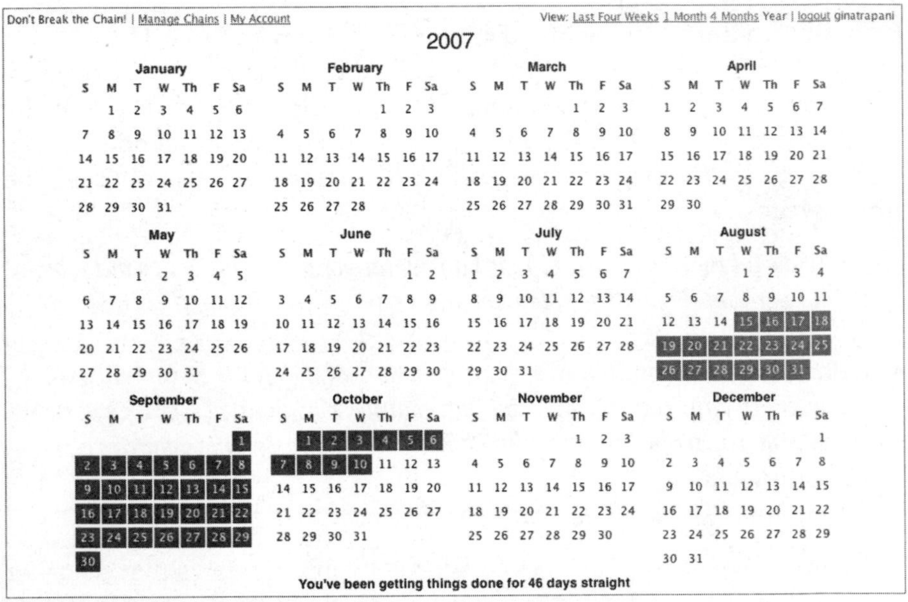

Figure 3-10 Manage your Seinfeldian chain at Don't Break the Chain (http://dontbreakthechain.com).

NOTE Benjamin Franklin used a system remarkably similar to Seinfeld's in his quest to form good habits. He marked the days he failed to espouse 13 virtues he laid out for himself on a weekly calendar. Over time, he "had the satisfaction of seeing [the marks] diminish."[10]

Using Seinfeld's method, you can easily form new habits day by day. Just remember: don't break the chain!

NOTE Special thanks to Brad Isaac for contributing the story of his run-in with Seinfeld to Lifehacker.com and this book.

Hack 28: Control Your Workday

Level. . . . . . . **Easy**
Platform. . . . **All**
Cost. . . . . **Free**

Getting out of the office on time is tough when there's always another task, project, or walk-by boss request to knock out before you leave. It's easy to lose a day checking email, going to meetings, and putting out fires only to find that at 5 or 6 or 7 p.m., you haven't gotten started on something critical.

Getting out of the office is as important to your state of mind — and productivity — as getting in is. But when you're not clear and focused on your highest-priority to-do items, getting out the door on a regular workday with a sense of accomplishment is impossible. Rush hour — that last hour (or two or three) of the workday — becomes your stressful closing window to get to the stuff that, a mere eight hours earlier, you thought you had all day to accomplish.

This hack presents some strategies for reigning in your workday schedule and getting out the door on time with your most important tasks completed.

Identify and Cut Back on Extra Work

It doesn't feel like it — especially at the beginning of what seems like a long workday — but your time is limited. There is only a certain number of hours in the day, and there is an unlimited number of things you could work on. Here's what to do:

Work on the most important tasks first.

Hack 23 covered how to spend the first hour of your day accomplishing the most important task of the day. Beyond that, look for other areas of inefficiency in how you spend your time. Sometimes it's easy to see unnecessary work you can weed out of your day; other times, it's a tougher decision.

For example, say that you're a freelance graphic designer who volunteers your time and expertise on mailing lists and at industry events to network, make contacts, and drum up business. This strategy has worked so well that in recent months, you've acquired a full roster of clients. Now, getting everything done — paying and nonpaying work — is difficult.

Instead of continuing to volunteer as always (whether out of habit or simply to live up to the expectations of others), decide what's more important: delivering your paying clients' projects on time, or volunteer work. These decisions are tricky; presumably you've built a reputation among your peers and gotten client work *because* of your volunteer work. You pride yourself on being a leader in your field, and enjoy being someone others come to for advice or consultation. However, the days don't get any longer. As your work life's demands increase in one area, others have got to give.

If you're having a hard time getting out the door on time or find yourself panicked at the end of the day because something critical is undone, it's time to reprioritize and reshuffle how you're spending your day. Maybe you don't have to meticulously pore over every receipt every month since you got yourself out of debt; instead, just skim the monthly statement and move on. Perhaps no one on staff really reads that detailed meeting summary you've typed up and emailed out every week for the past year — or maybe it could be shortened to four or five bullet points. People assign themselves duties that can become stale and unnecessary over time. Identify yours and cut them down or out completely.

Figure out what matters most, focus on that, and find ways to cut out anything extraneous. Some things may have to fall by the wayside, but you want to get the most bang for your time buck.

Stop Your Time Sinks

Using Hack 25, "Quick-Log Your Worday," identify the activities that take large amounts of time to complete. Does a particularly chatty client keep you on the phone for 40 minutes? Does your group always get into extended debates over email? Do staff meetings go off the rails and drone on and on and on?

Stop any team of wild horses you're hitched to by deleting, delegating, streamlining, or constraining tasks that take longer than necessary. Be prepared to firmly but politely cut off a call with Chatty Client. Call an impromptu group meeting to discuss whatever debate they're sending long missives about over email. Excuse yourself from meetings — or work with the leader to keep them short and focused on a definite agenda.

Make Post-Work Appointments

If your child has to be picked up at daycare at 5:30, or your buddy's waiting for you at the bowling alley, or you've got reservations with your other half for dinner, chances are you will be up and out of your desk chair on time.

Make dates with yourself or friends for the gym, a movie, or simply dinner at home at 6 o'clock sharp to get yourself out the door on time. Carpooling with a co-worker will not only cut off your day at a predetermined time; it'll save you money on gas and tolls, too.

Set Wrap-Up Alerts

At the beginning of the day, decide what time you're going to leave, and set a wrap-up timer. If your spouse is cooking you dinner tonight and you need to be out the door at 6 p.m., set alerts to go off at 5 p.m., 5:30, 5:45, and 5:55 (more, if necessary), saying, "Hey! Time to wrap up and get home!"

Prepare yourself mentally to start closing up shop ahead of time so that you're not surprised when your other half calls at 6:30, wondering where you are. Calendar software such as Microsoft Outlook or timer software (discussed in Hack 26) usually supports reminders at specific intervals before a scheduled event. Use them as your early-warning system — "Head home in 30 minutes!"

Hack 29: Turn Tasks into Game Play

Level. . . . . . . **Easy**
Platform. . . . **All**
Cost. . . . . **Free**

Marketers get you to do things using game play all the time: frequent-flier miles, those stamped cards at ice cream places that earn you a free cone after you buy eight, and under-the-soda-cap promotions that get you a free song download are all examples. You can use the same technique on yourself to psych yourself into getting work done.

Ever wish you could knock down the items on your to-do list with the same gusto you fit blocks together in Tetris or collect gold coins in Super Mario Bros.? Granted, cleaning out the refrigerator will never be as fun as taking out a sea of grunts in Halo, but if you reframe even the most dreaded task into a game with levels, points, rewards, and a bit of friendly competition, you'll be done before you know it.

Make It to the Next Level

Break your task down into chunks and track your progress to completion with a level-o-meter. Think of a fundraiser "thermometer" whose red marker rises as more money is raised. In like manner, you can draw yourself a personal progress bar to track your own road to completion. This technique works especially well for group projects.

Say that you have a 10-page paper due for class. Before you start writing, find a nearby whiteboard or poster board and draw out a progress bar split into 10 sections. Each time you write one page, color in one section of the bar. It's completely mental, but getting to the next level can be a huge motivator.

Collaborate, Compete, and Reward

The best way to knock the *dreaded* out of *dreaded task* is to work alongside someone. To help stay focused, create a friendly competition to help yourselves get through it, with a reward at the end of the work.

For example, my brother and I are both chronically late people. When we once worked in the same office, we'd drive in together, picking one another up on alternate days. We chose a time to be outside for pickup, and any time one of us was late, we marked it down. As we went on, the rules of engagement intensified, with synchronized watches and 60-second grace periods — and whoever accrued five more late marks than the other had to treat for lunch. The end result? We were on time — even early — at the office more than ever. The funny thing is, it became less about the lunch or even getting in on time, and more about the bragging rights and the game of it, enjoyable even at 6:45 in the morning. (Note: this works especially well with a competitive brother.)

Bribe Yourself

Tough tasks can be more fun when there's a reward or reason to enjoy them at the finish. For example, if you save the latest episode of *Lost* on your iPod to watch on the treadmill at the gym, you're much more likely to want to get there! If you've promised yourself a smoothie after your presentation's done, or even just a fancy coffee drink after you've finished leading that meeting you prepared for all week, you'll give yourself a much-deserved reward and create a pleasurable light at the end of the tunnel.

Time Yourself

One of the most effective techniques is to knock down big jobs in small, focused, time-based chunks. Set a timer for 60 minutes and dive in, and when the hour is up, stop. Just knowing that the clock is ticking makes you try to get as much as possible done before that timer beeps. This is great for computer-based tasks such as email triage as well as for cleaning out the closet or purging your file cabinet. You can even pick a goal of several items to accomplish in that hour and work to reach it; doing it this way hones your task/time estimation skills as well. See Hack 26 for more on timed dashes.

Whether you have to do your taxes, clean out the refrigerator, or finally sort through that monstrous pile of clothing that's been collecting in the corner of the bedroom for a month, turning any task into a game can ease the pain and help you psych yourself into knocking it out and checking it off your list as complete.

NOTE This hack was inspired by Amy Jo Kim's "Putting the Fun into Functional" presentation at O'Reilly's Emerging Technology conference in March 2006.

References

1. Science Daily, "Why Do We Overcommit? Study Suggests We Think We'll Have More Time In The Future Than We Have Today" (http://www.sciencedaily.com/releases/2005/02/050211084233.htm).

2. Steven Pressfield, *The War of Art* (Warner Books, 2002).

3. SARK, *The Bodacious Book of Succulence* (Simon & Schuster, 1998), 35.

4. Merlin Mann, 43 Folders, "Building a Smarter To-Do List" (http://www.43folders.com/2005/09/12/building-a-smarter-to-do-list-part-i/).

5. Merlin Mann, Macworld, "How to do a to-do list" (http://www.macworld.com/2006/07/secrets/augworkingmac/index1.php).

6. Julie Morgenstern, *Never Check Email in the Morning* (Simon & Schuster, 2004), 97.

7. Julie Morgenstern, *Time Management from the Inside Out* (Henry Holt, 2004), 181.

8. Kathy Sierra, Creating Passionate Users blog (`http://headrush`
   `.typepad.com/creating_passionate_users/2005/12/creativity_`
   `on_s.html`).

9. Brad Isaac, "Jerry Seinfeld's Productivity Secret," Lifehacker.com
   (`http://lifehacker.com/software/motivation/jerry-seinfelds-`
   `productivity-secret-281626.php`).

10. Benjamin Franklin. (1706–1790). His Autobiography. Available at
    `http://bartelby.com/1/1/4.html#179`.

Clear Your Mind

Your mind is a powerful computer. But sometimes it works *against* you instead of with you. Your brain makes complex decisions and stores years' worth of information, yet there's one thing it doesn't do well: think of what you need when you need it, and forget about nagging thoughts when you *don't* need them.

When you're walking past the dairy section at the grocery store, you don't realize you've got only a day's worth of milk left in the fridge at home. When do you remember the milk? When you're standing in the kitchen with a box of cereal in your hand.

Short-term memory is a lot like RAM, the temporary memory on a personal computer. It's where you keep all the things you see and experience, and the thoughts that pop into your head throughout the day: "Gotta call the vet when I get home." "Didn't realize that new Italian place is there, should invite her out to dinner this weekend." "Wonder how much a Spanish class would cost." "Darn, I never emailed Jim back about those forms!"

Productivity expert David Allen says these types of thoughts all represent unfulfilled commitments you've made to yourself — what he calls "open loops" — that distract and overwhelm you, creating stress, anxiety, and a constant sense that there's too much to do: "Your conscious mind, like the computer screen, is a focusing tool, not a storage place. You can think about only two or three things at once. But the incomplete items are still being stored in the short-term-memory space. And as with RAM, there's limited capacity; there's only so much 'stuff' you can store in there and still have that part of your brain function at a high level. Most people walk around with their RAM bursting at the seams. They're constantly distracted, their focus disturbed by their own internal mental overload."[1]

Today there are more tools than ever that can help you capture information, organize it, make it come back to you just the moment you need it, and access it from any computer or handheld gadget. After you create your "outboard brain,"[2] you'll have a system that you trust to get you what you need when you need it. That way, you can use all your available brain power on the task you're working on this very moment.

Whether it's remembering that you're due to make a dental appointment, or stowing away that tidbit you found online for next week's presentation, the only way to deal with all the stuff in your head is to get it off your mind and into a system that can help you recall it at the right time and in the right place.

This chapter explores various capture systems that offload distractions, pop-up thoughts, and to-do lists to your computer for easy recall, timely reminders, and, ultimately, a clear head.

Hack 30: Send Reminders to Your Future Self

Level. . . . . . . **Easy**
Platform. . . . **Web**
Cost. . . . . **Free**

Every day you've got a lot on your mind and a lot to do. As a result, it can be nearly impossible to remember mundane recurring tasks — such as when it's time to change the oil or go to the dentist — or even important yearly events, such as friends' and family members' birthdays.

Lots of PDAs and calendar software have some kind of reminder feature, but who knows what gadget or type of computer you'll be using next year when Mom's birthday rolls around. What you *do* know is that you'll be checking your email or carrying a cell phone.

There's a simple way to remind yourself of important events and tasks without being tied down to a particular software or device. The free, web-based Google Calendar (http://calendar.google.com) can send an email or text message to you with event and task information on the days and times you specify. You can create a time-based reminder file that emails your future self the data you'll need to know at just the right moment in time.

WEB-BASED CALENDAR AS TICKLER FILE

Productivity expert David Allen advises readers of his book *Getting Things Done* to keep a "tickler file" to track recurring or time-based tasks[3], such as that bill due on the 9th of each month. Allen's tickler file is a physical, paper accordion file that contains 43 folders: 12 folders (one for each month of the year) plus 31 folders (one for each day of the month). Allen says that every day, you should consult your tickler file and pull any paper reminders of time-based tasks out of it and do them. The first day of each month, you move the 31-day folders into the current month folder.

While Allen's tickler file concept is incredibly useful (especially for paper reminders), the physical folder implementation is "pull" technology. You (or your staff) must check it every day to see whether a bill or an assignment is due, even on the days when there isn't anything (which is a waste of time on those days). Additionally, it's too easy to forget to check your tickler or not be physically near it on the days you're out of the office.

The calendar-based reminder setup outlined in this hack serves the same purpose as Allen's tickler, except it is "push" technology. Instead of your having to check yet another place for tasks, your reminders come to you in your email inbox or on your cell phone, which you're already checking. This method doesn't require that you incorporate a new habit into your day and can also deliver you information "just in time." For example, directions to the office building you're headed toward can arrive on your cell phone exactly half an hour before the meeting.

To get your reminder file started, go to Google Calendar, sign into your Google account, and then follow these steps:

1. Click the Create Event link at the top left of the Calendar.

2. Name your event (Mom's birthday, for example) in the What text box.

3. Enter the date and time of the event. In the case of a birthday or due bill, check the All Day box. For recurring events, from the Repeats drop-down box, choose the time frame (that is, yearly, monthly, weekly, or daily).

4. Enter the reminder message you want to receive about your event in the Description text box. Include all the information you'll need to accomplish the task or manage the event.

5. In the Options section of the event, click Add A Reminder to set a message to arrive via email or text message anywhere from five minutes to one week in advance of the event. Choose how to receive the reminder (see Figure 4-1): an email, SMS message, or pop-up dialog (which appears when you're logged into Google Calendar on your computer).

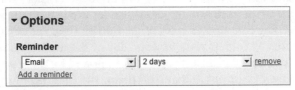

Figure 4-1 Configure your event reminder on the Add Or Edit Event page in Google Calendar.

6. Click the Save button at the bottom of the page to save your event.

NOTE Make sure your Google Calendar knows what time zone you're in so that you receive reminders when you expect them. Click the Settings link on the top right of any Google Calendar page to set your time zone.

That's it; you're guaranteed to always get a message from yourself before your mother's birthday: "Order flowers for Mom! Her birthday's in two days!"

Repeat these steps for each event or task you want to remind your future self about. Beyond birthdays, due dates, and oil changes, some other ways to use your Google Calendar reminder system include the following:

▪ **Remember tasks that need to be done far in advance.** You call the fireplace cleaner in February for an appointment and he tells you to try back in July. Add a summer email reminder that says, "Call Joe Fireplace Cleaner at 555-1212 for an appointment." Notice the phone number: make it as easy as possible for your future self to get the task done.

▪ **Send yourself info on the go.** On Monday, you make plans to go to the roller derby Friday night with friends. So you add an event to your Google Calendar for 5 p.m. Friday night that sends a text message to your mobile phone: "Gotham Girls roller derby tonight at Skate Key, 4 train to 138th street. Meet outside at 7:15." Directions and specific time are included — the more info, the better.

- **Interrupt yourself.** You're superinvolved in a project at work, but you have lunch plans at 1 o'clock across town. So you set up a pop-up reminder to trigger at 12:30 that says, "Lunch at Frank's! Get going or you'll be late!"

- **Don't forget the boring but necessary tasks.** Set up quarterly, monthly, biweekly, or weekly reminders for mundane tasks such as these:

  - Water the plants

  - Get a haircut

  - Send the rent check

  - Invoice client

  - Mail out estimated taxes

Google Calendar allows for pretty much any recurring timeframe for events.

- **Get in on events early.** When you find out that tickets go on sale in two weeks for your favorite band's next show, set up a reminder for the day before to round up the troops and storm Ticketmaster.com. Or send yourself a reminder to get reservations the very day they start accepting them for Restaurant Week, or SMS yourself an hour before an eBay auction is scheduled to end.

- **Create a long-term plan and stick to it.** Say that you commit yourself to a year-long savings plan to sock away $200 a month for that vacation to St. Croix. Send yourself an email each quarter that reads, "Hey, self, you should have $xxx in savings right now. Don't forget how great that Caribbean vacation will be!"

- **Reflect and review.** Each New Year's Day or birthday, write yourself an email describing your successes and failures of the past year, and your hopes for the next. Schedule it to arrive exactly one year later. Sure, this sounds like a lame high school writing assignment, but it's actually a fun way to surprise yourself with insight into where you are and where you've been.

NOTE Remember the Milk (`http://rememberthemilk.com`) **is another excellent personal organizer web application that includes an email or SMS reminder feature. See Hack 34 for more on using Remember the Milk to manage all your tasks, not just time-based ones.**

Hack 31: Build Your Personal Wikipedia

Level. . . . . . . **Advanced**
Platform. . . . **Windows XP and Vista**
Cost. . . . . **Free**

The collaboratively edited Wikipedia (http://en.wikipedia.org) is a vast, searchable repository of information, constantly written and re-written by its readers. Don't you wish you or your group could have your own editable encyclopedia of brain dumps and documentation like Wikipedia? You can clear your mind and build your collective offline memory using the same software that powers Wikipedia. MediaWiki (http://mediawiki.org/wiki/MediaWiki), the software that runs Wikipedia, is freely available for anyone to install. In this hack, you set up MediaWiki on your Windows PC and add and edit pages to your new, local *personalpedia*.

> **NOTE** MediaWiki is advanced wiki software that requires Apache web server, the PHP scripting language, and the MySQL database server installed to run. If the sound of that makes your head spin, try out the no-setup-required (though less-featured) free, hosted wiki application, PBWiki, located at http://pbwiki.com.

What You Need

- **A Windows computer**, not already running Apache web server.
- **WampServer software**, the all-in-one PHP/MySQL/Apache installation for Windows XP, available as a free download at http://www.wampserver.com/en/.
- **MediaWiki**, available as a free download at http://mediawiki.org/wiki/MediaWiki.

Set Up MediaWiki

Setting up MediaWiki involves configuring the Wamp web and database servers as well as the MediaWiki source files. Here's how to get all the components installed and working together.

WARNING Running a server on your personal computer can be
a security risk. Make sure you are behind a firewall that prevents
unauthorized access to your server. See Hack 102, "Firewall Your PC,"
for more information.

1. Download Wamp and install it in the c:\wamp\ directory. (If you
   want to install it elsewhere, make sure the folder you choose has
   no spaces or special characters in its name.) Check the Autostart
   option and the default DocumentRoot folder. Windows Firewall
   may ask whether it should block the web server; click the Unblock
   option. When the installation completes, visit http://localhost/
   in your web browser to see the front page of your new web server
   (see Figure 4-2).

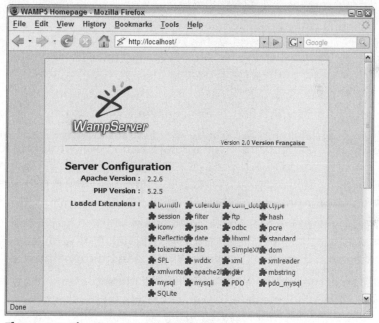

Figure 4-2 The Wamp server front page.

2. You're already behind or running a firewall (right?) but just to
   be on the safe side, you're going to assign a password to your
   new database server. (It's good to be healthily paranoid where
   security's concerned.) From the homepage of your Wamp installation (http://localhost), go to the Tools section and click the
   phpMyAdmin 2.11.0 link (your version may be more recent).

3. Then, click the Privileges link. Select all users except root and click Delete.

4. Click the Edit button next to the root user and change the password to something you'll remember and save. If you refresh phpMyAdmin or try to navigate to any other page, you'll get an "Access denied" error. That's because phpMyAdmin no longer has access to your database because it doesn't have your new password. Let's remedy that.

5. Open the `C:\wamp\phpmyadmin\config.inc.php` file in a text editor. Change the line that reads

    ```
    $cfg['Servers'][$i]['password'] = '';
    ```

    to

    ```
    $cfg['Servers'][$i]['password'] = 'yournewpassword';
    ```

    where `yournewpassword` is the password you just set up in phpMyAdmin. Refresh the phpMyAdmin interface in your web browser and you will be able to view your database information.

6. Extract the MediaWiki file package you downloaded, using a utility such as the free 7-Zip (`http://7-zip.org`), which handles both .zip and .tar archive file formats. Rename the resulting folder (probably called `media-wiki-1.11.0`, although your version may differ) to a folder called `mywikipedia` and move the entire directory to `C:\wamp\www\mywikipedia`.

7. Access your new MediaWiki installation at `http://localhost/mywikipedia`. Click the Set Up The Wiki link. The next screen is where you'll enter all of MediaWiki's configuration options.

8. This will seem like a long, complicated questionnaire, but it really isn't. Accept all the default values, *except* you must set a wiki name (mine is "Ginapedia"), WikiSysOp password, and your database password. The Database User can be root and the password you chose in Step 2. (Alternatively, create a non-root database user with fewer rights in phpMyAdmin and use that instead.)

9. When you've finished configuring your wiki, click the Install MediaWiki! button and let MediaWiki work its magic. If all goes well, you get a message at the bottom of the screen that reads, "Installation successful! Move the `config/LocalSettings.php` file into the parent directory and then follow *this link* to your

wiki." To do that, cut and paste the `C:\wamp\www\mywikipedia\` `config\LocalSettings.php` file to `C:\wamp\www\mywikipedia\` `LocalSettings.php`.

Then click the link to visit your new wiki installation, located at `http://localhost/mywikipedia`. Welcome to your new wiki!

10. You might notice that the default logo in the upper-left corner isn't very personal. To set it to something you like, crop and resize an image of your choice to 135 x 135 pixels and save it as `C:\wamp\` `www\mywikipedia\skins\common\images\mywikilogo.jpg`. Then, open the `c:\wamp\www\mywikipedia\LocalSettings.php` file and add a line that reads

    ```
    $wgLogo = "/mywikipedia/skins/common/images/mywikilogo.jpg";
    ```

    Refresh the wiki front page to see your new logo.

Test-Drive Your Wiki

Now you've got a clean, new, customized local installation of MediaWiki all ready to use however you please. Wikipedia is strong evidence that the best application of a wiki is group collaboration. However, wikis come in handy for individual use as well, to track lists, notes, links, images, or anything else you want to search or reference over time.

Wikis are especially good for writing projects because they keep every page's revision history and allow for easy adding and editing of pages. My co-editors and I at Lifehacker.com use a MediaWiki installation to collaborate on site ideas and drafts. I use a wiki to keep personal notes on programming techniques, to track software serial numbers, and to save quotes I like, as well as other relevant links and articles.

NOTE View a video demonstration of using MediaWiki to draft a novel manuscript at `http://lifehackerbook.com/links/mediawiki`.

To begin editing a page in your new wiki, simply click the Edit link at the top of a page, as shown in Figure 4-3.

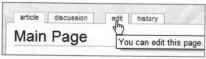

Figure 4-3 Click the link to edit your MediaWiki wiki.

Edit mode displays a page's text inside a text area. You'll see some square brackets and other markup around the text, too. This is the special formatting markup called Wikitext that lays out MediaWiki pages.

Brief Wikitext Primer

Using Wikitext, you can bold and italicize text, link text, add headers and subheaders, and link to other pages inside your wiki. Here are some common Wikitext markup usages:

- Denote a page's section header with two equal signs prefixed and suffixed around the section name, like so:

```
== Section Header Name ==
```

- A subsection uses three equal signs:

```
=== Subsection Name ===
```

- Links to a page inside your wiki — a page called Favorite Quotes, for example — would be achieved like this:

```
[[Favorite Quotes]]
```

- Create a link to an external web page with square brackets containing first the URL followed by the text of the link, like this:

```
[http://lifehacker.com Lifehacker]
```

- External links off of the MediaWiki site are followed by a little arrow, as shown in Figure 4-4.

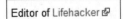

Figure 4-4 MediaWiki
link to another web site.

MediaWiki's User's Guide offers a full reference for MediaWiki markup at http://meta.wikimedia.org/wiki/MediaWiki_User%27s_Guide:_Editing_overview.

NOTE Later in the book, you'll find hacks that explain how to assign a domain name to your home web server and how to access a home server behind a router/firewall.

Hack 32: Develop Your (Digital) Photographic Memory

Level. . . . . . . **Easy**
Platform. . . . **Web- and email-enabled camera phone**
Cost. . . . . **Free for Flickr limited account, $29.95/year pro subscription**

The miniscule size and large memory capacity of modern digital cameras and camera phones can turn anyone into a constant, impromptu photographer. Documenting your world and the information in it has never been easier and faster than it is now. A ubiquitous capture device can change the way you remember (and forget) things for good. With a photo-sharing service such as Flickr (http://flickr.com), you can capture and file away your digital photographic memory in the Internet cloud from wherever you are.

NOTE Several photo-sharing services, such as Kodak Gallery and Snapfish, can publish your digital photos and serve the purpose detailed here. This hack uses Flickr as an example because of its useful tagging and upload-by-email feature.

Tag Your Photos on Flickr

When you add photos to your account on Flickr, you can assign keywords or tags to those photos, indicating what's in them or any other meta information you want to include. You can use the tags later to slice and dice your photos by keyword.

For example, you can view your own (or another user's, or all users') sunset tag to see all the photos of the sun going down (see Figure 4-5).

You can configure the privacy setting on any given photo to viewable only by you (private), by all (public), or only by contacts that you list as friends, family, or both.

Figure 4-5 All of ginatrapani's photos tagged "`sunset`" on Flickr.

Upload Photos to Flickr from Your Camera Phone

You can upload photos to Flickr through the web application or various uploading programs. But to publish photos from your camera phone, use Flickr's upload-by-email capability. To enable uploading by email, visit `http://flickr.com/account/uploadbyemail` while you're logged into Flickr. You'll be assigned a secret email address that will publish photos sent to it in your Flickr account.

Using a special message format, you can set the privacy and tag photos you email from your phone. Tag photos in a message by entering the tags: **x "y z"** syntax in the subject or on a new line in the body of a message. Also, entering suffixes such as **+private** or **+ff** added to the secret upload email address Flickr supplies will mark the photo as private or viewable by your friends and family.

For example, say that you're at Fry's Electronics and spot a hard drive you're interested in, but you want to research it more online when you get home. You could create a new message with the photo on your phone, and use the email address Flickr supplied you for upload. That message might look like this:

```
To: foo10bar+private@photos.flickr.com
Subject: Seagate 300GB tags: "to research" "frys" "to-do"
Body: [Photo attachment]
300GB, 7200RPM, USB 2.0, too spendy?
```

Adding +private to the address means you won't subject your friends to your blatant consumerism (it marks the photo as viewable by you only). Tagging the photo to-do, to research, and frys will help you remember to find out more about the drive and where you saw it when you get home.

WARNING Before you start uploading photos to Flickr from your camera phone, be sure that your mobile phone plan supports emailing photos and that it won't cost you an arm and a leg. When it comes to emailing photos, even 1 cent per kilobyte in data transfer adds up fast!

Your Photo Reference

Having mastered on-the-fly tagging and privacy settings, you'll want to check out some more creative uses for a personal photo database made with your camera phone on the go:

- **Business cards.** Instead of letting that stack of business cards you collected at the conference collect dust in your desk drawer, snap a picture of each and upload them all to Flickr with tags (people's names, conference name) and descriptions of who they were, where and when you met, and whether you want to follow up about something. Be sure to mark these as private!

- **Photo recipe box.** Eat something at a restaurant or a friend's house you'd like to try to make at home? Take a picture, add some details about the ingredients, and tag it cooking, as shown in Figure 4-6. Keep track of all your favorite meals with snapshots that make answering "What should we have for dinner tonight?" as simple as browsing your meals Flickr tag. You can even tag by ingredients such as chicken, vegan, or spicy so that you've got some ideas when your vegan brother-in-law comes over for dinner.

- **Wish list.** When you're out and about shopping, take a photo of the items you want to get or to price-compare. Possible tags include wishlist and to research.

- **Wine labels.** When your sweetheart remarks how much she loves the bottle of wine you got out at dinner, snap a photo of the label so that you can surprise her with a bottle at home. Start your personal wine database with label photos to keep track of what you liked and didn't like.

Figure 4-6 A Flickr photo of a recipe tagged `cooking`.

- **Text or URLs.** Maybe a sign at that landmark describes the history of the place. Or you'll never remember that web site address you saw on a billboard up the street. Take a pic and send to Flickr tagged `reference` or `to visit`.

- **Store hours of places you frequent.** Next time you're at the local post office or bank, snap a photo of the business hours so that you've got a quick reference for what's open when.

- **Home inventory.** A fantastic way to keep track of your home inventory is to snap pictures of serial numbers and include prices of your valuables. They'll come in very handy in case your laptop gets swiped or there's a fire or flood in your home.

- **Where you parked.** Was it level E or F? Snap a quick photo of the sign closest to where you put your car and save yourself a whole bunch of wandering through the parking lot or garage later on.[4] (Flickr isn't required for this one.)

Hack 33: Take Great Notes

Level. . . . . . . **Easy**
Platform. . . . **Pen and Paper**
Cost. . . . . **Free**

Like it or not, your work life involves meetings — status meetings, planning conference calls, brainstorming sessions, meetings for the sake of meetings. But a meeting is only as valuable as the action taken after everyone's left the conference room.

Whether you're headed to a business meeting, a university lecture, or a conference session, taking effective notes is a critical skill that moves your projects, your career, and your education forward. This hack covers three practical note-taking methods, as well as how to make your own custom notepaper.

Method 1: Symbolize Next Actions

Using notepaper or a simple text file on your laptop, indent each line of your notes in from the left margin. Then, use a simple system of symbols to mark off four different information types in the column space left in the margin. The following table describes the most useful symbols:

SYMBOL	DESCRIPTION
[ ] or ☐	A square check box denotes a to-do item.
( ) or o	A circle indicates a task to be assigned to someone else.
*	An asterisk is an important fact.
?	A question mark goes next to items to research or ask about.

After the meeting, a quick vertical scan of the margin area makes it easy to add tasks to your to-do list and calendar, send out requests to others, and check out further research questions.[5]

Method 2: Split Your Page into Quadrants

Another way to visually separate information types is to split your note-taking page into quadrants and record different kinds of information —

such as questions, references, to-do lists, and tasks to delegate — into separate areas on the page. Rumor has it that this is how Bill Gates — someone known for taking amazingly detailed meeting notes — gets it done.[6]

Method 3: Record and Summarize

The Cornell note-taking method works best for students or researchers digesting large amounts of information on a daily basis. The purpose of this system is to avoid recopying your notes after the fact; that is, to simply get it right the first time. To use this method, separate the page into different areas, as shown in Figure 4-7.[7]

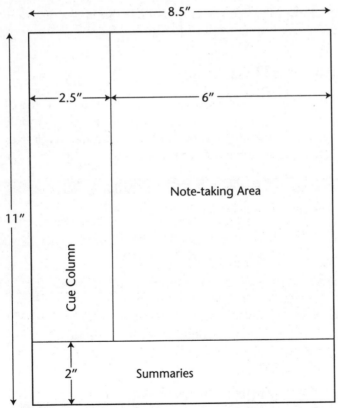

Figure 4-7 A page split into areas for use with the Cornell note-taking method.

Use the page sections as follows:

- **Note-taking area:** Record the lecture, discussion, or meeting as completely as possible using brief sentences in paragraphs. This area will contain the meat of the information to which you will refer later. Capture general ideas, and when the meeting leader or instructor moves on to a new point, skip a few lines and begin a new paragraph.

- **Cue column:** Jot questions and one-liners that connect main ideas in your notes in the cue column. Later, during a study or review session, cover up the right side of the page and use the left column's cues to help you recall facts.

- **Summary:** After the class or meeting, write a sentence or two at the bottom of the page summarizing the content of your page of notes. Use the summary section to scan your note pages and quickly find topics of discussion.

Print Custom Note Paper

There are a few free web applications out there that produce custom PDFs of formatted, lined note paper. Print several copies before your next meeting or class and put them in your notes binder.

- **The Notepaper Generator** (`http://simson.net/notepaper/`) at Simson.net creates a PDF file of a lined page with a small monthly calendar in the header and an optional summary box in the upper-right corner. Choose your font face and optionally include punch holes as well.

- **The Cornell Method PDF Generator** (`http://eleven21.com/notetaker`) prints pages split into the Cornell note paper style with unlined, ruled, or graphed sections. Optionally include your name, the date, and the name of your class, and up to four punch holes for use in a binder. Also, choose the line darkness on a scale from gray to black.

- **Michael Botsko's Notepad Generator** (`http://botsko.net/Demos/notepad_generator`; note the capital D in *Demos*) makes a PDF notes template that includes your name, the page number, date, and project name, and splits the page into two sections: one for notes (with lines) and the other for action items with due dates. It also has optional punch holes.

Hack 34: Organize Your Life with Remember the Milk

Level. . . . . . . **Medium**
Platform. . . . **Web**
Cost. . . . . **Free**

Even in this advanced age of software, keeping track of your work and personal to-do lists, projects, and due dates isn't easy. Chances are, you use a system at the office to track your tasks — such as Microsoft Outlook — and use something else at home — such as a whiteboard on the refrigerator. But the lines between work and life are blurring. You spend more time using different computers and handheld devices while you're on the go. You've got work, school, family, home, and side business matters to track. Now it's more important than ever to consolidate your lists into one, always-accessible place. There are dozens of robust, free online organizers out there, but one of the most stable and mature in the bunch is a web application called Remember the Milk (`http://rememberthemilk.com`).

Because it's a web-based service that you control, you can merge your personal, work, and family lists in a single place with Remember the Milk. Let's take a look at some of Remember the Milk's basic and then more advanced features.

NOTE If you're accustomed to storing your information in desktop software such as Microsoft Outlook, depending entirely on a web site like Remember the Milk may seem like a scary prospect. But as dynamic software moves off the desktop and onto the Web, the greatest advantage to users is its accessibility and portability. Using a web application such as Remember the Milk, you can get to your information from any Internet-connected computer with just a web browser.

Managing Tasks

After you've registered for a free account at Remember the Milk (RTM) and logged in, the home page displays tasks in three tabs based on when they're due: today, tomorrow, and overdue. Click the Continue To Tasks button on the upper right to start managing those tasks.

In the Tasks view, the tab labels switch to categories, by default: Inbox, Personal, Study, Work, and Sent. RTM automatically includes a starting task in your Personal list due today: Try out Remember the Milk. To add a new task to your Personal list, click Add Task and type in a description, as shown in Figure 4-8.

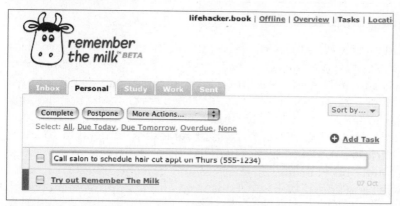

Figure 4-8 Enter a new task by clicking Add Task.

Press Enter to save the new task in your list. After you do that, a task box on the right side will contain editable details about that task. There you can set when it's due, whether it repeats, about how long it will take, and any associated web site addresses. You can even click the Notes tab and add more freehand text information about the task (such as directions to the salon or which stylist to request). A simple task such as calling the salon to schedule an appointment for a haircut probably doesn't need too many more details, but more complex tasks — or tasks you'll share with other users who may need more direction — are good candidates for the notes and URL fields.

Prioritizing Tasks

You can also prioritize tasks so that more important items show up at the top of the list in a particular color. To do so, select a task and press the 1, 2, or 3 key to assign priority. To remove already assigned priority, press the 4 key.

Completing Tasks

Now that you've added a task with details, you've officially completed your Try out Remember the Milk task. To mark it as complete, select the checkbox next to it, deselect any other tasks, and click the Complete button. It will disappear from your list. It's not gone forever, though. You can always see completed tasks for any list in the List box in the right sidebar. Click the 1 Completed link to view the Try out Remember the Milk task.

Managing Lists and Tags

As you add your to-do's to RTM, you may find that you don't use the lists it has set up for you (Personal, Study, Work). For example, if you're not in school, you probably don't need the Study list. You can delete that list and add other lists that do apply to you. To do so, click the Settings link on the top right of any page in RTM and then click the Lists tab. Here you can select any list to delete it, archive it, or set it as your default. To add a new list, click the Add List link. The RTM lists you create and manage depend entirely on your life, businesses, and current projects. I deleted the Study list and added Web Site, Book, and Home Improvement lists to RTM, as shown in Figure 4-9.

Figure 4-9 Enter a new list by clicking Add List, or edit an existing list by selecting it and choosing an action from the drop-down menu.

> **NOTE** You'll notice that the Inbox and Sent lists have lock icons next to them. That's because they're permanent lists that serve a special purpose: to act much the same as email does. The Inbox contains tasks that you've emailed or added to RTM without specifying a list, or that other users have sent you. The Sent list contains tasks you've sent to other RTM users, such as your co-worker or spouse.

In addition to categorizing your tasks into tabbed lists, you can also slice and dice task lists down further using tags. In the Tasks view, select any task from any list, and in the details box on the right side, click Tags to enter keywords for a task. For example, you may tag the tasks on your Home Improvement list by room, as shown in Figure 4-10.

Figure 4-10 Tag your tasks by specific keywords to subcategorize your to-do lists even further.

After your tasks are tagged, you can easily view the list of home-improvement items for the garage, or for the patio, or for the home office, for example.

WARNING It's easy to waste time organizing your tasks in a rich application such as RTM, which has lots of ways to categorize and input information about something. Remember: the purpose here is to actually get things done, not build a perfectly organized list. Use only the tags, fields, and lists that will help you, not just satisfy some innate desire to perfect a complex categorization system.

Setting Task Reminders

Remember the Milk can also notify you when tasks are due via a medium of your choice (email, text message, or instant messenger). For example, when you've got to pick up that package before the office closes at 5 p.m., RTM can send a text message to your cell phone with a reminder at 4:00. To set up task reminders in RTM, click the Settings link on the top right of any RTM page and then click the Reminders tab. There you can set how far in advance you want task reminders and through what medium(s) you'd like to receive them, as shown in Figure 4-11.

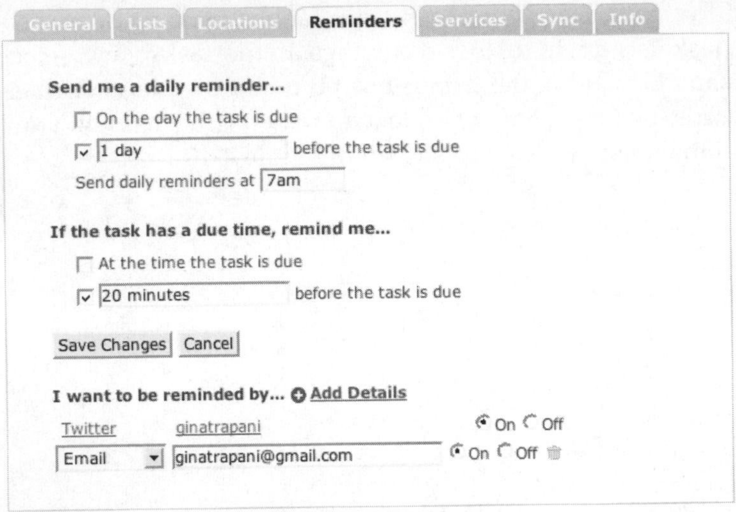

Figure 4-11 Set how and when you want RTM to send you reminders about tasks that have a due date or time.

RTM supports several instant messenger networks for IM reminders, including AIM, Google Talk, ICQ, Yahoo! Messenger, MSN Messenger, Jabber, and Skype. To receive text-message reminders on your cell phone, use the drop-down list to select your cell phone service and add your mobile number.

NOTE Make sure RTM knows what time zone you're in so that you receive reminders when you expect them. In the Settings area, click the General tab and make sure your time zone is correctly listed there.

Searching Tasks

Quickly search for tasks from RTM's search box, located on the upper-right side of any RTM screen. (You can use the Ctrl+Shift+/ keyboard shortcut to move your cursor into the search box so that you won't have to reach for the mouse.) By default, RTM searches only the main task line of currently undone tasks, not notes and not completed or archived tasks. To extend your search (or narrow it by date or list), click the Show Search Options link, which offers several input fields for tightening your search results, as shown in Figure 4-12.

To collapse the advanced search area, click the Hide Search Options link.

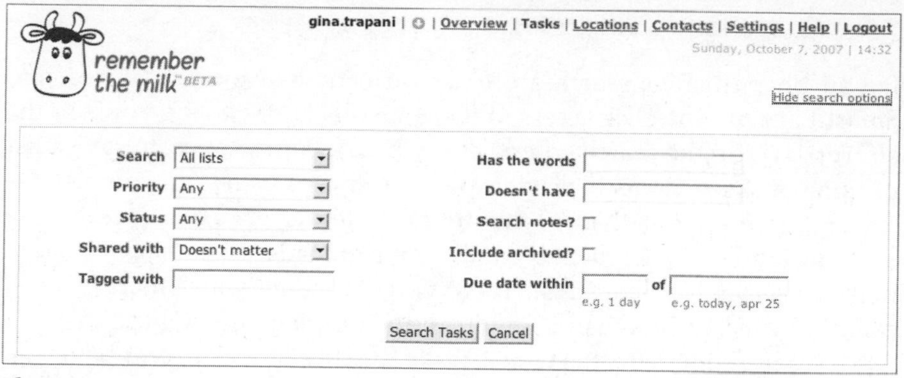

Figure 4-12 Using the search options form, narrow your results by specifying where and how RTM should search your lists.

Advanced Search Operators

You can also do a complex search in RTM from the single search box using advanced operators. For example, to search for the word *salon* in your Personal list, enter **list:personal salon** into the search box. Other useful advanced search operators include the following:

- **priority:** — Specifies the priority of the tasks you're searching. For example, `priority:1` searches the highest-priority tasks and `priority:none` returns all tasks that have no priority assigned.

- **dueWithin:** and **due:** — Specify a date range for due date. For example, `dueWithin:"3 days"` returns tasks due in the next three days. (Note: Enclose any descriptions that involve more than one word in quotation marks to associate the entire phrase with the `dueWithin:` operator.) Similarly, `due:"Oct 10"` will show you all the tasks due on the 10th, and `due:never` displays all tasks with no due date set.

- **timeEstimate:** — Specifies the estimated amount of time a task takes. For example, `timeEstimate:"1 hour"` returns tasks that will take an hour to complete; `timeEstimate:"< 1 hour"` returns tasks that will take less than an hour.

TIP Get the full list of available advanced search operators at `http://rememberthemilk.com/help/answers/search/advanced.rtm`.

Save Searches in Smart Lists

If you do particular searches often, you can save those searches into Smart Lists for one-click access to those results later (saving yourself the effort of typing the search criteria every time). For instance, to save a list of quick tasks — items that will take 20 minutes or less to complete — run a search for less-than-20-minute tasks (enter `timeEstimate:"< 20 minutes"` into RTM's search box). On the right side, click the Save tab to make this search a Smart List. There you can name your Smart List — I called my list of less-than-20-minutes-to-complete jobs Quick Tasks — and save it. From there, the Quick Tasks Smart List will appear below all lists and show you a subset of tasks that you can complete in less than 20 minutes each.

For more suggestions of great Smart Lists (such as tasks that have no due date or tasks that have the word *email* in them), see `http://rememberthemilk.com/help/answers/smartlists/whatare.rtm`.

Get Your RTM Tasks Offline

As you can see, Remember the Milk is a very robust web application. But one of the biggest fears and complaints people have about depending on a web-based application is that it's inaccessible during those times you're at your computer but not connected to the Internet — such as on a train commute to and from work or on an airplane. However, new technology from Google that works with the Firefox web browser can take your RTM data offline and let you view and edit your lists even when you're not on the Web.

A Firefox extension called Google Gears (available as a free download from `http://gears.google.com`) syncs web-based data to your computer so that it's available in your web browser regardless of whether you're connected to the Internet. Remember the Milk is Google Gears–enabled. To work with your RTM lists offline, you must be using the Firefox web browser. Install the Google Gears extension, and when you visit the RTM web site, you will be asked whether it can store data on your computer locally, as show in Figure 4-13.

Check the Remember My Decision For This Site box and click the Allow button. (If you don't have Gears remember the setting, it will ask you every time you visit the RTM web site.) After Google Gears can sync your RTM data, a small button will appear next to your username on the top of each page on the RTM web site. Click it to switch between offline and online mode. When you're offline (not connected to the Internet), you can interact with RTM as usual — add and modify tasks, lists, and tags. When you go back online, Google Gears will sync all your changes back to the RTM web site.

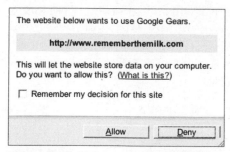

Figure 4-13 The Google Gears Firefox extension will ask whether it can save your Remember the Milk data to your computer.

NOTE As of this writing, the Google Gears Firefox extension is still an early beta release, so expect some instability until Google releases a final version.

More RTM Techniques

There are more useful Remember the Milk features — read on.

The Weekly Planner

Users who like to work with their to-do list on paper can print the weekly planner view at `http://rememberthemilk.com/printplanner/`*your* `.username`*.* (Substitute *your.username* with your RTM name in the URL.) Available from RTM's default homepage (click the Weekly Planner link), this page gives you a week's worth of tasks with priority and list information and large check boxes ready for you to X off with your pen.

Similarly, for any given list in RTM, use the Print link in the List box on the right side to print all the items on that list.

Add Tasks via Email

RTM users who live out of their email inbox (or have easy access to email on their mobile phone) can easily dash off tasks and send them to RTM via email. In the Settings area, go to the Info tab, and copy to your email application's address book the special, private inbox email address that RTM has assigned you. From there you can send tasks via email to RTM: simply put the special email address in your message's To: field and the name of the task in your message's subject line, and leave the message body empty. Send the message, and the task will appear in your RTM Inbox.

Advanced email users can even assign priority, tags, and notes using special message-formatting rules. (See `http://rememberthemilk.com/help/answers/sending/emailinbox.rtm` for more info on how to compose your task email messages for RTM.)

Keyboard Shortcuts

Switching between mouse and keyboard to navigate RTM's web interface can become tiring quickly. To get around faster and more efficiently, teach yourself RTM's extensive set of keyboard shortcuts that let you access almost all its features without reaching for the mouse. Print a copy of RTM's keyboard shortcut reference, available at `http://rememberthemilk.com/help/answers/basics/keyboard.rtm`.

View Your RTM Tasks on Your Calendar or Homepage

You don't have to be at the RTM web site to see your tasks and due dates. Subscribe to your due tasks in iCal or Google Calendar, or view them on your iGoogle personalized homepage or Netvibes. See RTM's Help section for where to find the iGoogle and Netvibes modules and the syndication feeds you can add to iCal or Google Calendar.

Hack 35: Organize Your Life in Text Files

Level. . . . . . . **Beginner to Advanced**
Platform. . . . **Windows XP and Vista (Cygwin), Mac OS X, Unix**
Cost. . . . . **Free**

Hack 34, "Organize Your Life with Remember the Milk," describes a rich application that can track your tasks, their priority, category, project, notes, due dates, and more. But all those bells and whistles can be too much of a distraction or learning curve when you just want a quick-and-dirty way to make a list fast, check off items on it, and be done. No matter how many new-fangled personal-organizer applications become available, new computer users and veterans alike still turn to the old standby for tracking to-do's: a file called `todo.txt`.

A plain-text file is an effective, no-frills way to capture and manage tasks, notes, and other lists. This hack covers some `todo.txt` best practices and ways to interact with your plain-text files.

Why Plain Text?

Plain text is application- and operating-system agnostic. It's searchable, portable, lightweight, and easily manipulated. It's unstructured. It works when someone else's web server is down or your Outlook `.pst` file gets corrupted. It's free, and because it's been around since the dawn of computing time, it's safe to say that plain text is completely future-proof. There's no exporting and importing and no databases or tags or flags or stars or prioritizing or Insert-Company-Name-Here–induced rules on what you can and can't do with it. It's small enough to fit on even the tiniest USB drive or email inbox size limit. It's also dead-simple to use with your favorite text editor.

MORE ON PLAIN TEXT

"Complicated applications crash, or get abandoned by their creators, or just keel over from feature-bloat and become unusable around version 5.0. Power users trust software as far as they have thrown their computers in the past.

"One way to think of text files is the grimy residue left over when an application explodes in your face. You put all your data into, say, Palm Desktop, and then one day you lose your Palm or move to a platform that can't read your desktop files. So you export it all into plain text, and try grimly to import it into the next big application. After a while, you just stay with the plain text because it's easier.

"Text files have some concrete advantages, too: you can get stuff into them quickly, and you can search them easily. Getting data in and out fast, and in a non-distracting way, is really the most important thing for a filing system. That is its very point."

—Danny O'Brien, Lifehacker researcher[8]

Using an Editor to Manage Your Text Files

The easiest and most common way to interact with your `todo.txt` and other text files is with a simple text editor, most likely the first tool you ever used on a personal computer. Although Windows comes with the Notepad text editor built in (and Mac OS X comes with TextEdit), neither of these has the two main useful features you need. To work with text-file lists effectively, install an editor that can open and edit multiple files at one time and sort the items on your lists. For Windows users, I recommend EditPlus, shareware available for download at `http://editplus.com`. Mac users, download and install a free copy of TextWrangler, available at `http://www.barebones.com/products/textwrangler`.

Allocate One Task Per Line

For any list-type file such as `todo.txt`, enter exactly one task on a given line. Although at first this may seem to be an unnecessary constraint, there's no limit to how long the line can be, and most text editors will wrap it automatically for easy reading. The advantage to the one-item-per-line rule is that you can easily prioritize and sort your items, as well as move items from one file to another.

Sorting Items

Advanced text editors such as TextWrangler and EditPlus come with the capability to sort the lines of text in a file alphabetically. This lesser-known feature is quite handy for lists such as `todo.txt`: simply mark off task importance using an alphabetical notation that will let you sort your list to get the high-priority items at the top. Use an uppercase letter surrounded by parentheses at the beginning of your task to enable easy sorting. For example, the following to-do list

```
Update web site news area with latest press release
FedEx status report by 3PM
Call dentist to make appointment for 6 month cleaning
```

could be prioritized this way:

```
(B) Update web site news area with latest press release
(A) FedEx status report by 3PM
(C) Call dentist to make appointment for 6 month cleaning
```

Now, with the `todo.txt` file open in your preferred editor, you can sort that list so that the highest-priority item shows at the top. For example, in EditPlus, choose Tools ➪ Sort (see Figure 4-14) to reorder the list.

The result will place the item prioritized (A) at the top, followed by (B) and then (C). To mark an item as complete, you can either delete it entirely from the file or place an X at the beginning of the line. Then, re-sorting places completed items at the bottom of the file.

Figure 4-14 Sort lines of text in your list from the Tools menu in EditPlus for Windows.

Transfer Tasks from One File to Another

If you're following Hack 22's recommendations for keeping your to-do list achievable, you've got other lists that contain items that don't belong there, such as `projects.txt` and `somedaymaybe.txt`. As you complete tasks and review your lists, you'll want to move items among them easily. Using EditPlus or TextWrangler, you can open all your text files in a single window and cut and paste lines between them to transfer items.

Say, for instance, you're putting the next action for a project onto your working `todo.txt`. Open both files in your editor, which will let you switch between them by clicking the filename or tab. Cut and paste the appropriate line from `projects.txt` into `todo.txt`, or from `todo.txt` to `somedaymaybe.txt`, and save all your changes.

Using the Command Line to Manage Text Files

Advanced users accustomed to working at the Unix command line know that there are several tools that can search, append to, and filter text files. For example, the `grep` command can list all the items in your `todo.txt` that contain the word *email*. Using the Mac OS X Terminal or the Cygwin Unix emulator on Windows, issue the following command (not counting the dollar sign, which represents the prompt):

```
$ grep email todo.txt
```

That will print to the terminal only the lines in `todo.txt` that contain the word *email*. Likewise, you can append a line to the file by using the following command:

```
$ echo "Drop off the dry cleaning" >> todo.txt
```

Similarly, the sort command can list your `todo.txt` by priority:

```
$ sort todo.txt
```

Remembering all those commands can be inconvenient, so over the past two years I've put together a singular command-line interface to a `todo.txt` file that contains one item per line.

Introducing todo.sh

A freely available bash script called `todo.sh` wraps the aforementioned Unix text commands (and several more) into an interface built specifically for `todo.txt`. Using `todo.sh`, you can automatically sort the contents of your `todo.txt` by priority, filter lines by keyword, add tasks, prioritize existing tasks using the (A), (B), (C) notation, and more. See `http://todotxt.com` to download the `todo.sh` script and get instructions on setting it up on your system.

A whole community of users and developers has come together to discuss and devise creative uses for `todo.txt` and shortcuts in doing so. Visit `http://todotxt.com` and join the mailing list to ask questions, make suggestions, and explore other ways you can put `todo.txt` to work for you.

References

1. David Allen, *Getting Things Done* (Penguin Books, 2001), 22.

2. Cory Doctorow, "My Blog, My Outboard Brain," O'Reilly Network (`http://www.oreillynet.com/pub/a/javascript/2002/01/01/cory.html`).

3. David Allen, *Getting Things Done* (Penguin Books, 2001), 173–175.

4. Merlin Mann, "How Do You Get Creative with Your Phonecam?" 43 Folders (`http://43folders.com/2005/09/21/how-do-you-get-creative-with-your-phonecam`).

5. Michael Hyatt, "Recovering the Lost Art of Note-taking," Working Smart (`http://michaelhyatt.blogs.com/workingsmart/2005/04/recovering_the_.html`).

6. Ron Howard, "Post BillG Review" (`http://weblogs.asp.net/ rhoward/archive/2003/04/28/6128.aspx`).

7. "The Cornell Note-Taking System," Brigham Young University (`http://ccc.byu.edu/learning/note-tak.php`).

8. "Interview: Father of 'Life Hacks' Danny O'Brien," Lifehacker.com (`http://lifehacker.com/software/interviews/interview- father-of-life-hacks-danny-obrien-036370.php`).

Firewall Your Attention

Your attention is your most endangered resource. The technical props of modern work life — email, instant messaging, mobile devices, and constant Internet connectivity — make limitless amounts of information always available at the press of a button. Every minute of every day, advertisements, software notifications, ringing phones, blinking voicemail signals, and buzzing pagers vie for your attention. But there is a finite number of minutes, hours, and days in your life.

Modern gadgets and software are designed to help you multitask: that's why you can have a dozen windows open on your screen simultaneously, each doing a different job. The problem is that modern computing devices have outpaced humans' capabilities to multitask.

Further, email software and cell phones and instant messenger make you reachable and interruptible at any moment in time. We live in a culture of constant connectivity, so we respond to those interruptions in kind. But this type of interruption-driven existence can have a devastating effect on your mental focus and your ability to perform. It makes for workers who are distracted, irritated, overwhelmed, and run ragged.

Psychiatrist Edward Hallowell calls the condition ADT (Attention Deficit Trait), a workplace-induced attention deficiency caused by the constant distraction of high-tech devices. He says, "It's sort of like the normal version of attention deficit disorder. But it's a condition induced by modern life, in which you've become so busy attending to so many inputs and outputs that you become increasingly distracted, irritable, impulsive, restless, and, over the long term, underachieving. In other words, it costs you efficiency because you're doing so much or trying to do so much, it's as if you're juggling one more ball than you possibly can."[1]

A University of California at Irvine study showed that businesspeople are interrupted once every 11 minutes on average during the work day.[2] A 2006 *Time* magazine article, which cited that study, points out that many well-known successful people make a point to shut out these types of interruptions:

> *Some of the world's most creative and productive individuals simply refuse to subject their brains to excess data streams. When a* New York Times *reporter interviewed several winners of MacArthur "genius" grants, a striking number said they kept cell phones and iPods off or away when in transit so that they could use the downtime for thinking. Personal-finance guru Suze Orman, despite an exhausting array of media and entrepreneurial commitments, utterly refuses to check messages, answer her phone, or allow anything else to come between her and whatever she's working on. "I do one thing at a time," she says. "I do it well, and then I move on."[3]*

Orman knows that the key to overcoming ADT is to fully focus on one task at a time. Give yourself the time and space to dig into a problem and reach that state of mind called *flow*, when you're fully immersed in your task, effortlessly successful, and oblivious to time and external factors.

To get into this zone, block out irrelevant distractions and let in only the information you need to get the job done. Like a computer-system firewall that blocks potential intruders, the techniques presented in this chapter will help you firewall your most precious resource — your attention.

Hack 36: Limit Visits to Time-Wasting Web Sites

Level. . . . . . . **Advanced**
Platform. . . . **All (Firefox)**
Cost. . . . . **Free**

Picture this: You sit down at your computer to write a report that's due the next day. You fire up a web browser to check the company intranet for a document. For a split second, you glance at your home page. "Wow!" you say. "The Red Sox won in the 17th inning! Let me see what happened. . ."

Three hours later, no report's been written, and you want to throw yourself out the window.

Sound familiar?

It's too easy to scamper down the rabbit hole of the Web when you've got pressing tasks to work on. At one point or another, you've probably burned a few hours clicking around Wikipedia, Amazon.com, eBay, Flickr, YouTube, or Google News when you had a deadline to meet. Surfing efficiently is an exercise in discipline and sometimes outright abstinence. This hack uses the LeechBlock Firefox extension to blank out certain web sites during times you're supposed to be working.

Install and Configure LeechBlock

Using the Firefox web browser, download the LeechBlock extension from `https://addons.mozilla.org/en-US/firefox/addon/4476` and install it. (For detailed instructions on how to install a Firefox extension, see Hack 85, "Extend Your Web Browser.") Restart your browser to complete installation.

Now you must determine which sites you burn the most unproductive time on. When you have even just one offending site in mind, you're ready to go. To set up which sites to block, in Firefox choose Tools ⇨ LeechBlock ⇨ Options. A detailed dialog box appears and you can set what sites to block, and when.

First, in the text area, enter the web site domains that you want to block, one per line. My first block list looked like this:

```
ask.metafilter.com
flickr.com
facebook.com
twitter.com
```

Second, set the time periods during which LeechBlock should get between you and these sites. The morning is a good time to slog through the bulk of the day's work, so let's say you want to allow yourself recreational browsing only after 3 p.m. on weekdays. In the input box under Enter the Time Periods Within Which to Block These Sites, use military time to enter time periods. For example, to block those sites between midnight and 3 p.m., enter **0000-1500**. Alternatively, you can set a number of minutes you're allowed to visit the sites per hour or day (that is, I can check my fantasy football team's progress for only 15 minutes per day).

Last, check off the days of the week that LeechBlock should apply. Then, you can optionally set a custom name for your set of sites, such as "Social Network Time Suckers," as shown in Figure 5-1.

Figure 5-1 Set what sites to block and when in LeechBlock's Options dialog box.

The advantage to giving a set of sites a custom name is that you can split your recreational browsing blocks into different categories. Facebook and Twitter might go into your Social Network Time Suckers category, but Wikipedia and Google News might go into the News Browsing category, whereas TMZ and Defamer might go into the Celebrity Gossip Mongers category. Each of these sets can have different block times and rules (all day, certain days, certain times of day, or so many minutes per day).

Visiting a Blocked Site

After you've saved your settings in LeechBlock, whenever you mindlessly hit that time-wasting bookmark, you'll see a message in your browser, as shown in Figure 5-2.

Figure 5-2 The LeechBlock block page.

That's your cue to get back to work and try again later in your allotted time.

Adding Sites to the Block List

When you have LeechBlock running, you can easily add another site to your block list using the right-click context menu as you surf. Say you find yourself on Google Video, wasting away minutes of your life watching the skateboarding dog the same way you used to on YouTube. Simply right-click the page (cmd+click for Mac users), and from the context menu, choose LeechBlock ⇨ Add This Site To [Block Set Name Here]. For example, if you've got an Online Video set of blocked sites, you could add it there, as shown in Figure 5-3.

Make It Difficult to Disable LeechBlock

Now, a particularly determined procrastinator might say, "If it's a block I can disable, I'll do it." If you find yourself blocked from a time-wasting site that you insist on visiting (and to hell with your deadline), you could go into LeechBlock's options and undo the block. However, LeechBlock comes with a clever feature built to prevent just that. In LeechBlock's options dialog, check off "Prevent access to options for this block set at times when these sites are blocked." That means if it's during blocked YouTube time, you can't change LeechBlock's settings to let you in after all.

Figure 5-3 Add sites to block lists using the LeechBlock context menu.

Along the same lines, you can set a password to get to LeechBlock's options area. (See the General tab of the Options dialog.) The purpose of the password is to throw up yet another roadblock on your way to procrastinating online. The LeechBlock developer says, "Note that the password feature is not intended for security purposes, but only to make it more difficult to bypass the blocking in haste — to delay you just long enough for your reason/conscience to wrest back control from your baser instincts! So a lengthy but memorable password will be most effective. Suggestion: Try `antidisestablishmentarianism`. It works for me!"[4]

Hack 37: Permanently Block Time-Wasting Web Sites

Level. . . . . . . **Advanced**
Platform. . . . **Windows XP and Vista, Mac OS X**
Cost. . . . . **Free**

Is there a web site that's utterly toxic to your mental state or ability to work? Maybe you grind your teeth over your ex's weblog, which details every moment of her happy new life without you. Maybe you've lost hours of your life trolling eBay auctions and you simply can't impulse-buy another autographed Neil Diamond record. Perhaps online backgammon can snatch away hours of your day at the office.

The preceding hack describes how to block time-wasting web sites during certain times of the day and week. Alternatively, you can block sites at *all* times, until you explicitly release the restriction. This hack fakes your computer into thinking that those problem sites live on your hard drive — although obviously they don't — and forces a Server Not Found error when your fingers impulsively type that tempting, time-sucking URL.

Here's what to do.

Windows

1. Using Notepad or some other text editor, open the file named hosts, which is located in the following directory:

   ▪ **Windows XP and Vista**: C:\WINDOWS\SYSTEM32\DRIVERS\ETC

   ▪ **Windows 2000**: C:\WINNT\SYSTEM32\DRIVERS\ETC

   ▪ **Windows 98\ME**: C:\WINDOWS\

2. Add the following on its own line in the hosts file:

   ```
   127.0.0.1 ebay.com games.yahoo.com evilex.com
   ```

Replace the sites listed with the domains that you want to block.

Mac OS X

1. In Finder, choose Go ➪ Go To Folder.

2. In the Go To Folder dialog, type **/etc/**.

3. From the /etc/ folder window, locate the hosts file and cmd+click on it. From the context menu, choose Get Info. In the Ownership & Permissions area, set You Can to Read & Write.

4. Now open the hosts file in a text editor.

5. Add the following on its own line in the hosts file:

   ```
   127.0.0.1 ebay.com games.yahoo.com evilex.com
   ```

Replace the sites listed with the domains that you want to block.

The Result

After you've completed the steps for your operating system, save the hosts file and quit your editor.

Now when you visit one of your blocked sites, you get a Server Not Found error. (If you're running a web server at home, as detailed in Hack 74, your own server's files appear.)

The advantage of this method over Hack 36 is that the sites are blocked from every browser, not just Firefox, on that computer,. The downside is that when you decide it's an okay time to browse eBay, you have to manually comment out the following line in the hosts file by adding a # to the beginning of the line, like this:

```
#127.0.0.1 metafilter.com flickr.com
```

That's a deliberately huge inconvenience — one that can help keep your wandering clicker in line when you're under deadline.

Hack 38: Reduce Email Interruptions

Level. . . . . . . **Easy**
Platform. . . . **All**
Cost. . . . . **Free**

In contrast to phone calls and instant messenger, email was never intended for real-time communication. However, most people treat it as if it were. You most likely work with your email program open all day long, letting it check for new messages every five minutes and notify you of unread incoming email on the spot.

It's so difficult to ignore that little unopened envelope, isn't it? Maybe those new messages contain juicy gossip, or photos of the baby, or heaping praise from the boss. Maybe they contain details of an emergency that has to be dealt with right this second. Most likely, they contain misspelled details of how to buy "cheap V1@gr@" but nevertheless, the impulse to look at them is powerful. Unread email is just another shot of the information drug your hungry mind craves. It cries out to you, "Open me! Open me!"

However, when you need to focus, do yourself a favor: actively control when you check your email. Two strategies can help.

Shut Down Your Email Program

The simplest (but perhaps least practical) way to stop letting your inbox run your day is to quit your email software. Make your default work mode email-free. Open your inbox only at designated processing times. Commit to just two or three times during a workday — say, first thing in the morning, just after lunch, and an hour before you leave — to check for and process unread messages. This means responding, filing, and taking any action those messages warrant on the spot.

NOTE Hack 2, "Decrease Your Response Time," provides strategies for processing email right off the bat to avoid a pileup of read-but-not-processed messages.

Set Your Email Program to Check for Messages Once an Hour

Your work situation may demand that your email program be open all the time — say, if you work in Outlook using its calendar and tasks lists. You can still reduce the constant interruption of the new mail notification: set your mail client to check for new messages once an hour.

By default, Microsoft Outlook checks for unread email every five minutes. That means — what with spam, cc-happy co-workers, mailing lists, and bored friends at work — you potentially can be interrupted 12 times an hour, or 108 times during a nine-hour workday by a new email message. Change this setting to every 60 minutes to reduce the number of interruptions from 108 to nine times a day.

The method for changing that setting varies, depending on your email program. If you use Microsoft Outlook, choose Tools ➪ Options. In the Mail Setup tab, click the Send And Receive button to change the frequency setting, as shown in Figure 5-4.

The amount of time you choose to let pass before checking for new messages is up to you, but even once an hour can be excessive. If you're truly ready to toss the email monkey off your back, try processing email two or three times a day, at times you determine.

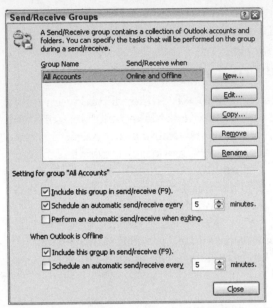

Figure 5-4 Microsoft Outlook Send/Receive options.

Hack 39: Split Your Work Among Multiple Desktops

Level. . . . . . . **Easy**
Platform. . . . **Windows XP, Mac OS X**
Cost. . . . . **Free**

The more space you have to lay out your materials, the easier it is to get a job done. Imagine a cook in a kitchen with restricted counter space. She has to remove the first ingredient from the refrigerator, put it on the counter, chop, measure, and add it to the recipe. To use more ingredients, she has to return the first to the refrigerator to make room for the second, and so on. But what if she had a larger countertop that could accommodate all the ingredients at one time? The chef could spend less time switching between ingredients and more time cooking.

The same concept applies to the amount of screen real estate you have on your computer monitor. Modern operating systems make multitasking with overlapping windows on one screen possible, but that requires some amount of task switching and window resizing to get to what you need. A second or even third monitor, however, gives you more space to work. A 2006 survey by Jon Peddie Research, cited in a *New York Times* article,[5] showed that multimonitor computer setups can increase a computer worker's productivity by 20 to 30 percent.

In fact, Microsoft Corporation founder Bill Gates splits his work onto three screens that make up one desktop: "The screen on the left has my list of emails. On the center screen is usually the specific email I'm reading and responding to. And my browser is on the right screen. This setup gives me the ability to glance and see what new has come in while I'm working on something, and to bring up a link that's related to an email and look at it while the email is still in front of me."[6]

To use physical multiple monitors, your computer has to have multiple video cards, or one video card capable of supporting multiple monitors. If you don't have that capability, use virtual desktops instead to separate your work into four distinct workspaces and focus on one at a time.

NOTE Hack 115, "Optimize Your Dual Monitors," has tips for putting more than one physical screen to best use.

For example, use one desktop for the task at hand; the second for your task resource documents, calendar, or to-do list; the third for web access; and the last for email. Here's how to get it set up.

Windows Vista and XP

Virtual desktop manager Dexpot is free for personal use and compatible with Windows Vista as well as XP. Download it from http://www.dexpot .de/ and install.

Dexpot can create and manage up to 20 virtual desktops (although you'll never need that many) and customize them extensively. Give each of your desktops a name, background image, screensaver, and other characteristics using Dexpot. Right-click the Dexpot icon in your system tray and select Configure Desktops to do just that, as shown in Figure 5-5.

For instance, I've created three desktops, named Email and Messaging, Writing, and Browsing. Using Dexpot's Desktop Rules feature, you can even create automatic actions based on what you're doing on a desktop — for example, if you launch your web browser on a desktop other than Browsing, Dexpot can automatically move it there.

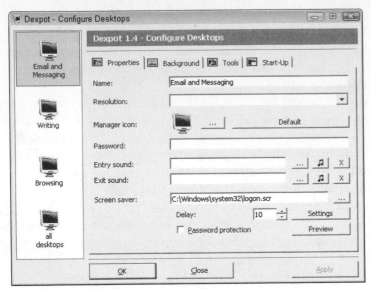

Figure 5-5 Configure your virtual desktops with Dexpot.

Windows XP

Download the free Microsoft Windows Virtual Desktop Manager (MSVDM) from http://microsoft.com/windowsxp/downloads/powertoys/ xppowertoys.mspx. After installing MSVDM, right-click your Windows taskbar and choose Toolbars ⇨ Desktop Manager. The MSVDM toolbar displays buttons labeled 1 through 4. Switch to another desktop by pressing a button, or use the Quick Preview button to see all four desktops in quadrants on your screen, as shown in Figure 5-6.

Assign a different desktop background to each desktop to distinguish them visually. To do so, right-click the MSVDM toolbar and choose Configure Desktop Images.

Mac OS X 10.4 (Tiger)

If you're running Mac OS X 10.4 (Tiger), VirtueDesktops (http:// virtuedesktops.info) is a free virtual desktop manager. Download the latest version, unzip it, and drag and drop it into your applications folder. Start up VirtueDesktops, and a virtual desktop menu appears in the status bar. Choose Preferences from that menu, and within the Triggers area, configure your preferred keyboard shortcuts for switching between desktops. By default, the Option+Tab key combination displays all four desktops (see Figure 5-7), which you can navigate using the arrow keys.

Figure 5-6 View all four virtual desktops using Microsoft Windows Virtual Desktop Manager.

Figure 5-7 Create and manage four virtual desktops on Mac OS X 10.4 with VirtueDesktops.

Mac OS X 10.5 (Leopard)

The latest version of Mac OS X 10.5 (Leopard) comes with a virtual desktops feature, called Spaces, built right in. To enable Spaces, from System Preferences choose the Exposé & Spaces pane. From the Spaces tab, select the Enable Spaces check box. (Optionally, also select Show Spaces In Menu Bar to add a Spaces button to the menu bar.)

By default, you get four virtual desktops, or Spaces. Use the + and – buttons next to Rows and Columns to add or delete Spaces. You can have as many as 16 Spaces and as few as two. To bind certain applications to certain Spaces, use the Application Assignments list. (This comes in handy if you always want to keep iTunes, for instance, in Space 2.) You can also set a certain application to show up on every Space, meaning it will be visible regardless of which Space you're in.

The most useful way to interact with Spaces is using the keyboard shortcuts, which you can also customize in Spaces' System Preferences pane, as shown in Figure 5-8.

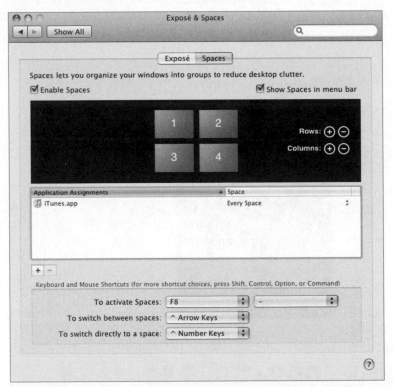

Figure 5-8 In System Preferences ⇨ Exposé & Spaces, choose how many Spaces you want, which applications should be associated with what Spaces, and your Spaces keyboard shortcuts.

By default, you can use the F8 key to invoke a birds-eye view — or complete grid — of your Spaces. Using the mouse, you can drag and drop application windows from one of your Spaces to another one here. You can also switch between Spaces using keyboard shortcuts; by default, Control+any arrow key will scroll through Spaces and Control+any number key will transport you directly to a specific Space.

More information on using Spaces is available at `http://apple.com/macosx/features/spaces.html`.

Hack 40: Build a No-Fly Zone

Level. . . . . . . **Easy**
Platform. . . . **All**
Cost. . . . . **Free**

Many modern office spaces have open layouts to "promote interaction between departments" — which means they're set up to distract you all day long. Low-wall cubes, side-by-side desks, required use of an instant messenger (IM) — all make for a workday that's interruption-driven instead of task-driven. Office seating arrangements that mix up personnel can place employees who do involved mental work such as programming or number-crunching next to loud sales people yammering away on the phone.

For anyone who doesn't have her own office with a door that can be closed, getting actual work done at the office can be a serious challenge. Co-workers stopping by, IM windows popping up, getting dragged off to meetings or hijacked to deal with the latest department crisis are all time-suckers that can leave you worn out at 6 p.m., wondering where the day went.

When you're just a cog in the machine, changing your office's culture might not be possible. But for your own sanity and productivity, do what you can to protect yourself from extraneous interruptions at the office.

Set Yourself Up to Get into the Zone

It takes 15 minutes of uninterrupted time to get into "the zone," that wonderfully productive place where you lose all sense of time and space and get a job done. Protect yourself from interruptions before you start on an involved mental task to give yourself that 15-minute runway.

Forward your office phone to voicemail and silence your cell phone. Shut down instant messenger. If it must be on, set your status to "Busy" or "Here but working, chat later." Shut down your email client. If you're waiting for a crucial message, set your email program to receive mes-sages quietly (with no audio or visual alerts) and forward any must-get-through email to your phone.

Shut down every application running on your computer that doesn't have to do with the task at hand. If you don't need the Web to complete your task, disconnect your machine from the network. I know — it's extreme, but I'm serious. If you're a programmer, download language documentation locally before you start to avoid the temptation of the web browser.

Make Yourself Inaccessible

If your office uses Outlook or a shared calendar, schedule an appoint-ment with yourself that shows you as busy when you're working on your task to avoid meeting requests during that time. (This is especially useful for recurring tasks such as writing weekly status reports.)

Signal to your co-workers in whatever ways are possible, that you shouldn't be interrupted unless absolutely necessary. If it's acceptable at your workplace, put on headphones — noise-canceling headphones are best — and listen to music to block out sound. (A former co-worker of mine once confessed that he put on headphones without anything play-ing on them just so that people wouldn't randomly address him.)

NOTE See Hack 44, "Drown Out Distracting Sounds with Pink Noise," for more on masking office noise.

If interruption by your manager or co-workers is a big problem, work out a way that you can signal that you're available to chat or that you're super-involved at the moment at your desk. Make an agreement with others that when the "Do Not Disturb" sign is up, they won't stop by asking if you want to get coffee or what you thought of last night's episode of *Survivor*.

Work at Quieter Times and in Zoned-Off Spaces

If all else fails, find times and space at your office where it's easier to get work done. Come in a little earlier or stay later or move your lunch break to the opposite time of your co-workers'. A couple of programmers I know who worked at a frenetic office used to schedule a two-hour meet-ing together in a conference room a couple of times a week, where they'd go with their laptops to code in peace and quiet. A complete change of scenery can help boost your productivity as well as keep you from the ringing phone and chatty cube mate.

Hack 41: Clear Your Desktop

Level. . . . . . . **Easy**
Platform. . . . **Windows XP and Vista, Mac OS X**
Cost. . . . . **Free**

It's amazing how fast your computer's desktop can fill up with shortcuts and files and turn into a virtual candy store of colorful icons beckoning your mouse pointer: "Click me! Click me!" Most modern software puts a shortcut to itself on your computer desktop by default when you install it. Your web browser and email program might save files they download directly to your desktop. It's tempting to leave documents on your desktop because you'll know they'll be in sight at all times. But at what cost?

A cluttered virtual desktop is as bad as a cluttered physical desktop. It's visually distracting and makes it easy to get derailed from the task at hand. ("Hey, lemme watch that funny video clip just one more time!")

Clear your virtual desktop by removing all the icons you don't need. To maintain a completely clear desktop with absolutely nothing taking up space, you can disable desktop icons entirely. Here's how.

Windows

1. Drag and drop all the files you've saved on your desktop into the My Documents folder. (See Hack 11, "Organize Your Documents Folder," for ways to get your My Documents folder under control.)

2. Delete all the shortcuts to software applications on your desktop that already exist in Windows' Start menu.

3. To disable desktop items entirely, in Windows XP, right-click the desktop, and from the Arrange Icons By submenu, deselect Show Desktop Icons. In Windows Vista, right-click the desktop, and from the View submenu, clear Show Desktop Icons.

4. Enable the Quick Launch toolbar to start up programs without having to navigate the Start menu. For easy access, add to this toolbar shortcuts to programs or documents you open often. The limited real estate is a good thing: Choose only the items you *launch* often. (For example, if you open the status.xls spreadsheet every other day, use a shortcut to that document instead of a shortcut to Excel.) As for all your other programs? Fear not: They're still accessible, safely tucked away in the programs folder.

Mac OS X

Mac applications are a lot less likely to add shortcuts to your desktop; however, it is still easy to save downloaded files to your Mac's desktop. Here's how to clear up things and still make all your favorite applications and documents accessible.

1. Drag and drop all the files on your desktop to your documents folder in Finder.

2. Delete any shortcuts left on your desktop.

3. Drag and drop your frequently launched programs to the Dock (to the left of the trash bin).

4. For easy access to your documents and applications folders, drag and drop them to the Dock as well. When clicked, the applications folder will reveal a vertical menu of items, as shown in Figure 5-9.

Make it a habit to file away programs and documents in folders rather than on your desktop to maintain a clutter-free virtual work environment.

Figure 5-9 Place the applications folder on the Dock as a menu to access all your software.

Hack 42: Make Your House a Usable Home

Level. . . . . . . **Easy**
Platform. . . . **All**
Cost. . . . . **Free**

Ever been on the way out the door and you can't find your keys? Dashing around the house tearing through every nook and cranny in a stressed-out frenzy isn't the best way to start the day, but we've all been there.

It's so easy to sabotage yourself every day without even realizing it. The moment you put your keys in the pocket of the jacket you tossed over the kitchen chair, you didn't think, "I'm going to make it really difficult for myself tomorrow morning when I have to leave for that big interview." Yet there are so many small ways in which you can unconsciously make life harder on yourself. Personal sabotage — whether it's in the form of convincing yourself you'll magically remember to pick up milk at the store or thoughtlessly surfing the Web when you've got a looming deadline — is a reversible habit with a little thought and planning.

Just the way a basketball teammate tips the ball when the slam dunker leaps to make the basket, you can be your own teammate and set yourself up for success in life and work.

Take a look at your living space with a focus on usability. Your home should be a tool that helps you get things done, a space that's a pleasure to be in, and a launch pad for daily tasks as well as your life goals. Whether you want to relax after work, phone a family member, or keep track of a dry-cleaning receipt, there are lots of simple ways to create a living space that makes getting things done a breeze.

Create a Place for Incoming Stuff

Every day you walk into the house with your hands full of mail, pockets full of change, and a cell phone that needs recharging. Instead of dumping that pile of bills onto the coffee table, scattering a mess of pennies and dimes on your dresser, and tossing the phone onto a table, create useful places to drop off stuff without having to think: a change jar that goes to Coinstar every few months, an indoor mailbox for you and your housemates, and a phone-charging center with an easily accessible plug. Fact is, after a long day at work, you don't want to have to think about where to put stuff when you walk in the door. So make it a no-brainer.

Put Items You Need to Remember in Your Path

Make it hard to forget where you put your keys, your cell phone, that check you're supposed to mail, or the dry-cleaning receipt. Section off a space near the door where you can easily pick up items on your way out. Hang a key rack. Place a snail-mail outbox nearby for letters and bills that need to be dropped at the post office. The door of my old apartment was metal, so I kept a few magnets stuck to it to hold receipts, mail, and notes I'd be sure to see on my way out the door.

Stow Away Stuff You Don't Use; Put Stuff You Do Within Easy Reach

Surround yourself with the things you use and either get rid of the things you don't or stow them away. For example, if you've ripped all your audio CDs to MP3 and listen to them only in that format, why line your living room walls with CDs that never get touched? Box up your CDs and store them up on a high shelf in the closet to make room for the things in the living room that you do use. In the kitchen, if you rarely make waffles but you're on a grilled-cheese kick, put the waffle-maker on the top shelf and leave the Foreman grill at eye level.

Strategically Place Items to Make Tasks Easy

Having all the things you need to complete a task on hand is half the battle. One of my favorite household life hacks is the sheet-folding trick: fold the flat and fitted sheets into a set and place them *inside* one pillowcase, along with any other pillowcases for those sheets. The convenient packaging precludes the need to rummage through the linen closet matching up sheet sets when the time comes to make the bed.

There are lots of ways to make tasks easier with strategic placement. If your telephone directory is digital, print a copy and leave it by the phone at home so that you don't have to consult your cell phone or boot up the computer to find a number. Make recycling easy by placing the bin in the area where the most paper or glass is generated — say, the home office or kitchen. If you're bleary-eyed and fumbling for the TV remote each day to check the weather, give yourself a break. Invest in a cheap thermometer and place it in the bedroom window near your closet so that you know what kind of outfit to choose without any hassle.

Alternatively, keep your laptop in the bedroom and use it as your alarm clock and weather notifier, in case of rain or snow. Use an

Alarm Clock widget (available at `http://widgetgallery.com/view`
`.php?widget=39123`) to start playing music at a time you determine.
Then schedule a task that launches a weather-report web page as well.
(See Hack 64, "Automatically Reboot and Launch Applications," for
more on launching a web page at a specific time.)

Make Task-Based Centers

Place all the items you need to complete a task in an area sectioned off for
that activity — such as a computer-repair center, a bill-paying center, or a
gift-wrapping center. Keep ink and paper next to the printer; folders and
tabs on the filing cabinet; and stamps, envelopes, and address stickers in
a mail center. Incorporate the defragging process — placing related items
next to one another — into your regular cleaning routine.

Leave Writing Material Everywhere

Keep pens and pads all over the house: by the phone, on the kitchen
counter, on the night table, in the bathroom. You never know when a
thought that needs to be recorded will strike. An idea, a forgotten to-do,
the solution to a problem you're having at work, a dream you want to
remember, an image or drawing, a phone number — all should be jotted
down without effort. Easily available capture tools keep nagging thoughts
from cluttering your mind.

Set Up an Inbox

Make a place to put real-life items that come streaming into your day so
that you can process them at times *you* determine instead of letting them
interrupt you. Snail mail, receipts, business cards, random paperwork,
notes you've scribbled to yourself should all be shuttled directly into
your inbox for later sorting and processing. A plastic or metal office inbox
does just fine; any kind of box or even designated desk space would
work. You get bonus points if you can get your housemate or partner to
get an inbox, too; that way, you can leave things for him or her to see
without having piles of stuff gathering around the house.

Collaborate with Housemates

Simple tools can make sharing household tasks easy. Place a magnetic
dirty/clean flippy sign on the dishwasher so that everyone knows when

it has to be emptied and when it can be loaded. Stick a magnetic white-board to the fridge with an ongoing shopping list. Use it to leave notes or to-do lists, too, such as "Call plumber about the toilet! 555-3456." A magnetic whiteboard calendar is also a handy way to keep track of household schedules, especially for busy families.

> **TIP** The Grocery Shopping Helper (available at `http://lifehackerbook` `.com/ch5/groceryhelper`) creates a list of shopping items with the aisle they're located in at your local store. Print a copy to keep on your fridge and list the quantity next to items you need. Then, sort needed items by aisle to make grocery shopping a breeze.

Hack 43: Sentence Stuff to Death Row

Level. . . . . . . **Easy**
Platform. . . . **All**
Cost. . . . . **Free**

Endless streams of information compete for your attention. RSS feeds, mailing lists, and news sites are all great ways to keep up with what's going on in the world and within your industry. However, because putting your ear to yet another new information channel is so easy, it's equally easy to find yourself swimming in a sea of unread items that pile up while you're focusing on other things. Prune your information chan-nels down to the ones most worth your time to keep up a solid attention firewall. One technique for doing so is sentencing certain information streams to a virtual "death row."[7]

Maybe it's the mailing list you once enjoyed but that has become more boring than informative. Maybe it's that weblog that seemed so fun and original six months ago that's slowly lost your interest. Whether you're decluttering your home or your digital space, sometimes it's hard to know what you can safely toss and what to hang onto. A simple method for choosing what goes and what stays is to make a folder called death row on your hard drive, in your email program, or in your RSS reader — or all three. Place any feeds, lists, or files you're not sure are useful to you anymore in there.

Give yourself six weeks. If within that time, you never looked up something in that feed, or list, or used one of those files, out it goes. If you did use an item, reinstate it into your regular rotation.

Hack 44: Drown out Distracting Sounds with Pink Noise

Level. . . . . . . **Easy**
Platform. . . . **Mac OS X, Windows**
Cost. . . . . **Up to $19.95**

If your co-worker's conversation down the hall is distracting you, or your downstairs neighbor's television is blaring up through your floor, block out the sound with neutralizing noise. The right concoction of nature sounds, white noise, or calm music can mask distracting ambient sounds such as passing car subwoofers or neighborhood industrial noise.

ChatterBlocker (Windows and Mac)

Desktop application ChatterBlocker neutralizes office noise with a variety of highly configurable sounds. Not just a white noise–maker, Chatter-Blocker lets you choose a preset recipe or customize your own theme by mixing and matching voices, music, and sound effects (see Figure 5-10) to create the most effective sound mask for you.

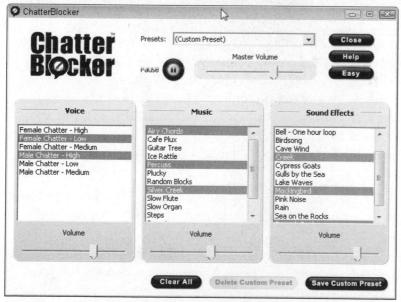

Figure 5-10 Mix and match neutralizing sounds to block out distracting noise.

ChatterBlocker is available for both Mac and Windows at `http://chatterblocker.com`. A 60-minute free trial is available and an individual license costs $19.95.

Noise (Mac OS X Only)

A free software application for Mac OS X, called Noise (see Figure 5-11), plays distraction-drowning pink noise continuously. You can download it from `http://blackholemedia.com/noise`.

Figure 5-11 Noise for Mac is a simple but effective white noise–maker.

References

1. Alorie Gilbert, "Why Can't You Pay Attention Anymore?" CNET News.com (`http://news.com.com/Why+cant+you+pay+attention+anymore/2008-1022_3-5637632.html`).

2. Jerry Useem, "Making Your Work Work For You," *CNN Money*, March 2006 (`http://money.cnn.com/magazines/fortune/fortune_archive/2006/03/20/8371789/index.htm`).

3. Claudia Wallis and Sonja Steptoe, "Help! I've Lost My Focus," *Time* magazine, Jan 10, 2006 (`http://time.com/time/archive/preview/0,10987,1147199,00.html`).

4. LeechBlock developer notes, Mozilla Add-ons (`https://addons.mozilla.org/en-US/firefox/addon/4476`).

5. Ivan Berger, "The Virtues of a Second Screen," *The New York Times*, April 20, 2006 (`http://nytimes.com/2006/04/20/technology/20basics.html`).

6. Bill Gates, "How I Work: Bill Gates," *Fortune Magazine*, Mar 30, 2006 (`http://money.cnn.com/2006/03/30/news/newsmakers/gates_howiwork_fortune`).

7. Michael Hyatt, "Sentencing Application Software to Death Row," Working Smart (`http://www.michaelhyatt.com/workingsmart/2005/11/sentencing_appl.html`).

Streamline Common Tasks

You can get your work done faster with the right shortcuts — for the price of *learning* those shortcuts, that is. Shortcuts get you where you want to go faster, but they're not obvious and it takes practice to incorporate them into your habits. The difference between taking main roads across town and taking the back roads is that the main roads are easier but take longer. If you drive across town every day, however, it's worth your time to learn the back-road shortcut.

The same principle applies to your work processes. No doubt you perform dozens of repetitive actions every day, such as typing www .google.com into your browser's address bar, or clicking the Start button and navigating to the Programs menu, or typing "Let me know if you have any questions" at the end of an email. These are opportunities for shortcuts that can add up to large savings over time. Every movement, every task, every action is a candidate for optimization and streamlining.

Imagine that working a few new shortcuts into your day saves two seconds on each of four tasks you perform 20 times a day. That amounts to about two and a half minutes of saved time a day, which adds up to 667 minutes or more than 11 hours a year (taking into account weekends and two weeks of vacation). All told, you can save more than an entire workday every year just by learning how to search Google or sign an email by taking the back roads.

The key is teaching yourself the shortcuts that will benefit you most. Identify the activities you perform most often, learn the shortcuts, and then train yourself to use them every time.

A WORD ABOUT KEYBOARD SHORTCUTS

One of the most common ways to streamline a computing task is to learn the keyboard command for an action. Moving your hand off your keyboard, placing it on the mouse, moving the mouse pointer over a button or menu, and clicking is inherently a time- and effort-intensive motion. Most modern software comes with keyboard shortcuts that can achieve the same end in half the time.

Many of the hacks in this chapter discuss keyboard shortcuts for useful applications such as Google search or Windows. These shortcuts may seem arcane and overly complicated. You may ask, "Why press Ctrl+Shift+M when I can just click the button?" As with the back roads, keyboard shortcuts take practice to learn but save you travel time on trips you take often.

The hacks in this chapter cover how to streamline common computer processes so that you can spend less time moving the mouse and tapping the keyboard and more time getting things done.

Hack 45: Search the Web in Three Keystrokes

Level. . . . . . . **Easy**
Platform. . . . **All (Firefox)**
Cost. . . . . **Free**

If you're online at work, chances are, you search for information on the Web several times a day. There are dozens of ways to do a web search from your desktop, but the most common method takes the longest:

1. With your web browser open, select the entire URL of the current page in the address bar.

2. Replace it by typing **www.google.com**.

3. Press Enter.

4. Type your search term — say, **lifehacker** — into Google's search box.

5. Click the Google Search button or press Enter.

You'd probably follow these same steps for lots of other web searches, too, such as at Yahoo!, Amazon.com, or Wikipedia.

There is a much faster way.

Run a Search with Keyboard Shortcuts

The free, open-source web browser Firefox (`http://mozilla.org/products/firefox`) comes equipped with a Google web search box built into its chrome, in the upper-right corner, as shown in Figure 6-1.

Figure 6-1 The Mozilla Firefox web browser comes with a search box built in to the right of the Go button.

You can execute a web search from this box without ever taking your hands off the keyboard; just use the key combination Ctrl+K. Here's how to Google Lifehacker using this shortcut:

1. With the Firefox web browser open, press Ctrl+K.

2. Type **lifehacker**.

3. Press Enter.

Firefox magically transports you to the search results page for Lifehacker without ever visiting the Google homepage. This method cuts your search down to three keystrokes plus your typed search terms — and no mouse movement.

The search bar doesn't work just for Google. It comes preloaded with Yahoo!, Amazon.com, eBay, Answers.com, and Creative Commons searches as well. Visit Firefox Add-ons at `https://addons.mozilla.org/search-engines.php` to get other useful engines such as the Wikipedia, IMDB (Internet Movie Database), the Merriam-Webster dictionary, Weather.com, and Ask.com.

To page to another search engine, use Ctrl+? or Ctrl+?. For example, to search for Lifehacker on Amazon.com do the following:

1. Press Ctrl+K to move the cursor to the Search box.

2. Press Ctrl+? twice to switch to Amazon.

3. Type **lifehacker** and press Enter.

TIP To open your search results in a new tab from the Firefox search bar, press Alt+Enter (instead of just Enter) after entering your search term.

There are several alternatives to the Firefox/Google search bar, including the Google Toolbar for Internet Explorer (available at `http://toolbar .google.com/T4`) and Google Desktop Search (see Hack 12, "Instantly Retrieve Files Stored on Your Computer," for more info).

Most application launcher programs such as Quicksilver for Mac (`http://quicksilver.blacktree.com`) and Launchy for Windows (`http:// www.launchy.net`) also support quick web search queries. See Hacks 46 and 47 in this chapter for more on those.

Now that you're searching the Web without taking your hands off the keyboard, you can extend your keyboard mastery to Google's page of search results. Google offers an alternative search-results view that listens to your keystrokes and lets you move up and down the list of links and open the ones you're interested in without clicking. Google's Keyboard Shortcuts search is one of several of its experimental search products, available at `http://www.google.com/experimental/index.html`. Click the Join This Experiment link next to Keyboard Shortcuts to give it a test drive. When you run a web search, you can move down and back up the list of link results using the J and K keys, respectively. To open a result, use the O key (for "open") or simply press Enter. The forward slash (/) key puts your cursor into Google's search box to run another search, and the Esc key removes it, as shown in Figure 6-2.

To combine the two techniques, install the Firefox Google by Keyboard search plugin for your browser's search box, available at `http://lifehacker .com/software/geek-to-live/useful-search-plugins-for-firefox- and-ie7-262602.php`. (Just click the Google By Keyboard link on that page to install the plugin.) If you make Google by Keyboard your default search engine, to run a web search and open the second result on the page, you do the following:

1. Press Ctrl+K to move your cursor to the search box (cmd+K for Mac users).

2. Type your search term and press Enter.

3. Press the J key once to move your cursor to the second search result.

4. Press Enter to open the link.

Getting to your destination without ever reaching for your mouse is much faster.

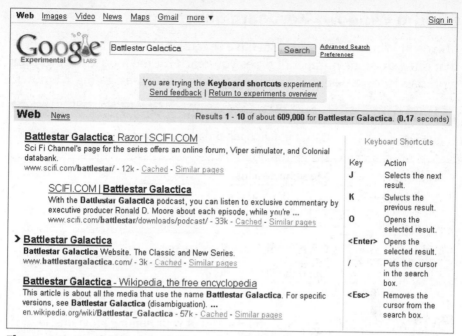

Figure 6-2 Google's Keyboard Shortcuts search experiment lets you move up and down the list of search-result links using the J and K keys, and open a link by pressing Enter.

Hack 46: Command Your Windows PC from the Keyboard

Level. . . . . . . **Medium**
Platform. . . . **Windows XP and Vista**
Cost. . . . . **Free**

The graphical user interface revolutionized personal computing because it made using a computer so much more visual. However, using the mouse is one of the most inefficient ways to drive a computer. Think about it: you must move your hand from the keyboard to the mouse pad, drag the pointer across the screen until it's over a button or icon, and then double-click to open a document or launch an application.

You can save an enormous amount of time by using keyboard shortcuts to navigate your computer's operating system and programs. This hack describes how to bypass the mouse and launch programs and documents on your Windows PC without ever taking your hands off the keyboard.

Built-in Windows Keyboard Shortcuts

Microsoft Windows XP and Vista have several built-in keyboard shortcuts that can reduce the number of times you reach for the mouse during your workday. Here are some of the essential shortcuts for navigating Windows:

SHORTCUT	RESULT
Alt+Tab	Cycle through open programs (release keys when you see the screen you want).
Windows+D	Show the desktop.
Windows+L	Lock your workstation.
Windows+R	Show the Run box.
Windows	Open the Start menu (Vista only).
Ctrl+Esc	Open the Start menu.

TIP Alt+Tab, which displays a mini menu of your running programs, is my most frequently used Windows key combination. The free Alt+Tab Windows XP Power Toy add-on — available for download at `http://microsoft.com/windowsxp/downloads/powertoys/xppowertoys.mspx` — presents a much more informative visual choice by displaying previews of the open windows as you cycle through them.

The following are indispensable editing shortcuts:

SHORTCUT	RESULT
Ctrl+S	Save the current document.
Ctrl+C	Copy selected text to clipboard.
Ctrl+X	Cut selected text or object and place on the clipboard.
Ctrl+V	Paste the contents of the clipboard into the current document.
Ctrl+Z	Undo the last action you performed.
Ctrl+Y	Redo the last action you undid.
Ctrl+B	Bold the selected text.
Ctrl+I	Italicize the selected text.
Ctrl+U	Underline the selected text.

You might use some of these shortcuts all the time and some none of the time. To find the key combinations most useful for your workflow, look over the complete list of Windows XP keyboard shortcuts at `http://support.microsoft.com/default.aspx?scid=kb;en-us;301583` and Windows Vista shortcuts at `http://windowshelp.microsoft.com/Windows/en-US/Help/2503b91d-d780-4c80-8f08-2f48878dc5661033.mspx`.

Launch Documents and Applications from Vista's Search Box

One of the most powerful and easiest-to-remember keyboard shortcuts in Windows Vista is very simple: one tap on the Windows key summons the Start menu, with your cursor in Vista's Start Search box. From there you can begin typing the name of any program, bookmark, or document — such as **Picasa** or **novel** — and Vista will automatically suggest matches in the menu, as shown in Figure 6-3.

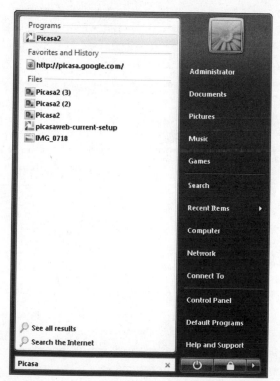

Figure 6-3 Tap the Windows key once to have Vista search as you type for any application, document, or bookmark.

Use your up and down arrow keys to traverse the list of search results. Press Enter when you've selected the one you'd like to start, such as the Picasa photo manager software.

Quickly Run Programs and Open Files with Launchy

Windows XP doesn't have the convenient Start menu search box that Vista does, but a free program called Launchy can give you similar functionality. Download Launchy from `http://launchy.net` and install it.

According to its developer, Launchy is "designed to help you forget about your Start menu, the icons on your desktop, and even your file manager," and it does. After you get into the habit of using Launchy, mousing through Start menu subfolders or clicking through Explorer window after Explorer window will seem like a quaint activity of the past.

When you've got Launchy installed and running, press Alt+Spacebar to invoke its plain-Jane black input field. Then type the name of any document, program, or bookmark, and Launchy will suggest a list of search matches. Use the arrow keys to move up and down the list. Open the one you need with a tap on the Enter key. Figure 6-4 displays Launchy in action, finding the Word document in which this chapter was written.

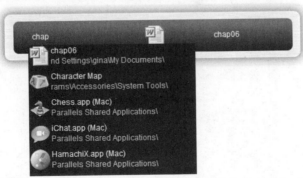

Figure 6-4 Invoke Launchy with its default key combination, Alt+Spacebar, and then begin typing the name of any program, file, or bookmark on your system.

To configure the directories Launchy indexes and other behavior, right-click the Launchy prompt and choose Preferences.

Launchy isn't just an application or file launcher. You can also use it to run a Google search, navigate your file system without Explorer, and interface with web applications such as Remember the Milk (`http://rememberthemilk.com`) and Google Calendar (`http://calendar.google.com`). For more advanced uses of Launchy, see `http://lifehacker.com/software/hack-attack/take-launchy-beyond-application-launching-284127.php`.

Hack 47: Command Your Mac from the Keyboard

Level. . . . . . . **Medium**
Platform. . . . **Mac OS X**
Cost. . . . . **Free**

Skip time-wasting point-and-click mouse movement on your Mac using free software called Quicksilver (`http://quicksilver.blacktree.com`), which is a keyboard interface to an astonishing variety of computing actions. At its most basic level of functionality, Quicksilver launches applications and opens documents, much the same as Launchy for Windows, as outlined in the previous hack.

Basic File and Application Launching with Quicksilver

Here's how to get started using Quicksilver as a keyboard launcher:

1. Download and install the latest version of Quicksilver from `http://quicksilver.blacktree.com`. As of this writing, beta 53 is the most recent version available.

2. To invoke the Quicksilver commander, press cmd+Spacebar (Quicksilver's default key combination). Begin to type the name of the application or document you'd like to open; for example, type **Wor**. Quicksilver suggests Microsoft Word as a match (or whatever files and programs you have installed that contain "Wor" in the title) and displays a drop-down list of other possible matches on the right, as shown in Figure 6-5.

3. Press Enter to open Microsoft Word, or press the down arrow key to choose another option. Quicksilver adapts its suggestions to your most-used applications and documents, so the next time you invoke Quicksilver with Ctrl+Spacebar and type **Wor**, it will suggest the item you've launched before at the top of the list.

Figure 6-5 Quicksilver launcher matches programs that contain "Wor" in the title.

Advanced Quicksilver Actions

In its most basic usage (just described), Quicksilver uses a two-paned interface that lets you select a subject in the first pane — the file or application — and an action (Open) in the second pane. But Quicksilver offers a wide variety of actions beyond Open that can take additional information in a third pane. Advanced three-pane Quicksilver actions come in the form of subject-action-object.

For example, you can select a file called chapter6.doc in the first pane, select Move To as the action, and tab to the third pane to choose the book folder. This three-paned action (see Figure 6-6) moves the file to that folder.

Figure 6-6 Quicksilver's three-paned subject-action-object actions can perform custom actions, such as moving a file to a destination folder.

Other actions that Quicksilver can perform on your Mac include the following:

- **Manipulate an iTunes music library.** Start playing an album, song, or playlist; browse your library by genre, artist, or album; or rate songs as they're playing on the fly without switching out of your current working application.

- **Email a document to a contact.** Select a document and choose Email To (Compose) as the action; select a contact in your address book as the recipient, without opening your email software (see Figure 6-7).

- **Append text to a file.** Invoke Quicksilver and press the period key (.) to start free-form entering text. In the Action panel, choose Append To and in the third panel, choose a text file, such as `todo.txt` or `shoppinglist.txt`, to add a line to the file without a text editor.

- **Look up a word in the dictionary.** Type a word to look up in the first panel and choose Dictionary as your action to get the definition.

Figure 6-7 Quicksilver plugins, such as the Apple Mail plugin, let you do more with Quicksilver — such as dash off an email to Mom.

NOTE Several of the actions listed here may require additional Quicksilver plugins to work as described. Check out the Quicksilver manual at `http://docs.blacktree.com/quicksilver/overview` to learn how to enable the actions you'd like to perform with Quicksilver.

As you can see, Quicksilver is not just a keyboard launcher; with the right plugins, it can do almost anything on your Mac via the keyboard that you do with your mouse. It would take an entire book just to describe all the things Quicksilver can do on your Mac. If this hack makes you want to learn more, get more Quicksilver tutorials and video demonstrations at `http://lifehackerbook.com/ch6`.

Hack 48: Reduce Repetitive Typing with Texter for Windows

Level. . . . . . . **Medium**
Platform. . . . **Windows XP and Vista**
Cost. . . . . **Free**

If you spend your day at a keyboard, chances are, you type particular phrases — such as "Thanks for contacting us" — several times throughout the day. Maybe you've acquired a maddening habit of typing *teh* instead of *the* when your fingers are really flying over the keys. Perhaps you enter the current date into documents all the time, or you tend to use Internet acronyms such as "imo" to stand for "in my opinion."

These are all situations in which text substitution can save you time. Define short abbreviations for phrases you use often, or misspellings you're prone to, and automatically expand those abbreviations to their full, intended form. This hack explains how to do that using the free Windows application Texter.

Set Up Texter Hotstrings

Download Texter from `http://lifehacker.com/software//lifehacker-code-texter-windows-238306.php` and save the `Texter.exe` file to a new folder, `C:\Program Files\Texter\`. Double-click `C:\Program Files\ Texter\Texter.exe` to run the program for the first time. You'll notice a green icon with the letters "LH" on it appear in your Windows system tray; right-click it and choose Manage Hotstrings to start configuring abbreviations that will do your typing for you.

Adding Hotstrings

To create a new hotstring, click the + sign. In the Hotstring field, enter your abbreviation — **btw**, for example. In the text area, type your hotstring's full replacement: **by the way**. Choose the key that will trigger the replacement (Enter, Tab, or Space) or select the Instant check box (see Figure 6-8) to make the replacement happen automatically.

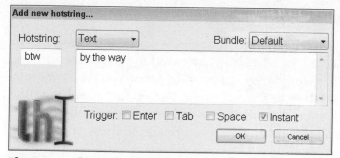

Figure 6-8 Adding a new hotstring — btw — that expands to "by the way" as soon as it's typed.

Click OK to save your new hotstring, which will appear in Texter's management dialog along with the rest of the hotstrings you set up, as shown in Figure 6-9.

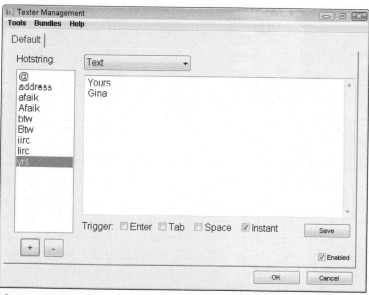

Figure 6-9 Managing Texter's default set of hotstrings.

After you've saved a hotstring, when Texter is enabled and running, type that hotstring and press the trigger key (not required for instant replacements), and Texter automatically expands it to your replacement. For example, the next time you type *btw*, Texter fills in *by the way*, producing 10 characters for the effort of typing three.

Choosing the Right Hotstring Trigger

Different trigger keys work better for different types of replacements. For example, if you'd like the word *address* to expand to your street address, you need to assign a specific trigger key — one that you wouldn't normally type, such as Tab — to the hotstring. Sometimes you'll type the word *address* and want it to remain *address* and not automatically expand, so the Instant replacement setting (or even Space or Enter trigger key) wouldn't work as well there.

For common typos, however, you want to use the Instant option as your trigger. For example, if you often type *teh* when you mean *the*, you want Texter to automatically correct you without your having to press a specific trigger key.

Configuring Bundles

You'll find many uses for text expansion, including the following:

- Email form letters or signatures (see Hack 9 about scripting repetitive email responses)
- Common misspellings (such as *teh* or *htis*)
- Common phrases (such as *as far as I know* or *Thanks for contacting us*)
- Document templates
- Personal data (such as name, address, phone number, or email address)

Using Texter you can divide your hotstrings into "bundles," or groups. For example, to create a Texter bundle for common misspellings, from the Bundles menu choose Add and name your bundle a single word (such as Typos). The Typos bundle will appear in its own tab in the Texter management dialog, where you can add hotstrings for *teh* and *htis* that automatically become *the* and *this*. To create another bundle for common phrases, choose Bundles ⇨ Add and name it Acronyms. There you can set up hotstrings such as *btw*, which expands to *by the way*, and *afaik*, for *as far as I know*. Bundles are just a way to organize and separate your Texter hotstrings by category or purpose (see Figure 6-10).

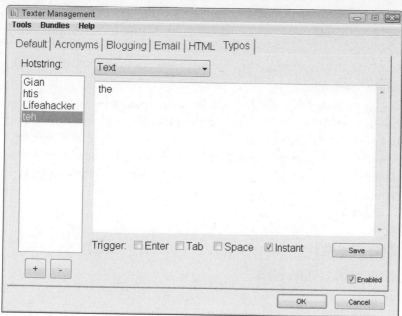

Figure 6-10 Managing multiple bundles of Texter hotstrings.

You can also export and import Texter bundles for easy sharing among colleagues.

More Texter Features

More ways to get the most out of Texter include the following:

- **Automatically start Texter when your computer does.** To make sure Texter starts working when you do, from the Tools menu, choose Preferences, and on the General tab, select Run Texter At Startup. Texter will launch automatically with Windows.

- **Print a cheat sheet.** Setting up three dozen hotstrings is one thing, but training your typing fingers to use them is another. Choose Preferences from Texter's Tools menu, and on the Print tab, click Create Printable Texter Cheatsheet to make a paper reference that you can pin to your bulletin board while you learn your Texter hotstrings and triggers.

- **Store and run Texter from a thumb drive.** Texter is a completely self-contained program that can live and run from an external USB thumb drive. If you use different computers throughout the day, just plug in the drive where Texter and its data are stored, launch it, and access all your hotstrings.

- **Create a new hotstring or manage hotstrings using keyboard shortcuts.** By default you can summon the New Hotstring dialog box by pressing Ctrl+Shift+H whenever Texter is running. Likewise, you can launch the Manage Hotstrings dialog box using Ctrl+Shift+M.

- **Revel in how much time Texter has saved you.** After you've come to depend on Texter to do your typing for you, check out how many hours of time it's saved you. In the Preferences dialog box (get to it from the Tools menu), check the Stats tab to see how many replacements Texter's made for you and how many characters and hours of time saved that translates into.

Hack 49: Reduce Repetitive Typing with TextExpander for Mac

Level. . . . . . . **Medium**
Platform. . . . **Mac OS X**
Cost. **$29.95**

In the same vein as Hack 48, Mac users can save thousands of keystrokes daily using the text-substitution application TextExpander. Everyone has phrases, information, or misspellings they type every day. With the TextExpander typing utility, you can automatically replace abbreviations such as *imo* with the phrase *in my opinion* or end email messages with two characters — say, *bt*, which magically turn into *Best, Tom*. Here's how.

Configure TextExpander Snippets

Download TextExpander (available at `http://www.smileonmymac.com/textexpander/index.html`) and install it on your Mac. An individual license costs $29.95, but you can try TextExpander for free. In System Preferences, launch the TextExpander pane, which is listed under Other. Here you'll set up a set of text *snippets*, or abbreviations, that TextExpander will replace with text you define.

Adding New Snippets

To create a new expanding snippet, click the plus sign on the bottom left of the TextExpander panel and choose New Snippet (or simply press cmd+N). On the right side of the panel, enter the expanded content — **by the way**, in this example — and at the bottom of the panel, in the Abbreviation field, type the snippet **btw**, as shown in Figure 6-11.

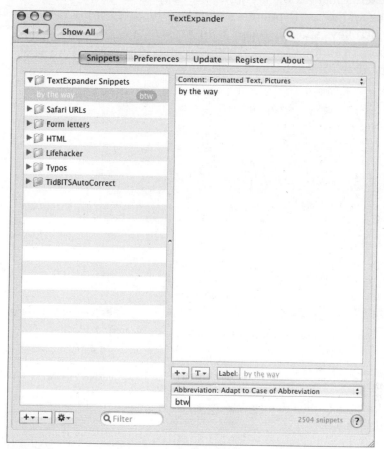

Figure 6-11 Create a new snippet, *btw*, that TextExpander replaces with *by the way*.

Your expanded content can be formatted text and pictures (such as your company logo or red, bold, warning text) as well as plain text. To insert a picture or color, or to size, bold, italicize, or otherwise format your text, select Formatted Text ⇨ Pictures in the Content drop-down list.

Set the Text Expansion Delimiter

By default, your TextExpander snippets are replaced as soon as you type them. However, if you use real words as your snippets, you may not always want them to expand. For example, if you use *email* to expand to your email address, you'll never be able to type just the word *email*.

To avoid this conflict, set TextExpander to use a delimiter key that triggers replacements instead of having them happen as you type. In the Preferences tab of the TextExpander pane, click the Set Delimiters button to specify which keys should trigger your replacement (the Tab key, for instance). Then, from the Expand Abbreviations drop-down list, choose At Delimiter (Abandon Delimiter), as shown in Figure 6-12.

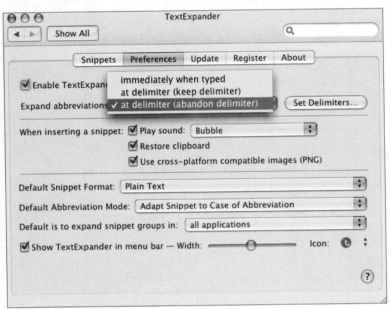

Figure 6-12 Set TextExpander to make replacements when you press the specified delimiter key.

NOTE Choosing At Delimiter (Keep Delimiter) will preserve the delimiter character after your replacement, such as a Tab, carriage return, or space. This means that if you type your snippet plus your delimiter key, TextExpander will replace the snippet and keep the delimiter after it. Otherwise, TextExpander will replace the snippet and remove the delimiter character.

You'll see more options in the Preferences area, such as limiting expansions to only certain applications, making your snippets case-sensitive, case-insensitive, or case-adaptive based on how you type the snippet (that is, *Btw* expands to *By the way* and *btw* expands to *by the way*).

Managing Snippet Groups

TextExpander can organize your snippets into folders by purpose, application specifics, or any other category. For example, you may keep a Common Misspellings group that automatically corrects typos for you, an Email Form Letters group that works only in your email software, or a Bookmarks group that fills in long web addresses in your web browser. Figure 6-13 shows some example categories.

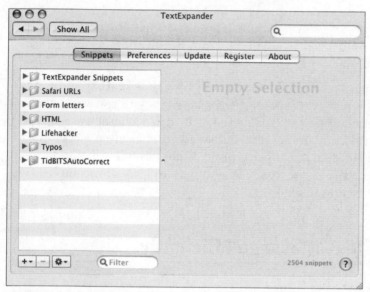

Figure 6-13 Organize your TextExpander snippets into groups.

SmileOnMyMac, the company that makes TextExpander, offers three useful prefab TextExpander groups you can import: the AutoCorrect snippet file (about 100 common typos and their corrections); the TidBITS AutoCorrect Dictionary (more than 2,400 misspellings and their corrections); and the HTML Code Snippet file (for bloggers or web site editors). They are all available as free downloads at http://www.smileonmymac .com/textexpander/snippets.html.

Advanced TextExpander Usage

Here are some more things you can do with TextExpander:

- **Program cursor movement.** Set your cursor's position within the replacement after it has been expanded using the special %| variable in your snippet content. Alternatively, program particular cursor movements (such as two taps to the left or three taps to the right). Use the Cursor item on the drop-down list to the left of the Label input field to insert cursor-movement variables.

- **Add variables that insert date, time, and Clipboard contents into your snippet.** From the drop-down list on the left of the Label input field, choose to insert special dynamic variables such as the current time, date, day of week, month, year, or contents of the Clipboard inside a snippet.

- **Synchronize your snippets with .Mac.** If you're a .Mac subscriber, you can update snippets on one Mac and then download your changes onto another when .Mac synchronization is enabled for TextExpander.

- **View the number of characters and time that TextExpander has saved you.** On TextExpander's Register tab, you can see the total number of snippets it's expanded, how many characters it's typed for you, and how much time it's saved you based on a typing speed of 400 characters per minute. Right now, TextExpander tells me it has replaced nearly 3,600 snippets and saved me almost five hours of typing time.

Hack 50: Text-Message Efficiently

Level. . . . . . . **Easy**
Platform. . . . **Mobile phone with SMS capabilities**
Cost. . . . . **Dependent on your plan**

More and more modern cell phones and plans feature Short Message Service (SMS), the capability to send a text message to another phone or email address.

To the uninitiated, texting can seem inconvenient, but text messages have numerous advantages over voice calls. Human beings read text faster than they can listen to speech. Text messages are archived, searchable, and can never be misheard or cut off by bad reception. Texting someone gets info into his hands when he's away from his desk without requiring that he stop everything to pick up the phone to talk. Text messages get right to the point, cutting out time-wasting small talk, throat-clearing, and the energy it takes to get back into the flow of what you were doing before the phone rang. Text messages, unlike the spoken word, are not affected by a noisy situation such as a party or concert. Texting various web services can retrieve helpful information you need on the go, such as directions, addresses, and phone numbers.

For those of you with an SMS-capable mobile phone, this hack presents a few power-texting tips that can help you get the most out of SMS.

What You Can Do with SMS

Texting can help you get things done. Here are a few examples:

- **Send reminders.** Text your spouse on her way home from work to *pick up milk at the store*. Remind your teenager to *call when you get there*. Text your future self reminders about to-do's or appointments.

- **Search the Web.** Several mobile search services such as Google SMS (http://www.google.com/sms) and 4INFO (http://4info.net) will text you information by SMS request. For example, you can text GOOGL (or 46645) the message *star wars 11215* to find show times for the latest Star Wars film in the 11215 ZIP Code. Get flight-arrival times, weather, sports scores, dictionary definitions, stock prices, and more via SMS. (See Hack 72, "Access Web Apps and Search via Text Message," for more.)

- **Find a friend in a loud place.** You're at a concert trying to meet up with a friend and you can't hear a thing. This is the time to text. SMS also comes in mighty handy in libraries, at parties, or at religious services, where talking is not possible or is a no-no. (Just make sure your phone SMS notification is set to vibrate!)

Quick-Start Guide for SMS Beginners

To send an SMS, create a new message and add a recipient from your mobile's address book. Sending a message to an SMS-capable phone requires only the recipient's phone number in the To: field. Then, to type the body of your message, use the numeric keys on your phone. Press each several times to cycle through the possible letters each number represents; stop when you've reached the one you need. For example, if you want the letter *B*, press 2 twice. You can see the key you're pressing scroll through all the letters associated with it. Pressing 2, for example, scrolls through *A*, *B*, and *C*.

Is this an insanely inconvenient way to type out text? Absolutely. But there are ways to make it more bearable.

Save Your Thumbs

Here are a couple of ways to make typing text on a numeric keypad easier and less time-consuming.

- **Use message templates.** After a while, you'll notice that you send the same kinds of messages over and over, such as *Running late, be there in...*, *On my way home*, and *Give me a call when you get a chance.* Set up templates for your most-used messages to avoid repetitive thumbing. The exact instructions on how to do this vary, so consult the user guide for your phone's model.

- **Turn on predictive text.** Many modern phones offer a predictive text feature, which precludes the need to press each numeric key multiple times to get the letter you want. Thumb out the numbers that contain the letters in your desired word by pressing each just once, and your phone will automatically predict the word you intend, saving dozens of key presses over time. See a short video demonstration of predictive text in action courtesy of Nokia at `http://nokia-asia.com/nokia/0,,79355,00.html`. (If your phone supports predictive text, it may look different, depending on your model.)

When you get the hang of it, text messaging is a convenient way to communicate when you're not at your computer with easy access to IM or email. But there are ways to use SMS from your desktop computer as well.

SMS from Your Computer

Several software applications and web sites can deliver text messages to phone numbers:

- **Send text messages from AOL Instant Messenger (AIM) to a phone.** Add a new contact to your Buddy List whose name is a phone number preceded by a plus sign (that is, +7185551212). An instant message sent to that buddy will be delivered as an SMS to that mobile phone.

- **SMS from the Web.** Yahoo! Mobile (`http://mobile.yahoo.com/sms/sendsms`) sends text messages to a mobile phone number of your choice from the Web.

- **SMS via email.** Many mobile service providers allow you to send a text message to a phone via email using a specific email address consisting of the phone number @ the service provider's email domain. If you don't know the domain, the free service Teleflip (http://teleflip.com) will route your email message for you. Simply send your message to 7185551212@teleflip.com, substituting your destination phone number before the @ sign.

WARNING Check how much text messages cost on your particular mobile phone plan. Many include unlimited SMS messages, but others can charge up to 10 cents a message, which can add up over time. You don't want to be surprised by a big cell phone bill the month after you start texting!

Hack 51: Batch-Resize Photos

Level. . . . . . . **Easy**
Platform. . . . **Windows XP**
Cost. . . . . **Free**

Everyone likes to email digital photos, but no one likes to receive pictures that are so huge they take forever to download and require you to scroll left and right and up and down to see the entire image. Luckily, with just two clicks, you can easily resize a large group of photos that you've downloaded from your digital camera.

Microsoft ImageResizer PowerToy is a free utility that plugs into Windows Explorer. Download and install ImageResizer from the right side of the page at http://microsoft.com/windowsxp/downloads/powertoys/ xppowertoys.mspx. Then, browse to the folder where you stored your digital photos.

Select the photos you want to resize, right-click, and choose Resize Pictures from the context menu to open the ImageResizer dialog box. Click the Advanced button to see all the options, as shown in Figure 6-14.

From there, choose one of the ImageResizer suggested dimensions, or enter your custom width and height. Be sure to select the Make Pictures Smaller But Not Larger option if you don't want to size up — and you won't, because making digital photos larger degrades quality. Click OK.

By default, ImageResizer creates copies of the files and adds the chosen size to the filename. For example, if your original photo filename was Jeremy001.jpg and you resized it using the Small setting, the new version will be named Jeremy001 (Small).jpg.

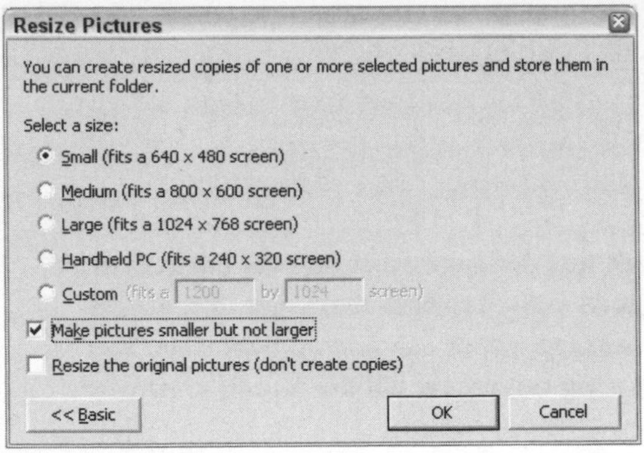

Figure 6-14 The ImageResizer options dialog box.

Alternatively, if you're looking for a complete photo manager that can do more extensive photo processing, including batch resizing, red-eye reduction, photo rating, keyword assigning, search, and lots of fun effects, download and install a copy of Google's free Picasa (http://picasa.com). After Picasa indexes all your photos, select the ones you want to resize so that they appear in the Picture Tray on the bottom left. Then click the Export button on the lower right. Here you can copy the photos at a new size to another folder on your hard drive for emailing, publishing online, or burning to CD. See Hack 17 for more on managing your photo collection with Picasa.

NOTE Windows Vista and Mac users should check out http:// lifehackerbook.com/ch6/ for your options when it comes to batch resizing photos.

Hack 52: Send and Receive Money on Your Cell Phone

Level. . . . . . . **Easy**
Platform. . . . **Cell phone (text messaging optional)**
Cost. . . . . **Free**

Popular online payment service PayPal (http://paypal.com) is a quick and easy way to email money to friends and co-workers — to cover your share of the dinner bill, pitch in on a shared gift, or send a payment for work done. PayPal's new mobile service now enables you to send and receive money directly from your cell phone when you're out and about.

Mobile-to-mobile payments can come in handy in lieu of cold, hard cash when purchasing something from someone you don't know (say, from Craigslist, `http://craigslist.org`) or when you can't find an ATM and your buddy's covering you. This hack explains how to initiate cash transactions via PayPal on your cell phone.

PayPal Mobile

You'll need a free PayPal account to get started. To add money to your PayPal account, link your checking account or credit card to it. To enable cell phone payments, you need to activate your mobile phone number within your PayPal account. Do so by entering your cell phone number on the PayPal web site in the mobile area (`https:// paypal.com/cgi-bin/webscr?cmd=xpt/cps/mobile/MobileOverview-outside`) and set up a mobile PIN (separate from your PayPal password). PayPal calls your phone on the spot and asks you to verify the PIN. When the PIN is matched, your phone is PayPal-enabled.

Then, to send someone else's phone $5.50 in cash, text-message PAY-PAL (or 729725) the following message:

```
send 5.50 to 7185551212
```

with the recipient's phone number in this example being (718) 555-1212.

The first time I tried this with my Nokia phone using Cingular, I got a text message back immediately saying that the recipient was invalid. Turns out only certain carriers — Alltel, Sprint, T-Mobile, and Verizon — support the SMS function.

Luckily, there's a plan B for folks not on those plans: you can call Pay-Pal's automated voice system to send cash as well. Dial 1-800-4PAYPAL and follow the instructions to send money to the destination cell phone number.

Either method results in a text message to the recipient's phone with instructions for picking up the money. In short, the recipient has to go to the web site and link her mobile phone number to her PayPal account to claim the payment.

The obvious question is, Why wouldn't a thief just steal your phone and text himself a few Benjamin Franklins? If you treat your PayPal mobile PIN the way you do your ATM PIN, that isn't possible because every single transaction initiated from your phone gets an immediate callback from PayPal asking that you enter your mobile PIN to proceed.

Send Money to an Email Address

If the payee doesn't have a cell phone (or doesn't want to associate it with his PayPal account), you can also text-message money to an email address. Just make your text message *send 5 to editor@lifehacker.com* instead (substituting an email address for the phone number). In this case, the recipient doesn't get immediate notification of the payment on his phone, but he doesn't have to associate his mobile number with his PayPal account, either.

You cannot use PayPal with someone's email address if you're using the 800 voice number — only if you're sending PayPal a text message (which means PayPal supports your mobile carrier). If you do use the voice system to send a payment to someone's phone and she doesn't want to link her mobile to PayPal, you can cancel the pending payment and reinitiate it through the PayPal web site.

The following table provides examples of all the PayPal Mobile SMS commands.

COMMAND	DESCRIPTION
send 10.99 to 2125551981	Send $10.99 to (212) 555-1981 phone number.
send 5 to name@example.com	Send $5.00 to name@example.com.
s 10.99 t 2125551981	Use the shortcuts s and t for send and to.
s 10.99 t 4150001234 note thx 4 dinn	Add a *thx 4 dinn* note with your payment.
send 5.43 EUR to 3105551212	Send your payment in Euros (CAD for Canadian dollars, GBP for British pounds, AUD for Australian dollars, or JPY for Yen also work).
send 10.99 to 4150001234 share address	Share your address with someone to have him ship you an item
send 10.99 to 3105551212 share phone	Share your phone number with the recipient.
send 5 to 2125551981 share info note send asap	Share your phone and address and send a note *send asap* to recipient.
Bal	Check your current PayPal balance.
Cancel	Cancel a pending payment.

PayPal Alternative

TextPayMe (http://textpayme.com) offers a service similar to PayPal Mobile Payments. TextPayMe's SMS payment address is a regular email address, so usage isn't limited to cell phone carriers. However, consumers are more likely to have a PayPal account than a TextPayMe account because PayPal's service has been established for many years and is linked with popular auction site eBay (http://ebay.com).

Hack 53: Bypass Free Site Registration with BugMeNot

Level. . . . . . . **Easy**
Platforms. . . **All**
Cost. . . . . **Free**

Ever more web sites require you to register on them for free and to sign in with a username and password to view their contents. An active surfer can easily accumulate dozens of logins for various sites across the Web. But what about when you don't want to go through the whole rigmarole of registering for a web site — you simply want inside?

The web site BugMeNot (http://bugmenot.com) maintains a public database of shared usernames and passwords for free web sites. If you come across a site that prompts you to log in to view its content, bypass the registration process by heading to BugMeNot to search for an already created username and password. Not all BugMeNot logins will work, but you can see the percentage success rate for a particular login and report whether it worked for you as well. If you can't find a BugMeNot login that works, create one and share it with the BugMeNot community.

There are four ways to use BugMeNot:

- Enter the address of the site you want to log into on http://bugmenot.com to get a list of possible logins.

- Drag and drop the BugMeNot bookmarklet to your web browser's links toolbar. When you come onto a site you'd like to log into, click the bookmarklet and get login detail suggestions in a pop-up window, as shown in Figure 6-15.

- Copy and paste the suggested login — in this example, username stupidideas and password asdfghjkl — into the nytimes.com login page to view a password-protected article.

- Download and install the BugMeNot Firefox extension, available at `http://roachfiend.com/archives/2005/02/07/bugmenot`. Restart Firefox. Next time you are presented with a username-and-password prompt, right-click inside the username text box and choose Login With BugMeNot, as shown in Figure 6-16.

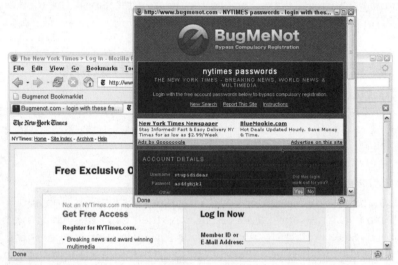

Figure 6-15 Using the BugMeNot bookmarklet to find a usable login for nytimes.com.

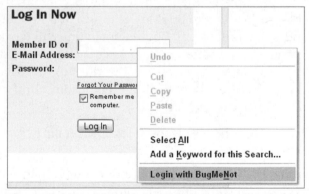

Figure 6-16 Log in with BugMeNot details directly from the context menu using the BugMeNot Firefox extension.

The extension is the fastest way to log in with a BugMeNot account because it doesn't require you to copy and paste the username and password into the login fields; however, it works only in Firefox (`http://mozilla.org/firefox/`).

NOTE See Hack 85, "Extend Your Web Browser," for more on how to install a Firefox extension.

BugMeNot does not work on web sites that require a paid subscription to view, and some sites block BugMeNot. The most popular BugMeNot sites include *The New York Times* (http://nytimes.com), *The Washington Post* (http://washingtonpost.com), and IMDB (http://imdb.com), the Internet Movie Database.

Hack 54: Speed Up Web Pages on a Slow Internet Connection

Level. . . . . . . **Easy**
Platform. . . . **All**
Cost. . . . . **Free**

It may feel as though centuries have passed since the last time you heard the unmistakable mating call of your computer's modem dialing into an ISP. But even in today's broadband-saturated world, dial-up remains an affordable and sometimes necessary connectivity alternative while traveling or when your high-speed connection isn't available.

When you're surfing the Web on a slow connection, it can seem as though grass grows faster than the download progress meter on your web browser moves. Still, it's not difficult to optimize your browsing setup for the fastest way to log on, get what you need done, and get off. This hack covers some strategies for squeezing the most productivity out of a limited flow of bytes over a slow Internet connection, be it via an analog dial-up line or a cell phone modem connection.

NOTE See Hack 79, "Turn Your Cell Phone into a Modem," for more on dialing into the Internet from your mobile phone on the go.

Configure Your Web Browser for a Slow Connection

Chances are, your web browser's setup assumes that your Internet connection is fast and ever present. A couple of small changes for your dial-in session can make a big difference:

- Increase the size of your browser's cache so that you re-download the same web page elements less often. The default cache size in Firefox, for example, is 50MB. Your hard drive probably has plenty of free space, so consider increasing this number to 100MB or more. To do so in Firefox, choose Tools ➪ Options ➪ Advanced and from the Network tab, set the number in the Cache section, as shown in Figure 6-17.

Figure 6-17 Increase the size of the cache to decrease the number of repeated downloads.

- If you want real speed and your inner aesthete won't be too offended, under Content, deselect Load Images Automatically. This, of course, takes away the pretty pictures on web pages, but it significantly speeds up page load on a slow connection. You can also specify sites that should be exceptions to the no-images rule using the — you guessed it — Exceptions button, as shown in Figure 6-18.

- To disable images in Internet Explorer, choose Tools ➪ Internet Options; go to the Multimedia section on the Advanced Tab, and deselect everything. In contrast to Firefox, Internet Explorer does not allow for exceptions to the rule.

Figure 6-18 Set Firefox to not download images or Java applets to speed up page load.

TIP Advanced users can employ the Firefox Profile feature to set up slow-connection preferences separately from your default profile, and switch to it as necessary. See more on how to manage profiles in Mozilla's Help section (`http://mozilla.org/support/firefox/profile`).

Block and Disable Bandwidth Hogs

Five minutes on a dialup connection and you begin to resent every unnecessary pixel, advertisement, and Flash movie on the Web. Install an ad blocker such as Adblock for Firefox (`https://addons.mozilla.org/firefox/10`) or FlashBlock (`http://flashblock.mozdev.org`) to avoid losing minutes of your life so that some web page can suggest you shoot the turkey and win an iPod in one of its banner ads.

Speaking of bandwidth hogs, if your podcasting software (such as iTunes) is set to automatically download new episodes when you connect to the Internet, you'll qualify for Social Security before you can view your browser's home page. Be sure to disable automatic podcast downloads when you're on a slow connection.

Use Tabs to Load Pages While You Work

The real beauty of tabbed browsing shows its efficient self in the face of a slow Internet connection. When searching the Web for information or clicking links from your RSS aggregator, click your mouse scroll wheel or Control/Command+click to open each page in a new tab. That way, you can read one page while others load in background tabs.

NOTE The web browsers that feature tabbed browsing are Firefox, Internet Explorer 7 (default in Windows Vista), and Opera. Internet Explorer 6 on Windows XP does not have tabbed browsing.

If the amount of time you're on the phone line is an issue, log on, open a bunch of pages in multiple tabs, disconnect, and read offline. Speaking of offline. . .

Work Offline Whenever Possible

Yes, always-online web applications are popular these days, but the fact is you're not always online. The capability to work offline makes a huge difference in productivity when you're dependent on a slow connection. Here's a quick list of offline work examples that can help you get things done when you're dialing in:

- Use a desktop RSS reader and download all unread articles for offline reading. (See Hack 82, "Subscribe to Web Sites with RSS," for more on using RSS.)
- Save web pages to your hard drive for reading later. (Chapter 9, "Master the Web," provides many hacks for improving your web experience.)
- Web mail users, install a desktop email client such as Mozilla Thunderbird (http://mozilla.org/products/thunderbird) and download your messages for offline reading and responding.
- Download bank transactions to Quicken or Microsoft Money instead of connecting to your bank's web site to pay bills.

A slow connection to the Internet can be an exercise in utter frustration, but tweaking your tools to fit the task can make it a lot more bearable.

Hack 55: Securely Save Web Site Passwords

Level. . . . . . . **Easy**
Platform. . . . **All (Firefox)**
Cost. . . . . **Free**

One of the most convenient features in Firefox is its capability to save the passwords you use to log on to web sites — such as your web mail and online banking — so that you don't have to type them in every time. Those saved passwords automatically fill in as asterisks in the Password field, but did you know how easy it is to see what they are? In Firefox, choose Tools ⇨ Options. In the Security tab, under Passwords, click the Show Passwords button. Then click the Show Passwords button in the dialog box — and there they are, all your high-security passwords in plain text and full sight.

Now consider how easy it would be for your Firefox-loving housemate to log onto your Gmail, or the computer-sharing temp at the office to get into your checking account, or for a laptop thief to log into your PayPal account. Not such a great feature anymore, eh? But you don't have to go back to retyping your passwords every time you visit a login-only site.

This hack describes how to secure your saved passwords in Firefox without requiring you give up the convenience of those auto-filled login details.

In Firefox, choose Tools ⇨ Options and, on the Security tab, under Passwords, select the Use a Master Password check box to set the master password (see Figure 6-19).

The master password is a single password that will lock the rest of your saved passwords away from prying eyes. It's a password you'll have to enter once a session — each time you restart Firefox.

When you set your master password, Firefox has a neat Password Quality Meter that displays how difficult your password is to crack. Try different combinations of words and numbers and symbols to get this secure-o-meter as high as possible. For example the password lifehacker scored low on the quality meter, but 11f3h4ck3r registered about 90 percent (see Figure 6-20), making it fairly hard to crack.

Figure 6-19 Set your master password in the Firefox Options dialog box.

Figure 6-20 The master password quality level.

Now, the trick is to pick something you will always remember, because if you forget your master password, you won't be able to access any of your saved passwords. That would be bad. (Hack 14, "Instantly Recall Any Number of Different Passwords," offers help in creating great passwords you won't forget.)

After you've set your master password, close Firefox. When you reopen and go to a page where you've saved a password — such as Yahoo! Mail — you get a security prompt, as shown in Figure 6-21.

Figure 6-21 The master password prompt.

Enter your master password, click OK, and your Yahoo! Mail login details fill in automatically.

The master password prompt is a bit of an inconvenience, but much less so than entering a password every time you visit login-only sites. It buys you the expediency of saved passwords with the security of having to be authorized to access them.

NOTE The Firefox Master Password is difficult — but not impossible — to crack. If there are passwords to web sites you absolutely don't want stored on your computer, when you enter them and Firefox asks whether it should save them, just click No.

Hack 56: Become a Scheduling Black Belt with Google Calendar

Level. . . . . . . **Easy**
Platform. . . . **Web**
Cost. . . . . **Free**

In Hack 30, "Send Reminders to Your Future Self," you learned how to schedule events and reminders using the web-based Google Calendar, or GCal. GCal has many more useful features that make it a strong candidate for your central work and life calendar application. This hack covers more advanced uses for GCal, such as adding and getting events from anywhere, subscribing to multiple calendars, sharing calendars, booking inanimate objects such as a conference room, and inviting multiple people to events.

Quickly Capture Events

When Google Calendar is loaded in your web browser, you can press the Q key to summon a single field to enter an event. Forget typing in 17 fields for all the event details; GCal understands natural language such as "tomorrow at 2PM," as shown in Figure 6-22.

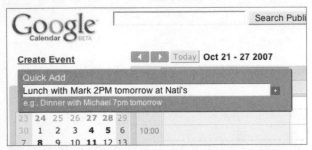

Figure 6-22 Use the Quick Add feature to add events to your Google Calendar by pressing the Q key and typing in event details in natural language, such as "Lunch tomorrow at 2PM."

To get that handy Quick Add box no matter what page you're looking at in Firefox, install the Google Calendar Quick Add extension, available for download at `http://torrez.us/archives/2006/04/18/433/`. With the extension installed, you can get a Calendar Quick Add box when you press the Ctrl+; key combination from any web page.

Subscribe to Shared Calendars

When's Passover this year? What day of the week does Cinco de Mayo land on? Browse GCal's list of shared public calendars to add sets of dates, from the phases of the moon to religious and regional holidays. Click the Manage Calendars link on the right side of GCal and then click the Add Calendar button. Choose the Browse Calendars tab to pick and choose from a list of shared calendars.

Share a Custom Calendar

You can also create and share your calendars such as your softball team's game schedule with co-workers and friends, or share a work-related calendar with your personal GCal. For example, my "Lifehacker editor vacations" calendar is accessible to my personal GCal account.

Google Calendar can display any calendar available in the iCal file format, like your favorite baseball team's schedule, most likely available on the Web. Web site iCal Share (`http://icalshare.com/`) is a growing, user-submitted repository of television, sports, and entertainment iCal calendars, accessible from your Google Calendar.

Book Conference Room B

GCal can even help you schedule the use of inanimate objects, such as the office projector or meeting space. Using GCal's auto-accept invitations feature, any invitation to the Conference Room B calendar that doesn't conflict with another meeting will automatically be entered. From Google's Help section, here's how to set up a calendar to manage conference room bookings:[1]

1. Create a secondary calendar named Conference Room B.

2. In the calendar list on the left, click the down-arrow button next to Conference Room B, select Calendar Settings, and then select the Calendar Details tab.

3. Enable the auto-accept invitations feature by selecting Auto-Accept Invitations That Do Not Conflict.

4. Click Save.

5. Click the down-arrow next to the calendar you created and select Share This Calendar.

6. Enter the email addresses of the users to whom you want to grant access to your resource.

7. Select the desired shared permission level (must be See All Event Details or higher).

Receive Your Daily Agenda via Email Automatically

If you live out of your inbox and not from a calendar, you'll love GCal's daily agenda to email feature. Get a simple list of the day's events emailed to you at 5 a.m. daily automatically. (Find the magic check box to turn that on in the GCal Settings Notifications tab.)

See This Week's Weather Forecast on Your Calendar

Wondering how to dress for the cookout this weekend? See how the weather might affect this week's upcoming events by turning on the forecast right inside GCal. To do so, in General Settings, enter your loca-tion and select whether you want to see the temperature in Celsius or Fahrenheit. Figure 6-23 shows the result: a small weather-forecast icon on each day right inside your calendar.

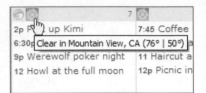

Figure 6-23 With the Google Calendar embedded weather forecast enabled, a small icon appears on each day of the upcoming week in your calendar. Hover your mouse pointer over the icon to get the forecasted high and low temperature.

Invite Your Friends to Events via GCal

Anyone else hate Evite? Yeah, me too. Google Calendar doesn't have that festive Evite feel, but it doesn't have the overbearing ads or busy design, either. GCal can send and manage event invitations, and the recipients can leave comments on an event as well.

Get Your Schedule Details via Text Message

Thumb-happy text-messaging fans will put GCal's SMS access to good use. Text the word *next* to short code GVENT (48368) from your cell phone to get the next event on your schedule. *Day* will get your day's agenda, and *nday* will send back tomorrow's events. You can SMS new event details (such as "Pumpkin picking Oct 25 at 3PM") to GVENT, too, to add them to your calendar.

Master GCal's Keyboard Shortcuts

The fastest way to become a black belt with most apps is to navigate them right from your keyboard. As does Gmail, GCal comes with a hefty set of keyboard shortcuts, detailed in Google's Help documents.[2] Here's a quick summary:

SHORTCUT KEY	DEFINITION
C	Create event
/	Search
P	Previous date range

SHORTCUT KEY	DEFINITION
N	Next date range
T	Jump to "Today"
D	"Day" view
X	Customized view
W	"Week" view
M	"Month" view
A	"Agenda" view
Q	Quick Add
Esc	Back to calendar

Hack 57: Scan Text to PDF with Your Camera Phone

Level. . . . . . . **Easy**
Platform. . . . **Web (digital camera or camera phone)**
Cost. . . . . **Free**

You're looking at a whiteboard full of notes or a paper document you want to copy quickly. Instead of manually transcribing the text, you can "scan" the information using a digital camera, including the one built in to your cell phone. Web application Qipit (http://qipit.com) turns digital photos that contain text into PDF files for you automatically. Here's how.

Register for a free account at http://qipit.com. To use your camera phone to scan text, enter your phone's model, number, and carrier, as shown in Figure 6-24. (Qipit needs your phone number so that when you send it images, it knows who you are.) If you don't want to enter your phone number or use your camera phone, select the I Will Use Qipit With My Digital Camera Only check box.

> **NOTE** Qipit will ask you to select which model handset you use. Qipit works with a wide variety of mobile carriers and handsets, but not all. If your phone isn't supported, you can still use Qipit with your regular digital camera.

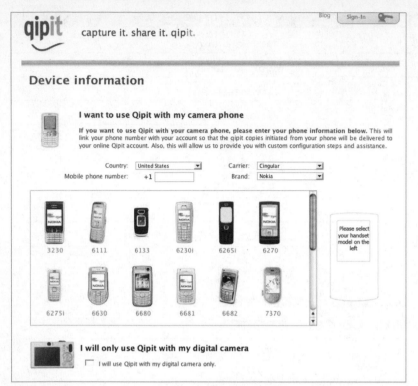

Figure 6-24 Enter your phone's number, service, and handset model for it to work with Qipit.

After you've set your phone's model, Qipit will tell you what types of documents it can scan. Different cameras produce different-quality images, so a camera phone that produces lower-megapixel images may be able to scan a whiteboard but not printed documents with small text on it. For example, Qipit tells me that my Nokia 6682 can scan whiteboards and hand-written notes but not printed documents, because the picture quality is too low, as shown in Figure 6-25.

Most consumer digital cameras (not camera phones) create images of high enough quality to scan printed documents, so even if your camera phone can't do that, your regular digital camera can.

Take Photos that Produce the Best Scan Results

When you take a photo to send to Qipit, put your camera phone on its highest quality setting. Make sure you've got ample light and get in close enough on the text so that is the only thing in the photo; avoid getting background edges in your photo. A nonphone camera doesn't have to be set to the highest quality setting — a 2- or 3-megapixel photo will do just as well as a 5-megapixel photo and will take less time for Qipit to process.

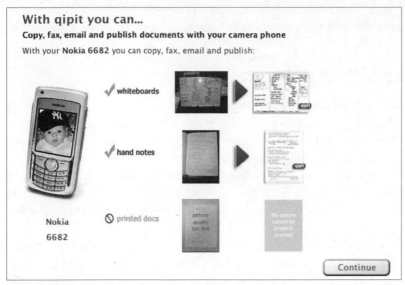

Figure 6-25 Qipit will tell you what kinds of documents your camera phone is capable of scanning.

Sending Images to Qipit

You have several ways to send Qipit your images for PDF conversion:

- **Email a photo directly from your camera phone.** The quickest and easiest way to send an image to Qipit is to snap a photo with your phone and send it via email to copy@qipit.com. Make the subject of your message the name of the document. (Your phone does have to have email capabilities to do this.)

- **Email your photo from your computer.** You can send any images that you've imported onto your computer to Qipit via your regular email program. Enter the copy@qipit.com address in the To: field and enter the document name in the subject line of your message. You can create multipage Qipit scans by attaching several images to one email. The pages will be scanned in the order in which they're attached to your message.

- **Upload your image via the Qipit web site.** Alternatively, you can log into the Qipit web site and click the Upload Picture button to add the image to your account.

After Qipit receives your image, it "scans" it to a PDF file, lightens any shadows, and makes the text clear and legible.

> **NOTE** Qipit does not perform OCR (Optical Character Recognition) on text documents. The PDF Qipit produces is legible, but it is an image, not text.

Working with Qipit Scans

After you've added document images to Qipit, click the My Documents link in Qipit to list them. From there, you can rotate the image (if, say, you shot a picture landscape and want to turn the text into portrait format). You can also email or fax the image file, merge several scans into one document, post it to your web site or blog, or publish a document at a certain web address. For example, you can view a Qipit scan of the introduction to this book at `http://www.qipit.com/public/lifehackerbook/book_intro_high_res`.

After you begin accumulating Qipit scans, you'll want to start organizing them. In the My Documents area of Qipit, you can add tags (such as `biologynotes` or `projectbrainstorming`) to an image. Click any tag on the right side to filter your list of scans by tag.

> **NOTE** As of this writing, you can store up to 100 pages of document scans to Qipit for free, at which point you either have to export pages and delete them from your Qipit account to make room for new ones or create another free account. Qipit representatives say they plan to offer more storage options in the future.

Hack 58: Poll Groups of People with Doodle

Level. . . . . . . **Easy**
Platform. . . . **Web**
Cost. . . . . **Free**

Anyone who's had to schedule a meeting or get-together for a large group of people knows how difficult finding a date that works for everyone can be. Whether it's a family reunion or a board meeting, when more than five people are involved, everyone's schedule gets in the way. Instead of sending around a group email with possible dates, which everyone responds to multiple times with what dates work for them, set up a group poll in one place with Doodle (`http://doodle.ch`). Here's how.

On the Doodle home page, click the Create Poll link under Schedule An Event. On the next screen, enter the details of your event: a title, a description, your name, and your email address, as shown in Figure 6-26.

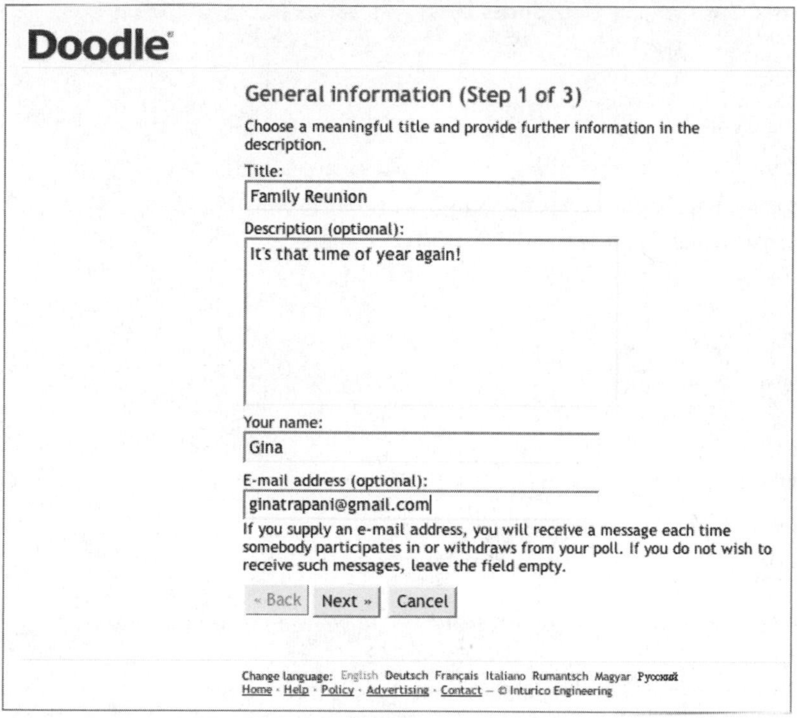

Doodle

General information (Step 1 of 3)

Choose a meaningful title and provide further information in the description.

Title:

Family Reunion

Description (optional):

It's that time of year again!

Your name:

Gina

E-mail address (optional):

ginatrapani@gmail.com

If you supply an e-mail address, you will receive a message each time somebody participates in or withdraws from your poll. If you do not wish to receive such messages, leave the field empty.

‹ Back | Next » | Cancel

Change language: English Deutsch Français Italiano Rumantsch Magyar Русский
Home · Help · Policy · Advertising · Contact – © Inturico Engineering

Figure 6-26 Create a new event poll at Doodle (`http://doodle.ch`).

Click Next and select the possible dates for your event. You can enter as many dates as you'd like. On the third and final screen, optionally enter times for each of the dates you chose. You can leave times blank for all-day events (such as family reunions).

After you've created your event, Doodle will email you a link to the event poll. Forward the link to all the event attendees, who will click it and mark off which days they can attend, as shown in Figure 6-27. Doodle will tally which dates work for the highest number of attendees, as shown in Figure 6-28.

Doodle can also poll groups about things other than possible event dates; ask your group members what restaurant they'd like to go to or which movie to see by using the Create Poll link on the Doodle home page under the Make A Choice heading.

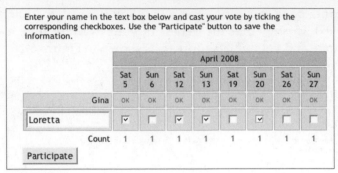

Enter your name in the text box below and cast your vote by ticking the corresponding checkboxes. Use the "Participate" button to save the information.

	April 2008							
	Sat 5	Sun 6	Sat 12	Sun 13	Sat 19	Sun 20	Sat 26	Sun 27
Gina	OK	OK	OK	OK	OK	OK	OK	OK
Loretta	☑	☐	☑	☑	☐	☑	☐	☐
Count	1	1	1	1	1	1	1	1

Participate

Figure 6-27 Each attendee enters her name and selects which dates (and times) she can make it.

Poll "Family Reunion"

Initiated by Gina.
It's that time of year again!

Summary:
Number of participants: 7
Most popular date: Saturday, April 12, 2008
Votes in favor: 7

Enter your name in the text box below and cast your vote by ticking the corresponding checkboxes. Use the "Participate" button to save the information.

	April 2008							
	Sat 5	Sun 6	Sat 12	Sun 13	Sat 19	Sun 20	Sat 26	Sun 27
Gina	OK	OK	OK	OK	OK	OK	OK	OK
Loretta	OK		OK	OK		OK		
Joey	OK		OK					OK
Andrew	OK	OK	OK	OK	OK			OK
Mom	OK		OK	OK	OK			
Margaret Mary	OK	OK	OK	OK				
Uncle Ken		OK	OK	OK		OK	OK	
Your name	☐	☐	☐	☐	☐	☐	☐	☐
Count	6	4	7	6	3	3	2	3

Figure 6-28 Doodle calculates which date is the most popular in the group.

A simple Doodle poll can reduce email back-and-forth between multiple attendees and provide an easy, visual map of who can make it when to your event.

References

1. Google Help Center, "Share & Manage Calendars," available at
   `http://www.google.com/support/calendar/bin/answer.py?answ`
   `er=44105&topic=8605`.

2. Google Help Center, "Calendar Basics," available at `http://`
   `www.google.com/support/calendar/bin/answer.py?answer=`
   `37034&topic=8556`.

Automate Repetitive Tasks

Thirty years ago, we thought that by 2008 we'd all have personal robots doing our laundry, cooking meals, and cleaning our houses — like the Jetsons' robot maid, Rosie. Although that scenario hasn't become reality yet, your personal computer *can* perform certain menial tasks, automatically and unsupervised, on a schedule you set. Your PC isn't as advanced or charming as Rosie, but it can clean up after itself and take the work out of repetitive computing jobs.

Let's face it: computers are built to relieve us of dull work, not create more work. Refrigerators switch on and off to maintain a certain temperature. Your paycheck gets deposited directly into your account without your having to visit the bank. Streetlights snap on at dusk so that humans don't have to canvass the neighborhood flipping switches. And you can automate personal computing tasks to run in the background automatically.

If you examine your work processes over time, you'll notice that certain activities come up repeatedly, whether it's filing certain email messages into the same folders, starting up those same three programs first thing in the morning, deleting old files you don't need, or downloading new songs from your favorite bands' web sites. The first step is to identify those repetitive actions. The next step is to program your computer to perform them so that you don't have to do them by hand again.

**RESISTANCE TO AUTOMATION AND THE
ATTRACTION OF BUSYWORK**

The type of work ripe for automation is busywork: well-defined tasks that happen the same way every time and require virtually no thinking at all. Although it may be boring, ironically, busywork's appeal is its simplicity. You can get it done with little mental effort, by just going through the motions, and get that rewarding feeling of accomplishment. With busywork, there's little chance of failure and there's a high degree of familiarity. But keeping busy with tasks that you could delegate to your computer (or another person) also keeps you away from the larger projects, decisions, and mental work only *you* can do. Next time you find yourself doing that same tedious job again by hand, ask yourself whether it's the best use of your time.

Chances are, you already have a few scheduled processes running on your computer. Certain types of software, such as virus and spyware scanners, come with prescheduled runtimes built in. But few users configure their own automatic processes and schedule them, and that's a shame. Granted, the initial time investment of automating a job can seem high, but in the long run, the payback more than makes up for it.

Almost every hack in this book involves automating life and work tasks in one way or another. This chapter covers automatic actions that take the work out of using a computer itself, such as backing up your files, opening programs, or searching the Web for the same terms more than once. All these are tasks your computer can do all by itself while you're asleep or at lunch or in a meeting. Save yourself from the doldrums of tedious computer work with the following hacks that automate important — but boring — tasks so that you can concentrate on more appealing work.

Hack 59: Automatically Back Up Your Files to an External Hard Drive (PC)

Level. . . . . . . **Medium**
Platform. . . . **Windows XP and Vista**
Cost. . . . . . . **$75 and up (for external hard drive)**

More and more, the fragments of your life exist as particles on a magnetic disk mounted inside your computer. The photos from your one-year-old niece's birthday, the interview you did with great-grandpa Gus, your working manuscript of the Great American Novel, the first email messages you exchanged with your spouse — not to mention crucial professional data — all reside on that spinning magnetic platter susceptible to temperature changes, power surges, fire, theft, static, and just plain wear and tear.

Hard drives fail. It's a fact of computing life. It's not a matter of *whether* your computer's disk will stop working; it's a matter of *when*. The question is how much it will disrupt your life — and it won't, if you have a backup copy.

Backing up your data is the dullest but most indispensable thing you do on your computer. But who remembers to do it? You don't have to.

In this hack, you'll automate nightly, weekly, and monthly backups for your PC using free software. This system will even email you if something goes wrong, so it's the ultimate "set it and forget it" situation. After you get this up and running, you'll never have to worry about losing data again.

What You'll Need

- **A Windows XP or Vista PC.**
- **SyncBack Freeware version 3.2.** Available as a free download from `http://2brightsparks.com/downloads.html`.
- **An external hard drive.** Purchase an external hard drive that connects via USB or FireWire, depending on your computer model. (Consult your PC's user guide for the ports available on your machine.) When deciding capacity, go for 10 times the amount of data you want to back up. For example, if the size of your My Documents folder is 10GB, then look to purchase a 100GB hard drive. (If a drive the size you need isn't available, calculate the size of your home directory without space-hogging subdirectories, such as My Music, My Videos, and My Pictures. You have the option to reduce the number of copies you keep of those large files to save space.)

Configure the Backup System

You can create multiple schedules and notifications and even back up over the Internet to remote servers with the SyncBack backup software. Although both Windows XP and Vista come with a built-in backup utility, neither offers the options and flexibility of SyncBack.

NOTE Vista's backup utility has one advantage over SyncBack — it displays a file's past versions inside its Properties dialog box, which is a nice perk.

To get your automated, worry-free backups up and running, follow these steps:

1. Get the SyncBack software — SyncBack Freeware v3.2 — available for download at `http://2brightsparks.com/downloads.html`. Install the application.

NOTE SyncBackSE version 4.0 is also available to buy for $25. This hack uses the free SyncBack version 3, which does not offer the advanced features of version 4, such as backing up open files, unlimited Zip file size, and encryption.

2. Connect your external hard drive to your computer. Turn it on. Name it `Backup` and browse to it in Explorer. (On my computer, for example, it's the `G:\` drive.)

3. Create four folders: `nightly`, `weekly`, `monthly-even`, and `monthly-odd`, as shown in Figure 7-1. You'll store your backups in these folders.

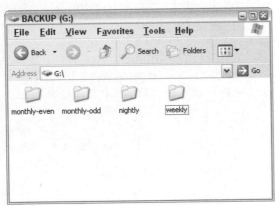

Figure 7-1 Backup folders on the external drive.

4. Fire up SyncBack. Create a new profile called `Local Nightly backup`. Set the Source to your `My Documents` folder (or wherever you store your important data), and the destination to your backup drive's `nightly` folder, as shown in Figure 7-2.

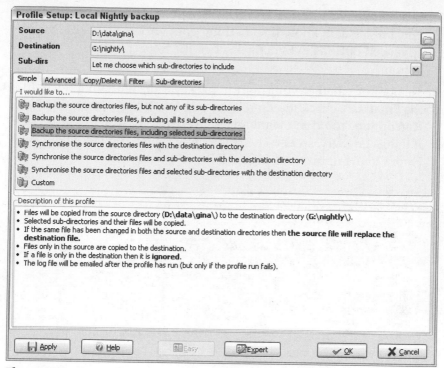

Figure 7-2 Local Nightly backup **profile window in SyncBack.**

5. Select the directory to back up. Choose to back up your entire Source directory or select specific subdirectories to get backed up. This option comes in handy, if, say, you have a few space-hogging directories (such as My Videos and My Music) and you don't have the space to keep four copies (one in each of the nightly, weekly, and two monthly folders) of those big files on your backup drive.

   To select which directories to back up, select Let Me Choose Which Sub-Directories To Include from the Sub-dirs drop-down list (just below the Destination field) and, on the Simple tab, choose Backup The Source Directories Files Including Selected Sub-Directories.

6. Click the Sub-Directories tab. If you have hundreds of subdirectories, it'll take SyncBack some time to traverse the tree and display them. Go grab a cup of coffee and come back to check off the directories you want backed up each night. That's when you tell SyncBack to ignore the My Music, My Pictures, and My Videos folders each night when it runs.

7. Really effective automation runs without intervention or interruption, but lets you know if something goes wrong. To enable the advanced options in SyncBack, click the Expert button at the bottom.

8. To monitor whether your nightly backup runs without a hitch, in the Email tab, check the Email The Log File When The Profile Has Run option. You don't want an email every day; you just want one if things go awry, so also check the Only Email The Log File If An Error Occurs option. See Figure 7-3.

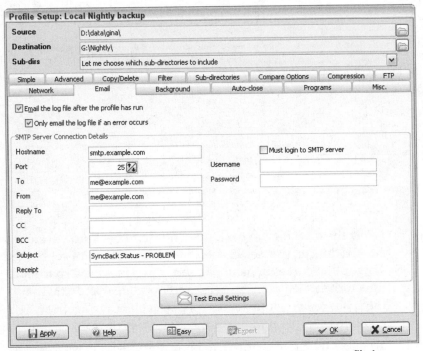

Figure 7-3 Email settings for the `Local Nightly backup` profile in SyncBack.

9. Set your SMTP server options as well and then click the Test Email Settings button (at the bottom of the Email tab) to make sure you can receive messages.

NOTE Your SMTP options specify what server you use to send mail. Check with your email service provider for your hostname and port information. The To and From fields should contain your email address.

10. Click the Misc tab and then click the Schedule button. Here you tell Windows to run this nightly backup every evening (or early morning) at, say, 2:00 a.m. Be sure to set the Windows password you use to log in to your computer for this scheduled task by clicking the Set Password button.

11. Wash, rinse, and repeat to create a profile called `Local Weekly Backup`. Set the Destination to your backup drive's `weekly` folder and set the profile to run once a week (say, at 3:00 a.m. Saturday morning). The subdirectory and email settings should remain the same for this profile.

12. Configure your bi-monthly local backup. You could set up a single monthly backup profile that runs once a month, but using that scheme, you run the risk of losing data. Here's how. Say you do a massive file deletion or update on the last day of the week and month. Those changes would replicate to all three backup copies (nightly, weekly, and monthly), and you'd have no backup of anything before your deletion or update.

To avoid this situation, set up two local bi-monthly backup profiles, one of which runs on even months, the other on odd months: `Local Bi-Monthly (even) Backup` and `Local Bi-Monthly (odd) Backup`, respectively. When you set up the schedule for the `Local Bi-Monthly (even)` profile, from the Schedule tab, select Monthly from the Schedule Task drop-down list and then click the Select Months button. Check off the even months of the year, as shown in Figure 7-4.

13. Set up the `Bi-Monthly (odd)` profile the same way, with odd months checked off.

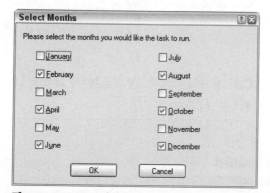

Figure 7-4 Run the `Local Bi-Monthly (even)` `Backup` on even months.

You can test your new backup profiles by doing a simulated run to see what files would be copied where without actually copying them. To do so, select a profile to test in SyncBack and choose Task ➪ Simulated Run. Depending on how much data you have, a test run can take a long time.

After all four profiles have run (in at most two months from setup), you'll have four copies of your most important data on your external drive: one gets updated every night, the other every week, and the last two every other month. If something goes wrong and the backups fail, you receive an email notification.

This means that if your hard drive fails, the most data you'll lose is a day's worth. And if you overwrote an important file — even if you did so a month ago — you can recover a backed-up copy.

Backup geeks and the curious should be sure to explore all of SyncBack's tabs and options. For example, in the Autoclose tab, you can set SyncBack to shut down any programs with a word you specify in the title bar before it runs a backup job. The Programs tab sets custom commands to run before and after backup happens, so you can schedule a database dump or file download right before your backup starts, for example.

LOCAL BACKUP VERSUS ONLINE BACKUP — WHY YOU SHOULD HAVE BOTH

You're now backing up your computer — congratulations! You're doing more than what 95 percent of all computer users do to protect their information. But your backup plan shouldn't stop here. Local external drive backups are great for quick recovery when you've accidentally deleted a file, or if your computer's internal hard drive crashes. But what if your house burns down or gets burglarized — including your backup drive? You also want your most important data located somewhere offsite. See Hack 61, "Automatically Back Up Your Files Online," for a set-it-and-forget-it way to back up your files over the Internet on secure, remote servers for extra data security.

Hack 60: Automatically Back Up Your Files to an External Hard Drive (Mac)

Level . . . . **Easy**
Platform . . . . **Mac OS X 10.5 Leopard**
Cost . . . . **$75 and up (for external hard drive)**

Mac users who thumb through Hack 59, which details how to back up your PC's files on a daily, weekly, and monthly basis, have a right to a smug laugh. The most recent version of Mac OS X 10.5, Leopard, ships with a comprehensive backup application called Time Machine that requires only two steps to set up. Here's how to turn on Time Machine and use it to restore deleted files on your computer.

Enable Time Machine Backups

All you'll need to start backing up your Mac with Time Machine is an external FireWire or USB hard drive. The larger the drive capacity, the more backups Time Machine can store on it, so purchase the largest drive that you can afford for best results. I recommend anything from a 300GB to 500GB drive, which retail for less than $200.

When you plug in your external hard drive to your Mac for the first time, Leopard asks whether you want to use that drive for Time Machine backups. Simply click Use As Backup Disk (see Figure 7-5) to turn on Time Machine.

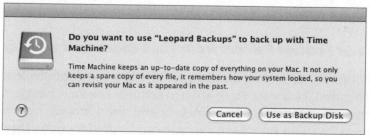

Figure 7-5 Time Machine asks whether it can use your external disk for backups when you plug it into your Mac.

Time Machine's first backup takes a long time because it copies all your Mac's files to the external drive. Every backup after that will happen on its own, without your intervention, and will copy only files that have changed, so it will complete much more quickly. The only way you'll know Time Machine is working is by the sound of your hard drive spinning.

What Time Machine Does

In short, Time Machine performs automatic, incremental backups of your Mac over time. *Incremental* means that it copies only files that have changed since the previous backup, instead of making a whole, full new copy. (Therefore, incremental backups save disk space.) As long as your external drive is connected and Time Machine is enabled, it will save hourly backups of your Mac's files automatically and keep a backup of the last 24 hours, as well as daily backups for the past month and weekly backups older than a month. The only files that might not get backed up with Time Machine are files you create and delete inside the space of an hour.

If you put your Mac to sleep or shut down in the midst of a Time Machine backup, when you wake or restart it, it will automatically resume where it was when it left off . If your external drive isn't connected to your Mac, Time Machine backups won't happen again until the drive is present, and then it will copy all the files that changed since the last backup.

When your external hard drive is full, Time Machine will alert you and delete the oldest backup that it has stored (presumably, if you have a spacious drive, a weekly backup older than a month ago.) Time Machine's backups aren't stored in any special format, either; you can browse to your external drive in Finder, where you'll see a folder named `Backups.backupdb`. That folder contains dated subfolders of Time Machine's backups, with all the files available to copy, view, or otherwise manipulate like any other file on your Mac.

Switch Disks or Exclude Folders from Time Machine's Backup

The beauty of Time Machine is that it has so very few user options that need to be configured. However, there are two settings you can change in System Preferences' Time Machine panel. Using the Options button (shown in Figure 7-6), you can opt to exclude certain folders from Time Machine's backup process (such as space-hogging video files that you back up or store elsewhere, or photos you automatically upload online anyway). You can also change the disk Time Machine uses to store backups by clicking the Change Disk button (also shown in Figure 7-6).

Restore Deleted or Overwritten Files

When Time Machine is on and backing up your Mac, you'll likely not give it another thought — until you've accidentally deleted or overwritten an important file. To restore a past or deleted file, start Time Machine, which will display the backups it has stored of your Mac in a dramatic line of Finder windows that extend back in space. Use the timeline on the right side of the screen to fly back and forth between Time Machine backups of a folder. When you've found the files you need in a past backup, select them and click the Restore button on the lower-right side of the screen, as shown in Figure 7-7.

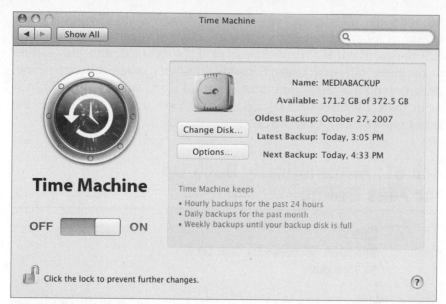

Figure 7-6 Exclude directories from Time Machine's backups using the Options dialog box, or change the disk Time Machine uses in the Time Machine area of System Preferences.

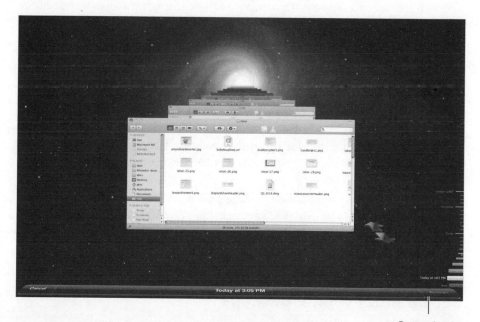

Restore button

Figure 7-7 Fly back in time and find the past version of a file; then click the Restore button to copy it back to your Mac.

As with the backup system for PCs described in Hack 59, Time Machine saves snapshots of your Mac only to a local external drive, which means that if that drive breaks or if it's lost or stolen, you lose all your backups. Although using Time Machine only is better than nothing, to ensure that your important data is backed up in case of a natural disaster or theft, consider backing up to an online storage service over the Internet. See Hack 61 for more on setting that up.

Hack 61: Automatically Back Up Your Files Online

Level. . . . . . . **Easy**
Platform. . . . **Windows (all versions), Mac OS X**
Cost. **$4.95/month**

Hurricane Katrina victims can tell you that no matter how diligently you back up your computer to a local hard drive — as detailed in Hacks 59 and 60 — you will still lose your photos, documents, and other important files if you don't keep a copy offsite, preferably out of state. Some users keep an extra hard drive with a copy of their important files at the office or at their mother's house in case of theft or fire. But that requires manually transporting your hard drive back and forth on a regular basis, and you want to set it and forget it.

Instead, automatically back up your files to an online backup service such as Mozy (http://mozy.com) over the Internet. Unlimited backup at Mozy costs $4.95 per month per computer, and works with Macs and PCs. As of this writing, Mozy offers 2GB of free storage for personal use, so you can try the service without paying for unlimited backup. Read on to see how to set up the ultimate insurance for your data: automatic, offsite backup.

> **TIP** If you already have a web hosting plan with FTP access to a server with lots of space, you can use SyncBack, the Windows software detailed in Hack 59, to back up your files online instead of getting another online account at Mozy. In SyncBack's interface, go to the FTP tab to set it up.

Set Up Mozy Online Backups

Register for your free MozyHome account online at http://mozy.com and download the free Mozy software appropriate for your system. (As of this writing, Mozy offers a home-use client for Windows Vista, XP, and

2000, and beta software for Mac OS X. This hack uses screenshots from the Windows version.)

When you install the Mozy software, you log in with the account information you set up online. The Mozy software tests your broadband Internet connection to make sure it's fast enough to transfer your files. Then the software scans your system, suggests which directories it should back up, and lets you know how much of your Mozy quota those files will use. If you don't want to go with Mozy's suggestions, you can manually choose which files and folders it backs up. To do so, click the Mozy icon in your PC's status bar. From the dialog box, click the Configure button and go to the File System tab (see Figure 7-8).

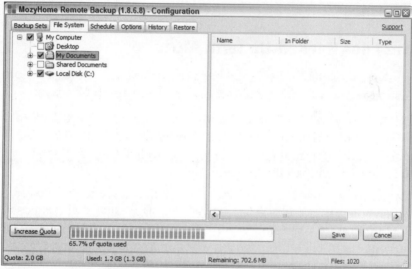

Figure 7-8 Choose which folders Mozy should back up.

Mozy's configuration dialog box also contains settings for your automatic backup schedule (by default once a day, when your computer's not busy) and other options, such as how it should notify you and how much bandwidth and computer power it should use to get its job done. After you've configured Mozy the way you want, click the Save button. To run a Mozy backup manually, click Mozy's system tray icon to open its Status dialog box and then click the Start Backup button.

What Mozy Does

Mozy's backup process encrypts the files on your computer using either an encryption key it chooses or your own private key. (You get the option to input your own key when you set up the software.) Then it transfers your files over an encrypted connection to its servers.

If you delete a file on your computer, Mozy marks it as deleted and holds onto a copy on its side for 30 days. After that time, Mozy deletes it. That way, you can recover a deleted file for up to a month.

Mozy does differential — or incremental — backups; that is, it backs up only portions of your files that have changed since the last time they were backed up. This means that the first backup you do with Mozy may take a long time, but backups after that will be much faster, assuming that you're not changing every file in your backup set. Your best bet is to run Mozy's first backup overnight, or at a time you plan to have your computer on for an extended amount of time, depending on how many files you're backing up.

Restore Files Backed Up with Mozy

After you've completed at least one backup with Mozy, you can restore files copied to its servers in one of three ways. Here are those ways:

- On the Mozy web site, from the My Account page, select Restore Files. If you're on a computer that does not have the Mozy software installed, from the Web Restore area, click Choose Files To Restore to download the files you need.

- On your Windows PC with Mozy installed, browse to the file for which you want to recover a past version, right-click it, and choose Restore Previous Version. You'll see a list of the files on Mozy's servers. Right-click the one you want and choose Restore. Or choose Restore To save the restored file somewhere other than its original location.

- Click the Mozy software icon in your system tray and click the Restore button to pick and choose the files you want to copy back to your system from Mozy's servers (see Figure 7-9).

MOZY ALTERNATIVES

Since the dawn of computing, businesses have been concerned about data backup. But now, as consumers generate more data, there's a new market for individual online backup, and you have several good choices of service. If Mozy isn't for you, consider **Carbonite** (http://carbonite .com), **Xdrive** (http://xdrive.com), **or Apple's .Mac service** (http://www .apple.com/dotmac/, **Mac only).**

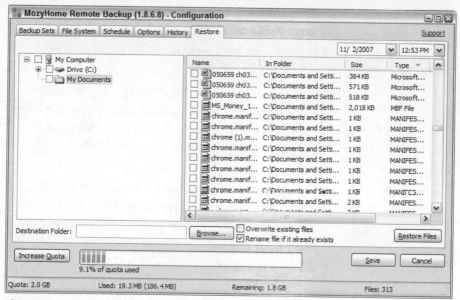

Figure 7-9 Choose which backed-up files on Mozy's servers to restore.

Hack 62: Automatically Empty Your Digital Junk Drawer (PC)

Level. . . . . . . **Advanced**
Platform. . . . **Windows XP and Vista**
Cost. . . . . **Free**

During the course of a workday, you save all sorts of disposable files on your computer: video, images, and songs meant for a single viewing or hearing; PDF files you have to print; software installers and Zip files you extract and do whatever you need with the contents. The end result is a lot of digital detritus clogging your hard drive for no good reason. But you don't want to clean up after yourself every time you work with a set of files you don't need to keep.

In this hack, you schedule a virtual janitor script that sweeps through your hard drive every night and deletes any files in your digital junk drawer that have been sitting around for more than x days, like old garbage starting to stink. This program constantly recovers space on your hard drive so that you don't have to worry about getting the dreaded Low Disk Space message while you're in the middle of something important.

WARNING This script and the instructions for use require comfort with executable script editing and automated file deletion, which are not to be taken lightly. Pointed at the wrong directory, this script could damage your PC.

To put your janitor to work, you must first create your virtual junk drawer folder. Then you'll configure the janitor to clean out the files older than a number of days you determine from that folder. Finally, you'll schedule the janitor to clean up at a regular, convenient time.

Here's what to do:

1. Create a directory in your main documents directory that will serve as a holding pen for temporary, disposable files. Mine is in `D:\data\gina\junkdrawer`, so that's how I refer to it for the rest of this hack.

2. Download the `janitor.vbs` script, available at `http://lifehackerbook.com/ch7/janitor.vbs`. Save it in your documents. (Mine is located in `D:\data\gina\scripts\janitor.vbs`.)

3. Set your web browser and email client to save downloaded files and message attachments to your junk drawer.

   Firefox users, choose Tools ⇨ Options. In the Main tab, set the directory to which Firefox should download automatically in the Downloads section, as shown in Figure 7-10.

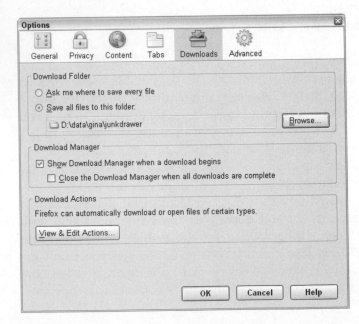

Figure 7-10 The Firefox Downloads dialog box set to save to the `junkdrawer` directory.

4. Using a plain-text editor such as Notepad, open the `janitor.vbs` file and edit the following sections to set the path to your `junkdrawer` directory, and to set how many days old files should be when they get deleted.

```
''''''''''''''''''''''''''''''''''''''''''''''''''''''''''''''''''''''''''''
'
'ENTER THE PATH THAT CONTAINS THE FILES YOU WANT TO CLEAN UP
''''''''''''''''''''''''''''''''''''''''''''''''''''''''''''''''''''''''''''
'
'Path to the root directory that you're cleaning up
PathToClean = "D:\data\gina\junkdrawer"
'^^^^^^^^^^^^^^^^^^^^^^^^^^^^^^^^^^^^^^^^^^^^^^^^^^^^^^^^^^^^^^^^^^^^^^^^^^^^^^
'^


''''''''''''''''''''''''''''''''''''''''''''''''''''''''''''''''''''''''''''
'
'ENTER THE NUMBER OF DAYS SINCE THE FILE WAS LAST MODIFIED
'
'ANY FILE WITH A DATE LAST MODIFIED THAT IS GREATER OR EQUAL TO
'THIS NUMBER WILL BE DELETED.
''''''''''''''''''''''''''''''''''''''''''''''''''''''''''''''''''''''''''''
'
'Specify how many days old a file must be in order to be deleted.
numberOfDays = 7
'^^^^^^^^^^^^^^^^^^^^^^^^^^^^^^^^^^^^^^^^^^^^^^^^^^^^^^^^^^^^^^^^^^^^^^^^^^^^^^
'^

    .
    .
    .
```

In the line that begins with `PathToClean`, replace `D:\data\gina\junkdrawer` with the path to your junk drawer folder. Also, change the line `numberOfDays` to your preferred time frame. I'm happy deleting stuff that's seven days old, but you might want to start with a month (30) or two weeks (14).

WARNING This script deletes files from your hard drive, from any directory that you specify. If you enter `C:\Windows\system32`, for example, you could do irreparable damage to your computer. So make absolutely sure that the `PathToClean` is set to a directory with files Windows does not need to function and files you don't care about losing.

Also, this script deletes files x days older than the files' Last Modified date. It is possible that a file's Last Modified date is already older than the number of days you specify, even if you've just downloaded the file. Keep this in mind when you're saving files to your junk drawer. Save only stuff in your junk drawer that's okay to lose.

When you have set up your junk drawer and configured the script, double-click janitor.vbs to run it. It will check your junk drawer and all its subdirectories for old files and delete any it finds. Empty subdirectories will be deleted as well. If all goes well, you see a pop-up box that reads, "The directory has been cleaned up!" as shown in Figure 7-11.

Figure 7-11 Janitor completion pop-up.

NOTE If you get a message along the lines of "no script engine for file extension .vbs," download the Windows XP Scripting Host from http:// microsoft.com/downloads/details.aspx?FamilyID=C717D943-7E4B-4622-86EB-95A22B832CAA&displayLang=en. This installation requires a restart of your computer.

When your script is pointed to the right place and you've run it and are happy with the results, you want to schedule your virtual janitor to sweep through every day.

Go to the Control Panel and choose Scheduled Tasks ⇨ File ⇨ New. Name your new task Clean Out Junk Drawer. Double-click the task and set the Run line to where your script lives, as shown in Figure 7-12.

Click the Set Password button and enter your Windows password. Doing so authorizes Windows to run the script on its own.

On the Schedule tab, set the job to run each day at a convenient time. On a computer that stays on all night, you can run the script in the wee hours of the morning. To test the new job, right-click Clean Out Junk Drawer in Scheduled Tasks and choose Run. You should get the "The directory has been cleaned up!" message again.

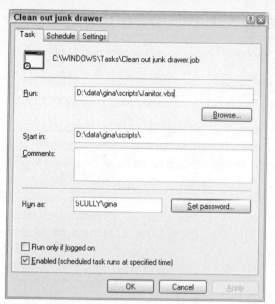

Figure 7-12 Make the janitor script a scheduled task.

ABOUT VISUAL BASIC

Many viruses and spyware use Visual Basic, the language this script is written in, to do bad things such as spam your friends and steal your credit card number. This doesn't mean Visual Basic is inherently bad; it means it's oft been used for evil. As a result, many spyware scanners and virus protection-programs will sound off all sorts of alarms and even disable Visual Basic scripts entirely in the name of protecting you. This script is benign. It does nothing harmful except delete files from a directory you specify. Allow it to execute no matter what your virus protection and spyware cleaner says; it's kosher.

Now your virtual janitor is set to clean up after you. Remember, the key to this system is to move files out of your junk drawer if you'll need them over the long term. Otherwise, they will be irrecoverably lost.

NOTE Danny O'Brien developed the concept of the janitor script, and programming help was generously provided by Brian Plexico. Variations on this script with extra features are available at http://lifehackerbook.com/ch7/.

Hack 63: Automatically Clean Up Your Mac

Level. . . . . . . **Medium**
Platform. . . . **Mac OS X**
Cost. **$21.95**

Just as in the physical world, it's easy to let digital clutter accumulate on your Mac. Chances are, your Downloads folder contains no-longer-relevant files, or your Desktop is covered in documents, images, and songs you finished with last week. Hack 62, "Automatically Empty Your Digital Junk Drawer (PC)," offered a Windows script that cleans files of a certain age from a given folder. Mac users have an even simpler, graphical alternative: the automated, rules-based file manager Hazel. Download a 14-day free trial of Hazel 2, available at http://www.noodlesoft.com/hazel.php. (A license costs $21.95.) Here's how Hazel can keep your Mac's hard drive free of files you don't need anymore.

Empty Your Downloads Folder with Hazel

After you've installed Hazel, go to its pane in System Preferences (it will be listed under the Other heading). To add a new folder rule, click the + button under the Folder list (bottom-left pane) and choose a folder, such as Downloads, to add it to the list. Select it and then, to create a new rules-based action, click the + button under the Rules box (bottom-right pane). Here you can set up automatic actions based on file criteria, as shown in Figure 7-13.

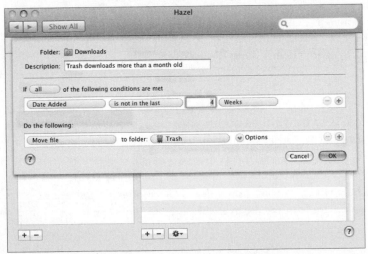

Figure 7-13 Set up a Hazel rule to delete files in the Downloads folder that haven't been opened in more than a month.

Think of Hazel's rules as email filters: they work according to simple if-then logic. The rule pictured in Figure 7-13 says that if a file in the Downloads folder was added (that is, downloaded and saved there) more than four weeks ago, Hazel should delete it. When Hazel is running, it will automatically recover space in your Downloads folder occupied by files you saved there more than four weeks ago.

You can use similar rules on any folders you set up as temporary work-spaces to keep them clean and tidy.

Take Out the Trash with Hazel

Hazel can also automatically manage your Mac's Trash bin, so you don't have to empty it by hand, or worry that the files there are taking up too much space on your hard drive. In Hazel's System Preferences pane, go to the Trash tab. There you can set Hazel to automatically delete files that have been sitting in the Trash for more than a certain amount of time, or set it to keep the total size of the Trash under a certain file size, as shown in Figure 7-14.

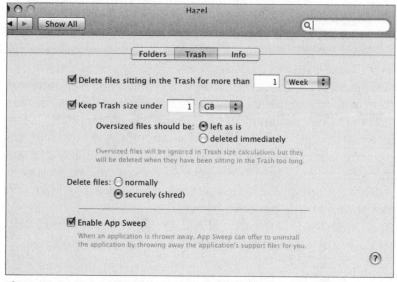

Figure 7-14 Set up Hazel to automatically keep your Trash bin under control.

Also in the Trash tab, you can enable Hazel's App Sweep feature, which monitors the applications installed on your Mac and the related settings and files it adds to your system. When you delete a program, Hazel will prompt you to delete any related files that application would otherwise leave behind.

More Automatic File Processing

Hazel can do much more than just delete old files. Experiment with its rich criteria options and possible actions to see what's useful for you. To see some examples, choose Load Sample Rules from the drop-down list beneath the Rules area. With Hazel, you can

- Automatically move media files such as MP3s, videos, or photos to your iTunes library or iPhoto library. (This works well in conjunction with Hack 66, "Automatically Download Music, Movies, and More.")
- Automatically sort images into subfolders named by date.
- Label or add a keyword to any file based on any rule ("added in the last hour," for example.)

Hack 64: Automatically Reboot and Launch Applications

Level. . . . . . . **Easy**
Platform. . . . **Windows XP and Vista**
Cost. . . . . **Free**

Windows PC users know that every once in a while, your computer can slow down or run into problems that are magically resolved when you restart. A PC that's on continuously 24 hours a day — especially when it's hard at work at night running the automated tasks outlined in this chapter — can benefit from a regular reboot to clear out memory and end any hanging software processes. Furthermore, chances are, you start your workday with a set number of software applications, such as Microsoft Outlook and your morning-paper web sites.

In this hack, you schedule an early morning reboot and launch the software you need to get to work before you even sit down at your desk.

Automatically Reboot Your Computer

It's the middle of the night. Your computer has backed itself up, defragged the hard drives, and fetched you new music from all over the Web. Now it's time to begin the new day with a fresh start.

Choose Start ➪ Control Panel ➪ Scheduled Tasks. In the Scheduled Tasks window, choose File ➪ New ➪ Scheduled Task. Name the new job

Reboot. Right-click the task and choose Properties. In the Run text box, enter the following, as shown in Figure 7-15.

```
C:\WINDOWS\system32\shutdown.exe -r -t 01
```

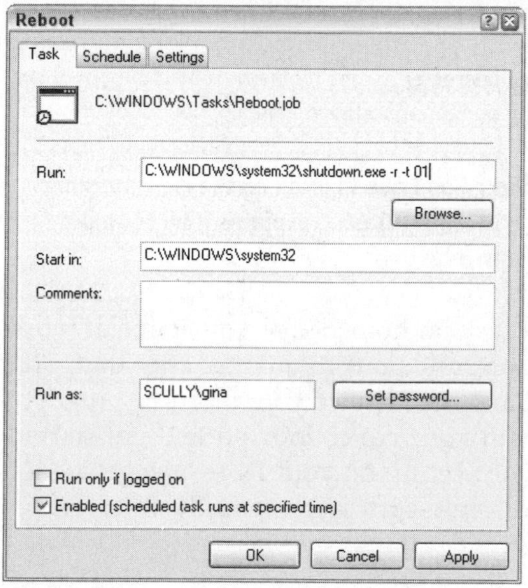

Figure 7-15 The Reboot scheduled task.

You don't want your PC to reboot if it's in the middle of something else, so on the Settings tab, select the Only Start This Task If The Computer Has Been Idle For At Least option, and enter a time frame, such as 10 minutes. If your Windows login has a password, you have to enter it to authorize Windows to run the task with your username's system rights.

Set the task schedule to Daily, one hour before you usually sit down at your computer. If the Reboot job doesn't run because the computer is busy at that time, it shouldn't try again after you start working, so on the Settings Tab, make sure the Retry Up To option is set to 60 minutes.

Automatically Launch Software or Documents

Schedule the applications you normally launch by hand to start on their own before you sit down at your computer in the morning as well. Enter the path to any software program in a newly scheduled task's Run text box. For example, provided that it has been installed in the default location, Microsoft Outlook 2003 launches with the following command:

```
"C:\Program Files\Microsoft Office\OFFICE11\OUTLOOK.EXE"
```

Additionally, you can launch specific documents rather than just programs. For instance, if you absolutely must start the day editing Chapter 7 of your book, create a task that is simply the path of the document:

```
"D:/data/gina/docs/lifehacker-book/chapter7.doc"
```

Doing so will open the `chapter7.doc` file in Microsoft Word automatically. Or schedule a WinAmp or iTunes playlist to launch and begin playing first thing in the morning for a custom alarm clock.

NOTE Set the most important thing you have to work on the next morning automatically. Hack 23, "Set Up a Morning Dash," explains how to make the first hour of the day the most productive.

If you schedule your Reboot task an hour before you arrive at work, have the auto software launch job run about 15 minutes after that. That way, your computer will restart and then launch your morning programs so that you can just walk in with your coffee in hand and get started. (However, if you have a password set up on your PC — always a good idea security-wise — programs can't start automatically after reboot until you've logged in by hand.)

Automatically Start a Web-Browsing Session

If you spend time browsing the Web at work, chances are, you have a set of pages that you visit to start the day, like your morning paper. Your computer can easily fetch your favorite web pages before you reach your desk so that your morning reads are waiting for you.

Set up a task to open the Firefox web browser the same way as you did with Outlook. Then add all the pages you'd like to load automatically, separated by a space, to the Run line. The resulting command could look something like this:

```
"C:\Program Files\Mozilla Firefox\firefox.exe" lifehacker.com
nytimes.com gmail.google.com
```

NOTE The free Firefox web browser is available for download at `http://mozilla.org/products/firefox`.

In this example, when you arrive at your computer, a Firefox window will be open with all your morning sites preloaded.

NOTE Special thanks to Lifehacker.com senior editor Adam Pash for his contributions to this hack.

Hack 65: Make Google Search Results Automatically Come to You

Level. . . . . . . **Beginner**
Platform. . . . **Web**
Cost. . . . . **Free**

Keeping up with any news published online about a certain topic used to mean searching the Web for it every so often, or checking various online news sites. But not any more. Google now offers free email alerts when certain search terms appear on web pages, as they are published.

For example, you want to know whenever the product your company makes gets mentioned online — in the news, on blogs, or on any web page out there. Instead of searching the Web for your product's name every week, let Google Alerts do that for you. To set up an alert, go to http://google.com/alerts and click the Sign In To Manage Your Alerts link. Log in with your Google account (free registration) and click the Create Alert link. Next, enter your search term, the type of alert you want to receive, and the email frequency, as shown in Figure 7-16.

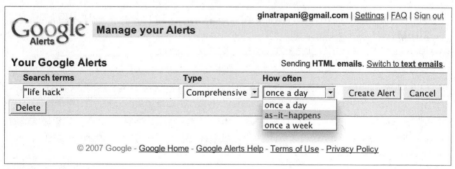

Figure 7-16 Enter your search term, type of alert, and email frequency in Google Alerts.

Your Google Alert will let you know when your term appears in news pages, blogs, general web search results, Google Groups, Google Video, or all of the above. After you've created your alert, click the term(s) you entered to preview the kind of content the email you receive will contain.

Watch out: if you enter very popular search terms, you will get inundated with frequent or very long messages, so make your searches as specific as possible. To avoid getting too much email, I recommend the Once A Day or Once A Week frequency setting, instead of As-It-Happens (which is better suited for very time-sensitive temporary news alerts).

TIP Narrow your alert results by using advanced search operators such as AND, OR, and enclosing phrases in quotation marks. See Hack 81, "Google Like a Pro," for more on pinpointing results you really want with the right search term.

By default, your Google Alerts will be sent to your Gmail account, but you can use Gmail's filters to forward them to any email address you'd like (such as your company email address). Just create a filter that forwards all messages from googlealerts-noreply@google.com to your desired destination address.

Hack 66: Automatically Download Music, Movies, and More

Level. . . . . . . **Advanced**
Platform. . . . **All**
Cost. . . . . **Free**

Your web browser does a good job of fetching web documents and displaying them, but there are times when you need an extra-strength program to get those tougher download jobs done.

A versatile, old-school Unix program called wget is a handy tool that makes downloading tasks very configurable. Whether you want to mirror an entire web site, automatically download music or movies from a set of favorite weblogs, or transfer huge files painlessly on a slow or intermittent network connection, the wget program — the noninteractive network retriever — is for you.

Install and Run wget

Download the Mac or Windows version of wget from http://lifehackerbook.com/links/wget. After downloading, extract the files to C:\wget in Windows or /Applications/wget on the Mac.

To run wget, launch a command line (the Mac Terminal or Windows Command Prompt). At the command-line prompt, switch to the directory where wget is installed by typing

```
cd c:\wget\
```

on Windows, or

```
cd /Applications/wget/
```

on the Mac. Then type the wget command you want from the examples described in the upcoming sections and press Enter.

The format of wget commands is as follows:

```
wget [option]... [URL]...
```

URL is the address of the file(s) you want wget to download. The magic in this little tool is the long menu of options available that make some highly customized and scriptable downloading tasks possible. This hack covers some examples of what you can do with wget and a few dashes and letters in the [option] part of the command.

NOTE For the full take on all of the wget program's secret options sauce, type wget --help at the command line or check out the complete wget manual online, available at http://gnu.org/software/wget/manual.

Mirror an Entire Web Site

Say you want to back up your blog or create a local copy of an entire directory of a web site for archiving or reading later. The following command saves all the pages that exist at the example.com web site in a folder named example.com on your computer:

```
wget -m http://example.com
```

The -m switch in the command stands for "mirror this site."

To retrieve all the pages on a site and the pages to which that site links, you'd go with the following command:

```
wget -H -r --level=1 -k -p http://example.com
```

In plain English, this translates into Download all the pages (-r, recursive) on http://example.com plus one level (--level=1) into any other sites it links to (-H, span hosts) and convert the links in the downloaded version to point to the other sites' downloaded version (-k). Also, get all the components, such as images, that make up each page (-p).

WARNING Those with small hard drives, beware! This command downloads a *lot* of data from large sites with several links (such as blogs). Don't try to back up the Internet, because you'll run out of disk space!

Resume Partial Downloads on an Intermittent Connection

Say you're using the wireless connection at the airport, and it's time to board the plane — with just a minute left on that download you started half an hour ago. When you make it back home and reconnect to the network, you can use the -c (continue) option to direct wget to resume a partial download where it left off.

For example, you want to download the 89MB installer file for free office-suite software OpenOffice.org (http://openoffice.org). Use the following wget command:

```
wget http://ftp.ussg.iu.edu/openoffice/stable/2.0.2/OOo_2.0.2_↵
Win32Intel_install.exe
```

Mid-download, you get the boarding call and have to close your laptop and get on the plane. When you reopen it back home, you can add a -c to your wget command and resume fetching the partially downloaded file, like this:

```
wget -c http://ftp.ussg.iu.edu/openoffice/stable/2.0.2/OOo↵
_2.0.2_Win32Intel_install.exe
```

This feature comes in handy when you're sharing bandwidth with others or need to pause a download while you work on another bandwidth-intensive task. For instance, if that movie download is affecting the quality of your Internet phone call, stop the download and after you've hung up the phone, resume the download using the wget -c switch.

NOTE Most — but not all — servers on the Internet support resuming partial downloads.

Also, if the URL of the file you're downloading contains ampersand (&) characters, be sure to enclose the URL in quotation marks in the command, like this:

```
wget -c "http://example.com/?p1=y&p2=n"
```

Automatically Download New Music from the Web

These days, there are tons of directories, aggregators, filters, and weblogs that point to interesting types of media. You can use wget to create a text-file list of your favorite sites that, say, link to MP3 music files, and schedule it to automatically download any newly added MP3s from those sites each day to your computer.[1]

Here's how:

1. Create a text file called mp3_sites.txt and list URLs of your favorite sources of music online (such as http://del.icio.us/ tag/system:filetype:mp3 or http://stereogum.com), one per line.

2. Use the following wget command to go out and fetch those MP3s:

```
wget -r -l1 -H -t1 -nd -N -np -A.mp3 -erobots=off -i
mp3_sites.txt
```

That wget recipe recursively (-r) downloads only MP3 files (-A.mp3) linked from the sites (-H) one level out (-l1) listed in mp3_sites.txt (-i mp3_sites.txt) that are newer (-N) than any you've already downloaded. There are a few other specifications in there — such as to not create a new directory for every music file (-nd), to ignore robots.txt (-erobots=off), and to not crawl up to the parent directory of a link (-np).

When this command is scheduled with the list of sites you specify, you get an ever-refreshed folder of new music files that wget fetches for you. With a good set of trusted sources, you'll never have to go looking for new music again — wget will do all the work for you.

TIP Use this technique to download all your favorite bookmarks for offline usage as well. If you keep your bookmarks online in del.icio.us, use wget to download the contents of your favorite pages to your hard drive. Then, using Google Desktop Search, you can search the contents of your bookmarks even when you're offline.

Automate wget Downloads on Windows

To schedule a wget download task to run at a certain time, open a new document in a plain-text editor such as Notepad. Type the wget command you want to schedule, and save the file with a .bat extension, such as getnewmusic.bat.

In Windows Task Scheduler, browse to `getnewmusic.bat` in the Programs section and set the schedule as usual.

> **NOTE** See Hack 64, "Automatically Reboot and Launch Applications," for more details on setting up a recurring job in Windows Task Scheduler.

Hack 67: Automatically Email Yourself File Backups

Level. . . . . . . **Advanced**
Platform. . . . **Windows XP and Vista**
Cost. . . . . **Free**

When my sister-in-law asked me how she could back up her master's thesis without any special equipment or software, I had to think for a minute.

"Email it to yourself," I finally told her.

Emailing yourself important documents that change often is a quick-and–dirty — yet very effective — form of backup, especially if you're using a web-based email solution such as Gmail (`http://gmail.google.com`) or Yahoo! Mail (`http://mail.yahoo.com`).

By regularly emailing yourself a copy of a file you've been slaving over for months — or hours — you're storing it offsite on your mail server, where it'll be safe in case of drive failure, theft, fire, or flood. Plus, you build up a directory of document versions over time, all in your inbox. Even if you're using the more complex and thorough backup system detailed earlier in this chapter, having a few copies of that key document in your email inbox can give you an extra sense of security and accessibility.

Of course, you don't want to go through the work of attaching a document to a new email and sending it manually four times a day. In this hack, you'll use a scriptable Windows program to do it for you. Schedule this program to run daily or hourly, or however often you need, for quick-and-easy versioned, offsite backup of your most important working documents.

Set Up the Email Script

The main act in this emailing show is a small, free utility called Blat, available for download at `http://blat.net`. Blat sends email with attachments from the command line. Unzip Blat into the `C:\Blat250\` directory.

Using Notepad or another text editor, make a list of all the files you want to email yourself, separated by commas. Save that file as `C:\Blat250\full\files-to-backup.txt`. Here's a sample `files-to-backup.txt`:

```
D:\data\Important Document01.doc, D:\data\Career-changing-
Presentation.ppt
```

List as many files as you like — just make sure there are commas between them.

Now you have to set your email SMTP server and From: address. To do so, from the Windows command line (in Windows XP, choose Start ⇨ Run, type **cmd** and press Enter), switch to the Blat directory (type **cd C:\blat250\full**). Then run the following command, substituting your SMTP server and your address for `smtp.example.com` and `yourname@example.com`:

```
Blat -install smtp.example.com you@example.com
```

That tells Blat how to send the message and from whom.

NOTE Check with your Internet service provider for your SMTP server settings.

Now, create your auto-email backup script by entering the following into a new text document:

```
C:
cd \
cd Blat250\full\

Blat -body "Just in case." -s "[backup] Important files" -to ↵
you@example.com -af files-to-backup.txt
```

Replace `you@example.com` with the email address where you will store your backups.

(Remember, ↵ indicates that the code line continues on the next line. It should all be on one line in your editor.)

Finally, save this new file as `C:\Blat250\full\email-file-backups` `.bat`. (Make sure this file has the `.bat` extension and that it's not a `.txt` file.)

You're ready to test the email script. In Windows Explorer, browse to the `C:\Blat250\full\` directory (see Figure 7-17). Double-click your new script, `email-file-backups.bat`.

Figure 7-17 The contents of the `C:\Blat250\` `full\` directory.

A command window pop ups, with Blat doing its thing. Within a few seconds, all the files you listed in `files-to-backup.txt` should appear in your email inbox.

Why Not Just Save Files to Flash Drives or a CD?

The key advantage to this method is that the files become available from anywhere you can get your mail. In the case of web-based mail such as Gmail or Hotmail, that's any Internet-connected computer with a web browser. If your laptop is stolen, thumb drive is lost, CD goes bad — you have your files up in the cloud. This works especially well for work files you've edited at home.

More on Emailing Yourself Backups

Here are some more tips and notes that will help you make the most of this hack.

Email Backup Filtering

You'll notice that the subject line of your email is `[backup] Important files` (that's set by the `-s` switch in the `Blat` command in your `.bat` file).

Use message filters and the word *[backup]* in the subject line to dispatch these messages from your inbox to a `backups` folder automatically so that they don't get in your way.

> **NOTE** See Hack 10, "Filter Low-Priority Messages ('Bacn')," for more on using email filters.

Scheduling

Finally, you can use Windows Task Scheduler to set your script to run at certain times. If you're rapidly changing a set of documents throughout the day, once an hour might be an appropriate recurring schedule; otherwise, once a day could work. Other considerations include your email provider's storage capacity and how many versions of your documents you want to store.

File Size and Type Limitations

Keep in mind that this method is not meant for use with very large files. Your email host provides only so much disk space, and some SMTP servers limit the size and number of attachments you can send at a time. Limitations depend on your provider. (For example, if you're a Gmail user, note that `.exe` file attachments don't make it through the Gmail spam filters.)

The bottom line is that this hack is not for backing up more than just a handful of smallish files, such as Office documents.

Troubleshooting

If your script doesn't work, from the command line, change directories with this command: `cd c:\Blat250\full`. Then run the script from there (just type **email-file-backups.bat**) and watch the output. If there's a problem connecting to your SMTP server, it'll be listed there. There are tons of switches and options for Blat — for example, you can specify a non-default mail port, or username and password to log on to your SMTP server. Run `Blat -h` to see the full rundown.

Also, the Blat Yahoo! Group (`http://groups.yahoo.com/group/blat`) is active, and its archives contain a lot of helpful troubleshooting information and tips.

Hack 68: Automatically Update a Spreadsheet

Level. . . . . . . **Medium**
Platform. . . . **Windows XP or Vista with Microsoft Excel**
Cost. . . . . **Free**

A spreadsheet is a great way to track progress on any type of undertaking that involves numbers — such as how much weight you've lost, how many widgets you made, how many miles you ran, or how many cigarettes you smoked. But who remembers to update his spreadsheet by hand?

Instead, use a simple scheduled script that prompts you to add data to your spreadsheet log. For example, if you're trying to lose weight, you could use this script to automatically remind yourself to record your current weight with the dialog box shown in Figure 7-18.

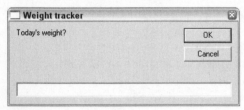

Figure 7-18 Spreadsheet log update dialog box.

Simply enter your current weight into the text box, click OK, and the script automatically appends the current date and your weight to a two-column Excel spreadsheet — without your ever having to open Excel.

Schedule this script to run when you log on every morning or once a week. With it, you'll never forget to log your current weight again, and you can make shiny line charts graphing your diet progress in Excel after you've added enough data.

Here's how to set it up:

1. Download the `weightlogger.vbs` script from `http://lifehackerbook.com/ch7/weightlogger.vbs` and save it to your computer. Here's the complete code listing (you'll edit the bold line):

```
'''''''''''''''''''''''''''''''''''''''''''''''''''''''''''''''''''''
''
'TITLE:    Weight Logger
```

```
'DESCRIPTION:     Appends your current weight to an Excel↵
spreadsheet with today's date
'CREATED BY:    Gina Trapani - lifehacker.com
'CREATE DATE:    07/28/2005
'
'INSTRUCTIONS:    Enter the filename you'd like to append your↵
weight to; make sure to only change the text that currently reads
' "C:\Gina\logs\weight.xls". The path must be surrounded by quotes.
'''''''''''''''''''''''''''''''''''''''''''''''''''''''''''''''''''
' '


Dim xlApp, xlBook, xlSht
Dim w, filename, currentRow, lastVal


filename = "C:\Gina\logs\weight.xls"


w = InputBox("Today's weight?", "Weight tracker")

Set xlApp = CreateObject("Excel.Application")
set xlBook = xlApp.WorkBooks.Open(filename)
set xlSht = xlApp.activesheet

xlApp.DisplayAlerts = False

'write data
currentRow = 2
lastVal = xlSht.Cells(2, 2)
while lastVal <> ""
    currentRow = currentRow + 1
    lastVal = xlSht.Cells(currentRow, 2 )
wend

xlSht.Cells(currentRow, 1) = Now
xlSht.Cells(currentRow, 2) = w

xlBook.Save
xlBook.Close SaveChanges = True
xlApp.Quit

'deallocate
set xlSht = Nothing
Set xlBook = Nothing
Set xlApp = Nothing
```

2. Create a new spreadsheet called `weight.xls`. The Column A header is Date and the Column B header is Weight.

3. Using your favorite text editor, open the `weightlogger.vbs` file you just downloaded. Change the line that reads

```
filename = "C:\Gina\logs\weight.xls"
```

to contain the path to where your `weight.xls` spreadsheet resides on your hard drive. Save your changes. Be sure to enclose the file path in quotes.

TIP If you're using `weightlogger.vbs` to track progress on something other than weight loss, you can modify the script to reflect that. For example, the line that reads

```
w = InputBox("Today's weight?", "Weight tracker")
```
could be changed to
```
w = InputBox("Miles run today?", "Running log").
```

4. Double-click the `weightlogger.vbs` script. A dialog box prompts you for your weight. Enter a number and click OK. Your current weight is entered into `weight.xls`.

NOTE The free Windows XP Script Engine is required to run VBS scripts. If you get a message along the lines of "no script engine for file extension .vbs," download the engine from `http://microsoft`
`.com/downloads/details.aspx?FamilyID=C717D943-7E4B-4622-`
`86EB-95A22B832CAA&displayLang=en`. **The installation does require you to restart your computer.**

5. Schedule regular weigh-in prompts using Windows Scheduled Tasks. Set the `weightlogger.vbs` script task to run every day or every week, at your discretion.

Reference

1. Jeffrey Veen, "MP3 Blogs and wget" (`http://veen.com/jeff/archives/000573.html`).

Get Your Data to Go

To get things done today, you need the right information at your fingertips — no matter where you are. You will travel, relocate, switch jobs, use more computers, and generate larger quantities of data in your lifetime than any previous generation has. The capability (or inability) to access that information on the go can make the difference between success and failure in work and life.

Every day you create a digital trail that details your life. Your Sent mail folder describes your professional and personal relationships. Your digital photo and video archive documents family vacations, graduations, births, and the car accident you got into last year. You've got your college papers, your résumé, and professional documents created at your last three jobs stowed away on your hard drive.

Ten years ago, you may have been able to store all the data you needed on a 1.44MB floppy disk. Now, in the age of MP3 players, ubiquitous broadband, personal camcorders, and digital cameras, you create and collect dozens of gigabytes of data per year. There are three main ways to get to this data when you're not sitting at the computer it lives on:

- **Storing it "in the cloud" using web applications (webapps).** Hack 69, "Manage Your Documents in a Web-Based Office Suite" and Hack 80, "Use Gmail as an Internet Hard Drive," cover ways to use web applications to store your data online, and even revise and collaborate on documents using only a browser.

■ **Taking your software and files with you on a portable device.** That iPod's good for more than just playing music and video, and with the right software installed on your USB drive, you may not need to take your laptop everywhere. Hack 78 covers how to use your iPod as an external hard drive, and Hacks 70 and 71 describe how to run Windows as well as your favorite portable applications directly from a flash drive.

■ **Turning your home computer into a personal server and connecting to it from anywhere.** If your home computer is your central digital nervous system and you've got always-on broadband Internet access at home, you can get to your home files from anywhere — across town or an ocean. Hack 73 details how to create a personal virtual private network to access your home computer from anywhere securely. Hacks 74 and 75 walk you through creating a home web server to browse and download files and to control your home computer's desktop remotely over the Internet.

Your data is your life. Secure, easy access to it — no matter where you are — is a must. Whether it's taking it with you on a keychain, storing it up in the cloud, or connecting to your home server from anywhere, this chapter's hacks cover several ways to get your data on the go.

Hack 69: Manage Your Documents in a Web-Based Office Suite

Level. . . . . . . **Beginner**
Platform. . . . **Web**
Cost. . . . . **Free**

A profound shift in modern computing is afoot: a move from desktop software to the Web. Mature web browsers, always-on broadband Internet connections, and an increase in mobile users has spurred a new breed of web sites that aren't just static pages — they're hosted software applications (web applications, or webapps) that you access from your browser.

Typing a memo, calculating charts in a spreadsheet, or designing a slideshow presentation used to require specialized and expensive software, such as WordPerfect or Microsoft PowerPoint, that you'd install on your computer. Today, a new crop of completely web-based office applications can create and manage those types of files, and you need only a web browser to use them. Several hacks in this book have encouraged you to move from desktop software to web applications — such as controlling your email with Gmail or managing your schedule in Google Calendar. You can do the same with your word processor documents, spreadsheets, and slideshows. This hack covers how (and why).

Why Move from Desktop Software to Web Applications

All you need to start using an online office suite is a computer with a web browser connected to the Internet and a free account at the service you choose (such as Google Docs at `http://docs.google.com` or Zoho at `http://zoho.com`). There are several advantages to abandoning your expensive desktop office suite in favor of web applications:

- No special software is required to create, revise, open, and save a new spreadsheet or slideshow, which eliminates the need to purchase or install Microsoft Office.

- You can access online office suites from any computer with a web browser and Internet connection, regardless of operating system or location.

- The most recent revision of your document is always available in one place, eliminating the need to copy your documents to a disk to take them with you or to back them up.

- You can easily collaborate on documents stored in a single place with several other people, whose edits will be saved in that one place. You don't need to send emails with document attachments for others to revise and risk having to deal with confusing multiple versions.

For example, as I wrote this book, I kept a spreadsheet detailing the revisions and additions I made to the first edition. At first I emailed a copy of this spreadsheet to my editor, but then a few hours later I made several changes. Finally, instead of emailing a copy every time I revised the sheet, I uploaded it to Zoho Sheet (`http://sheet.zoho.com`) and invited my editor to view it. That way, any revisions I made were immediately available to her, with no email or attachment required. Figure 8-1 shows the spreadsheet accessed via Zoho.

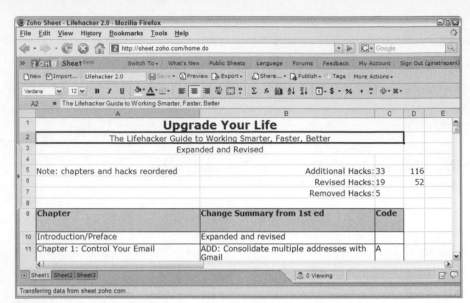

Figure 8-1 Viewing a spreadsheet in a web browser created and maintained with the web-based Zoho Sheet.

Working with web-based office applications probably sounds like a mobile, multicomputer user's nirvana, right? But there are some downsides; here's a look of some of them:

- The full-featured version of Microsoft Word, for instance, has many more features than any online word processor does. (Most likely the majority of Word documents don't employ those features, but some documents might.) You'll be surprised at how many features online office suites do support: advanced formatting; spreadsheet formulas; What You See Is What You Get (WYSIWYG) layouts. But you couldn't do a mail merge, for example, from a web-based word processor.

- Working in a web browser has some interface limitations and differences from installed, rich, desktop applications. For example, you can't drag and drop toolbars or files inside a web application. I have a habit of pressing Ctrl+S to save my documents as I work, and that doesn't work in some web-based office suites. Journalist Michael Calore worked exclusively in web applications for a full month and missed particular actions that are possible on the desktop but not in the web browser. In April of 2007, he wrote,

"A web-based user interface isn't as snappy as a desktop app. Menu navigation is much different, and tool palettes can't be customized or dragged around [...]. The one aspect of the desktop environment that I began to miss the most was drag-and-drop functionality. It seems so simple, but after years of interacting with my software in a very specific manner, dragging files from the desktop into applications had become an integral part of my work flow."[1]

- Your data is stored on someone else's server. The advantage is that it will still be there if your computer crashes, but some users might be concerned about privacy and security, especially if your documents contain confidential information.

- You must be connected to the Internet to access your documents (for now, that is — see the sidebar for more information). If you're on a cross-country flight and want to edit a document stored online, unless you exported it to your local desktop first and have the right desktop software installed to open it, you can't access it.

WORKING OFFLINE WITH WEB APPLICATIONS

Web-based applications like Zoho Office Suite, Gmail, and Google Calendar are all online, so they require a constant Internet connection to use them, right? Not necessarily. A new browser add-on, Google Gears (`http://gears.google.com`), aims to solve that problem. When you install and enable Gears, it downloads your information (such as documents or a to-do list) and saves it on your local computer for offline access. When you're disconnected from the Internet, you can edit your information using your browser as though you were online. Next time you connect, Gears syncs your changes back up to the webapp. As of this writing, Gears is still in beta, and only a handful of webapps work with it, such as the Remember the Milk task manager (detailed in Hack 34) and Zoho Writer. Presumably, more webapps will become Gears-enabled in the coming months (perhaps even before this book makes it into your hands). Additionally, makers of the Firefox web browser have discussed the possibility of offline web application access in upcoming releases of the browser. In short, offline access to web application data is on the horizon.

Web Application Alternatives to Desktop Office Software

You have several options for managing and storing your office documents online. Two major players — Google Docs and Zoho — offer suites of multiple applications such as word processors, spreadsheets, and presentation apps (the online answer to Microsoft PowerPoint). Other companies specialize in a single type of office applications. Here's a partial list of web applications you may use the next time you want to create a certain type of office document.

DESKTOP	WEBAPP ALTERNATIVE
WORD PROCESSORS	
Microsoft Word	Zoho Writer (http://writer.zoho.com)
WordPerfect	Google Docs (http://docs.google.com)
	ThinkFree (http://thinkfree.com)
	Approver (http://approver.com)
SPREADSHEETS	
Microsoft Excel	Zoho Sheet (http://sheet.zoho.com)
Lotus 1-2-3	Google Docs (http://docs.google.com)
	NumSum (http://numsum.com)
PRESENTATIONS	
Microsoft PowerPoint	Zoho Show (http://show.zoho.com)
Keynote	Google Docs (http://docs.google.com)
	Thumbstacks.com (http://thumbstacks.com)
	Preezo (http://preezo.com)

NOTE Google Docs and Zoho offer very similar office suites with a subtle difference. Google Docs is aimed at consumers, whereas Zoho is intended for business users. Both are free for individual use. Although many users may opt for Google Docs because of familiarity with the Google brand and an existing Google account (no separate registration required), overall, Zoho's suite includes more features within its applications.[2]

What You Can Do in an Online Office Suite

Web-based document editors have several features that separate them from and complement desktop software. Most office webapps let you do the following:

- **Import and export files for use on the desktop.** You use Zoho Writer but your co-worker uses Microsoft Word? Not a problem.

You can draft your document in Writer and click the Export button to download a Word document (.doc file), OpenOffice.org document (.sxw file), PDF, text, HTML, or rich-text document that can be edited on the desktop as usual. Likewise, if you have an existing Word document, for example, you can import it into a web-based office app for viewing or editing. Figure 8-2 shows this chapter's Word document as it appears uploaded to Google Docs.

Figure 8-2 Upload existing Microsoft Word documents to an online word processor such as Google Docs to back it up, share, or edit it from any web browser.

- ■ **Collaborate or share with specific people.** For any given document, you can email co-workers, friends, or family members and give them view-only or edit rights to the document in progress, which allows you to easily collaborate without clunky email attachments. Several online apps (such as Zoho Writer and Google Presentations) let users chat in-document while editing and viewing it.

■ **Publish your document.** Make your document viewable by anyone who visits its URL, or embed documents you create onto your weblog or company intranet page. Rather than send emails around with a document attached, you simply include the link to the published document to share it with others, as shown in Figure 8-3.

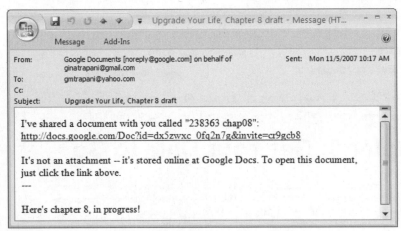

Figure 8-3 Share your document by emailing a URL instead of a file attachment.

Hack 70: Replace Your Laptop with a Portable Drive

Level. . . . . . . **Medium**
Platform. . . . **Windows XP (with a USB drive, iPod, or external hard drive)**
Cost. . . . . **Free**

You're headed to your in-laws' for the holiday week and you don't want to drag your laptop with you. Instead, take along a small hard drive that you can plug into their PC and get your own custom Windows desktop, applications, and files. Free software MojoPac (http://mojopac.com) creates a "PC on a stick" that borrows a host PC's hardware and runs Windows directly from a flash drive or iPod.

Plug your MojoPac-enabled portable drive into your mother-in-law's PC, launch Windows from it, and use any application or document directly from the drive, leaving no footprint behind on the host PC. Great for everyone who works on several PCs on a regular basis — or who just wants to separate certain apps and documents from a computer he uses — MojoPac is a convenient, portable Windows virtual machine.

Uses for MojoPac

You can do all sorts of things on the go with your MojoPac "PC on a stick," including the following:

- Listen to your music library, watch videos, and download podcasts from any PC with iTunes installed on your MojoPac.

- Watch downloaded video such as movies or TV shows with your media player of choice from any PC.

- Play PC games such as World of Warcraft, EverQuest, or Half-Life from any PC and take the game and its current state with you.

- Use expensive PC software you have limited licenses for, such as Microsoft Office or Photoshop, from any computer.

- Surf with your preferred browser, storing your passwords and other sensitive data separate from an untrusted host PC.

- Back up working copies of your essential software so that if your computer crashes or hard drive fails, you can plug your MojoPac into another PC and have a working environment ready to go.

Sound good? Let's get it running.

Install MojoPac

To get MojoPac set up, you'll need:

- **A USB flash drive or disk-mode–enabled iPod.**

- **A Windows XP PC that lets you log on as an administrator.**

- **The MojoPac software.** MojoPac Freedom is free to download for individual use; upgrade to MojoPac Deluxe ($49.99 as of this writing) to get technical support and automatic updates.

Here's how to install MojoPac.

1. Prepare your portable drive. You can install MojoPac on any external drive, including iPods with disk use enabled and USB flash drives. Flash drives are smaller but run MojoPac more slowly, so opt for a hard drive instead of a flash drive. If you're installing

MojoPac on a USB flash drive, clear off as much disk space from it as possible. Then, optimize it for fast reading and writing. In My Computer, go to the Properties panel of the portable drive. In the Hardware tab, choose the drive and click Properties. Then, on the Policies tab, select Optimize For Performance, as shown in Figure 8-4. You will need to restart your computer to save this setting.

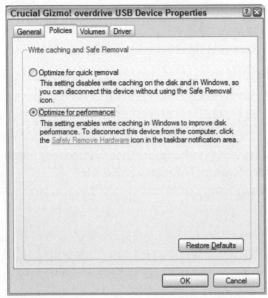

Figure 8-4 Set your MojoPac flash drive to be optimized for better performance.

If you're using an iPod, make sure the Manually Manage Music option is selected in iTunes, and that Enable Disk Use is also selected.

2. Download MojoPac from `http://mojopac.com` and run the installer, which will ask which drive it should put the MojoPac on. Choose either your flash drive, iPod, or external hard drive from the drop-down list.

3. Launch MojoPac for the first time. Either choose Launch MojoPac Now! at the end of the installation process or browse to the drive contents and click the `MojoPac Start.exe` file. MojoPac will prompt you to log in, as shown in Figure 8-5.

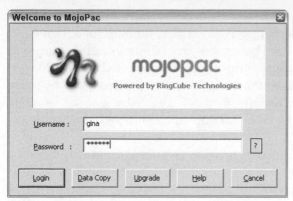

Figure 8-5 Clicking the `Start.exe` file will launch the MojoPac login dialog box.

The initial setup will ask you to name your MojoPac device and set a username and password to log in to it (in case it's lost or stolen). You also have to register for a free account at `http://mojopac.com` and enter your web username and password during the device's setup.

When the device setup it complete, click the Start Mojo button and enter the login information you set up (for the device, not on the web site). MojoPac's first boot takes a few extra minutes to get your portable Windows installation in order, so grab a drink while it gets everything set up.

Now you'll be sitting at your MojoPac Windows desktop, which resides entirely on your portable drive but "borrows" the CPU, video drivers, Internet connection, keyboard, and mouse from the host PC. Across the top of your desktop, you'll see a MojoPac toolbar that lets you switch back and forth between host PC and MojoPac. In MojoPac, the button reads Switch To Host, and on your host PC's desktop, it's Switch to Mojo, as shown in Figure 8-6.

Figure 8-6 Toggle between the host PC's desktop and MojoPac using the toolbar at the top of your desktop while MojoPac is running.

Inside MojoPac, browse to My Computer and notice that the portable drive you're running from is MojoPac's `c:` drive. In contrast to most virtual machines, you cannot access the host PC's disks while in MojoPac; however, while you're in the host PC, you can write to your MojoPac drive.

While you're in MojoPac, you can install any Windows application you want — not just portable apps. Photoshop, iTunes, VLC media player, any PC game, full-on Microsoft Office — you're limited only by how much space is available on your portable disk. MojoPac turns your portable disk not only into a data backup but also a working software application backup.

Speaking of data, MojoPac also provides a useful Data Copy utility that moves your documents onto your MojoPac. To get into it, quit MojoPac (while you're in MojoPac, right-click the system tray icon and choose Exit MojoPac) and then restart it. Instead of clicking the Start Mojo button, click the Data Copy button. Choose the folders on your host PC that you want to move into your MojoPac installation, as shown in Figure 8-7.

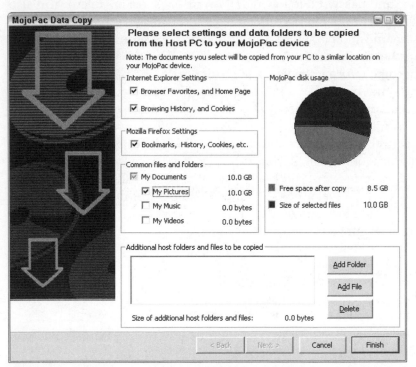

Figure 8-7 Copy your PC's files to your MojoPac drive using its built-in Data Copy utility, which displays how much space your portable drive has for folders you choose.

MojoPac's Pros, Cons, and Notes

Overall MojoPac is an excellent plug-and-play solution for Windows users who don't want to lug their laptops everywhere. But there are a few things to know when travelling with a MojoPac drive:

- MojoPac advertises itself as a solution for folks who are limited by IT restrictions on software — say, at the office or a café. However, you must be logged in to the host PC as an administrator to run MojoPac, something most users in IT lockdown are not.

- MojoPac's speed depends entirely on how fast the computer can read and write to the disk. Even with a fast disk, this will be slower than working on the host PC itself.

- Although major Windows software packages such as Microsoft Office do work with MojoPac, some software applications may not. See a comprehensive list of software known to work with MojoPac at http://mojopac.com/portal/content/what/apps.jsp.

- As of this writing, MojoPac does not yet support Windows Vista, so you must be working on a Windows XP PC with MojoPac. Vista support is on its way.

- For extra security, you can encrypt your MojoPac drive using True-Crypt's File Container option. See Hack 19, "Create a Password-Protected Disk on Your PC," for more on how to do this.

- A clean installation of MojoPac is about 52MB, not including any applications or user data saved on the drive, so the bigger hard drive you use with MojoPac, the more software and documents you can take with you.

Portable operating systems aren't limited to just MojoPac and Windows. Other free, Linux-based options include Damn Small Linux (http://damnsmalllinux.org) and Puppy Linux (http://puppylinux.com).

Hack 71: Carry Your Life on a Flash Drive

Level. . . . . . . **Medium**
Platform. . . . **Windows XP and Vista (with a flash drive)**
Cost. . . . . **Free**

Portable hard drives such as USB flash drives and iPods get cheaper, smaller in size, and larger in capacity by the day. Instead of lugging around your laptop or emailing yourself files, store your favorite software applications and important data on a thumb (flash) drive about the size of a car key. Then plug it into any computer for quick and easy access on the go.

This hack covers popular portable applications and some practical uses for these small drives.

Here are a few scenarios in which a USB drive loaded with your favorite applications and important documents might come in handy:

- You work on a set of files on several different computers (such as at the office and at home, on the laptop and the desktop) and you want easy access to them from one place.

- Your IT department doesn't give you administrative rights to install your favorite software on your office computer.

- You'd like to back up your files and store them offsite, such as home files at the office or work files at home. (You can store USB drives in a safety deposit box or mail one to Mom in Florida every few months, too.)

- You don't want to download and install your favorite application at every computer you use.

- You want to avoid using your in-laws' hijacked web browser to download virus scanners and spyware cleaners; instead, you want to take the tools you'll need to fix their computer along on your flash drive.

- You want to bring the latest episode of *Heroes* with you on the airplane, or create a digital music mix to use when you're the DJ at a friend's party. (USB drives are more portable and durable than DVDs, CDs, or VCR tapes.)

NOTE Later in this chapter, Hack 78, "Back Up Data to Your iPod," shows you how to use the iPod as an external hard drive from which you can also run portable applications and store your data.

Portable Applications

When you install software on your computer, the setup program makes changes to the Windows registry and stores special files (called DLLs) throughout your PC's file system so that the program can run. Portable apps — software programs meant to run from a single hard drive — don't require any changes to the operating system. They are self-contained and stand alone on one drive. Portable applications meant for use on flash drives are often stripped down to the bare essentials to take up the least amount of disk space possible. However, program size becomes less of an issue for software makers as larger-capacity drives become cheaper and more available. (As of this writing, thumb drives up to 16GB in size are available on the market.)

When purchasing a flash drive, keep in mind that size does matter. The more space you have, the more programs and information you can store.

Some popular portable software applications include the following:

- **Web browser:** Portable Firefox, 7.55MB installed. Includes all Firefox profile information such as bookmarks and extensions.

  ```
  http://portableapps.com/apps/Internet/browsers/portable_
  firefox
  ```

- **Office suite:** Portable OpenOffice.org, 90.6MB installed. Spreadsheet, word processor, and presentation software.

  ```
  http://portableapps.com/apps/office/suites/portable_
  openoffice
  ```

- **Email:** Portable Thunderbird, 21.7MB installed. Email, address book, and mail filters.

  ```
  http://portableapps.com/apps/Internet/email/portable_
  thunderbird
  ```

- **Instant messenger:** Trillian Anywhere, about 34MB installed, depending on the size of your Trillian profile. Multiprotocol instant-messaging client works with AIM, Yahoo! Messenger, MSN Messenger, ICQ, and IRC.

  ```
  http://trilliananywhere.com
  ```

- **Virus scanner:** Portable ClamWin, about 15MB installed (with definitions). Open source Windows virus scanner.

  ```
  http://portableapps.com/apps/utilities/antivirus/
  portable_clamwin
  ```

- **Remote login:** TightVNC (viewer executable only), 159KB installed. Log in to your remote VNC (virtual network computing) server with the TightVNC viewer. (See Hack 75, "Remotely Control Your Home Computer," for more information on using the TightVNC viewer.)

  ```
  http://tightvnc.com/download.html
  ```

What kind of space are we talking about? Those six portable programs total 327.85MB, or about 33 percent of a 1GB flash drive, which leaves plenty of space for work files.

For a constantly updated directory of software fit for toting around on a thumb drive, keep an eye on John Haller's web site, Portable Apps (`http://portableapps.com`).

The Portable Apps site also offers an entire suite of software packages for your flash drive in a single download. The suite includes a web browser, email client, web editor, office suite, word processor, calendar/scheduler, instant-messaging client, and FTP client, ready to save to your flash drive and use. Two flavors are available for download: Standard and Lite (smaller file size). Download it for free at `http://portableapps.com/suite`. The Standard version, unzipped and installed, takes up 256MB; the Lite, a mere 99 MB.

Several other software applications discussed in other hacks in this book are small enough to fit on a thumb drive or offer a portable version:

- **KeePass password manager:** See Hack 15, "Securely Track Your Passwords," for more on using KeePass.

- **TrueCrypt data encryption utility:** See Hack 19, "Create a Password-Protected Disk on Your PC," for more on making your files inaccessible in case your thumb drive is lost or stolen.

- **Texter text replacement:** See Hack 48, "Reduce Repetitive Typing with Texter for Windows," for more details on creating custom abbreviation replacement and common misspelling correction programs with the free, portable-drive-friendly Windows program called Texter.

Carry a System-Recovery Toolkit on Your Flash Drive

Tech-support warriors should add a thumb stick loaded with the prefab PC Repair Kit (available at `http://www.dailycupoftech.com/usb-drive-systems/3/`) to their toolbox. The PC Repair Kit offers a menu of 37 Windows diagnose-and-fix utilities for your (or your co-worker's) spyware-addled PC.

Useful Data to Store on Your Thumb Drive

Software is worthless without data. Store your important files on your flash drive for access on any computer. That includes your

- To-do list.

- Address book.

- Passwords: Be sure to encrypt this file for security! (See the following section, "Secure Your Drive," for more information.)

- Multimedia: Photos, music, and video (depending on the size of your drive).

- Office documents.

- ReturnIfLost.txt file with your contact information.

- Web site bookmarks.

- Web browser configuration (see Hack 92, "Take Your Browser Configuration with You," for more information).

Secure Your Drive

Flash drives are tiny and convenient, which means they're easily lost, damaged, stolen, and transported. More and more cases of stolen laptops and hard drives have spelled disaster for companies and individuals who handle sensitive customer data or private company documents.

Here are a few strategies for securing the data on your thumb drive.

Lock Sensitive Text Files

Free software LockNote, available at http://locknote.steganos.com, is a standalone text-file encryption program. Save the LockNote.exe file to your thumb drive. Launch it and enter any textual information you'd like to secure — passwords, addresses, phone numbers, account numbers, and so on — and then close the document. LockNote prompts you for a password and scrambles the file so that anyone without the password can't open it.

The LockNote.exe file weighs in at about 296KB — about 0.29 MB — and is worth the space if you're dealing with sensitive, confidential material.

Encrypt Your Data

If you have different types of existing files, you can create a password-protected ZIP archive of them. Using free software 7-Zip, available at http://7zip.org, add the files you want to save on your flash drive to a new ZIP archive, and set a password to open them, as shown in Figure 8-8.

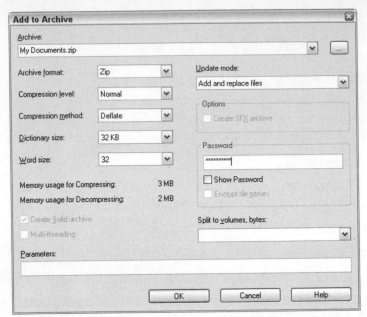

Figure 8-8 Set a password on the zipped files for security.

Make sure you change the Archive Format from `7z` to `zip` so that Windows can extract the file without 7-Zip. Finally, move the resulting archive (`.zip` file) to your thumb drive.

You can browse the file and folder names within a password-protected ZIP file, but the individual files cannot be extracted or the contents viewed without entering the password. A stronger, alternative encryption method employs the free software TrueCrypt (`http://truecrypt.org/downloads.php`). For detailed instructions on how to encrypt an entire thumb drive — or just a particular folder or set of files with True-Crypt — see Hack 19.

Make Your Drive Returnable

Place an "If found, please return" text file with contact information on your flash drive to increase the chances that it'll be returned in case of loss. But don't encrypt this file — it should be readable by anyone!

Using Your Thumb Drive

When your flash drive is loaded, plug it into any computer with a USB drive and access it the same as any other internal hard drive. All the usual

Mac/PC compatibility issues apply (for example, an .exe file won't launch on a Mac), but Office documents, PDFs, and text files are cross-platform.

WARNING If you're not sure the computer you're using is free of spyware and viruses, assume that it is not. USB drives are the perfect way to spread computer nasties, so be extra cautious with a promiscuous thumb drive. For this very reason, network administrators sometimes disable the capability to mount a thumb drive on public computers (such as at libraries).

Hack 72: Access Web Apps and Search via Text Message

Level. . . . . . . **Medium**
Platform. . . . **A mobile phone with text messaging**
Cost. . . . . **Dependent on your mobile phone plan**

You're out and about town and you need movie times at theaters nearby, a reminder to feed the parking meter in 60 minutes, to quickly capture how much gas you just put in the tank, or to check the weather forecast. You don't need a laptop or even a tricked-out PDA to access the Web on the go: you can do it directly from any phone that can send text messages. More and more, modern web applications are offering access to their services via text message.

Here's how it works: You send a text message that contains a short code — such as w 90210 or m 11215, to check the weather or get movie times. Then, you receive a message response back on your mobile phone immediately (within a minute). Let's take a look at a few SMS-enabled web search engines and applications.

NOTE For more on how to send a text message from your SMS-enabled phone, see Hack 50, "Text-Message Efficiently."

Web Search via Text Message

Major web search engines Google and Yahoo! — and a smaller, new company, 4INFO — offer SMS search results to your cell phone via text message on the spot. All you need to know is where to send your query. The following table provides a list of common tasks, the numbers to message, the queries to send, and example replies.

TASK	TO	MESSAGE	REPLY
Find a Wi-Fi hotspot	YAHOO (92466) 4INFO (44636)	wifi 11215	Naidre Miller Incorporated 718-965-7585, 382 7th Ave, Brooklyn, NY
Find a local business	GOOGL (46645) YAHOO (92466)	taxi Marietta, OH pizza 11215	Ohio Valley Cab Co 330 Franklin St # B Marietta, OH 740-374-2736 4 mi, SW
Check flight status for American Airlines flight 810	4INFO (44636) GOOGL (46645)	AA 810	American Airlines #810 Landed D:SAN A:ORD-115p
Sports scores, stock prices, and horoscopes	GOOGL (46645) 4INFO (44636) 4INFO (44636) 4INFO (44636)	yankees mlb yhoo virgo	MLB *Minnesota*: 6 NY Yankees: 1 Final, Sep 2 Recent game: Sep 1 Minnesota: 1 *NY Yankees*: 8
Dictionary definitions	GOOGL (46645) YAHOO (92466)	d philomath	Glossary: * philomath: a lover of learning
Drink recipes	4INFO (44636)	Drink cosmo	Cosmo 2 oz. Vodka 1 oz. Triple Sec 1 oz. Cranberry Juice Juice 1 Lime Shake with ice and strain over ice into your favorite cocktail glass and serve.

TASK	TO	MESSAGE	REPLY
Weather	GOOGL (46645) 4INFO (44636) YAHOO (92466)	w asbury park, nj w seattle,wa w york, pa	Weather: Asbury Park, NJ 66F, OvercastWind: E 5mph Hum:73%Sa:63-66F, Rain Su:59-75F, Showers M:60-77F, Mostly Sunny Tu:63-76F, Showers
Movie times	Specific movies: GOOGL (46645) Movies in a ZIP Code: 4INFO (44636)	pirates 92037 m 11228	* Pirates of the Caribbean: Dead Man's ... 2hr 31min,PG-13, Action/Adventure/Comedy , 3.4/5 AMC La Jolla 1211:50am 3:00pm 6:45 10:008657 Villa La Jolla Dr.La Jolla, CA858-558-2262 x087
Translations	GOOGL (46645)	translate beautiful in italian	Google Translation: 'beautiful' in English means 'bello' in Italian
Comparison shopping	GOOGL (46645)	Price battlestar galactica season 1 dvd	Products. * Battlestar Galactica (2004): Season 2.0 [3 Discs] -, $44.99, Best Buy * Battlestar Galactica - Season 1 - DVD BOXSET *NEW, $31.96, MovieMars.com
Look up location of a ZIP or area code	GOOGL (46645) YAHOO (92466)	718	718: area code for Brooklyn, Queens, Staten Island, New York
Driving directions	GOOGL (46645)	San Francisco ca to Santa Cruz ca	(See text following table.)
Currency conversion	GOOGL (46645)	5 usd in euro	Currency Conversion: 5 U.S. dollars = 3.89650873 Euro

Driving directions messages are long and may come in multiple message installments. Here's the reply to the example message:

```
(1/3)Directions:
Distance: 72.5 mi (about 1 hour 9 mins) 9 steps.
1. Head SE from 11th St (0.3)
2. (L) at Folsom St (0.1)
3. (R) at 10th St (0.2)


(2/3)4. Bear (L) into US-101 S entry ramp to San Jose (35)
5. Take CA-85 S ramp to Cupertino/Santa Cruz (13)
6. Take CA-17 ramp to San Jose/Santa Cruz (0.2)
(3/3)7. Take CA-17 S ramp to Santa Cruz (23)
8. Bear (L) at Chestnut St (0.2)
9. (L) at Church St (0.1)
```

TIP Add GOOGL, YAHOO, and 4INFO to your phone's address book for quicker message addressing.

Get Help

No one expects you to remember all the search codes listed in the preceding table. Luckily, each service provides a help command that returns a listing of all the possible commands it supports. Text GOOGL, 4INFO, or YAHOO the word `help` to get a command reference texted back to you. Save the message to your phone so that you can refer to it any time you want to conduct an SMS search.

Test-Drive SMS Search on the Web

All three mobile search services offer web-based demonstrations of SMS search via phone. Test-drive a text message search at the following locations on the Web:

- ▪ 4INFO: `http://4info.net/howto`
- ▪ Yahoo! SMS: `http://mobile.yahoo.com/search/smsdemo`
- ▪ Google SMS: `http://google.com/sms`

Preschedule Search-Result SMS Alerts

4INFO offers a particularly useful feature: prescheduled, automatic search results that come to your phone on a regular basis. For example, if you want to get a text message whenever the status of your FedEx package changes, you can set up alerts from 4INFO to do just that. Get fantasy sports team updates, your horoscope, stock prices, or scores texted to your phone automatically on a schedule. Visit `http://4info.net/waysto/waystoalert.jsp` to set it up.

Web Applications via Text Message

In addition to regular web search, several personal-organizer web applications, such as calendars, budgeting, and reminder services, offer SMS access.

Calendar

Not only can Google Calendar text-message you event notifications (as detailed in Hack 30, "Send Reminders to Your Future Self"), but you can also retrieve and add to your Google Calendar by text-messaging the short code GVENT. First register your phone number in Google Calendar. Then use the following text-message commands to see and add events to your calendar:

- Send the word `next` to GVENT get a notification regarding your next scheduled event.
- Send `day` to get a notification containing all your scheduled events for the present day.
- Send `nday` to get a notification containing all your events for the following day.
- To add an event, send GVENT the details; for example, `Lunch at Josie's 2PM Saturday`.

Get a full rundown of Google Calendar's text message support and setup at `http://www.google.com/support/calendar/bin/answer.py?answer=45351&topic=8568`.

Twitter Universal SMS Interface

Micro-blogging service Twitter (`http://twitter.com`) lets users post short status updates about their lives and send messages to other Twitter users via SMS (as well as via the Web and IM). What most Twitter users don't know is that you can also send messages to various "bots" that perform different tasks for you, such as send timed reminders or interact with your to-do list. To use any Twitter bot, you need to register for a free account at Twitter and enable your mobile phone number for direct messages from Twitter.

Instant Reminders

Schedule a "wake-up call"-like timed text message to remind yourself to feed the parking meter or put the laundry in the dryer. Add the Twitter user named `timer` to your Twitter friends list, and direct-message the Twitter `timer` user reminder details. A Twitter message that reads `d timer 45 pay parking meter` will trigger an SMS back to your cell phone in the specified number of minutes (in this case, 45) with your reminder message.

To-Do List

Additionally, the `rtm` Twitter bot acts as a middleman between Twitter and the Remember the Milk task manager (described in Hack 34). Add the `rtm` Twitter user to your friends, and direct-message it to add, update, and retrieve your Remember the Milk to-do list via SMS commands. Here are some examples:

- Add to-do's to your list with task and optional time, such as

```
d rtm pick up the milk
d rtm call jimmy at 5pm tomorrow
d rtm return library books in 2 weeks
```

- Get today's to-do list with `d rtm !today`.
- Retrieve all tasks for a specific context with `d rtm !getlist shopping`.

Get more details about Remember the Milk's full-featured Twitter bot at `http://blog.rememberthemilk.com/2007/07/twitter-your-tasks.html`.

Money

The key to sticking to a budget is writing down exactly what you spent on what. If you use a web-based money manager, such as Buxfer (`http://buxfer.com`), you can email expenditure details to your account from your phone on the go so that you don't forget you just dropped 18 bucks on toiletries or that your roommate owes you a portion of the rent. Buxfer's email commands get pretty detailed; you can use them to add tags, amounts, and people who are in on a given transaction. For example,

```
toilettries 18.00 tags: household acct:wamu
```

adds an $18 expenditure from the account named WaMu tagged `household`. If your phone doesn't have email but does have SMS, you can use Buxfer's Twitter bot, named `bux`. Add `bux` to your Twitter friends and direct-message it like this:

```
d bux starbucks 12.00 tags:coffee
```

to add a 12-buck coffee purchase at Starbucks. More details on SMS interaction with Buxfer are available at `http://www.buxfer.com/faqs.php?cat=sms`.

Gas Mileage

Another useful personal tracking tool with SMS support is webapp My Mile Marker (`http://mymilemarker.com/`), a gas purchase/mileage tracker that calculates your vehicle's MPG. My Mile Marker's SMS interface is also available via the `mymm` Twitter bot. To record your gas and mileage info via text message from the pump, your message should be in the format d `mymm [miles] [gallons] [price]`. For example, after you've filled your tank with gas, from the station you could send this text message to the `mymm` Twitter bot:

```
d mymm 15476 15.34 3.129
```

which means the odometer read 15476 when you filled up with 15.34 gallons at $3.129/gallon. Back at the My Mile Marker web site, you can generate charts and reports of gas prices and mileage and calculate your fuel economy over time and distance traveled.

Hack 73: Create a Virtual Private Network (VPN) with Hamachi

Level. . . . . . . **Advanced**
Platform. . . . **All**
Cost. . . . . **Free**

You can do things between computers on your local network that you can't from out on the Internet, such as listen to a shared iTunes library or access files in shared folders. But using the free, virtual private network application Hamachi (`https://secure.logmein.com/products/hamachi/vpn.asp`), you can access your computer from anywhere on the Internet as if you were home on your local network.

This hack uses Hamachi to create a virtual private network between a PC and a Mac and listen to a shared iTunes library over the Internet.

What's Hamachi VPN?

The free Hamachi desktop application gives you a secure, zero-configuration LAN over the Internet. Any application that works over a local network can be used with Hamachi over the Internet, such as Windows file sharing, iTunes, Remote Desktop, FTP, VNC, and gaming. All Hamachi's connections are secure, encrypted, authenticated, and peer-to-peer. Although Hamachi acts as a mediator between your computers and creates the tunnel for their communication, Hamachi's servers don't listen in on or log your activity.

You might use Hamachi in the following situations:

- You're on the road with your laptop and want secure access to your PC's files.

- Your office or dorm-room computer is behind a restrictive firewall that doesn't let you reach it from the Internet.

- You want to add encryption to insecure network protocols such as VNC.

- You want to set up a shared folder of files for friends and family to access.

Sound useful? Read on to get started.

Set Up Hamachi

The following sections lead you through downloading and installing Hamachi's VPN as well as setting up your Hamachi network.

Download and Install Hamachi

Download the right version of Hamachi for your operating system from `https://secure.logmein.com/products/hamachi/list.asp`. (Although Hamachi is available for Windows, Linux, and Mac OS X, this hack addresses the Windows setup specifically.) For the most part, the Windows installation is a regular wizard — just click Next to step through it. When asked, opt to use the Hamachi Basic service, which is free for individual use.

During installation, Hamachi will attempt to install a virtual network adapter, which Windows may say is not supported. Just click the Continue Anyway button at that point. If you have Windows Firewall enabled (or any firewall, for that matter), the firewall program will ask whether you want to allow traffic to and from the Hamachi client. You do. Click the Unblock button to allow Hamachi traffic through your firewall.

For Mac users, the Hamachi version offered for download is command-line only. For a graphical interface to Hamachi, download and install HamachiX, available at `http://hamachix.spaceants.net`. (As of this writing, HamachiX is not compatible with Leopard, but from the looks of things, upgrades are on their way.)

Create Your Hamachi Network

When Hamachi is installed, it will walk you through a quick tutorial to get you started. Read it — it's worth it. Then, click the Network button (bottom-right corner, second button to the left) and choose Create New Network from the menu. Give your network a name (mine was `gtrap-home`) and a password (if you'd like), as shown in Figure 8-9. Click the Create button.

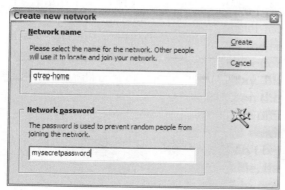

Figure 8-9 Set your new virtual private network's name and the password. Any computers that join your network must enter these.

Now your computer will be a member of the new network and get its own Hamachi IP address (in addition to its regular IP address). It will also have a nickname that will identify it on your network. Mine was `dell-pc`.

Invite Others to Join Your Hamachi Network

Right away, you can tell your friends or co-workers your Hamachi network's name and password so that they, too, can join it with the Hamachi client installed on their computers. Alternatively, you can join your own network from another computer (such as your PC at the office). Using HamachiX, I connected my Mac (nicknamed `nyx`) to the `gtrap-home` network, and the Hamachi client on my PC displayed the Mac online, as shown in Figure 8-10.

Figure 8-10 Like an instant-messenger window, the Hamachi client displays what computers in your network are online.

You can also administer your Hamachi network from its web interface when you're not running the Hamachi client itself. Log into the Hamachi web site (at `http://my.hamachi.cc`) and click the Networks tab to view a list of networks you own (see Figure 8-11). Click a network name to see all the computers on that network; you can even evict computers to which you want to deny access.

Figure 8-11 View the list of computers connected to your Hamachi network from the control panel at `my.hamachi.cc`.

Now you're ready to put your private network to good use.

What You Can Do Over Hamachi VPN

Anything you can do over a local network — your home wireless network, for example — you can do over the Internet between two computers on a Hamachi VPN. Share files and printers, or stream your iTunes library from your home Mac to your office PC. Browse shared Windows folders, FTP into a home media server, remotely control your computer over VNC, or access a private home web server over Hamachi VPN, which adds an extra layer of security and privacy. See Hacks 74 and 75 in this chapter for how to set up a home web server and remotely control your computer, and couple those techniques with Hamachi to encrypt and restrict access to your home computer.

Hack 74: Run a Home Web Server

Level. . . . . . . **Advanced**
Platform. . . . **Windows XP and Vista**
Cost. . . . . . . **Free**

A web server is software that continuously runs on a computer and allows other computers to download documents from it. Any web page you view has traveled over a network connection from the site's hosting web server to the browser on your computer. Web servers are usually loud, scary, headless machines in cold, windowless rooms, but you can run one under your desk at home.

Why would you want to run a home web server? Maybe you want to download files — perhaps some of your digital music collection — on your home computer from anywhere. Maybe you want your friends and family to have access to your music or photo collection from anywhere, too.

In this hack, you set up a home web server that enables anyone (with the right password) to connect to your computer and download your MP3 files from it. It gives you an easy way to share your music collection with friends, or play a song from your home machine for co-workers at the office.

There are tons of uses for your personal web server beyond a password-protected jukebox: You can publish your weblog at home, host a personal wiki, and share video files and photos. Basically, any file you want to publish as read-only is a good candidate. A home web server has the advantage over special server/client software because it requires only a web browser to connect to it.

WARNING Running a server on your home computer is a risky undertaking. Before you start, ensure that your computer has all the latest patches and security updates (visit `http://windowsupdate.microsoft.com` to make sure) and that you've done a thorough spyware and virus scan. This hack is for advanced users who feel comfortable editing textual configuration files and exposing port 80 on their home computers to the Internet. You should be running a strong firewall with explicit user-set rules.

Here's what you need to get started:

- A Windows PC
- An always-on broadband (DSL or cable) Internet connection

Step 1: Disable Other Servers or Firewall Software

Disable and stop any firewall or server software you may have running, including Windows Firewall, Skype, Trillian, or any other instant-messaging applications. This is extremely important, and if you don't do it, you can cause the server installation and startup to fail miserably. These programs and services can be started and used again as usual when you're done setting up the web server.

Step 2: Install Apache HTTP Server

Download the Apache HTTP server, available at `http://httpd.apache.org/download.cgi`. Use the link under Best Available Version next to Win32 Binary (MSI Installer). If the Windows binary is not available on the home page, click the Other Files link and go to the `binaries` folder, and from the `win32` folder, download the most recent `.msi` file. As of this writing, that file is `apache_2.2.3-win32-x86-no_ssl.msi`.

Click the downloaded file to start the installation wizard. Accept the license agreement and use the default location for the Apache files, which is `C:\Program Files\Apache Software Foundation\Apache 2.x\`. When you reach the screen prompting for server information, enter your own email address and **homeip.net** as the domain information, as shown in Figure 8-12.

It doesn't matter what domain you put here. I chose `homeip.net` because it's descriptive is and one of the DynDNS home domains. (See Hack 76, "Give Your Home Computer a Web Address," for more information on DynDNS.)

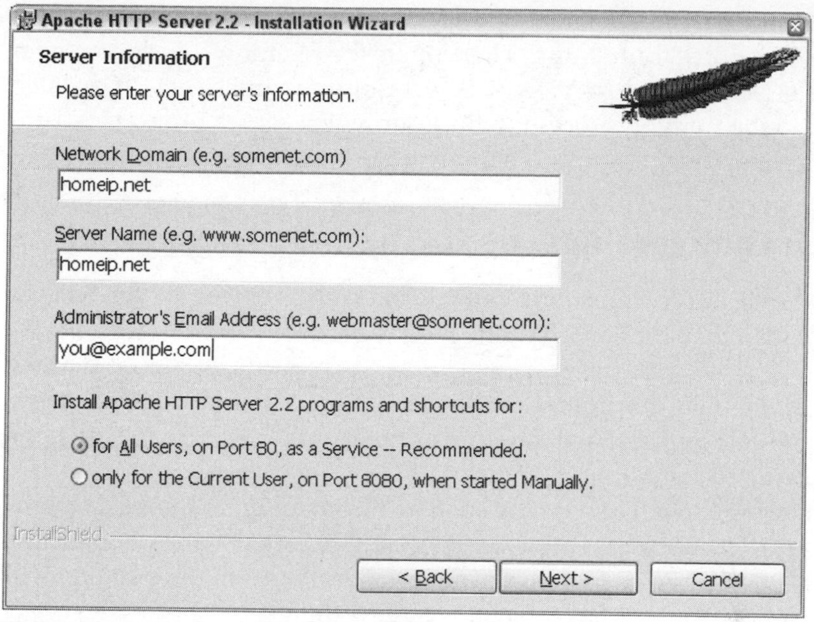

Figure 8-12 Set the web server options.

Complete the Installation

Complete the installation wizard using the Typical Installation setting. Set the server to run on port 80 for all users. If Windows Firewall (or any other firewall you may be running) asks what it should do about the server running on port 80, choose to unblock or allow Apache to run on it.

When the installation is complete, open your web browser and go to `http://localhost/`. If the page you see reads something along the lines of "If you can see this, it means that the installation of the Apache web server software on this system was successful" — or, more simply, a page that declares "It works!" — you're golden.

Common Problem

A common installation error with Apache reads, "Only one usage of each socket address (protocol/network address/port) is normally permitted. : make_sock: could not bind to address 0.0.0.0:80 no listening sockets available, shutting down. Unable to open logs." This means that some other server program (such as Skype) is interfering with Apache. To figure out what program it is, open a command prompt and type

```
netstat -a -o
```

Find the PID (Process ID) of the program running on your local machine on port 80 (or http). Then open the Windows Task Manager (Ctrl+Alt+Delete). Choose View ⇨ Select Columns and select PID. Match the PID to the running process to find out which server program is running; then stop that program. Then retry the Apache installation.

Step 3: Configure Apache to Share Documents

To make your music collection available via your new web server, browse to the folder that contains Apache's configuration files, located at `C:\Program Files\Apache Software Foundation\Apache 2.x\conf\`. Make a copy of the main configuration file, `httpd.conf`, before you make any changes — just in case. Save the copy as `httpd.backup.conf` in that same directory.

Then, using a plain-text editor such as Notepad, open the `C:\Program Files\Apache Software Foundation\Apache 2.x\conf\httpd.conf` file. The contents of this file look long and scary, but most of the defaults will work just fine. You just have to change a few things.

First, comment out the line that starts with `DocumentRoot` by adding a # at the beginning of the line and add another with your directory, like this:

```
#DocumentRoot "C:/Program Files/Apache Group/Apache2/htdocs"
DocumentRoot "C:/Documents and Settings/penelope/My Documents/My
Music"
```

where `C:/Documents and Settings/penelope/My Documents/My Music` corresponds to the location of your music files.

> **NOTE** While Windows directory structure normally uses backslashes, Apache's default `httpd.conf` uses forward slashes, so that's what I use in this hack.

Then, comment out the line that starts with `<Directory "C:/Program` and add another line with your directory, like this:

```
#<Directory "C:/Program Files/Apache Group/Apache2/htdocs">
<Directory "C:/Documents and Settings/penelope/My Documents/My
Music">
```

Last, about 20 lines later, there's a line that reads

```
AllowOverride None
```

Change it to

```
AllowOverride All
```

When you're done, save `httpd.conf`. Then click the Apache icon in your taskbar and choose Restart. If Apache restarts successfully, you edited your the file correctly. Visit `http://localhost/` in your web browser. This time, you should see a listing of your music files.

> **NOTE** If Apache doesn't start correctly, it's because it can't read the `httpd.conf` file, which means you probably had a typo in your changes. Check your changes carefully, save, and restart Apache to try again. If necessary, copy `httpd.backup.conf` to `httpd.conf` to start all over again.

Step 4: Password-Protect Your Web Site Documents

You don't want just anyone to be able to download your music. Your bandwidth and files are private and precious, so you want to secure things a bit. You can use a VPN (virtual private network) to restrict access to your home web server; see Hack 73 for more information on how to do that. If you don't want to make everyone who accesses your web server have to run special VPN software, you can create a simple browser password prompt instead. Here's how:

1. Open a command prompt (choose Start ➪ Run, type **cmd**, and press Enter). Change to the Apache bin directory by typing

   ```
   cd "C:\Program Files\Apache Software Foundation\Apache 2.x\bin"
   ```

   where `Apache 2.x` matches the version you installed (Apache 2.2, for example).

2. Create a password file by typing

   ```
   htpasswd -c "C:\Documents and Settings\penelope\My Documents\; ↵
   web-server-pass-file" penny
   ```

   Replace the path with wherever your password file should be located (which can be any folder *except* the web server's document root that you set up previously). Replace `penny` with your preferred username.

3. When prompted, enter the password you want to set up. After you've done that, a password file will be created.

Now, follow these steps to apply that login to your music directory:

1. Open a new file in a plain-text editor such as Notepad. Enter the following text into it:

```
AuthType Basic
AuthName "This is a private area, please log in"

AuthUserFile "C:\Documents and Settings\penelope\My Documents\;
web-server-pass-file"
AuthGroupFile /dev/null

<Limit GET POST PUT>
require valid-user
</Limit>
```

Make sure you replace C:\Documents and Settings\penelope\My Documents\web-server-pass-file in the text with the path to the password file you created.

2. Name the file .htaccess and save this new file in the web server's document root you set earlier (in this example, C:/Documents and Settings/penelope/My Documents/My Music). Don't forget the dot in the beginning, before htaccess. In other words, you are saving the file as C:\Documents and Settings\penelope\My Documents\My Music\.htaccess.

NOTE If you're using Notepad to create your .htaccess file, put quotation marks around the filename — ".htaccess" — when you save the file so that Notepad doesn't automatically put a .txt extension on the file. (If the file has a .txt file extension, your password won't work!) Alternatively, choose All Files from the Save As Type drop-down list before you save the file.

3. Point your web browser to http://localhost/. You are prompted to log in as shown in Figure 8-13.

4. Enter the username and password you set up in your password file, and you're in.

Congratulations! You've got a home web server running.

If you are not behind a firewall, you can access your web server from other computers by typing your computer's IP address into a web browser's address bar. (If you're not sure what your IP is, visit WhatIsMyIP at http://whatismyip.com to find out.) If your IP is 12.34.567.890, type **http://12.34.567.890** into a browser's address bar.

Figure 8-13 The password prompt for your local web server.

NOTE Depending on your Internet service provider, your computer's IP address may change, but there's an easy way to set up a memorable name that doesn't change. See Hack 76, "Give Your Home Computer a Web Address," for more information.

If you are behind a firewall (such as through a wireless router), you'll need to open port 80 on the firewall and forward it to your computer. Consult your router's manual, or for more information on port forwarding, go to http://lifehackerbook.com/links/portforward.

In the meantime, enjoy accessing the files on your home computer from anywhere via your home web server!

Hack 75: Remotely Control Your Home Computer

Level. . . . . . . **Advanced**
Platform. . . . **Windows XP and Vista, Mac OS X 10.4 and later**
Cost. . . . . **Free**

Ever been at a friend's house and wanted to show off a photo you left saved on your home computer? Want to check from the office that your daughter's doing homework and not instant messaging with friends at home? Need to grab a file on your home hard drive when you're miles away? With a relatively old protocol called VNC and some free software, you can remotely control your home computer from anywhere.

In this hack, you set up a VNC server on your home computer, which will enable you to connect to your desktop and drive it from any Internet-connected computer.

WARNING As mentioned earlier, running a server and opening a port on your home computer to the Internet is a risky undertaking. Make sure your computer has all the latest security patches, has been checked for spyware and viruses, and that you're using strong passwords. The VNC protocol is not inherently secure. This hack assumes that you're comfortable with basic networking concepts. In case this fine print has scared you off, LogMeIn (`http://logmein.com`) is a web-based application that also provides remote desktop control, which may be a better option for some folks. VNC is preferable because it's free, it doesn't require third-party intervention, and it works across operating systems.

The VNC protocol remotely controls another computer over a network. Think of it as a window into your home computer's desktop from any other computer (see Figure 8-14).

Figure 8-14 An open VNC connection to a Windows PC from a Mac.

Your key presses and mouse clicks travel over the network and happen on the remote computer — your home computer — in real time, and anyone at the remote computer can watch the action as it happens.

A few things you can do with a VNC server running at home:

- Start downloading a large file, such as a movie, in the morning so that it's there when you get home in the evening

- Search your home computer's IM logs, address book, or file system for important information from the office.

- Help Mom figure out why Microsoft Word doesn't start without having to go to her house (even though Mom would like to see you more often).

- Control a headless (monitor-less) machine such as a media center or file server in another room in the house from the laptop on the couch.

VNC requires two components for a successful connection: the server on your home computer and the viewer on the remote computer. Ready to set them up?

Step 1: Install the VNC Server

There are several free VNC servers for Windows and Mac, so pick the section that you need.

Windows

TightVNC (http://tightvnc.com) is a free Windows VNC server and client software package. TightVNC is a nice choice because it also allows for file transfers and high compression levels for slow connections. Download TightVNC from http://tightvnc.com/download.html and run the installation on your home computer. Start the server and set a password for incoming connections.

If you're running a firewall, it may prompt you about whether to allow the VNC server to run; allow it.

TightVNC can be set to run as a Windows service, which means your Windows usernames and passwords can be used to authenticate on the VNC server connection. If you choose this option, be sure all your Windows passwords are set and strong, and that any password-less guest accounts are disabled.

Mac

Mac OS 10.5 (Leopard) users have a VNC server built into their computer already, but Apple calls it Screen Sharing. To turn on the server in Leopard, in System Preferences, go to the Sharing pane and select Screen Sharing, as shown in Figure 8-15. You can also limit which users can remotely control your Mac and set a screen-sharing password by clicking the Computer Settings button.

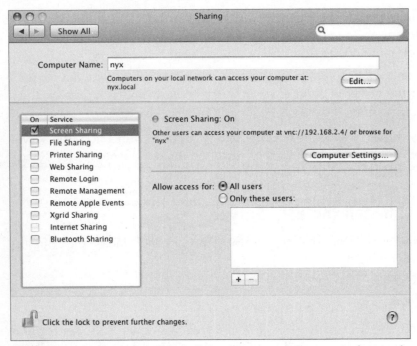

Figure 8-15 Turn on Leopard's built-in VNC server in System Preferences' Sharing pane.

NOTE If you plan to remotely control your Mac running Leopard from a Windows VNC client, be sure to click the Computer Settings button and set a password for VNC viewers. Otherwise, you will run into a security error on non-Leopard viewers.

Mac users may also try the free Vine Server (http://www.redstonesoftware .com/products/vine/server/vineosx/). Download, install, set up a password, and start the server.

About the Server

If your VNC server is connected directly to the Internet, it is now listening for Internet requests on port 5900, VNC's default port (which is also configurable). Visit WhatIsMyIP (http://whatismyip.com) from your home computer to determine its IP address, and write it down.

If your home computer is behind a home network router with a firewall, remote computers cannot connect. You must open a port on your router's firewall and forward requests to your computer. Consult your router's manual for more information on how to do that, or check out the article "How to access a home server behind a router/firewall" at http://lifehacker-book.com/links/portforward.

Step 2: Install the VNC Client

On the remote Windows computer, also download and install TightVNC (http://tightvnc.com), but this time, start the viewer instead of the server. If you're on a Mac, download the free Chicken of the VNC (http://sourceforge.net/projects/cotvnc) Mac viewer to connect to your home PC. Enter your home computer's IP address and password to connect.

> **NOTE** Alternatively, you can enter your home computer's domain name. Then, when connecting using the VNC viewer, you can enter a URL like pennyscomputer.dyndns.org **instead of an IP address.**

When connected, you're virtually sitting at your home desktop from anywhere in the world.

More VNC Considerations

A few extra VNC tips to consider:

- VNC is not a secure protocol — connection information is sent over the network "in the clear," which means someone listening on the network can see your transmissions. Also, you may not be able to make the connection if the server computer is behind a firewall you don't control (such as at the office). If you set up VNC to work across a virtual private network, however, the connection will be encrypted and can bypass any restrictive firewalls. See Hack 73 for how to set up Hamachi, or refer to http://lifehackerbook.com/links/vncvpn for detailed instructions on pairing Hamachi and VNC.

- For slower network connections, set the compression to Best. The window image quality will be lower, but the connection response will be snappier.

- Bring a VNC viewer with you on a USB memory stick so that you don't have to download and install it on every computer you want to use to connect to your server.

- Avoid having to install a server on Mom's computer; email her the 166K self-extracting SingleClick UltraVNC server, available at `http://www.uvnc.com/addons/singleclick.html`, for your next tech-support phone session.

Hack 76: Give Your Home Computer a Web Address

Level. . . . . . . **Advanced**
Platform. . . . **All**
Cost. . . . . **Free**

Accessing your home computer from the Internet is a lot easier if a memorable, permanent web address such as `yourname.com` points to it.

Depending on how your Internet service provider works, your home computer's IP address may change over time, which means you need to keep track of the current one to reach your home computer. To avoid that, you can get a permanent web address that is made up of words (not numbers, as the IP address is) and automatically resolves to a dynamic IP. This way, addressing your home computer is much simpler.

Why would you want to assign a domain name to your home web server? Maybe you want to start a blog that you're going to host at home instead of buying a web-hosting plan and you want the URL to be unforgettable. Maybe you want to set up a personal home page at `yourname.com` for business purposes or so that folks can easily find your web site. Or maybe your home computer's IP address changes and you don't want to have to worry about keeping track to access your server.

NOTE This tutorial assumes that you already have a web or VNC server running at home. If you don't, check out the preceding two hacks for getting one set up.

A dynamic DNS service, such as DynDNS (http://dyndns.com), is a constantly updated database of IP addresses and domain names. For free, you can get one of the available DynDNS domain names plus a custom subdomain (such as lifehacker.getmyip.net); or, for a small fee, you can register your own domain (such as joesmith.com) and set it to resolve to your home-computer web server with DynDNS.

WARNING Some corporate and university networks and ISPs don't allow computers that are outside the network to access computers with internal IP addresses. To test whether your home computer's IP address is accessible from the outside, visit Network Tools (http://network-tools .com) from your home computer and choose the Ping option. If the ping is successful (meaning it doesn't time out), your computer is accessible from the outside.

Let's get started.

Step 1: Set Up Your DynDNS Account

From your home computer, register for a free account at DynDNS (http://dyndns.com). Agree to the site's terms and use a legitimate email address to complete registration. (Once in a while, DynDNS will send an email asking you to confirm that you want to continue maintaining your computer's IP record, so to continue your service, make sure you use an address you check regularly.)

Log into your new account. Go to the My Services area and under My Hosts, click Add Host Services. There, click Add Dynamic DNS Host. DynDNS will autofill your current IP address. Enter a custom subdomain (such as your name) and choose from a list of domains. The result can be anything from lifehacker.dyndns.org or john.is-a-geek.com to gtrapani.homeip.net. In Figure 8-16, I've typed in the custom subdomain "gtrapani" and chosen homeip.net from the drop-down list.

Step 2: Set up Your Computer to Update DynDNS

Now that your computer is registered with DynDNS, each time its IP address changes, it will let DynDNS know. You can have this updating done either with free updater client software or through your router.

If your computer is connected directly to the Internet, download the DynDNS updater client for Mac or Windows, available at https:// dyndns.com/support/clients. Install and enter your DynDNS information so that your computer can send its current IP address to the DynDNS database when it changes.

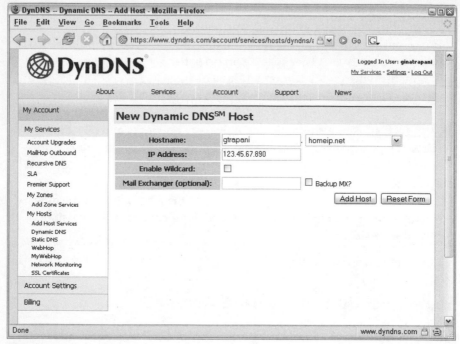

Figure 8-16 Configure your dynamic DNS host.

If you are behind a router, you're in luck: most modern routers support dynamic DNS services. Consult your router's manual to find out how to set the dynamic DNS service provider (in this case, DynDNS.com), the host name (whatever you chose at DynDNS.com), and your DynDNS.com username and password.

Step 3: Give Your New Domain a Spin

Enter your new, full domain name (in this example, mine is `http://gtrapani.homeip.net`) in your web browser's address bar, and your home web server's home page should appear. From here you can publicize or bookmark your server's new domain name no matter how often your IP address changes.

DynDNS Options

DynDNS has a couple of options to consider.

- **Enable wildcard:** Allows you to set up sub-subdomains. For example, `blog.johnsmith.mine.nu` can resolve to a weblog, whereas `jukebox.johnsmith.mine.nu` can resolve to a music directory. Virtual hosts must be configured for your Apache web server to display the right site when addressed by different subdomains. Get more information on setting up virtual hosts at `http://lifehackerbook.com/ch7/`.

- **Custom domain name:** Upgrade your account to use a custom domain name like `yourname.com`. Assign a domain name you've purchased to your home server for about 25 bucks a year (DynDNS's fee) plus the cost of the domain registration. See more info on Custom DNS at `https://dyndns.com/services/dns/custom`.

Hack 77: Optimize Your Laptop

Level. . . . . . . **Easy**
Platforms. . . **All**
Cost. . . . . **Free**

You just got a shiny new laptop to use on your commute to the office, on business trips and vacations, and at the coffee shop down the street. You'll be a productivity powerhouse! Just hold your horses for a minute there, bucko.

More folks than ever are hitting the pavement with a notebook computer under one arm, but any road warrior can tell you that life with a lappie isn't always easy. This hack provides some hints and tips for extending the life of your laptop and easing the pain of the never-ending outlet and hotspot hunt.

Extend Your Battery Life

Laptop productivity on the cold, cruel, and often electrical outlet-less road depends entirely on how much juice your battery's got left. Here are a few ways to increase the life of your laptop battery when there's no outlet in sight:

- **Dim the display.** The screen draws the most power from your laptop's battery. Dim it to the lowest setting you can stand to preserve battery life.

- **Turn off unnecessary processes.** If you don't need them, disable Wi-Fi and Bluetooth detection, spyware and virus scanning, and desktop search file indexing (such as Google Desktop) while you're on battery power. Eject any CD, DVD, or other unneeded disk to prevent your computer from spinning or scanning it for no reason.

▪ **Enable the power-saver profile.** Use the Microsoft Windows Max Battery Power Option (in Control Panel) and Mac OS X Energy Saver (in System Preferences), which set your computer to use resources as sparingly as possible when battery life is most important.

▪ **Recalibrate your battery's fuel gauge.** Do a deliberate full discharge of your laptop's lithium-ion battery every 30 charges or so, then recharge to calibrate the battery-life gauge. If it isn't recalibrated, the gauge can read inaccurately and cut off your laptop's operation prematurely because it thinks the battery is depleted when it's not.

Save Your Keyboard and Screen

There are crumbs at the coffee shop, sand at the beach house, and right now your fingers are covered in Doritos dust. Use a protective cover on your keyboard to prevent stray crumbs from getting into the cracks. It will do double duty by also protecting your laptop's screen from scratches caused by the keys when the top is closed. The iSkin (http:// iskin.com) is a thin, rubbery cover that fits Apple laptops (iBooks and MacBooks) and stays on while you type.

Alternatively, you can cut a piece of rubberized shelf liner to fit inside your laptop when you close — sort of like the bologna in a sandwich. Some people also use a thin piece of cloth cut to fit the keyboard.

If your laptop keyboard is already a hideout for crumbs and pet hair, purchase a can of compressed air to blow out any debris stuck between the keys.

Keep It Cool

After an hour or so of usage, a laptop computer can burn one's unprotected thighs and wrists. In fact, the Apple User Guide for the new MacBook Pro model states, "Do not leave the bottom of your MacBook Pro in contact with your lap or any surface of your body for extended periods. Prolonged contact with your body could cause discomfort and potentially a burn."

If laptop heat is a problem, get material that doesn't conduct heat well between your skin and your lappie, such as a lap desk or your laptop sleeve. Long-sleeved shirts with big cuffs help on wrists when the top of your keyboard gets hot to the touch, too.

Additionally, overheating is one of the most common reasons for laptop hardware failure. Be aware of how hot your machine gets.

Set Yourself Up to Work Offline

You have 10 hours to kill on that transatlantic flight without Internet access. Or your favorite coffee shop's wireless network is down. It's not always easy to get online with your laptop, so be prepared to work offline as much as possible.

For example, don't depend entirely on web-based email on your laptop. The Mozilla Thunderbird email client (`http://mozilla.org/products/thunderbird`) is must-have software that enables you to download your email locally and work with it offline. Thunderbird 2 also has excellent SMTP server management, so you can quickly switch which server you send your mail through when you *do* get online. Using a NetZero dial-up account that requires you use `smtp.netzero.net`? Need to use the secure SMTP server at the office for work mail? No problem. You can set up multiple SMTP servers and associate them with different email accounts with Thunderbird.

Secure Your Data

While you're out and about and on open wireless networks, make sure you've got a secure firewall installed on your laptop and that its settings are extremely restrictive. (See Hack 102, "Firewall Your PC," for more on running a software firewall.)

Also, turn off folder sharing and any local servers you have running (such as a web, FTP, or VNC server) to keep others from peeking in on your data. Make sure your laptop's logins have strong passwords assigned.

Lastly, consider encrypting the data on your disk in case of theft; you can use a utility such as Mac OS X's FileVault to do so.

NOTE Hack 19, "Create a Password-Protected Disk on Your PC," and Hack 100, "Truly Delete Data from Your Hard Drive," provide practical methods for making your documents inaccessible to laptop thieves and snoops.

Carry with Care

Your laptop spends a lot of time swinging over your shoulder, banging around on your back, bumping into the guy next to you on the subway, and sliding around on your car's back seat. Wrapping it up in that spare Linux T-shirt and shoving it into your messenger bag full of gadgets probably isn't a good idea, either. Make sure your laptop is snug as a bug in a rug. Invest in a padded sleeve or bag made to carry laptops that'll protect it if your bag falls over or is accidentally kicked.

Back Up

Portable computers deal with a lot more wear and tear than desktops, which increases the risk of hard-drive failure. Make sure you back up the data on your laptop regularly — and often. Create a lappie docking station at home where you can plug in to recharge the battery and hook up an external drive to back up your data.

Pack Helpful Extras

If you have a CD-R or DVD-R drive in your lappie, keep a few spare blanks or a USB drive for easy backup on the road. A two-prong-to-three-prong electrical-plug adaptor, an extra battery (charged), an Ethernet cable or phone cord, and an extra mouse might all be helpful additions to your portable arsenal.

Find a Hotspot

A few web sites and desktop software applications can help you find wireless hotspots while you're online and off, including the following:

- **JiWire** (http://jiwire.com/search-hotspot-locations.htm). Results include pay-for and free hotspots all over the country. JiWire also offers a downloadable Wi-Fi directory that's accessible when you're offline and looking for a hotspot, available for Windows and Mac OS X at http://jiwire.com/hotspot-locator-frontdoor.htm.

- **ILoveFreeWifi** (http://ilovefreewifi.com). Includes only free wireless hotspots for a select number of cities.

- **NetStumbler** (Windows only, available as a free download at http://www.netstumbler.com/downloads/). View all the wireless networks within range of your computer and find out whether they require a password and how strong the signal is. The main advantage to using NetStumbler instead of the Windows built-in wireless network listing is that NetStumbler displays wireless signals that do not broadcast their name (these signals are *not* included in the Windows default list).

▪ **iStumbler** (Mac only, available as a free download at `http://istumbler.net/`). As does NetStumbler for Windows, iStumbler lists all the wireless networks in range (broadcasting their SSID or not), as well as Bluetooth devices and Bonjour networks.

Hack 78: Back Up Data to Your iPod

Level. . . . . . . **Easy**
Platforms. . . **Windows XP and Vista, Mac OS X (with Apple's iPod music player)**
Cost. . . . . . . **Free**

Your iPod isn't just a music player — it's a giant external hard drive that can store any kind of digital data in addition to music. That makes it a convenient place to back up and store your important files. You can carry around your documents along with several dozen CDs' worth of music on that little white music player by enabling what's called *disk mode*.

Turn Your iPod into a Hard Drive

To access your iPod as you do any other external drive connected to your computer, you have to use iTunes. Here's how:

1. Connect your iPod to your computer and open iTunes.

2. At the bottom of iTunes Preferences pane's iPod tab, select Enable Disk Use (see Figure 8-17).

   If you're an iPod Shuffle owner, you can use a storage allocation slider to set the amount of space you want to use for music and for other files.

3. Your iPod will appear in Windows Explorer or Mac Finder, as shown in Figure 8-18.

Now you can save and read files to your iPod as if it were any other disk drive. When you're finished, be sure to eject the iPod disk before disconnecting it from your computer. (To do so, right-click it in My Computer and choose Eject from the menu; Mac users can simply drag the iPod icon on the Desktop over to the Trash Bin and drop it there.) Then, you can connect the iPod to any other computer with disk mode enabled to access the files on it there, too.

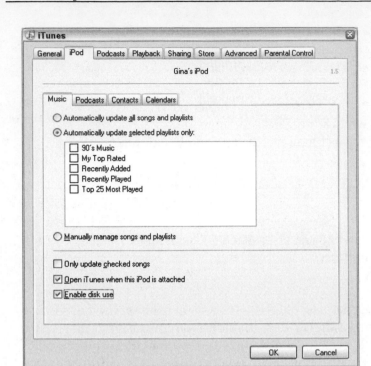

Figure 8-17 Setting the iPod to work as a disk in iTunes.

Figure 8-18 The iPod named Gina's iPod appears as an additional disk in Windows Explorer.

Encrypt Your Data

iPods are a hot commodity that get smaller and more easily lost — and more easily stolen — with each new model. You don't want your data to drive off in that cab without you or make it into the hands of a mugger, so do encrypt the data you store on it.

Mac OS X

Using OS X's built-in Disk Utility, make an encrypted, password-protected disk image of your home directory and then drag and drop it onto your iPod. If it has enough space on it, the iPod can preclude a need to back up to an external hard drive — because it is one. Be sure to exclude your music collection from the disk image; iTunes put that on your iPod once already.

Windows

See Hack 19 for how to password-protect sensitive files you want to store on your iPod.

Take Your Software with You on the iPod

Not only can you back up your data and take important documents with you on the iPod; you can also run software from it. Hack 71 points out several portable software applications that you can also copy and run from an iPod mounted as an external disk drive.

Hack 79: Turn Your Cell Phone into a Modem

Level. . . . . . . **Medium**
Platform. . . . **Windows XP and Vista, Mac OS X (with mobile phone)**
Cost. . . . . **Dependent on your mobile phone plan**

You're stuck with the laptop in the land of no Internet, but you have unlimited minutes or a great data plan on your cell phone. What to do? Plug that phone into your laptop, of course, and get surfing!

   In this hack, you transform your cell phone into a modem that gets you online even when there's not a Wi-Fi hotspot, landline, or Ethernet jack in sight.

What You Need

You will need the following items for this hack:

- **A PC or Mac.**
- **A mobile phone with built-in modem.** Most newer mobile phones can be used as Internet modems; check your model's user guide for more information.
- **A cell phone plan that includes data transfer.**
- **(Optional) A phone-to-computer data cable (if your phone and computer don't both support Bluetooth).**

Configure Your Cell Phone as a Modem

Here's how to get online with your mobile phone:

1. Connect the phone to your laptop using a USB cord or through Bluetooth.

   If your phone didn't come with a cord, check Google Product Search (`http://google.com/products`) or Cellular Factory (`http://cellularfactory.com/data_cable.jsp`) for the right cable, which most likely will set you back between $10 and $40. If your phone is Bluetooth-enabled but your laptop is not, you can purchase a USB Bluetooth adapter for about $15.

2. If necessary, install the phone's modem driver.

   When the phone is connected, Windows knows you just plugged in something new and wants to know what it is, so the Add New Hardware wizard appears, eager to get the question settled. If you're lucky, your phone came with a handy CD that contains your drivers. Alternatively, you can download them from your phone manufacturer's web site. Point the Add New Hardware wizard to the location of the drivers. When the drivers are installed, your cell phone modem will appear in the modems list in Control Panel.

   NOTE When I tried this with a Samsung A920 and a Nokia 6682, Mac OS X recognized the phone as a modem right away, without needing additional drivers.

3. Connect to your ISP through the modem.

   You'll need connection software provided by your carrier. Again, this might be on that CD that came with your phone, or you can download it from your plan's web site (such as Sprint PCS Connection Manager or Nokia PC Suite). When the software is installed, it's probably a matter of pressing the Go or Connect button and you'll be online using your provider's data network.

   If you don't have connection software or you're on a Mac (and the software isn't available for you), simply enter the phone number for your mobile phone's network in the modem's dial-up properties. The Sprint data network can be reached by dialing #777 from a Sprint phone. Check with your provider for your details if you have a data plan. Alternatively, you can dial into an AOL, NetZero, or Earthlink account for regular old 56K dial-up speeds.

If software isn't available, you can set up your connection manually. Here's how:

1. When the mobile is installed as a modem on Windows, choose Start ⇨ Control Panel ⇨ Network Connections.

2. Click the Create A New Connection link in the left panel.

3. In the New Connection wizard, do the following:

   Select Connect To The Internet and click Next.

   Select Set Up My Connection Manually and click Next.

   Select Connect Using A Dial-Up Modem and click Next

   Select your newly installed cell phone modem (see Figure 8-19).

4. Click Next. Then enter your ISP's access number, username, and password. Consult with your cellular provider to obtain these details.

5. Click Finish.

Keep an Eye on the Meter

Some data plans provide connections that don't come near broadband speeds but beat out classic 56K dialup any day — such as the Sprint Power Vision network, which reaches speeds of about 230K.

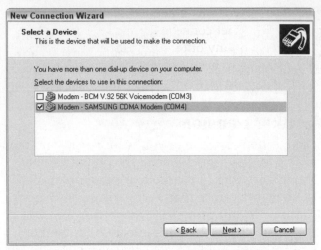

Figure 8-19 Select your cell phone modem in the dial-up connection wizard.

WARNING Check your mobile plan to avoid insane charges for downloading data. If you are paying per megabyte of data transferred, the cost can quickly become exorbitant. Some wireless service providers quote in terms of cents per kilobyte of data, but remember, a seemingly low 2¢ per kilobytes equates to a hefty $20 per megabyte. Spend any amount of time surfing the Internet or downloading large emails with attachments, and in no time you'll have to pay for multiple megabytes of data.

Before you disconnect your home broadband connection in favor of using your cell phone modem all the time, be warned: cell connection speeds will vary based on your location, and will slow you down when sending large attachments or downloading bigger files. For casual surfing and email checking on the road, however, your cell phone can provide all the connectivity you need. (See more ways to optimize your cell connection in Hack 54, "Speed Up Web Pages on a Slow Internet Connection.")

Hack 80: Use Gmail as an Internet Hard Drive

Level. . . . . . . **Easy**
Platform. . . . **Windows XP and Vista, Mac OS X (with Gmail)**
Cost. . . . . **Free**

Google's web-based email service, Gmail (http://gmail.google.com), offers more free storage space for messages and attachments than any other service does (4.6GB as of this writing — and rising). An easy way to make files available from any Internet-connected computer is to simply email them to yourself (at Gmail or any other web-based email service). But a free software application makes keeping your files up in the Gmail "cloud" and accessible from any web browser even easier.

Windows: GMail Drive Extension

The GMail Drive shell extension accesses your Gmail web-based email account as if it were another hard drive on your computer.

Download the GMail Drive shell extension, available at `http://viksoe` `.dk/code/gmail.htm`. Extract the files and run `setup.exe`. The shell extension will add a disk called GMail Drive to your computer (see Figure 8-20).

Figure 8-20 The GMail Drive appears as an additional disk in My Computer.

To access files on the GMail Drive, double-click it. You will get a prompt for your Gmail username and password, as shown in Figure 8-21.

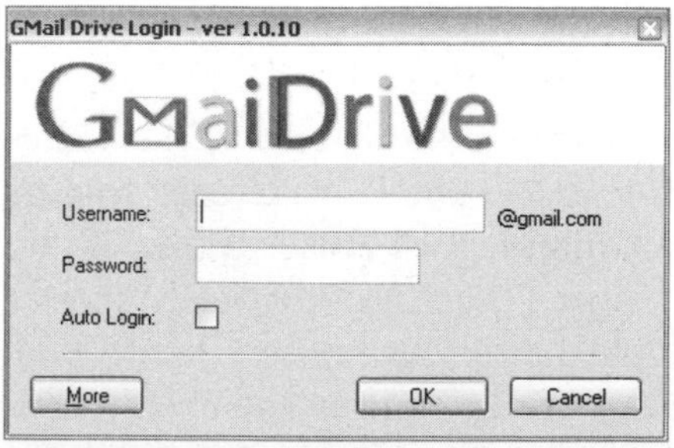

Figure 8-21 GMail Drive login prompt.

After you've logged on to your Gmail account, you can create folders and drag and drop files to the GMail Drive as if it were any other hard drive. The files are whisked away to your Gmail account and appear as attachments to new email messages from yourself in your inbox, as shown in Figure 8-22.

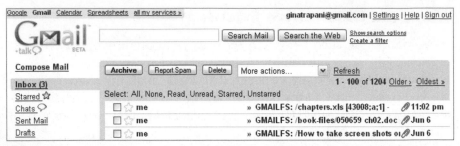

Figure 8-22 GMail Drive shell extension files appear in your Gmail inbox as new messages with attachments.

The GMail Drive extension (and Gmail itself) doesn't support message attachments 10MB in size or greater, so this works well only for photos, Microsoft Office documents, and other small- to medium-sized files. In an attempt to stop email viruses, Gmail also does not allow attachments with a .exe extension, so if you save an executable file to your GMail Drive — say, setup.exe — it appears in your Gmail account as setup .exe_renamed. To use an executable file that's been renamed as such for storage in Gmail, download it and change the name back to its original (by removing the _renamed from the file extension).

TIP Configure a Gmail filter that archives and labels incoming GMail Drive files. To do so, set the search criteria to any messages with GMAILFS: / in the subject line. See Hack 6, "Master Message Search," for more information.

Mac OS X: gDisk

Mac users can find similar functionality in the free software gDisk, available for download at http://gdisk.sourceforge.net. Create folders inside the gDisk interface that map to Gmail labels. For example, if you create a photos label in gDisk, the files stored there automatically appear in the photos.gDisk label in your Gmail inbox. As is the GMail Drive extension, gDisk is slower to copy files, but unlike how the shell extension is accessed in Windows Explorer, it is not integrated into Finder.

For more on using email as data backup, check out Hack 67, "Automatically Email Yourself File Backups."

References

1. Michael Calore, "Livin' la Vida Google: A Month-Long Dive Into Web-Based Apps," Wired News (`http://www.wired.com/software/softwarereviews/news/2007/04/lavidagoogle`).

2. "Lifehacker Faceoff: Zoho Suite vs Google Docs," `http://lifehacker.com/software/lifehacker-faccoff/zoho-suite-vs-google-docs-315256.php`.

Master the Web

Never before have humans had ready access to such a vast repository of information in their households as we do today with the World Wide Web. That storehouse of information (and misinformation) grows by leaps and bounds every day. With the proliferation of publishing tools and capture devices such as blogging software and digital cameras, anyone can publish online, and millions do.

But that kind of information access is useless unless you can hone your searching, filtering, and researching skills. Mastering the use of a web browser, finding what you need quickly, navigating engines and indices, determining a set of trusted sources, and judging the quality and authority of new sources are all skills anyone who uses the Web to his advantage needs. In effect, on the Web you are your own personal research librarian.

Memorizing facts is less important than the capability to look them up quickly. The Web acts as the outboard memory of millions of people. Now more than ever, you can depend on it to have the information you need, whether it's the current population of New York City or a review of that ice-cream maker you're interested in. You just need to know how to fashion a query that will extract those facts from the endless virtual shelves of information.

Additionally, in contrast to books, film, TV, and magazines, the Web is participatory media (or read/write, if you like). You not only consume it; you can just as easily produce it, and that capability becomes ever more key in an age in which web search engines are the overarching directory of topics, people, and places. (In fact, right now, a potential employer or date or long-lost high-school friend may be typing your name into Google. What comes up when she does?)

This chapter's hacks provide tips, tricks, and shortcuts for searching and navigating the Web, customizing your web browser for an optimal experience, and sharing and publishing information about yourself and your area of expertise most effectively.

Your best bet is to read this chapter with a computer that's online nearby, because it's full of web site URLs and services you'll want to try right away. If transcribing web site addresses from the book into your browser's address bar isn't your idea of fun, visit `http://lifehackerbook.com/ch9/` to get a clickable list of links to all the resources mentioned in this chapter's hacks.

Hack 81: Google Like a Pro

Level. . . . . . . **Easy**
Platform. . . . **Web**
Cost. . . . . **Free**

When you search the Web using Google (`http://google.com`), you're likely to get tens of thousands of web page results that contain your search terms. But who has time to go through them all? Instead, make the engine narrow its answers down for you. Google's single, one-line input box conceals a host of functionality that can decrease web search results down to the most relevant pages. Clicking through thousands of links is time-consuming and unnecessary. Get fewer, more relevant search results with Google's advanced search operators.

You have two ways to issue queries with Google's advanced methods:

- Use the Advanced Search form by clicking the small, blue Advanced Search link on the right of the Google search box.

- Use Google's advanced search operators inside the single Google search box.

A page full of input boxes (the Advanced Search form) is the easier way to use Google's advanced operators, but it isn't the most efficient. Google's operators, which usually appear in the form `operator:criteria`, and special characters such as quotation marks, plus and minus signs, and the tilde (~) enable you to easily fine-tune your query from the single search box.

This hack covers only a few of the most useful Google search query formats; refer to Google's Help Center (`http://google.com/intl/en/help/basics.html`) for a Search Guide that details all the options.

Exact Phrase with Quotations

To find web pages that contain an exact phrase, enclose the phrase in quotation marks. This functionality comes in handy when you want to only see pages that contain a specific sequence of words — especially common words.

For example, searching for `the course has been set` may return any number of odd results. The words are all quite common.

A search for `"the course has been set"` returns pages containing that exact phrase. Adding a second phrase, for example

```
"the course has been set" "summon your courage"
```

can zero in on exactly the result you're looking for — in this case, that swashbuckling box office disaster *Cutthroat Island*.

Here are some other examples of effective searching by phrase:

- Computer error messages:
    ```
    "cannot delete file"
    "filename too long"
    ```

- Quotes:
    ```
    "I cannot tell a lie"
    ```

- Song lyrics:
    ```
    "in a pear tree"
    ```

- Names:
    ```
    "John Smith, Ph.D"
    "Anne Rice"
    ```

Include and Exclude Words Using + and –

Force your search results to contain or omit words using + and – signs. This is especially useful for getting more specific about context. Here are two examples:

- Search for information on the Java programming language:

  ```
  java -coffee
  ```

- Find pages that contain the words *computer* and *virus*:

  ```
  computer + virus
  ```

Search Within a Site

Many web sites either don't have a built-in search feature or have one that doesn't work very well. Google can search the contents of a single site with the `site:example.com` operator. Specify an entire domain name or just the suffix. Consider these examples:

- Search the Microsoft web site for information on Windows security:

  ```
  site:microsoft.com windows security
  ```

- Search Lifehacker.com for keyboard shortcuts:

  ```
  site:lifehacker.com keyboard shortcuts
  ```

- Search only Irish web sites that mention the BBC:

  ```
  site:ir BBC
  ```

- Search only government web sites for tax forms:

  ```
  site:gov tax forms
  ```

Search Certain Types of Files

Google doesn't just search web pages; it also indexes PDF files, Microsoft Office documents, and other file types. To search for a specific file type, use the `filetype:ext operator`. Here are a couple of examples:

- Find Excel-based budget templates:

  ```
  filetype:xls checkbook
  ```

- Find PDF search-engine cheat sheets:

  ```
  filetype:pdf search cheat sheet
  ```

Calculations

Google search can also perform mathematical equations and currency and other conversions. Here are some examples:

- Find out how many teaspoons are in a quarter cup:

  `quarter cup in teaspoons`

- Multiply 16,758 with 921:

  `16,758 * 921`

- See how many seconds there are in a year:

  `seconds in a year`

- Convert dollars to yen:

  `$5 in yen`

- Not sure of the international currency? This also works:

  `25 Australian money in Italian money`

- Compare gas prices by doing a double currency and measurement conversion:

  `$2.85 per gallon in British money per liter`

- Convert kb to gigabytes:

  `13233434 kb in gigabytes`

Synonyms

Search for synonyms using the tilde (~) next to keywords. This comes in handy when you are searching for a concept rather than for a specific word or sequence. Here are a few examples:

- `~nutrition ~information muffins` returns exact matches as well as matches on pages that contain muffins food facts and muffins vitamin information.

- `~car` turns up information on trucks and vehicles.

- A search for `~pen` yields pencils, graphite, and sketch.

Combine Criteria and Operators

You can combine all of the preceding techniques into one query, as in these examples:

- Search for information about privacy and Google that appears on sites *not* including google.com:

```
google + privacy -site:google.com
```

- View any contributions by a specific person on a site:

```
site:digitaljournalist.org "P.F. Bentley"
```

- Find pages with the title of a film and the words *movie* and *review*:

```
"Inconvenient truth" + review + movie
```

- Find pages with the word *lifehacker* in them that are not on life-hacker.com:

```
lifehacker -site.lifehacker.com
```

- Find Creative Commons–licensed Excel spreadsheets on Lifehacker.com (see Hack 88, "Find Reusable Media Online," later in this chapter for more information about Creative Commons):

```
site:lifehacker.com filetype:xls "Creative Commons"
```

- Get pages that display directory listings of .wma or .mp3 music files by the Kleptones[1]:

```
-inurl:(htm|html|php) intitle:"index of" +"last modified"
+"parent directory" ↵
+description +size +(wma|mp3) "Kleptones"
```

TIP Print the Google Search Cheat Sheet, available at `http://google .com/intl/en/help/cheatsheet.html` and place it near your desk to help you incorporate advanced search techniques into your everyday web searching. A complete list of Google's Advanced Search operators is available at `http://googleguide.com/advanced_operators.html`.

Hack 82: Subscribe to Web Sites with RSS

Level. . . . . . . **Medium**
Platform. . . . **All**
Cost. . . . . **Free**

Information from web sites such as newspaper sites or weblogs updates frequently throughout the day, week, or month. You could waste time visiting each site you like, looking for new content, much as you'd go to the newsstand to check whether your favorite magazine's newest issue is out yet.

But checking every site you like every day is tedious and unnecessary. As with a magazine subscription that automatically brings each new issue to your door, you can subscribe to web site feeds that push information to your online door.

Web site feeds are special XML files that contain all the latest updates to a web site or to a section of it. Place the address of any number of these feeds into feedreader software (also called a news aggregator) and you can see, all in one place, when new items have appeared on your favorite sites.

This hack explains how to subscribe to feeds and lists the different types of information they can provide you.

How to Subscribe to Web Site Feeds

To start building your web site subscription list, you first need a feedreader, either in the form of desktop software or a web-based application. A feedreader lists the newest content available on the sites you choose all in one place. This hack uses Google Reader (http://google .com/reader) — an excellent, web-based feedreader — as an example. (See the following "Other Popular Feedreaders" section for other options.)

If you use Gmail or Google Calendar, your existing Google account information will work for Google Reader. After you've signed into Google Reader (or set up your desktop or other web-based feedreader), you're ready to build your subscription list.

To subscribe to *The New York Times* Sunday Book Review, for example, go to its site (http://nytimes.com) and click the Add New York Times RSS Feeds link (near the bottom of the right column). Doing so opens an entire page listing all the available feeds (one per section), as shown in Figure 9-1. (You can also go directly to that RSS feeds page: `http://nytimes.com/services/xml/rss/index.html`.)

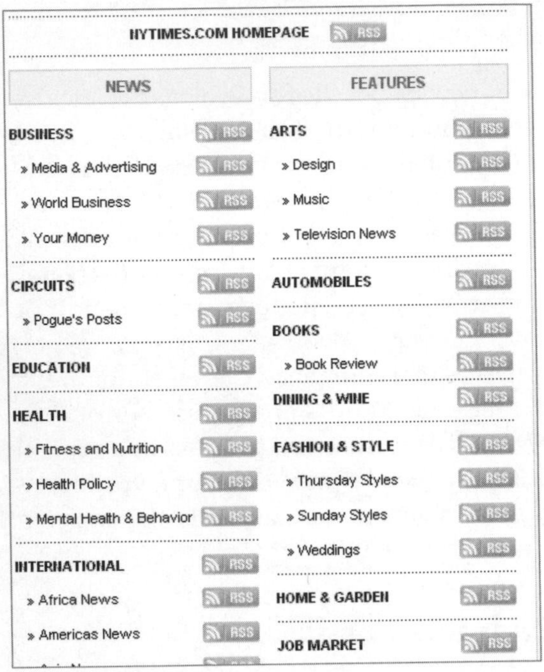

Figure 9-1 *The New York Times* available feeds.

To subscribe to the Book Review, right-click the orange RSS icon and select Copy Link Location. (If you click the feed link as if it were a regular web page, you will view the raw XML, which is meant to be read by a news aggregator, not a human.)

After you've copied the feed location to your Clipboard, switch to Google Reader or your desktop feedreader. Go to the area to add a new feed (in Google Reader, click the Add Subscription link), paste the feed URL into the input box, and then click the Add button. From there, you can place your subscription into a folder if you'd like. Repeat the process for any other feeds you're interested in. Many web sites will display the orange RSS icon somewhere on the page; on others, if a feed is available, the icon will appear on the far right of your browser's address bar, as shown in Figure 9-2. Click it to get the feed URL you need to add to your reader.

Figure 9-2 In Firefox, the feed icon on RSS-enabled web sites appears on the far right of the address bar.

After you're subscribed to one or more web sites, Google Reader's left panel lists the number of unread items in each site subscription displayed next to its title (see Figure 9-3), much like your email inbox displays unread messages.

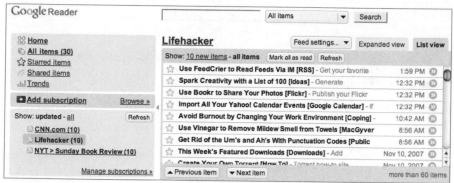

Figure 9-3 Tracking three web site feeds on one page using Google Reader.

Click a subscription to display the latest content from that feed in the right panel.

I use Google Reader to keep up-to-date with more than 200 web sites for research purposes — an impossible feat if I had to visit each one individually.

Other Popular Feedreaders

If you already use a portal such as My Yahoo!, My AOL, or iGoogle to read news, you don't have to set up a separate feedreader. They all can display web site feed updates as well.

Additionally, here are some of the more popular desktop feedreaders:

- Bloglines: Web-based reader; free to use. http://bloglines.com

- NetNewsWire: Mac OS X only; free; `http://apple.com/downloads/macosx/internet_utilities/netnewswire.html`

- Mozilla Thunderbird: Mac/Windows/Linux; free; `http://mozilla.org/products/thunderbird`

- NewsGator: Windows only (runs inside Microsoft Outlook); $29.95; `http://newsgator.com/home.aspx`

- Sharpreader: Windows only; free; `http://sharpreader.net`

Search and Track Dynamic Information with Feeds

Web site feeds don't just contain headlines from news and blogs. Some feeds can track ever-changing information such as weather, library books, your Netflix queue, and more. Some dynamic feeds you may want to subscribe to include the following:

- Weather: http://www.accuweather.com/rss-center.asp

- Craigslist listings: `http://craigslist.com`

- Library book availability: `http://libraryelf.com`

- Sports scores and news: `http://sports.espn.go.com/espn/rss/index`

- Tides: `http://tides.info`

- Deals: `http://dealcatcher.com`

- Horoscopes: `http://dailyhoroscopes.com`

- Vehicle traffic updates: `http://developer.yahoo.com/traffic/rss/V1/index.html`

- News keyword searches: `http://news.search.yahoo.com`

You can also subscribe to feeds for search-term results — for example, all the new web pages in Google search results where your name, company, or product appears. To set up more than 22 search result feeds for terms you enter, visit the MonitorThis web site at `http://alp-uckan.net/free/monitorthis`. For more details on setting up "ego feeds," see `http://lifehackerbook.com/links/egofeed`.

Hack 83: Add Engines to Your Browser's Search Box

Level. . . . . . . Beginner
Platform. . . . All (Firefox/Internet Explorer 7)
Cost. . . . . Free

One of the most convenient features of modern web browsers such as Firefox and Internet Explorer 7 is the built-in search box in the upper-right corner of the window, as shown in Figure 9-4.

Figure 9-4 In Firefox, you can search Google directly from the search box on the right of the location bar.

In Hack 45, you learned how to search the Web in three keystrokes using this search box. By default, Firefox now comes with Google, Yahoo!, Amazon, eBay, Answers.com, and Creative Commons installed. But you can add several more useful engines for quick results without visiting individual pages first to run your search.

Adding Search Plugins

The easiest way to install a new search plugin is to click a link to install it from the various sites that offer it. Firefox users can pick and choose from a large list of search destinations, from BBC News and ESPN to Lonely Planet and the Merriam-Webster Dictionary at `https://addons .mozilla.org/en-US/firefox/browse/type:4`. Internet Explorer 7 users should visit `http://microsoft.com/windows/ie/searchguide/en-en/ default.mspx`.

In addition to those resources, you can use the list I've compiled of eight click-to-install engines for both Firefox and Internet Explorer, located at `http://lifehackerbook.com/links/searchplugins`. Click any of the links on that page, using Internet Explorer 7 or Firefox, to add each engine in your browser's search box.

NOTE Only Firefox and Internet Explorer 7 (not Internet Explorer 6) can install engines using these links.

After you click, you get a confirmation box, shown in Figure 9-5.

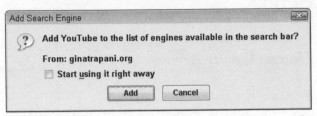

Figure 9-5 Click a search plugin and click Add to install it.

Click the Add button and you're on your way. Now, on to the list of additional plugins you can install:

- Google by keyboard: Search Google and navigate results using Gmail-like keyboard shortcuts. Use J and K to move up and down the results list; press Enter to open a selected link.

- GCal (Firefox only): Search your Google Calendar's events. (You must be logged into your Google account to run this search.)

- Gmail: Search your Gmail for messages. (You must be logged into your Gmail account to run this search.)

- Google Maps: Map a location using Google Maps.

- Wikipedia: Search the English Wikipedia.

- YouTube: Search YouTube for videos.

- EveryStockPhoto.com: EveryStockPhoto.com searches stock and Creative Commons–licensed images from Flickr, stock.xchng, and other free image sources.

To find and install more search engines for Firefox — such as BitTorrent searches, IMDb (Internet Movie Database), and word lookups such as Thesaurus.com and Dictionary.com — check out the Mycroft project at `http://mycroft.mozdev.org/dlstats.html`.

Search-Box Basics

To edit your existing plugin list, click the search-box drop-down arrow and select Manage Search Engines, as shown in Figure 9-6.

In the Manage Search Engine List, you can edit and reorder your engines, as shown in Figure 9-7.

Figure 9-6 In Firefox, edit your search-engine plugin list through Manage Search Engines.

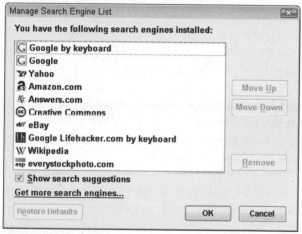

Figure 9-7 Add, delete, and reorder the available search-engine plugins.

Get to the Search Box by Keyboard

You don't need your mouse to use the search box, either. Hack 45 details how to run a search using keyboard shortcuts in Firefox. If you're using Internet Explorer 7, you can do the following:

- Send the cursor into the search box using Ctrl+E.
- Navigate up and down the engine list using Ctrl+Up Arrow and Ctrl+Down Arrow.

Hack 84: Quick Search from the URL Bar

Level. . . . . . . **Medium**
Platform. . . . **All (Firefox)**
Cost. . . . . **Free**

Hack 83 describes how to add engines to your browser's built-in search box, but that's not the only quick method of searching the Web. Another keyboard-driven way to search web sites is what Firefox calls Quick Searches — customizable, keyword-based searches from the Firefox address bar.

If you're a Firefox user who eschews the mouse where possible, give a Quick Search a try. In Firefox (`http://mozilla.org/firefox`), key up to the location bar (Windows: Alt+D; Mac: Cmd+L), type `dict eschew`, and press Enter. You're automatically transported to the definition of eschew ("to avoid, shun"). That's a Quick Search in action.

Firefox comes with the `dict` search preinstalled, along with the predictable `google` keyword search, but you can set up any number of Quick Searches. This hack includes 15 useful Firefox Quick Searches of dependable search engines, all ready to run from your keyboard.

> **NOTE** The Firefox search box can also contain any number of engines, and to use them you must key up and down through the list. However, the Quick Search interface is more like using a command line instead of a drop-down list. As always, it's a matter of preference.

To set up a Quick Search, use Firefox to go to any search engine page with an input box (the Flickr photo search page at `http://flickr.com` is used in this example). Right-click inside the search input box and choose Add A Keyword For This Search, as shown in Figure 9-8.

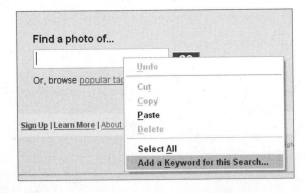

Figure 9-8 Right-click in the search box and select Add A Keyword For This Search.

The Add Bookmark dialog box opens. Enter a title for the search and a keyword you'll use to execute it, as shown in Figure 9-9.

Figure 9-9 Assign a title and, most important, a keyword to your Quick Search.

Press OK. In Firefox, press the Ctlr+L key combination to move your cursor to the address bar. Then type `flickr puppies` to search Flickr photos for — you guessed it — puppies.

Now you can go through and assign keywords to each search engine you use on a regular basis, or you can download the Lifehacker Bookmark set discussed in the next section.

Download the Bookmark Set

My favorite Firefox Quick Searches are available for download. The file includes 15 keywords I use on a daily basis.

Here's how to get them installed:

1. Using Firefox, go to the Quick Search bookmarks file at `http://lifehackerbook.com/ch9/quicksearch.html`.

2. Choose File ➪ Save As and save the file somewhere on your computer.

3. Choose Bookmark ➪ Manage Bookmarks.

4. From the Bookmarks Manager File menu, choose Import ➪ From File. Browse to and open the `quicksearch.html` file you just saved.

Now you have a Lifehacker Quick Searches folder in your Bookmarks, which includes all sorts of keyword searches, described in the following section.

Lifehacker Quick Searches

Here's the full list of Quick Searches included in the Lifehacker file:

QUICK SEARCH	TYPE THIS	DESCRIPTION
Acronym Finder	`acronym <acronym>`	Finds an acronym for your word.
Amazon.com	`amazon <product name>`	Looks up an item on Amazon.com.
Dictionary.com	`dict <word>`	Finds the definition of your word.
EBay	`ebay <item>`	Finds the item you want on eBay.
Flickr	`flickr <search term>`	Finds all the tags, titles, and descriptions of images at Flickr that match your search term.
Google Product Search	`Google Product Search <product name>`	Looks up your product on the shopping search engine Google Product Search.
Google Maps	`Map <address>`	Produces a Google map of a street address or location.
Google Image	`image <search term>`	Finds images that fit your search term.
Lifehacker	`lh <search term>`	Searches the Lifehacker site for information.
Technorati	`technorati <search term>`	Finds weblogs that are posting about your search term.
Thesaurus	`thes <word>`	Finds synonyms for your word.
Urban Dictionary	`slang <expression>`	Defines your slang expression.
Wikipedia	`wikiped <person|place|thing>`	Looks up your search item in the collaboratively edited encyclopedia Wikipedia.

QUICK SEARCH	TYPE THIS	DESCRIPTION
Yahoo! Creative Commons	`cc <word>`	Finds Creative Commons–licensed items available for reuse.
Yahoo! Local	`local <business>`	Finds a local business listing.*

*This bookmark must be edited to work in your area. Replace 92037 in the URL with your ZIP Code.

Customize your Quick Searches using the Bookmarks manager (choose Bookmarks ➪ Manage Bookmarks). Browse to the Lifehacker Quick Searches subfolder and choose Properties for any bookmark. Here you can change a keyword shortcut or edit a URL. (Remember to edit the Yahoo! Local Search URL to include your ZIP Code.)

Hack 85: Extend Your Web Browser

Level. . . . . . . **Medium**
Platform. . . . **All (Firefox)**
Cost. . . . . **Free**

The best feature of the popular Firefox web browser is its openness: the browser was built so that anyone can write a feature-adding extension for it. As a result, developers all over the world have made thousands of plug ins available to enhance and streamline the way you use your browser.

Block banner ads, synchronize your bookmarks across several computers, track exactly how much time you spend on the Web, and back up files to your Gmail account with time-saving and feature-enhancing Firefox add-ons. You've already seen some of them in action in earlier hacks.

How to Install a Firefox Extension

In this example you install the excellent Foxmarks Firefox extension, which saves your bookmarks online and synchronizes them with all the computers you use. Here's what to do:

1. Using Firefox, click the Install Now button on the Foxmarks extension home page at `https://addons.mozilla.org/en-US/firefox/addon/2410`, and then from the dialog box, click the Install button.

NOTE If you're installing an extension from anywhere except Firefox's official add-ons site, Firefox may display a message across the top of the page that reads, "To protect your computer, Firefox prevented this site from installing software on your computer." To install extensions hosted on nonofficial Mozilla sites, click the Options button and then click the Allow button for the site address. Keep in mind, however, that Firefox extensions from unverified sites can include malware. Mozilla Add-ons verifies and tests all the extensions it hosts before publishing them.

2. Restart Firefox to complete the installation and enable the new extension.

When Firefox starts up again, Foxmarks' setup wizard launches automatically to start saving and syncing your bookmarks. But not all extensions work the same way. When your new extension is installed, it may not be obvious what it does or how it works. If you don't see changes to Firefox's buttons, toolbars, or menus, choose Tools ⇨ Extensions. From your list of installed extensions, you can right-click one and choose Visit Homepage to read the extension's instructions and, often, view screenshots of it in action. The Options menu item usually lets you configure the extension as well.

NOTE As with all good software, Firefox is a work in progress, so new versions of it are constantly being released, which means extensions have to keep up. At the time of this writing, Firefox 3.0 is slated for release in the near future, and it incorporates the functionality of many extensions by default. If you upgrade Firefox soon after the new release comes out, chances are that some of your extensions will be disabled because they haven't yet been updated for the new version. Go to the Add-ons dialog box (choose Tools ⇨ Add-ons) to update your extension versions (press the Find Updates button).

Recommended Firefox Extensions

New versions of Firefox are released every few months, so the types and availability of extensions for the version you're running may vary. That said, the following table describes some examples of Firefox-enhancing extensions (for Firefox 2.0).

EXTENSION	DESCRIPTION
Googlepedia `https://addons.mozilla.org/firefox/2517`	Add search results from Wikipedia automatically alongside your Google search results.
Adblock Plus `https://addons.mozilla.org/firefox/1865`	Block banner advertisements from all or certain web sites with Adblock.
Tab Mix Plus `https://addons.mozilla.org/firefox/1122`	Enhance Firefox's tab behavior with an unread tab style and a Close button on each individual tab.
BugMeNot `http://roachfiend.com/archives/2005/02/07/bugmenot`	Route around free web site registration and sign-ins with this community database of auto-filled usernames and passwords. (See Hack 53, "Bypass Free Site Registration with BugMeNot.")
DownThemAll! `http://downthemall.net`	Easily download all the files linked to a web page, pause and resume large file downloads, and increase speed and download performance. (See the following hack, "Supercharge Your Firefox Downloads with DownThemAll!")
TinyUrl Creator `https://addons.mozilla.org/firefox/126`	Convert long web site addresses into short, more email-friendly URLs. (See Hack 3, "Craft Effective Messages.")
Auto Copy `https://addons.mozilla.org/firefox/383`	Bypass Ctrl+C and just select text on a web page to automatically add it to the Clipboard. (Great for researchers, bloggers, and writers who quote web pages often.)

(continued)

(continued)

EXTENSION	DESCRIPTION
Gspace `http://getgspace.com/`	Embeds an FTP-like interface inside Firefox to your Gmail email account for easy backup and file saving within Gmail.
Greasemonkey `http://greasespot.net`	Customize web pages to your liking with JavaScript that can change the look and functionality of web sites.

Foxmarks
`https://addons.mozilla.org/`
`firefox/2410`
	Synchronize your Firefox bookmarks across several computers.

TimeTracker
`https://addons.mozilla.org/`
`firefox/1887`
	Track how much time you spend browsing the Web with this Firefox-based timer that runs only while Firefox is in focus.

Be sure to visit the Firefox extension home base at `https://addons` `.mozilla.org` to find the most up-to-date extension recommendations and top downloads.

Hack 86: Supercharge Your Firefox Downloads with DownThemAll!

Level. . . . . . . **Advanced**
Platform. . . . **All (with Firefox)**
Cost. . . . . **Free**

When it comes to heavy-duty download jobs, Firefox's default downloads manager just doesn't cut the mustard. If you need closer control of multiple, large downloads, you need the DownThemAll! Firefox extension. This extra-strength download manager can speed up, queue for later, and download sets of files in batches from the Web based on patterns you define in one click.

In this hack, you'll learn how to finely control and prioritize downloads with DownThemAll, as well as batch-save all the MP3s from a web page in one shot. Before you get started, install DownThemAll for free using Firefox at `https://addons.mozilla.org/en-US/firefox/addon/201`.

NOTE Hack 85 covers how to install a Firefox extension such as DownThemAll.

Download Individual Files with DownThemAll!

In DownThemAll's most basic usage, download a particular file from a web page by right-clicking it and choosing DownThemAll (dTa) from the context menu. (Depending on what you've selected — a video, a link to another web page, an image — this item may read Save Link With dTa as well.) Set the destination directory for where dTa should save the files. After you click the Start button, dTa will open a window that displays all your downloads, their transfer progress, and several buttons that can pause, resume, cancel, and reorder the priority of your downloads, as shown in Figure 9-10.

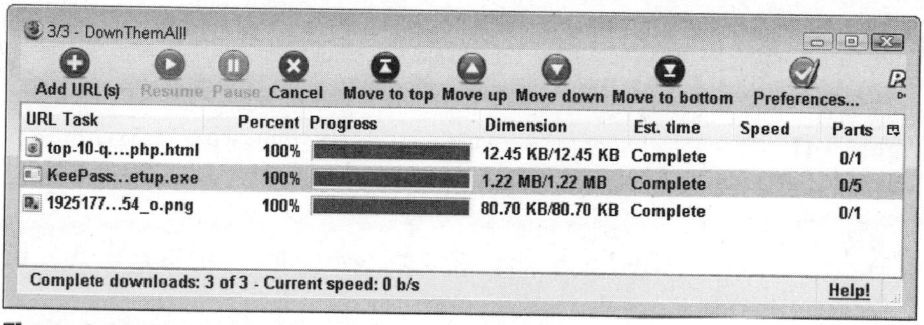
3/3 - DownThemAll!
Add URL(s)
Resume
Pause
Cancel
Move to top
Move up
Move down
Move to bottom
Preferences...
URL Task
Percent
Progress
Dimension
Est. time
Speed
Parts
top-10-q....php.html
100%
12.45 KB/12.45 KB
Complete
0/1
KeePass...etup.exe
100%
1.22 MB/1.22 MB
Complete
0/5
1925177...54_o.png
100%
80.70 KB/80.70 KB
Complete
0/1
Complete downloads: 3 of 3 - Current speed: 0 b/s
Help!

Figure 9-10 Pause, resume, reorder, and cancel downloads in progress with DownThemAll.

Batch-Download Files with Filters

When you have a large set of files to download, it's too tedious to right-click each one to start the transfer. Instead, DownThemAll! can help you select a large set of files and start their transfer quickly and easily based on certain criteria. It does that by listing all the media available on a web page (such as images and video clips) as well as all the files that page links to.

To see these lists, right-click any web page in Firefox with dTa installed and choose DownThemAll to open the selection dialog. Use the Links and Pictures and Embedded tabs at the top to toggle between lists. Then, from a given list, you can manually select the files you want, or automatically select a subset using filters — such as the preset Archives (`.zip`

and .rar files), Video (.mpeg, .avi, .wmv) and Images (.gif, .jpg, .png) filters, as shown in Figure 9-11.

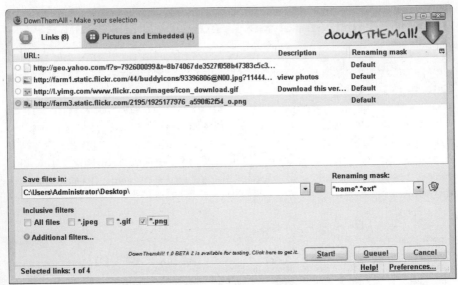

Figure 9-11 Use a preset filter (such as Videos, Images, or file extensions such as
.png) to select files to download in DownThemAll!

When you're satisfied with the file selection, click the Start button to
begin downloading.

Customize a Filter to Download All the MP3s on a Web Page

When you right-click and choose DownThemAll (dTa) from the context
menu on a web page, dTa presents a list of possible downloads from that
page — every single link that exists there, whether it's to another web
page or a piece of media, such as an image, video or MP3. The power in
dTa is the Filters area, where you define a pattern that selects the files you
want to download from the often long and crowded list.

If you were visiting a music site that features MP3 downloads (such as
at http://del.icio.us/tag/system:filetype:mp3), you might just
want to suck down all the music from the page in one click. Here's how
to do so:

1. **Define your filter.** Open DownThemAll's Preferences dialog box
   by right-clicking any web page, choosing DownThemAll from the

context menu, and then clicking the Preferences link at the bottom right of the dialog box. In the Preferences area, go to the Filters tab. There you'll see several predefined file filters, such as Archives (.zip and .rar files) and Videos (.mpeg, .avi, .wmv). The Extensions column contains a regular expression that defines the file filter. Click the Add New Filter button to add one for MP3 files. Set the caption to *.mp3, check the Reg. Ex. box, and set the Filtered Extensions to /\/[^\/\?]+\.mp3$/, as shown in Figure 9-12. Click the OK button to save your new filter.

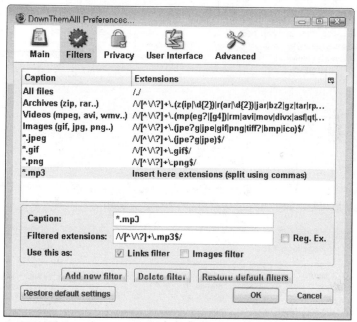

Figure 9-12 Configure a filter to automatically select all the .mp3 files linked on a web page.

2. **Select all the MP3s with your filter.** Then, on the page that links to music files, such as http://del.icio.us/tag/system:filetype:mp3 or your favorite MP3 blog, right-click and choose DownThemAll. Click the MP3 filter check box to select only the music files linked on the page for download — just 10 out of 90, as shown in Figure 9-13. Be sure to select the destination directory on your hard drive as well in the Save Files In: area.

3. **Custom-rename files.** Another useful dTa feature is the capability to set the downloaded filenames using different variables, such as date and time and order number. In the Renaming Mask drop-

down list, choose the pattern the downloaded filenames should use. Click the little paper-clip note button to see the Renaming Tags reference table, as shown in Figure 9-14.

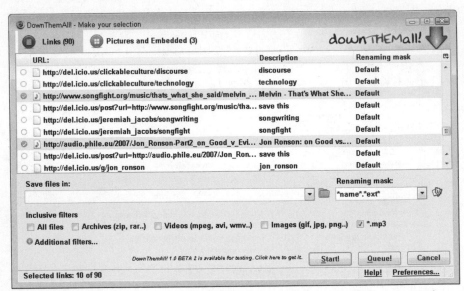

Figure 9-13 Select the *.mp3 filter that you created to automatically select only the MP3 files linked on the current web page for download.

Renaming Tags

Tag	Description	Tag	Description
name	File name	*refer*	Referrer URL
ext	Extension	*hh*	Hours
url	Base URL	*mm*	Minutes
curl	Full URL	*ss*	Seconds
subdirs	URL subdirectories	*d*	Day
num	Progressive number	*m*	Month
text	Link description	*y*	Year

Figure 9-14 Configure a filter to automatically select all the MP3 files linked on a web page.

4. **Queue or start your download.** From there, click the Start button to begin downloading the tracks from the Web. Alternatively, if you don't want to use the bandwidth now, click the Queue button (a kind of light download bookmarking tool) to set up the files in dTa for downloading later on.

One-Click Access to dTa Settings

When you have a set of dTa preferences set up that you want to reuse — say, if you want to download MP3s from several different pages — you want to use dTaOneClick!, also available on your right-click context menu. From the Help page:

> *dTaOneClick! will start downloading all the links/pictures of the current webpage that will match the filters used in the last dTa! session. Downloads will be saved in the last set destination path and will be renamed using the last set renaming mask.*

As can the command-line program wget, detailed in Hack 66, "Automatically Download Music, Movies, and More," dTa can easily download large sets of files. In contrast to wget, however, you can't schedule regular, recurring downloads with dTa, but most will find DownThemAll!'s graphical interface and Firefox integration a lot easier to deal with than wget's command-line parameters.

Hack 87: Get 10 Useful Bookmarklets

Level....... **Easy**
Platform. .... **All**
Cost........ **Free**

A bookmarklet is a snippet of JavaScript that you can bookmark (or save as a favorite) on your web browser's bookmark toolbar. Bookmarklets can enhance web pages, add special functionality, and make your browsing experience much more efficient by offering one-click access to useful tools.

The following 10 bookmarklets will streamline work in your browser. Access them at http://lifehackerbook.com/links/bookmarklets.

- **Acronym lookup:** LOL, RTFM, YMMV AFAIK! If you stumble upon one of those nutty Internet-speak acronyms online, highlight it, click this bookmarklet, and automatically look it up using the Acronym Finder.

- **Translate text:** What do you do when you stumble across a web page that's definitely saying something you want to know, except it's in a language you don't speak? You translate it, of course. This bookmarklet runs a web page through Google's translation service, which automatically detects the language of the page and translates it to English. (Note: When it comes to translating language, machines never do as clear and correct a job as humans, but automated translations can give you the main idea.)

- **Urban Dictionary lookup:** Similar to the acronym lookup, this bookmarklet looks up selected text on a web page in the Urban Dictionary, the collaboratively edited slang dictionary. Cool beans.

- **Wikipedia lookup:** Highlight text on any web page and perform a Wikipedia search.

- **Alexa site profile:** Find out everything you ever wanted to know about any web site you're currently viewing using Alexa's profile page. View traffic stats and charts, related sites, and inbound links to that site.

- **del.icio.us linkbacks:** See which del.icio.us users bookmarked a web page and what del.icio.us tags they assigned to it with one click.

- **View cookies:** Cookies are small text files that web sites plant on your hard drive to save the state of things, track where you have been on that site, or keep you logged in. Check out all the cookies a site has set for you with this bookmarklet.

- **Toss cookies:** When you see all the cookies a site has set for you, you may want to discard them using this bookmarklet. Warning: many sites may not work the way you expect without the cookies they set, and this bookmarklet dumps all the cookies, not selected ones.

- **TinyURL:** Sometimes web page URLs are just too long to easily remember or type. Sometimes you want to email a web page address and it's so lengthy that it wraps around in the message, rendering it unclickable. That's where TinyURL comes in. Go to any web page with an extralong address and hit up this bookmarklet to create a — well, tiny — URL for emailing, IMing, and sharing without the wrap.

- **View passwords:** You know when you're typing a password into a web page form, and it's displayed as *******, and when you try to log in you're told the password is incorrect? Double-check what you've typed with this bookmarklet, which reveals the contents of a password field. This bookmarklet is secure and client-side, so no worries about revealing your password to evildoers. It's just an easy way to verify that you didn't accidentally hit that pesky Caps Lock key.

NOTE Several of these bookmarklets are from Jesse's Bookmarklets Site
(http://squarefree.com/bookmarklets), **a fabulous index of all sorts
of bookmarklet fun.**

To install a bookmarklet, drag and drop the link that contains the
JavaScript to your browser's Bookmarks toolbar (see Figure 9-15).

Figure 9-15 The Acronym Lookup and Translate Text bookmarklets
on the Firefox Bookmarks toolbar.

If this toolbar is not visible in your web browser, simply enable it. In
Firefox, choose View ⇨ Toolbars and select Bookmarks. In Internet
Explorer, choose View ⇨ Toolbars and select Links.

To save toolbar real estate, create a bookmarklets — or the narrower
bkmrklt — folder and drag and drop your bookmarklets there.

TIP Technology journalist and screencaster Jon Udell published a
**short film that demonstrates how bookmarklets work and how to
install them. It's available at** http://weblog.infoworld.com/
udell/gems/bookmarklet.html.

Hack 88: Find Reusable Media Online

Level. . . . . . . **Easy**
Platform. . . . **Web**
Cost. . . . . **Free**

You're designing a new brochure, PowerPoint presentation, web site, or
flyer and you need the right image to use with it fast. Put your hands in
the air and step away from the cheesy clip art, now. Thanks to organiza-
tions such as Creative Commons, licenses such as the GNU Free Documentation License, and the public domain, there are tons of photos,

songs, movies, and documents freely available for you to download and republish without fear of the copyright police.

What's Reusable Media?

Traditionally photographers, artists, writers, musicians, and other creatives copyright their work to restrict usage by others, and charge fees or royalties to do so. But in recent years, the new "free culture" movement arose on the Web, advocating the benefits of proactively permitting others to republish creative work. A new set of licenses that give explicit permission to reuse and republish media (versus restrict it) was born.

NOTE Lawrence Lessig's Creative Commons–licensed book, *Free Culture*, inspired and fully explores the free-culture movement.

If you're looking for an image to include in your published work — whether it's a movie, brochure, or e-book — you can't use copyrighted material without the permission of the copyright holder. But media licensed for reuse (or that's in the public domain) is now widely available online, there for the taking in your own projects. This hack covers a few places you can find it.

Six Reusable-Media Search Engines and Sources

The following are some of the best reusable-media search engines and sources online:

- **Creative Commons (CC)** search interface (`http://search.creativecommons.org`)

  What you'll find: Video, music, images, and documents

  Creative Commons' tabbed search interface looks up CC-licensed photos from Flickr, any file type on Yahoo! and Google, audio on OWL Music Search and SpinXpress, and videos on Blip.TV in one convenient place. (Before you go republish Creative Commons–licensed work, be sure to check exactly which CC license that perfect photo carries — whether it can be modified, used for commercial purposes, or should include attribution.)

- **Wikimedia** (`http://commons.wikimedia.org/wiki/Main_Page`)

  What you'll find: Video, music, images, documents

User-edited Wikimedia Commons contains more than 700,000 pieces of freely available, modifiable (even for commercial purposes) media that's categorized and tagged by users. Need a photo of the moon for your blog? Type `Category:Moon` into the Wikimedia search box.

- **CCHits** (`http://cchits.ning.com/recent`) and **CCMixter** (`http://ccmixter.org`)

  What you'll find: Music

  Find podcastable, remixable, put-your-iMovie-to-it music at the CCHits and CCMixter listings of Creative Commons–licensed songs.

- **EveryStockPhoto** (`http://everystockphoto.com`)

  What you'll find: Images

  There are dozens of stock photo sites out there, but EveryStock-Photo (ESP) aggregates photos licensed for reuse from several sources. ESP is the first place I turn for images to publish on Lifehacker.com, and rarely am I disappointed with search results there.

- **Google** (`http://google.com`)

  What you'll find: Images, documents

  Although Google has an Advanced Search option to find reusable content (as does Yahoo!), some advanced Google search techniques work as well. For instance, to find Creative Commons–licensed Excel documents with the words *time map* in them, try

  ```
  filetype:xls time map "this work is licensed under a Creative
  Commons"
  ```

  Similarly, to find PDFs licensed under the GNU FDL, try

  ```
  filetype:pdf "published under the GNU Free Documentation
  License"
  ```

  See Hack 81, "Google Like a Pro," for more on advanced search operators.

- **Public Domain Torrents** (`http://www.publicdomaintorrents.com`)

  What you'll find: Video

  This collection of public-domain A and B movies is available for download via BitTorrent. Use it to spice up your indie film with a clip of *Dr. Jekyll and Mr. Hyde* or *Tom and Jerry*.

Hack 89: Get Your Data on a Map

Level. . . . . . . **Easy**
Platform. . . . **Web**
Cost. . . . . **Free**

The launch of Google Maps (http://maps.google.com), the search engine's online geographical mapping application, ushered in a revolution in visualizing location-based data. Not only do Google Maps' built-in features help you find establishments, addresses, and driving directions (as does its predecessor, MapQuest), but Google opened its maps interface to third-party developers for their own use. The result is a host of Google Maps mashups, which plot sets of data onto web-based maps.

These map mashups are an incredible way to see geographical information in a new manner. This hack points you to several of the best mashups that can help you adjust your commute home from work for traffic, decide where to live, help you find a nearby used car for sale, and figure out how far your jog across the bridge this morning really was.

- **GeoWhitePages** (http://geowhitepages.com): Look up an individual person's phone number and address in this maps-based white pages, or see census data for big cities, as shown in Figure 9-16.

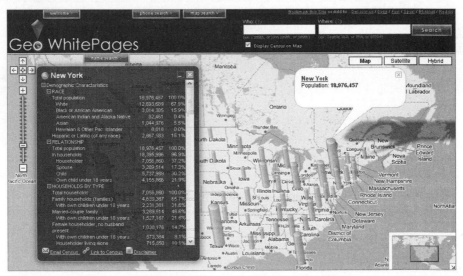

Figure 9-16 The Geo WhitePages maps more than census data.

- **Dude, Where's My Used Car?** (http://dudewheresmyusedcar .com): In this eBay car auction maps mashup, browse used cars on eBay for sale near you.

- **GarbageScout** (http://garbagescout.com): — Dumpster divers in San Francisco, Philadelphia, and New York can find where someone just discarded an old couch on the curb with GarbageScout's constantly updating map of useful trash.

- **Gchart** (http://gchart.com): Look up the local time and area code of any location on the globe.

- **MapMyRun** (http://mapmyrun.com): Plot running routes and calculate the distance and your speed based on time.

- **HomePriceRecords** (http://homepricerecords.com): See how much homes sold for near a specified address or within a certain ZIP Code.

- **Fast food restaurants** (http://fastfoodmaps.com): View all the locations of popular fast-food chains by area.

- **WeatherMole** (http://weathermole.com/WeatherMole/index .html): See the weather for a particular place on the map, as shown in Figure 9-17.

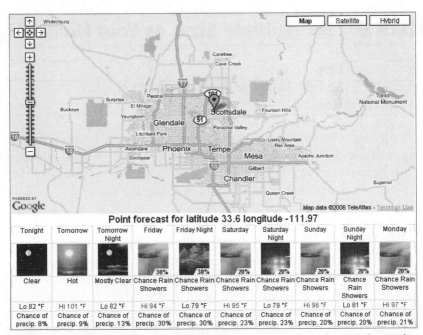

Figure 9-17 The weather for Scottsdale, AZ, displayed on the WeatherMole maps mashup.

- **Universal Package Tracking** (`http://isnoop.net/tracking`):
  View the progress of your DHL, UPS, USPS, or FedEx package as
  it travels to your doorstep. This tracker also generates a feed you
  can subscribe to for updates.

NOTE New maps mashups appear every day. Two good sources to use
for keeping up with the latest and greatest maps development are the
Google Maps Mania weblog (`http://googlemapsmania.blogspot`
`.com`) **and Lifehacker.com's maps tag** (`http://lifehacker.com/`
`software/maps`).

In addition to plotting various sets of data, Google Maps' open API
allows a new breed of user-generated maps to flourish. Several of those
applications enable users — or groups of users — to create annotated
maps with photos and video. For example, a knitting group may publish
a map of all the best yarn stores across the country. Or someone who just
moved to Seattle may want to share a map with photos and videos of
new favorite spots. These things are all possible with this new breed of
web application. See more on creating your own annotated online map in
the Lifehacker.com feature "Map Yourself," `http://lifehacker.com/`
`software/google-maps/geek-to-live-map-yourself-165157.php`.

Hack 90: Set Multiple Sites as Your Home Page

Level. . . . . . . **Easy**
Platform. . . . **All (with Firefox or Internet Explorer 7)**
Cost. . . . . **Free**

The advent of tabbed browsing enables web surfers to work with sets of
pages rather than individual web sites. You can set several web pages as
your home page in tabbed browsers (such as Firefox and Internet
Explorer 7) as well as bookmark and open sets of tabs.

Multitab Homepage

Say, for example, that when you launch your web browser, you look at
three sites first thing: your Google Reader subscriptions, your Gmail
account, and CNN.com. To make your three regular morning reads open
automatically when you launch Firefox or IE7, set them as your home page.

Firefox

To set multiple home pages in Firefox, choose Tools ➾ Options ➾ General, and in the Location(s) field of the Home Page section, enter the addresses of the sites separated by a pipe (|), as shown in Figure 9-18.

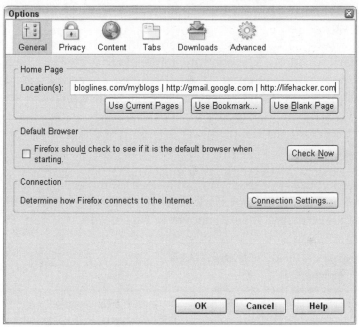

Figure 9-18 Separate multiple URLs with a pipe (|).

Alternatively, you can open all the web pages in tabs and then click the Use Current Pages button, shown in Figure 9-18 below the Location(s) field.

Internet Explorer 7

Internet Explorer 7 also supports multiple tabbed home pages. To set them, choose Tools ➾ Internet Options and, in the General tab, enter the URL of each page on its own line (not separated by a | as in Firefox). Alternatively, you can open the pages in tabs and click the Use Current button.

Bookmark Sets of Tabs

You can also save and open sets of tabs. For example, say you're working on a research project for the next few months. The project involves a company intranet web page, an external client login page, and a weblog that you and your teammates use to keep each other updated. You can save this set of pages and easily launch them with a click when it's time to work on the report.

To bookmark a set of tabs in Firefox, open them and choose Bookmarks ⇨ Bookmark All Tabs. Then enter the name of the folder in which the set should be stored. In Internet Explorer, choose Favorites ⇨ Add Tab Group to Favorites and then enter a folder name in which the set should be stored.

Open a Set of Tabs

After you've saved your set of tabs, you can launch all those pages with one click in Firefox. From the Bookmarks menu, navigate to your set's submenu and choose Open In Tabs, as shown in Figure 9-19.

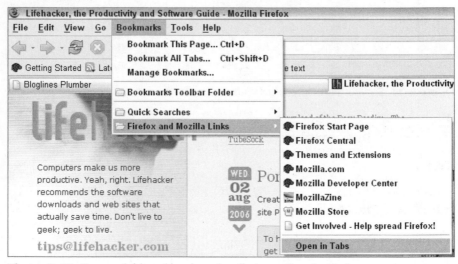

Figure 9-19 Open a folder of bookmarks all at one time in Firefox.

As of this writing, Internet Explorer 7 does not offer the set-of-tabs feature.

Hack 91: Access Unavailable Web Sites via Google

Level. . . . . . . **Easy**
Platform. . . . **Web**
Cost. . . . . **Free**

Web sites go offline. They move, occasionally suffer from temporary unavailability or errors, or become slow to respond because of technical difficulties or a period of high user demand. Some web sites may not be reachable from your particular Internet connection or network. In those cases, when you need the information right away, you need a mirror of that web site's content.

Unless a site explicitly denies it, Google creates a full copy of a site's pages on its servers. When you do a Google search, you'll notice that there are light blue links on the bottom right of each result. One of these — the Cached link — is the doorway to Google's copy of a site.

For example, if Lifehacker.com is down (although that never happens!) but you need the article published there about creating a DVD photo slideshow for Mom's birthday tomorrow, you'd need only to execute a Google search to find that article (`site:lifehacker.com DVD photo slideshow`). The results will look something like Figure 9-20; click on the Cached link to see the article that you need, courtesy of Google.

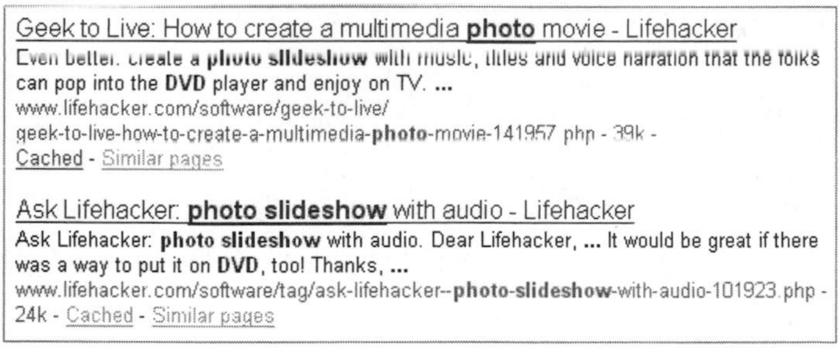

Geek to Live: How to create a multimedia **photo** movie - Lifehacker
Even better, create a **photo slideshow** with music, titles and voice narration that the folks can pop into the **DVD** player and enjoy on TV. ...
www.lifehacker.com/software/geek-to-live/
geek-to-live-how-to-create-a-multimedia-**photo**-movie-141957.php - 39k -
Cached - Similar pages

Ask Lifehacker: **photo slideshow** with audio - Lifehacker
Ask Lifehacker: **photo slideshow** with audio. Dear Lifehacker, ... It would be great if there was a way to put it on **DVD**, too! Thanks, ...
www.lifehacker.com/software/tag/ask-lifehacker--**photo-slideshow**-with-audio-101923.php -
24k - Cached - Similar pages

Figure 9-20 Search results with Cached links to Google's copy of those web pages.

Alternatively, you can simply view Google's copy of a site's front page by using the `cache:` operator. That is, simply search for `cache:lifehacker.com`.

Hack 92: Take Your Browser Configuration with You

Level. . . . . . . **Medium**
Platform. . . . **Windows (with Firefox)**
Cost. . . . . **Free**

Now that you've tricked out your copy of Firefox with extensions, book-marklets, sets of bookmarks, and Quick Searches, the last thing you want to do is have to set it all up again at another computer. If you get a new computer, or want to transport your settings at home to the office, a handy utility called MozBackup can help.

MozBackup packages all the Firefox settings, bookmarks, extensions, and other customizations that you've worked hard to perfect, and makes them available to a fresh, new copy of Firefox.

Here's how to take your Firefox browser configuration with you using MozBackup:

1. Download MozBackup from `http://mozbackup.jasnapaka.com/download.php`.

2. Install the application. Quit Firefox and launch MozBackup.

3. Choose the Mozilla program you're backing up. (MozBackup can also package Thunderbird email settings, contacts, and other configuration information.) Choose the version of Firefox you're running from the list, as shown in Figure 9-21, and click Next.

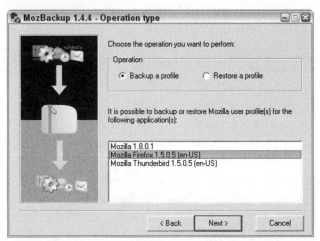

Figure 9-21 Backing up a Firefox profile using MozBackup.

4. Choose which Firefox profile you're backing up. Most likely, you will see only one choice: Default. Select it and click Next.

5. Assign a password to your profile file to add extra security — a useful option for someone who carries files around on a thumb drive (see more on that in Hack 71, "Carry Your Life on a Flash Drive").

6. Choose which of your Firefox settings you'd like to back up, as shown in Figure 9-22.

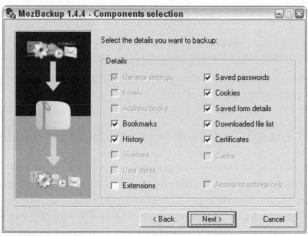

Figure 9-22 You choose what to back up.

WARNING MozBackup's extensions backup does not support all extensions, so use this option with that in mind. To be sure you'll have the information you need to restore your extensions, export any extension data, and if MozBackup is not compatible with an extension of yours, install the extension freshly and import the data.

The backup file will be named something like Firefox 2.0.0.9 (en-US) - 2007-11-14.pcv, including the software name, version, language, and date of the backup. That naming style makes it easy to back up often; the file won't be overwritten, provided that you don't back up the settings more than once each day.

When you want to restore a backed-up profile at your other computer — or simply revert to an earlier configuration — launch MozBackup and select Restore A Profile from the Operation Type choices. Choose your .pcv backup file and restart Firefox.

That sets up Firefox exactly as you backed it up.

TIP Every time you consider installing a new extension — especially one in active development — back up your working copy of Firefox with MozBackup for extra insurance.

Hack 93: Find Out About a Web Site

Level. . . . . . . **Medium**
Platform. . . . **Web**
Cost. . . . . **Free**

When you find information on the Web at a site you've never seen before, it's difficult to assess how trustworthy that source is. Although ultimately the decision is yours, several services provide information about other web sites that can help you decide.

View Site Traffic and Related Information with Alexa

Web site rankings service Alexa (`http://alexa.com`) provides quite a bit of meta information about sites, including related sites, incoming links, traffic rank, screenshots, and ratings. To view information about a site — Wikipedia, in this example — at Alexa, go to `http://alexa.com/data/details/main?q=&url=http://en.wikipedia.org`. To check out another site, just replace the `en.wikipedia.org` portion of that URL with the site you'd like to find out about.

Alexa also offers endlessly interesting web site traffic information and enables you to compare sites' traffic against one another. You can do so through the Alexa site, but an easier-to-use interface is a site called Alexaholic (`http://alexaholic.com`), where you can enter up to five sites and compare their traffic. For example, Figure 9-23 displays an Alexaholic traffic comparison between Dell.com, Apple.com, HP.com, IBM.com, and Sun.com.

NOTE Alexa's traffic graphs' accuracy is hotly debated because the graphs are generated using data by web surfers who have the Alexa toolbar installed, a very small and most likely targeted segment of the Internet-surfing population at large. Take Alexa's traffic numbers with a grain of salt.

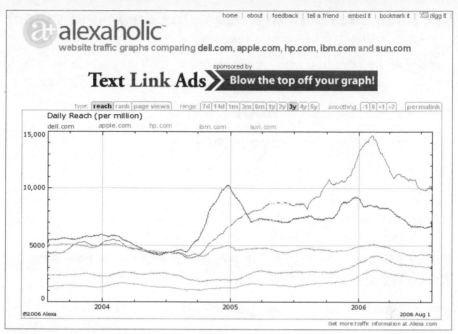

Figure 9-23 Comparing Alexa traffic graphs of five web sites.

See What Others Are Saying about a Site on Technorati

Technorati (http://technorati.com) is a blog search engine that indexes weblog posts across the Internet. You can use it to search for what bloggers are saying about a particular web page. For example, baseball fans can look for a list of blog posts that link to MLB.com on Technorati by using the URL http://technorati.com/search/mlb.com. Substitute the mlb.com bit of that URL with the web site you're researching. (Technorati specializes in weblogs, so it does not list every web site that links to a site.)

View Past Versions of a Site in the Internet Archive

The Internet Archive is a nonprofit project that's been saving snapshots of the Web since 1996. The Internet Archive's Wayback Machine search engine enables you to view a past incarnation of a site by entering its URL in the search box at http://archive.org/web/web.php and clicking the Take Me Back button. Then, choose from a dated list of site versions to view a snapshot from the past.

See What Sites Link to a Site with Google and Yahoo!

Search engine giants Google and Yahoo! provide search operators that display which sites link into a particular site. On Google, use the `link:` operator. Here's a query that displays the sites that link to WSJ.com:

```
link:wsj.com
```

On Yahoo!, use the `linkdomain:` operator:

```
linkdomain:wsj.com.
```

Of course, not everyone is interested in links to *The Wall Street Journal*, but you can easily substitute another URL for `wsj.com`.

Get 25 Meta Lookups for a Web Page with the About This Site Firefox Extension

If you're checking web site backgrounds with the services listed here and you're using the Firefox web browser, download the free About This Site Firefox extension, which I developed, available at `https://addons .mozilla.org/en-US/firefox/addon/3673`. About This Site comes pre-loaded with lookups and other bookmarks that give you more information about a web site, its popularity, the technology running it, and what others are saying about it. After About This Site is installed, right-click any web page and choose About This Site Bookmarks from the menu to do a lookup.

Hack 94: Have a Say in What Google Says About You

Level. . . . . . . **Medium**
Platform. . . . **Web**
Cost. . . . . **Starting at $10 a month**

Someone out there's trying to find information about you right now, whether it's a potential employer, a date, or a long-lost friend. What happens when she Googles you?

More than half the time, she'll get information about someone else with the same name or a web site that you don't control. This hack provides the ins and outs of setting up a nameplate web site that makes you "Googleable" with a web page whose content *you* control.

But I Already Have a Web Site

You may already have a personal blog with photos of your kids on it or a page dedicated to your monstrous LEGO collection that comes up when your name is searched. But is that the first point of contact you want a Google cold-caller to have? Consider your nameplate site your Internet business card, where you publish contact and professional info in a context-insensitive way that'll help Googlers get a bird's-eye view of who you are and what you do — beyond the LEGO collection.

Get Your Domain

Do what you can to register a *yourname*.com (or .org) domain. This will cost a small yearly fee, starting at around $10, depending on the top-level domain you choose (.com, .net, .org, .tv, and so on). There was a time you may have thought one domain to one individual person was egotistical and unnecessary, but that time is over. You will change jobs, move, go freelance, and switch email addresses more in your lifetime than any other past generation did. Personal findability is more important than ever. Investing in a *yourname*.com domain is worth it. If you can't get *yourname*.com or .org, try .net, or even .name.

A NOTE ABOUT NAMES

There are many people in the world who probably have the same exact name as you, and there will be more and more coming online each year. Do what you can to brand yourself uniquely online, either by including your middle name, initial, or using your full first name (James instead of Jim or Deborah instead of Deb). Of course, you want to use the name people will most likely use to search for you, but if you decide to go with a more formal (read: unique) form of your name, be sure to also use it as your email name (james@jamesdoe.com) and on your resume and other paperwork.

You lucky people with unique names? Your domain name is waiting — its availability is payback for all the years of misspellings and mispronunciation.

You don't absolutely have to get *yourname*.com to set up your nameplate site, but it's a better option than a page on a free host with a predetermined URL, as at a university or Geocities, because someday that service might change its address or go away. If you own *yourname*.com, you control it forever and you can point it anywhere you like — blog, static page, whatever — for as long as you pay for it.

> **NOTE** Lifehacker.com readers recommend domain registrars at
> `http://lifehacker.com/software/ask-the-readers/ask-`
> `lifehacker-readers-good-domain-registrar-152014.php.`

Author Your Nameplate

Now's the time to decide what to put on your "web business card." Your profession, location, and email address is a good start, maybe with links to your kids' pictures and your LEGO-collection site. Needless to say, do not give away your physical address, Social Security number, or phone number here — this is general info so that others can identify you (as in, "Oh, yes, John Smith the architect in Santa Cruz"). Figure 9-24 shows an example of a well-done site.

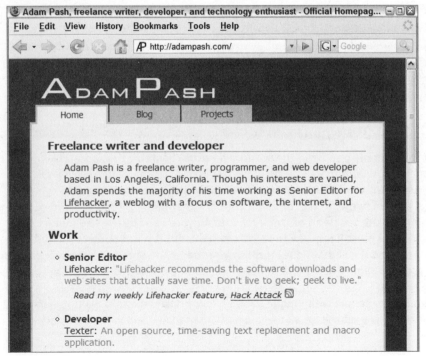

Figure 9-24 A Google-friendly nameplate site includes your name, location, profession, and any other information you want to advertise about yourself.

An HTML tutorial this hack is not, but do make sure that your full name is prominent within a header tag (`<h1>`) at the top of the page, and within the title (`<title>`) of the document. Ensure that all the content of the page you want Google to know about is in text (not in images or Flash). Finally, be sure to mask your email address to keep it from spammers. (Google "email address obfuscator" for web sites that will help you mask your email address from spammers online.)

Find a Web Host

The next thing to do is find a web host, which will entail a monthly fee. If your nameplate site is only one page (and it doesn't have to be more), this cost will be minimal. (See Lifehacker.com readers' recommendation for web hosting providers at `http://lifehacker.com/software/web-publishing/ask-lifehacker-readers-web-hosting-provider-139504.php`.) A nice side benefit of having your own domain and host is having a memorable email address, such as joe@joesmith.com, which you can use as a future-proofed email address (see Hack 7, "Future-Proof Your Email Address," for more). Upload your new nameplate and associate it with your new domain name according to your hosting provider's instructions.

Dedicated do-it-yourselfers with always-on broadband can host their nameplate web site at home, but go this route only if your site is very low on bandwidth (no images), your computer is always on, and you're not concerned about site responsiveness, which will be slow for typical cable and DSL connections, especially if many visitors go to your site at one time.

Link Up Your Name Site

Just because you build it doesn't mean that Google will come. Search engines will find your nameplate site and associate it with your name only if it is linked to your name on other, indexed pages. For example, if you're a member of an online community such as MySpace, MetaFilter, or Slashdot and you want Google to find your nameplate site, just add it to your profile pages in those communities. You can also send a request to the webmaster of other sites that mention you to link your name to your new site.

Hack 95: Capture Web Clippings with Google Notebook

Level. . . . . . . **Medium**
Platform. . . . **All (with Firefox or Internet Explorer)**
Cost. . . . . **Free**

Collecting bookmarks just isn't enough when you're doing serious web research. web pages disappear, or the information you need is just one paragraph halfway down the page, or you want to annotate a page with your own notes for later reference.

Whether you're scouring the Web for information on your next vacation, a research paper, or an important client presentation, you can use Google Notebook (`http://google.com/notebook`) to store and annotate your personal library of web clippings. Here's how:

1. Register for a free Google account and log in to Google Notebook.

2. Google Notebook prompts you to install a notebook add-on for Internet Explorer or an extension for Firefox, depending on your browser. Click the Agree And Download button to do so.

3. Now you're ready to add a web page clip to your Google notebook. Say you're collecting quotes on aviation. From the Amelia Earhart page on the Wikipedia (`http://en.wikipedia.org/wiki/Amelia_earhart`), select an Earhart quote, right-click, and choose Note This (Google Notebook) from the context menu, as shown in Figure 9-25, to save the clipping.

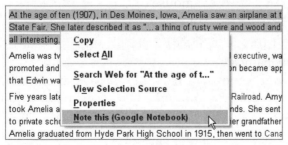

Figure 9-25 Add a snippet of text on a web page to your Google Notebook.

In the bottom right of the current page, a Google Notebook dialog box appears. To add your own notes to the clipping, click the Edit button.

Otherwise, simply click the X to close the dialog box. Your clipping (and the address of its source page) is neatly tucked away in your notebook for later reference.

At the Google Notebook site, you can manage your notebook. There you can create multiple notebooks; edit and rename your current notebook; add section headings and notes; and move, edit, and delete current clippings. For example, you could rename the default My Notebook to Quotes on Aviation and then create a section called Amelia Earhart. Simply click, drag, and drop the Earhart quote to that subsection to organize your clippings.

You can also make your Google Notebook(s) public for others to view. Search your own notebooks or all public notebooks by keyword using Google's world-class search technology as well.

WARNING Although it's convenient to make your Google Notebooks public to share information with others, do be careful when clipping text from private web pages, such as email messages or your company's intranet. You don't want to inadvertently publicize confidential information.

The advantage of using Google Notebook is that your clippings are available online from any computer, and you can use Google's excellent searching capabilities with them.

However, you can also save a personal web-clippings library on your own computer. The Scrapbook extension for Firefox is an excellent alternative to Google Notebook; it's free, and you can download it at `http://amb.vis.ne.jp/mozilla/scrapbook`. Scrapbook has many features that Google Notebook does not, such as the capability to capture whole web pages plus several levels of links, add yellow sticky notes onto a saved web page, insert inline comments on sections of text within a web page that appear when you mouse over them, and save all the pages you have open in tabs. Watch a video demonstration of Scrapbook in action at `http://lifehackerbook.com/links/scrapbook`.

Hack 96: Clear Your Web Browsing Tracks

Level. . . . . . . **Easy**
Platform. . . . **All (with Internet Explorer or Firefox)**
Cost. . . . . **Free**

Your web browser saves a lot of information about where you go and what you do online while you're surfing the Web. The sites you visit, copies of the images and text you view, cookies, and information you type into form fields (such as username and password or your mailing address and credit card number) are all saved to your computer's hard drive and web browser cache for the sake of convenience so that those pages will load faster or your browser can suggest auto-filling the address of a site you visited before.

However, if you're using a shared or public computer, you may not want the web browser to remember your web site logins, history, or even your usernames. Maybe you don't want your spouse to discover you ordered flowers for her at FTD.com when she types *f* into the address bar. Maybe you don't want your roommate to know that you searched for "apartments for rent" on Google last night.

This hack explains how to sweep away your browsing tracks after you're done surfing the Web.

Internet Explorer 6 (Windows XP)

In Internet Explorer 6, select Tools ➪ Internet Options. On the General tab (see Figure 9-26), use the Delete Cookies, Delete Files, and Clear History buttons to wipe out your cookies, temporary files, and browsing history that IE6 saved while you surfed.

Figure 9-26 Delete your saved browsing history and cookies in IE6.

To delete form-field data — such as your shipping address at Amazon or your Yahoo! username and password — that you may have entered while surfing, go to the Content tab in the Internet Options dialog and click the AutoComplete button. Here you can delete saved form information and passwords as well as web-address suggestions based on sites you've already visited, as shown in Figure 9-27.

Figure 9-27 Clear saved AutoComplete information in IE6.

Simply check the items you want to delete, click the Clear Forms and Clear Passwords buttons, and then click Ok.

Internet Explorer 7 (Windows Vista)

Internet Explorer 7 (which comes with Windows Vista) consolidated the interfaces for clearing your browsing tracks into one place. Choose Tools ⇨ Internet Options, and under Browsing History on the General tab, click the Delete button. In the Delete Browsing History dialog box (see Figure 9-28), you can remove all your browsing-session information by clicking the Delete All button at the bottom.

You've erased your web tracks in one fell swoop.

Mozilla Firefox

To delete your browsing tracks in Firefox, choose Tools ⇨ Clear Private Data. Check the items you want to delete — Browsing History, Saved Form Information, Saved Passwords, Download History, Cookies, Cache, and Authenticated Sessions — and click the Clear Private Data Now button.

Figure 9-28 Delete your browsing history in
Internet Explorer 7.

If you regularly use a shared computer with Firefox, configure the Clear
Private Data tool to delete your tracks automatically at the end of every
browsing session. Choose Tools ⇨ Options, and on the Privacy tab, click
the Settings button next to the Clear Private Data tool information. Select
the Clear Private Data When Closing Firefox box in the Settings area.

You can also use the Ctrl+Shift+Del keyboard shortcut (Cmd+Shift+Del
for Mac users) to clear your private data in Firefox without navigating
any menus or dialog boxes.

Reference

1. Search recipe courtesy of The Google Tutor & Advisor article,
   "Voyeur Heaven" (`http://googletutor.com/2005/04/15/`
   `voyeur-heaven`).

CHAPTER 10

Hone Your Computer Survival Skills

Computer disasters happen, but when they do, you don't have to pay the local computer repair shop hundreds of dollars to recover from them. Whether you delete an important file by accident, get infected with a computer virus, face the "blue screen of death," discover your hard drive is dead, or find that your computer has slowed down over time, plenty of free, easy, do-it-yourself fix-it options are available to help you get back to a speedy, secure, and stable system.

In an age of always-on PCs connected to the open Internet at high speed, rogue software tries to install itself on your computer at every turn. Viruses sent via email with inviting subject lines such as "Anna Kournikova pics ;)" and "I love you" threaten home computers as well as entire office networks. Pushy programs put themselves in your computer's startup process and slow down overall performance. Toolbars install themselves in your web browser and redirect you to advertising web sites. Your nine-year-old downloads and installs malicious software that looks a lot like Tetris on your PC. Your toddler gets hold of the mouse and deletes a critical folder in one click.

Your computer is an essential tool in your work and life now more than ever before. The more dependent you become on it, the more wear and tear it suffers, and the more adept you should be at protecting, maintaining, and rescuing it from an unwanted end.

This chapter's hacks include simple methods for protecting your computer from malicious software; getting the most out of the disks that house your important data; reverting your broken PC to a past, working state; freeing much-needed disk space; and restoring accidentally deleted files. Some of the hacks cover ways to proactively insure your computer against possible system failures or infections — such as creating a mirror image of your computer in a known, working state (Hack 107) or firewalling it against unwanted network connections (Hacks 102 and 103.) Others describe reactive fixes for already problematic PCs, such as cleaning a spyware-laden system (Hack 97) or recovering data from an unbootable hard drive (Hack 108.) Still others can help you speed up your system (Hacks 98 and 104) and free space on your hard drive (Hacks 101 and 105). Although this chapter has far more Windows-related than Mac-related hacks, Mac users can find tips in Hacks 100, 103, and 105.

Several utilities are built right into modern operating systems to perform these tasks, but not all of them are the best ones available. These hacks contain information your operating-system vendor won't tell you about, and they use some of the best (and usually free) software tools out there to keep your computer in tip-top shape.

Hack 97: Rescue Your PC from Malware

Level. . . . . . . **Medium**
Platform. . . . **Windows**
Cost. . . . . **Free**

The scourge of personal computing in recent years has been malware: malicious software that installs itself without your consent and undermines your computer's operation for various nefarious purposes, ranging from identity theft to aggressive advertising to common vandalism.

There are several different types of malware, but none of them is desirable. *Spyware* tracks what you do on your computer and sends information about that back to its originating service, which then uses that information to target ads to you, or worse, steal your credit card or identity. *Adware* pops up constant, unwanted advertising on your computer even when you're not browsing the Web, interrupting your work. *Browser hijackers* take over your web browser's site requests and redirect them to unintended web sites, usually advertisements. *Viruses* (a different animal than spyware, but just as destructive) are usually spread via email (but not always) and can also wreak havoc on your PC's files and operation, and replicate by emailing themselves to all the addresses in your contacts list.

Symptoms

Some unexpected behaviors you may see on a malware-infected system include the following:

- Constant advertising pop-ups
- Unfamiliar or unknown programs running in the taskbar (that may or may not log your activity on the computer)
- Unknown web browser toolbars, or plug-ins that cause web pages to redirect to unintended web sites automatically
- An overall system slowdown, or processes running in the background that were not started with your consent

You can remove all these types of malware from your PC and protect it from future infection with a set of free software tools available for download.

Malware-Removal and -Prevention Tools

Anti-spyware software cleans existing spyware, prevents new malware installations, or both. Here are some of the tools:

- **Lavasoft Ad-Aware** (must-have removal tool; free but with paid upgrades available; `www.lavasoft.com/products/ad_aware_free.php`): Ad-Aware SE Personal is the most popular malware-removal tool on the market. It scans and cleans infected computer systems. Pay for versions of Ad-Aware include preventative protection and scheduled spyware scans.
- **Spybot Search and Destroy** (removal; free; `http://spybot.info/en/spybotsd/index.html`): As does Ad-Aware, Spybot Search and Destroy scans your system for existing spyware and removes it.
- **SpywareBlaster** (preventative; free; `http://javacoolsoftware.com/spywareblaster.com`): SpywareBlaster is preventative software that keeps browser hijackers and adware from installing themselves on your system.
- **Windows Defender** (removal and prevention; free with Windows Vista): Windows Defender is Microsoft's built-in spyware detection, removal, and prevention tool. Windows XP users should download Defender for free from `http://microsoft.com/athome/security/spyware/software/default.mspx`. Defender is built into Windows Vista.

Each of these malware tools has two components: the scanning engine and the malicious-software definitions. Because new types of malware are released every day, scanning software such as Ad-Aware must have the latest list of known offending software to clean it up. Every single one of these tools has an Update feature that downloads the latest malware definitions for the engine to use.

How to Clean an Infected System

A system that displays the symptoms listed previously is most likely infected with malware. To clean it, download Ad-Aware and Spybot Search and Destroy (to start). When the cleaners are installed, launch each and select Update to get the latest definitions.

NOTE If your web browser is hijacked, you may be unable to use the infected machine to download the software. Alternatively, download the software on a clean machine and burn it to CD or save it to a USB drive. If no other machine is available, try downloading it using a non-Internet Explorer–based web browser, such as Mozilla Firefox (`http://mozilla .org/firefox`), which is less likely to be hijacked.

Before you scan your computer, unload any spyware processes that are already up and running on your machine. To do so, disconnect your PC from the Internet connection and shut down. Start the computer again and press the F8 key while it is booting up (before you get to the blue-toned Windows welcome screens). Choose to start the computer in Safe Mode, which runs only the bare-essential processes and drives to make a system work.

When the computer is up and running in Safe Mode, open Ad-Aware. Select Scan ⇨ Full System Scan and click the Start button. The scanning process can take a while to run, but when it's finished, it displays a list of possibly malicious objects it found on your system, as shown in Figure 10-1.

Click the Next button to browse the list of detected adware and remove it from your system.

Quit Ad-Aware and launch Spybot Search and Destroy. Choose Check For Problems. This scan might also take some time. Remove anything Spybot finds.

While you're still in Safe Mode, go to Add/Remove Programs in Control Panel and comb through your installed software list. Uninstall anything you don't recognize or need. Any piece of software whose title contains the words *bargain*, *tracker*, *snoop*, or *monitor* should be removed immediately (and their authors roasted for long, painful hours over a hot fire).

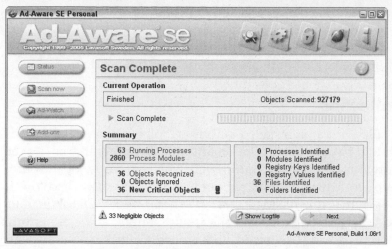

Figure 10-1 Lavasoft Ad-Aware SE scan results.

Then, reestablish your Internet connection and reboot your computer normally (not in Safe Mode).

When you're back in Windows, download Spyware Blaster and then install and run it. Also, visit Windows Update (http://windowsupdate .microsoft.com) to make sure your copy of Windows has all the latest security patches and updates — at least all the critical updates, if not all recommended upgrades. This process can take a long time, depending on the speed and age of your computer, and it may require rebooting your PC (sometimes more than once). When given the option, turn Automatic Updates on, as shown in Figure 10-2.

Figure 10-2 Microsoft Windows Automatic Updates keep your PC's system patched and secure.

If it isn't already on your computer, install and run Microsoft Windows Defender. Fix any problems it finds.

Finally, weed out any unnecessary programs that are starting up with your computer. (The next hack provides more on how to do that.)

Virus Protection

Most PCs ship with a preinstalled antivirus tool, one that usually starts nagging you to pay for a subscription after the three-month trial is over. Pay-for antivirus solutions do a fine job, but less costly, open-source options also work well without a price tag. My favorite, ClamWin, is available as a free download at http://clamwin.com. ClamWin integrates into Windows Explorer and Microsoft Outlook and can perform scheduled virus scans. Download and launch ClamWin to scan your computer for viruses. Select the disks you want to scan (such as your hard drives and removable disk drives) and click the Scan button (see Figure 10-3).

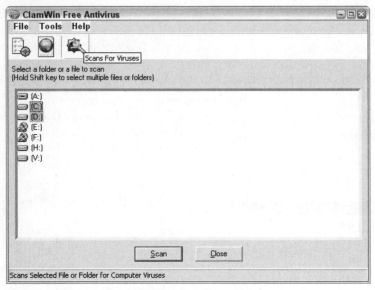

Figure 10-3 The ClamWin Free Antivirus console.

NOTE One disadvantage of the free ClamWin is important to know: in contrast to many popular commercial products, ClamWin does not provide an on-access, real-time file scanner. You must manually scan your files for viruses with it, or schedule a scan to run on a regular basis.

Web-Browser Hijacking

The best indicator that your PC is host to malicious software is unexpected web-browser behavior. If an unfamiliar toolbar has suddenly appeared, if your home page has mysteriously changed, if the built-in search functionality uses "Joe's Super-Duper Marketing-Enhanced SearchIt!" instead of your usual search engine, chances are, your web browser has been hijacked.

If scanning with Ad-Aware and Spybot Search and Destroy doesn't resolve your web browser's erratic behavior, a free diagnosis tool called HijackThis is available at `http://spychecker.com/program/hijackthis.html`.

The HijackThis freeware does not identify browser-hijacking programs but only lists all the add-ons, buttons, and startup items associated with your browser. Using it, you can disable whichever items you choose — the trick is identifying unwanted items. The list includes every browser startup object, including the benign ones, so using HijackThis requires research or expert review of your log before you decide what to remove. A free tool that will analyze your HijackThis log and point out known malicious browser add-ons listed there is available at `http://hijackthis.de/#anl`.

Typically, malicious browser-hijacking programs target the Microsoft Internet Explorer web browser. A good way to avoid future infection is to switch your system's default web browser to Firefox, available as a free download from `http://mozilla.org/firefox`. (Fear not: Firefox can easily import your current Internet Explorer bookmarks.)

Hack 98: Clean Up Your Startup

Level. . . . . . . **Easy to Advanced**
Platform. . . . **Windows**
Cost. . . . . **Free**

Does your computer seem a lot slower starting up now than it did the day you took it out of the box? When it comes to computer slowdowns that get worse over time, one of the biggest culprits is software installations that plant themselves in your PC's login sequence and start up automatically with your computer. These programs — which you may or may not use during your session — are taking up memory and CPU cycles that they don't have to.

Say you install a media player such as Apple's popular QuickTime player. QuickTime wants to be your media player of choice, and it wants to start up fast whenever you need it. To that end, QuickTime places a link to start itself up in the background *whenever you start your computer*, whether or not you need to run QuickTime, so that it can detect when you come across a QuickTime playable file and run. When several different pieces of software also do this, the result is a much longer lag between the time you log into your PC and the time it's ready to get to work for you.

A few simple methods and utilities are available to prune those unneeded programs from your computer's Startup directory and speed it up again.

Start Menu (Easy)

A special folder in your PC's Start ⇨ Programs menu contains shortcuts to programs that start automatically when you log in. This folder is called, appropriately, Startup (see Figure 10-4).

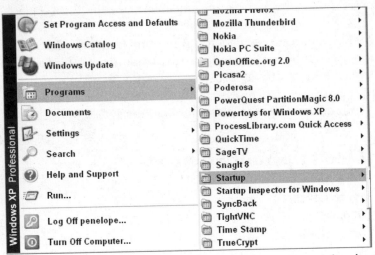

Figure 10-4 The Startup group in the Programs menu contains shortcuts to programs that automatically start with your computer.

To edit these auto-starting programs, right-click the Start button and choose Explore. Browse to your user's Programs folder and then the Startup subfolder. You can delete any shortcuts that appear there. Then, go to the Startup folder for All Users, which is located at C:\Documents and Settings\All Users\Start Menu\Programs\Startup by default. Audit the programs listed there, deleting anything you don't use on a regular basis.

System Configuration Utility (Medium)

Not every auto-starting program is listed in the Startup folder. View additional startup items using the built-in Windows System Configuration. To get to it, choose Start ➪ Run, type MSCONFIG, and press Enter.

In the Startup tab of the System Configuration Utility (see Figure 10-5), deselect anything you don't need to load automatically on boot.

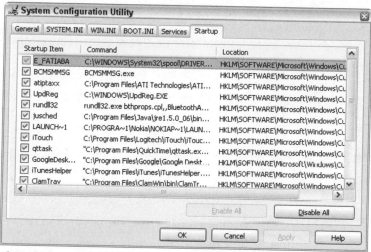

Figure 10-5 View the items that start up automatically using the System Configuration Utility.

You'll notice that most of these programs have opaque names that give little hint as to what they do or whether you really need them. One strategy for deciding is expanding the width of the Command column and viewing the entire path. If qttask is in the Program Files/QuickTime folder, chances are, it starts QuickTime. If you don't want QuickTime to start automatically (there's little reason you would; it works without getting started first), deselect that task.

Using the System Configuration Utility is a bit of a hit-or-miss proposition. Many of the programs listed there are unidentifiable on sight. If the file path doesn't help, Google the process name for more information. When in doubt, keep it checked.

TIP It's a great idea to create a system restore point first — before you make any system changes — just in case you have to roll back to the original state. Hack 99, coming up next, provides more information on that.

Autoruns (Advanced)

A third-party freeware utility called Autoruns can also help you weed out any unneeded tasks from starting automatically. Download the free Autoruns from `http://technet.microsoft.com/en-us/sysinternals/default.aspx`. When Autoruns is installed and running, view items that automatically start up with your computer in several different categories, including services, drivers, Internet Explorer add-ons, Start menu items, scheduled tasks, and more, as shown in Figure 10-6.

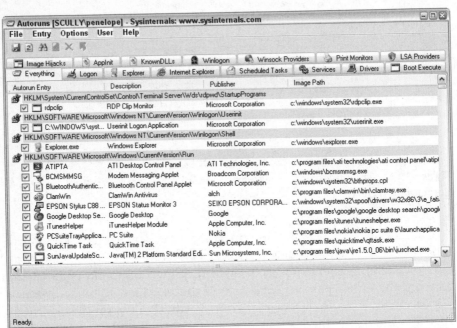

Figure 10-6 Autoruns provides a thorough, detailed list of items set to automatically start with your computer.

One of the more convenient features of Autoruns is a built-in Google lookup for an entry. To use it, select an entry for which you'd like more information and choose Entry ➪ Google to go directly to Google search results for it.

Hack 99: Undo System Configuration Changes

Level. . . . . . . **Medium**
Platform. . . . **Windows**
Cost. . . . . **Free**

You installed buggy software or changed a setting on your PC, and things got ugly — now nothing works. But all is not lost. Luckily, you can save your PC from that bad decision with a powerful tool that's built into Windows XP and Vista. It's called System Restore.

You know how it goes: you're editing your registry, you're installing beta — okay, alpha — software, you're throwing caution to the wind and testing unstable applications and drivers all willy-nilly. But one false move can render your machine unusable — or make it start popping up 30 `missing` `.dll` alerts every time you log in.

System Restore takes snapshots of your computer's configuration over time. In the event of a disastrous installation or configuration change that didn't go your way, System Restore can roll back a current Windows state to a working version without affecting any of your data.

By default, System Restore in Windows is turned on for all your computer's hard drives if you had more than 200MB (300MB for Vista) of disk space available after Windows was installed (and most likely, you did). To see whether System Restore is enabled, do the following:

- Windows XP: Open the Control Panel and choose Performance and Maintenance ➪ System. On the System Restore tab, deselect the Turn Off System Restore On All Drives check box.

- Windows Vista: Open the Control Panel and select System Maintenance ➪ Backup and Restore Center. Under Restore Files Or Your Entire Computer, click Use System Restore To Fix Problems And Undo Changes To Windows.

Make sure that your computer's drive — at least the one that contains your system and program files (usually the `c:` drive) — status is listed as Monitoring, as shown in Figure 10-7.

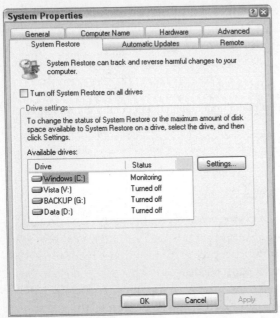

Figure 10-7 Enable System Restore in the System Properties dialog box.

> **NOTE** If your hard drive doesn't have enough space to enable System Restore, see Hack 105, "Free Up Hard-Drive Space."

System Restore tracks changes in the Windows registry, user profiles, .dlls, and other internal Windows files over time. If you have multiple drives or partitions on your computer, but only one runs Windows, it makes sense to set System Restore to monitor just the drive on which your operating system and applications reside.

Create or Restore a Saved Point with System Restore

To run System Restore, choose Start ⇨ Programs ⇨ Accessories ⇨ System Tools ⇨ System Restore. From there, choose whether you want to restore a previous state or create a new saved state, which you can name — for example, Prestartup cleanup.

If you restore your computer to a previous state, note that current documents, files, and email are *not* affected. Choose your previous state from a calendar, as shown in Figure 10-8.

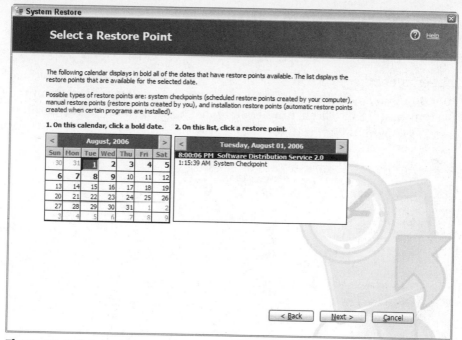

Figure 10-8 Return your system to a past working state with System Restore.

Also, a restoration can be undone. To reverse your restoration, start System Restore, choose Undo My Last Restoration, and click Next.

WARNING System Restore is not a replacement for file backup; it takes snapshots of your computer's configuration and program files, not your personal data and information. (See Hack 59, "Automatically Back Up Your Files to an External Hard Drive (PC)," for more on backing up your personal data.)

When System Restore Takes Snapshots

System Restore takes system snapshots every day the computer is on during idle time, as well as *before* system changes such as Windows Automatic Updates, driver installations, software installations, and system restorations take place. The Microsoft web site lists specific times and instances in which System Restore snapshots are taken at `http://lifehackerbook.com/links/systemrestore`.

Limit System Restore's Disk Usage

One of the gripes about System Restore is that its snapshots can take up a significant bit of hard-drive space. By default, System Restore is given 12 percent of disk space in Windows XP (15 percent in Vista). To reduce that amount, right-click My Computer and choose Properties. From the System Restore tab, adjust the Disk Space To Use slider in the Settings area, as shown in Figure 10-9.

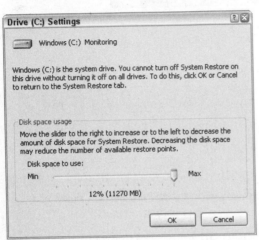

Figure 10-9 Adjust the amount of disk space allocated to System Restore points.

New shapshots overwrite old ones, so if you can spare the maximum 12 percent (or 15 percent), do so. The more space you allocate to System Restore, the more restore points you'll have available in the event of a system misconfiguration.

Hack 100: Truly Delete Data from Your Hard Drive

Level. . . . . . . **Medium**
Platform. . . . **Windows, Mac OS X**
Cost. . . . . **Free**

You're about to sell, donate, pass on, or give away your old computer. Did you know that file-undelete software can easily resurrect those files you just emptied out of the Recycle Bin? Even though it *looks* as though you've erased the files, in reality your computer has only marked the space they took up on disk as available — the ones and zeros that make up those deleted files still exist.

The only sure way to securely and permanently delete sensitive files — such as a customer database, secret company documents, or personal photos you don't want the guy who buys your hard drive on eBay to see — is to overwrite them several times with new data. Utilities to do this are available for both Mac and Windows systems.

Windows

Free, open-source Windows software Eraser (http://heidi.ie/eraser/download.php) permanently deletes files from disk using your choice of methods, including a Defense Department standard (DoD 5220.22-M). Eraser can do both on-demand and scheduled scrub-downs of unused disk space on your entire hard drive; either way, it permanently deletes files.

If you're passing a computer on to a co-worker or family member or selling it, delete your data as usual and then use Eraser to permanently remove any trace of that data from the free space on your disks. To do so, open Eraser, and in the On-Demand section, choose File ➪ New Task. From the drop-down list, choose the drive, folder, or file you want to permanently delete and click OK. The location is added to Eraser's task list, as shown in Figure 10-10.

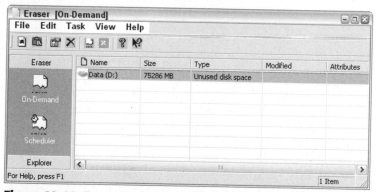

Figure 10-10 Eraser can permanently delete any trace of files on the unused portions of a disk, or delete specific existing files.

To go ahead with the delete action, choose Task ➪ Run All.

Eraser is also integrated with Windows Explorer. With Eraser installed, right-click any file, choose Erase from the context menu, and confirm deletion.

> **WARNING** When you erase a file with Eraser, it does not go into the Recycle Bin, nor can it be recovered using undelete software. It is permanently deleted, so use it sparingly and with caution.

Mac OS X

To permanently delete sensitive data in the Trash on a Mac (OS X 10.4 and higher), choose Finder ⇨ Secure Empty Trash. (That menu option is enabled only if the Trash bin contains any files.)

In Mac OS 10.5 (Leopard), you can set your Mac to always securely empty the Trash. To do so, choose Finder ⇨ Preferences and select Empty Trash Securely.

To white out all the current free space on your Mac, launch Disk Utility and choose your Mac's hard drive. Then, on the Erase tab, click the Erase Free Space button to choose your erasing method, as shown in Figure 10-11.

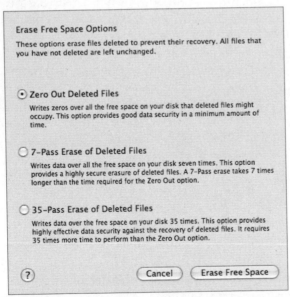

Figure 10-11 The built-in Mac OS X erase feature scrubs deleted file fragments from unused disk space.

Hack 101: Compare and Merge Files and Folders with WinMerge

Level. . . . . . . **Medium**
Platform. . . . **Windows XP and Vista**
Cost. . . . . . . **Free**

When several people work on the same set of files — making changes and copies — multiple versions can blossom out of control. Figuring out what's been updated on which version and merging it all back together can be a gargantuan task, but it doesn't have to be. If your kids downloaded images from the digital camera repeatedly to different locations on the computer, or you and your co-worker lost track of who made the latest changes to that PowerPoint presentation, you need the free, open-source Windows utility WinMerge. WinMerge can compare and merge documents and folders on your computer.

Download WinMerge (available at http://winmerge.org) and install it on your PC. During installation, select the Windows Explorer integration option, which comes in very handy later.

At first glance, WinMerge is a little intimidating — especially to users who haven't worked with file diff utilities before — but it's quite helpful after you make it your friend.

Compare and Merge Folders

You've got two directories of photos downloaded from the camera. Some were cropped and had the red-eye removed, some weren't; new photos were taken and old ones redownloaded. Here's how WinMerge can help.

First, in Windows Explorer, select the two directories of photos (in this example, C:\photos\ and C:\pics\) and choose WinMerge from the context menu. You'll get a file listing that displays all the files in both folders, including which ones are identical, which are different, and which exist on the "left" or "right" folder, as shown in Figure 10-12.

From the file listing, you can right-click any entry to open it (or its other version) to view the differences. Alternatively, you can copy files that exist on one side to the other using the Copy Left and Copy Right buttons in the toolbar (or key combinations Alt+Left Arrow and Alt+Right Arrow).

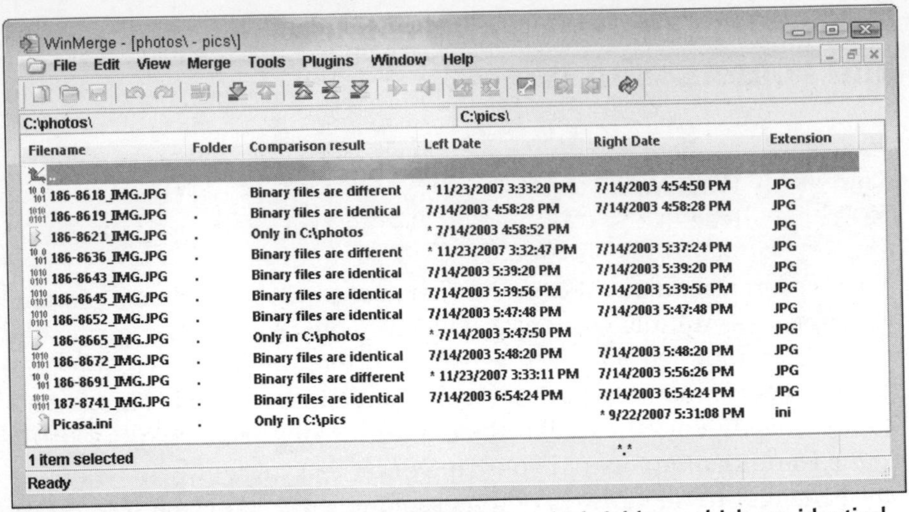

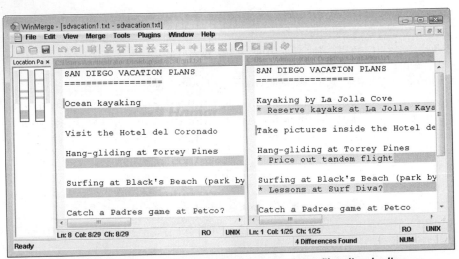

Figure 10-12 WinMerge lists which files exist in which folders, which are identical, which are different, and the last time each version was modified.

Diff and Merge Text Files

WinMerge can not only detail differences in file listings but also visually identify differences within files it understands, such as text files. Figure 10-13 shows the differences between two text files with notes on vacation plans.

Figure 10-13 WinMerge can compare the contents of text files, line by line.

In this text-file comparison three-pane interface, the leftmost pane displays a map of the file differences. The orange areas indicate lines that differ, the grey areas show lines that exist in one file but not the other, and the white area shows identical lines in the file. Click any one of those areas to skip directly to that section of the two files, which are shown in the two right panes. Using the toolbar buttons, you can merge all or selected changes from the left to the right file.

Compare and Merge Office Documents

Most people don't work exclusively in text files, but WinMerge can also compare proprietary file formats, such as Microsoft Office files. Supposedly, WinMerge comes with Word and Excel support out of the box, but I had limited success in getting that to work. If you, too, get the error message saying that WinMerge is unable to compare binary files, download and install the xdocdiff WinMerge plugin (available at `http://freemind .s57.xrea.com/xdocdiffPlugin/en/index.html`). The xdocdiff plugin can compare Word, Excel, PowerPoint, PDF, Outlook Email, and RTF documents as well as OpenOffice.org and Lotus 1-2-3 files. The plugin installation isn't a one-click process; be sure to extract the `.zip` file and copy the appropriate files into the WinMerge program folder according to the instructions on the plugin page.

Figure 10-14 shows what a comparison of two Word documents (drafts of this chapter in progress) looks like in WinMerge.

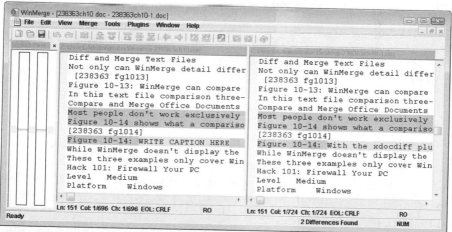

Figure 10-14 With the xdocdiff plugin enabled, WinMerge can compare the text contents of Office documents, such as Microsoft Word and Excel, as well as PDF and OpenOffice.org documents.

The downside is that WinMerge doesn't display the document formatting, just the contents of the file in a straight textual display. But all the same text-comparison features listed previously apply. Move all or selected changes left or right and navigate the differences using the leftmost pane. Then you can save your changes to a new document.

These three examples cover only basic usage of WinMerge. Be sure to check out the WinMerge online manual to roll up your sleeves and really get down and dirty with this useful utility. It's available at `http://winmerge .org/2.6/manual/index.html`.

Hack 102: Firewall Your PC

Level. . . . . . . **Medium**
Platform. . . . **Windows**
Cost. . . . . **Free**

A home PC connected directly to the Internet — especially with an always-on broadband connection such as cable or DSL — is a prime target for malicious software attacks. Predatory software constantly scans public networks (such as your ISP's network) looking for insecure computers to attack, take over, and use for their own purposes. A criminal hacker can use an unsecured home PC to send out spam email, steal credit card or other identity information, or simply delete data or crash the machine for the fun of it.

A firewall can protect your computer against these types of attacks. Without a firewall, your PC connected directly to a cable modem is exposed to the wilds of the Internet — which runs rampant with infected PCs just waiting to spread their viruses and key-log your credit card numbers.

Does Your Computer Need a Firewall?

If you're on a secure network — like at the office — or if your home computer is connected to a wireless router with a built-in firewall, it may already be protected. If not, running a software firewall can greatly reduce the chances of an outsider's gaining access to your PC without your knowledge or consent.

Open ports on your computer represent possible entry points and vulnerabilities on your machine. Test out how secure your PC is by using a free online port scan application at `http://www.t1shopper.com/tools/ port-scanner/`.

If your machine has open ports, run a firewall to explicitly allow and disallow traffic from the Internet in and out of your computer.

NOTE If you're running a home server as described in Hacks 74 and 75, you will have purposefully opened ports on your machine. Make sure those servers are secured with difficult-to-guess passwords. When you're not using the servers, shut them down to close their open ports.

If you can, get a hardware firewall to protect your home desktop computers. (Most modern wireless network routers come with a firewall built in.) A hardware firewall is ideal because it frees up CPU cycles (because your computer doesn't have to run the firewall itself) and is often more effective than a software firewall. However, software firewalls are sometimes necessary, especially for roaming laptops that connect to open wireless networks such as at the local coffee shop or airport.

ZoneAlarm Software Firewall

Several commercial firewall applications are available for home use. Zone Labs offers a free version of its feature-full ZoneAlarm firewall for download at `http://zonelabs.com/store/content/catalog/products/sku_list_za.jsp`.

When ZoneAlarm is installed, it monitors and asks you to confirm or deny incoming and outgoing Internet traffic from your computer. Also, for troubleshooting purposes (and a great sense of satisfaction), ZoneAlarm reports the details and total of how many possible intrusions it blocked — attempts from other computers to connect to yours, as shown in Figure 10-15.

Control What Programs Can Connect to the Internet

After ZoneAlarm is installed and you've begun using your computer as usual, you'll notice that it will interrupt you every time a program tries to connect to the Internet. (These days, most software applications do — mostly for legitimate purposes, such as checking to see whether you're using the most updated version.) Allow or deny Internet access to those programs using ZoneAlarm's (somewhat annoying) pop-ups, such as the one shown in Figure 10-16, which appears when you click a link in a Microsoft Word document.

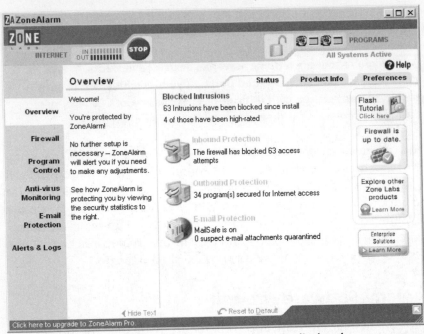

Figure 10-15 The ZoneAlarm firewall's main console displays how many possible intrusions it has blocked and how many programs are secured for Internet access.

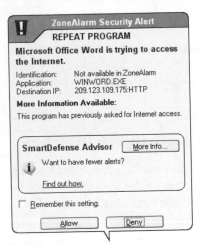

Figure 10-16 ZoneAlarm asks you to authorize or deny individual programs' access to the Internet.

To avoid constant ZoneAlarm interruptions, edit the program whitelist and blacklist all at one time. In ZoneAlarm's Program Control section, choose the Programs tab. There, click each program and choose Allow, Deny, or Ask, as shown in Figure 10-17.

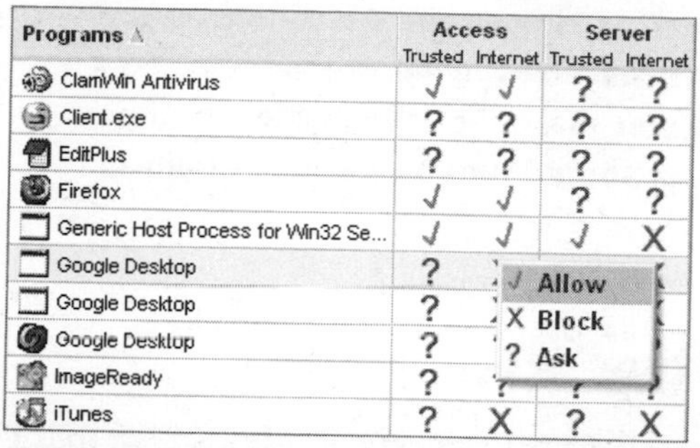

Programs ∧	Access		Server	
	Trusted	Internet	Trusted	Internet
ClamWin Antivirus	√	√	?	?
Client.exe	?	?	?	?
EditPlus	?	?	?	?
Firefox	√	√	?	?
Generic Host Process for Win32 Se...	√	√	√	X
Google Desktop	?	√ Allow		
Google Desktop	?	X Block		
Google Desktop	?	? Ask		
ImageReady	?	?	?	?
iTunes	?	X	?	X

Figure 10-17 Update the Access control setting for each program on your computer within ZoneAlarm.

With ZoneAlarm running, you can rest easy, knowing that no one can connect to your computer without your explicit permission.

NOTE Starting with Windows XP Service Pack 2 and continuing to Windows Vista, a built-in firewall is available in the Control Panel Security Center. The Windows Firewall offers similar protection as ZoneAlarm, but it's not as informative or configurable. Get more information about the Windows Firewall and the benefits of firewalls in general at http:// microsoft.com/athome/security/protect/firewall.mspx.

Hack 103: Firewall Your Mac

Level. . . . . . . **Easy**
Platform. . . . **Mac OS X 10.5 (Leopard)**
Cost. . . . . **Free**

Surprisingly, your new Mac doesn't ship with its firewall turned on by default. That's not a problem if your Mac accesses the Internet through another device that has a firewall on, such as a wireless router. But if you connect your Mac to the Internet at public wireless hotspots, or plug it directly into your broadband Internet connection, you should enable the firewall to avoid unwanted connections from other computers.

NOTE Macs are advertised as and generally known as being more secure than PCs. Instances of malware, such as viruses and Trojan horses, are extremely rare in Mac OS X — but they have happened. Because Mac OS X includes several services that help you share files and connect to other computers, the security-minded user should turn on the Mac's built-in firewall.

Choose Your Firewall Setting

To turn on Mac OS X's firewall, in System Preferences, choose Security. On the Firewall tab, you'll see three possible settings, as shown in Figure 10-18.

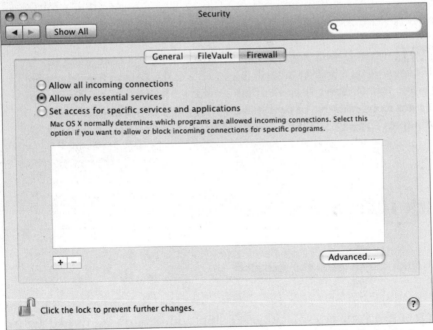

Figure 10-18 Turn on Mac OS X's firewall by choosing System Preferences ⇨ Security.

NOTE Figure 10-18 displays the firewall settings in Mac OS X 10.5.1, the most updated version of Leopard as of this writing. If you bought a brand-new Mac without applying any updates to it, this pane might not look the same on your system. To download the Leopard update, from your Mac's Apple menu, choose Software Update. By the time you read this, the minor version number will very possibly be even higher than 1.

Allow All Incoming Connections

Allow All Incoming Connections is the Mac OS X default setting and means that the firewall is off. Any computer on the same network as your Mac could make incoming connections to your Mac and "see" that your Mac exists on the network.

Allow Only Essential Services

When you select Allow Only Essential Services, the firewall is on and lets only a limited list of services "essential to the operation of your computer" through. Apple calls this choice the "most conservative mode,"[1] and it's your best bet when you get on at a public wireless hotspot with your Mac.

Set Access For Specific Services And Applications

If you know of certain programs to which you want to give explicit permission to pass through the firewall, choose Set Access For Specific Services And Applications. Then you can click the plus sign to add an application to the application whitelist. For example, if you turn on file sharing (in System Preferences' Sharing panel), File Sharing will automatically appear in the allowed services list in the firewall settings under this choice.

Get Stealthy

Computers running rogue software usually scan open networks for potential victims — all the computers that exist on them. Even with your firewall on, your Mac is still visible to this type of software. For added security, you can turn on Stealth mode — which is essentially an invisibility cloak for your Mac. To do so, in the firewall settings, click the Advanced button and select Enable Stealth Mode. In Stealth mode, other computers on the network won't be able to detect that your machine is there at all, meaning that uninvited connections won't receive any response or acknowledgement.

Hack 104: Speed Up Windows Vista with a Thumb Drive

Level. . . . . . . **Easy**
Platform. . . . **Windows Vista**
Cost. . . . . **Free**

The best way to make a computer run faster is to add more system memory, or RAM. But not all computers have expansion slots available for additional memory, and installing internal memory sticks can be an intimidating undertaking for those who've never opened their computer and faced its silicon innards. That's why Microsoft introduced a new feature into Windows Vista called ReadyBoost, which lets you add memory to your PC with a regular USB flash drive. If you have a spare USB drive with unused space on it and you'd like your Vista PC to be more responsive, ReadyBoost is for you. Here's how to set it up.

Enable ReadyBoost for a Flash Drive

When you plug a USB drive into your Vista PC, the AutoPlay dialog box comes up by default, asking what you'd like to do with the drive. This dialog box contains a Speed Up My System option, as shown in Figure 10-19.

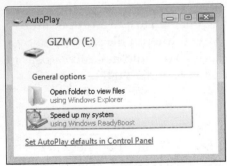

Figure 10-19 When you plug a thumb drive into a Vista PC, the AutoPlay dialog box offers a Speed Up My System option that turns on ReadyBoost.

Click Speed Up My System to enable ReadyBoost for the flash drive. ReadyBoost isn't compatible with *all* flash drives, but only with drives that meet a certain speed requirement. If it's a relatively new and roomy flash drive, ReadyBoost should work.

Allocate How Much Space ReadyBoost Uses

You can use the same flash drive for both ReadyBoost *and* file storage. To allocate a certain amount of space on your flash drive for ReadyBoost, in My Computer, right-click the USB drive. In its Properties dialog box, choose the ReadyBoost tab, shown in Figure 10-20.

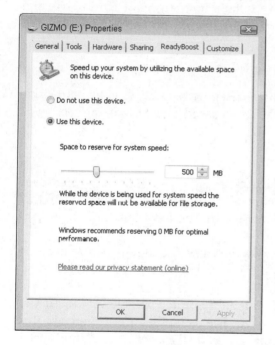

Figure 10-20 Adjust ReadyBoost settings for a USB drive in the ReadyBoost tab of its Properties panel. (Right-click the drive to get there.)

Use the slider to set how much space Vista should reserve on the stick to use for ReadyBoost. If you change your mind about ReadyBoost, here you can also disable it by selecting the Do Not Use This Device option.

Read more about ReadyBoost in Windows Vista at `http://www` `.microsoft.com/windows/products/windowsvista/features/details/` `readyboost.mspx`.

Hack 105: Free Up Hard-Drive Space

Level. . . . . . . **Easy**
Platform. . . . **Windows, Mac OS X**
Cost. . . . . **Free**

When you bought your computer two years ago, you thought it had a much bigger hard drive than you'd ever need. However, as your computer aged, all that space got eaten up by who knows what. Hard-drive space is cheap and plentiful, but you don't have to run out to buy a whole new drive the minute you start pushing your current disk's space limits. There are easy ways to inventory what's hogging your hard drive, and then you can offload some of it to external disks or simply delete it.

Visualize Disk Hogs

Two utilities — WinDirStat and JDiskReport — analyze your hard drive and map its usage statistics. They're discussed in the following sections.

WinDirStat (Windows)

The free, open-source utility WinDirStat (`http://windirstat.sourceforge .net`, Windows only) displays your disk usage in a color-coded map that shows what file types and folders take up the most space on your hard drive.

Using WinDirStat, you can easily identify the biggest space hogs on your disk. The utility provides a three-paned view: tree view, list view, and treemap view (see Figure 10-21).

The treemap represents each file as a colored rectangle, the area of which is proportional to the file's size. The rectangles are arranged so that directories make up rectangles that contain all their files and subdirectories. Select files by folder name, file type, or colored rectangle, and delete or move them from within WinDirStat.

JDiskReport (Windows or Mac)

Freeware JDiskReport (`http://jgoodies.com/freeware/jdiskreport`, Mac/Windows/Linux) provides graphical disk-usage statistics as WinDirStat does, but JDiskReport uses more common pie/line/bar charts, as shown in Figure 10-22.

JDiskReport is a cross-platform program but does require Java (http://java.com/en) to run.

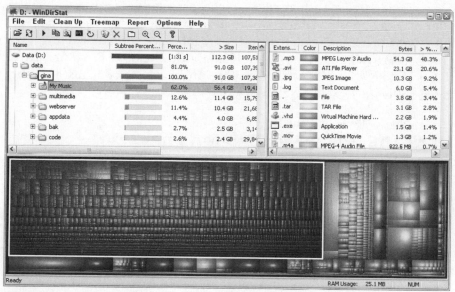

Figure 10-21 WinDirStat graphs disk usage based on a color-coded map.

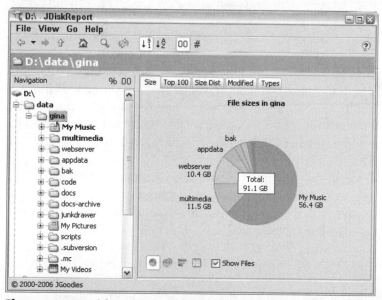

Figure 10-22 JDiskReport, for Mac, Windows, or Linux, charts disk usage to easily identify hard-drive space hogs.

Clean Your Entire System with CCleaner

Another free utility for Windows, CCleaner (which stands for Crap Cleaner), identifies system files — such as Internet browsing history, temporary setup files, and logs — that can be deleted to free up space on your hard drive. CCleaner includes an interface for uninstalling programs (also available in the Control Panel Add/Remove Programs area), fixing broken shortcuts, and removing unused registry items and outdated software. Download it from `http://ccleaner.com`.

Hack 106: Resurrect Deleted Files

Level. . . . . . . **Medium**
Platform. . . . **Windows**
Cost. . . . . **Free**

When you delete files from your computer's hard drive, the data is not actually erased. In reality, the space it occupies is marked as available for your operating system to overwrite with new data.

As a result, special file-recovery undelete programs can often resurrect deleted files from the space on your disk marked as free (which still holds fragments of the old file). Although sometimes you don't ever want your deleted files to see the light of day again, in the case of accidental deletion, an undelete process can retrieve what you thought was permanently lost data.

The moment you realize you've accidentally deleted files you want back, stop. Those files may still be on disk, but any computer activity that writes to disk may overwrite whatever's left of them and render them unrecoverable. Don't restart your computer (boot up writes temp files to disk) and don't do any other work on the machine; instead, get straight to the recovery process.

Download free undelete utility Restoration from `http://snapfiles.com/get/restoration.html` and unzip it, preferably using a computer other than the one where your deleted files live. If that's not possible, save and unzip the file to an external drive (such as a USB drive).

Restoration can restore deleted files on your Windows PC's hard drive or on external disks such as a digital-camera memory card and USB stick.

TIP **Restoration is an excellent addition to a PC helper's USB drive, along with spyware- and virus-cleaning utilities. (See Hack 97, earlier in this chapter, and Hack 71, "Carry Your Life on a Flash Drive.")**

Launch Restoration and choose the disk and filename of the document you want to recover. Say you deleted a Word document called `chapter10` `.doc` from the Desktop and emptied the Recycle Bin. In Restoration, enter some part of the filename — even if it's just the extension, such as `.doc` — and its location (drive), as shown in Figure 10-23.

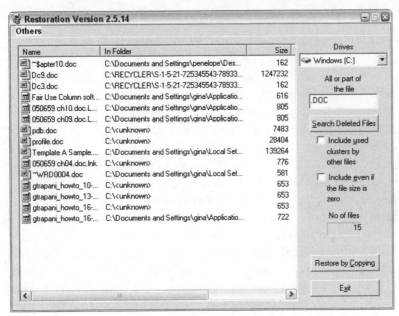

Figure 10-23 Searching deleted files in Restoration.

Restoration lists all the deleted files that match your search term. (Alternatively, view all the available deleted files by not entering any search term.) To get a deleted file back, select it, click the Restore By Copying button, and choose a location for the restored copy.

TIP If you've accidentally deleted photos from your digital camera, connect it to your PC. Many modern digital-camera memory cards will appear as an external hard drive in My Computer. Use Restoration to scan your camera as if it were an external disk and recover deleted pictures.

Keep in mind that restoring deleted files is a hit-or-miss operation that can miss often, especially in the case of large files such as video or music that Windows might overwrite quickly.

This type of file restoration is no excuse for not having or replacement for a solid backup system.

Hack 107: Hot Image Your PC for Instant Restoration

Level. . . . . . . **Medium**
Platform. . . . **Windows**
Cost. . . . . **Free**

Over time and with heavy usage, your PC can become slow and unstable, bogged down with programs you don't use and victim of system changes that make it behave in ways you never intended. If you've ever encountered the "blue screen of death" — that is, had your Windows PC crash entirely — you may know what a tedious job rebuilding your computer can be. Reinstalling the operating system and applications and restoring your documents can take time you don't have.

However, if you saved a mirror image of your PC in a known, working state first, you could restore it from a crash or slowdown quickly and easily. Commercial software such as Norton Ghost and Acronis True Image take complete snapshots of your PC for insurance in case of crash. Although these programs retail for between $50 and $70 each, a free program called DriveImage XML also acts as a virtual copy machine for your PC. DriveImage XML takes a snapshot of your entire computer's hard drive; that is, Windows itself, its configuration, and your software and documents. You can use this snapshot to copy back individual files that have since been overwritten or deleted, or restore your entire computer to its past state. Here's how.

> **NOTE** Hack 99, "Undo System Configuration Changes," describes how to use a built-in Windows utility to roll back changes you make to your computer over time. DriveImage XML is a more comprehensive hard-drive imaging program that you can use as both a file backup and a system-restore utility.

Create a New System Image

First, download DriveImage XML for free from http://www.runtime.org/dixml.htm and install it as usual. You can store your system image anywhere you'd like, but I highly recommend saving it on a disk *other than* the one you're imaging. So if you plan to image your c: drive, purchase an external hard drive to store c:'s image; or, right after you create the image, burn the files to CD or DVD. This way, if your c: drive fails or breaks, you still have your image available on a separate physical disk.

When you launch DriveImage XML (DiX), click the Backup button on the lower left of the screen. It will scan your PC and list all the hard drives connected to your system. To image your c: drive (most likely your system's primary, active disk), select it and click the Next button to launch DriveImage XML's backup wizard. Click Next again to set where DiX should save your image, and a few additional options, as shown in Figure 10-24.

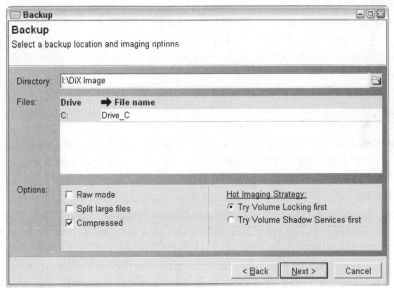

Figure 10-24 Set various options, such as where DriveImage XML should save your image, in the Backup wizard.

These settings will affect how large your image file is and how it can be restored. Here's a rundown of what each does.

Raw Mode

In raw mode, DriveImage XML makes a sector-by-sector copy of your drive, including unused space. This means your image file will be the same exact size of the drive, and it can be restored only to a drive of that same exact size. For most home-use situations, leave this box unselected. (No sense backing up blank disk space.)

Split Large Files

If you plan to burn your disk image to CDs or DVDs, select Split Large Files, which will break your image file down into smaller chunks so that you can easily save them to smaller-sized disks later. If you don't select Split Large Files, you'll get one giant image file, either as large as the disk itself or as large as the used space on the disk (depending on whether Raw Mode is enabled).

Compressed

If space on your destination drive is at a premium, select the Compressed option to make your image file up to 40 percent smaller than in normal mode. Compression slows down the imaging process, but it helps save on disk space.

Hot Imaging Strategy

The best feature of DriveImage XML is that it can image your drive while you work — but that means that files you're using while it does its thing have to be locked to be copied correctly. DiX will try two strategies: locking the drive entirely (if you're not using the computer and saving files) or using the Windows built-in Volume Shadow Services to get the last saved state of the drive. Leaving this at the default (Try Volume Locking First) is fine for home use.

Click the Next button to start creating the drive image file. Depending on the speed of your computer, the size of your hard drive, and the amount of used space, this process can take a significant amount of time. Consider starting it before you leave your computer for the evening, or during your lunch break. DriveImage XML will keep a running counter of how much time it has been copying the disk and how much time is left until it completes, as shown in Figure 10-25.

DiX isn't fast, especially if you have a lot of data to image. On my PC, about 12GB of used space took about 35 minutes to image. When the imaging process is complete, you'll have two types of files stored on the destination: a single XML file (hence DriveImage XML's name) and either one or several DAT files (depending on whether you selected Split Large Files). The .xml file is a list of all the files in the image. The .dat file(s) contain the actual image data. Figure 10-26 displays the file listing on my external drive after my image was complete.

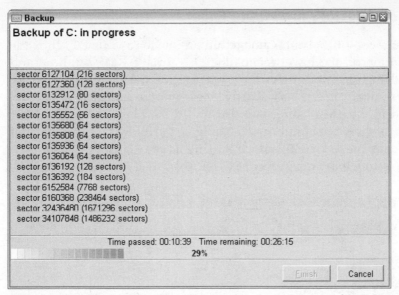

Figure 10-25 Monitor how long the process of creating your drive's image will take.

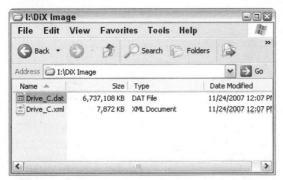

Figure 10-26 DriveImage XML's image files consist of a single XML file and DAT file(s).

Restore Your System Image

After you've saved a system image, you can use it in three ways: to restore individual files from their saved state, to restore your PC to the exact state it was when you saved the image, or to make an exact copy of the drive to another partition or hard drive.

Browse and Restore Individual Files

To view and copy files contained within an image to your PC, click the Browse button on the lower left of the DriveImage XML window and click Load Image. Then select the .xml file for the image you saved. (Remember, every image has exactly one XML file associated with it.) DiX will read the XML listing and display all the files contained within the image, as shown in Figure 10-27. Navigate the folder tree as usual and right-click any file to view it, launch it using its associated application, or extract it (restore it to your current PC setup).

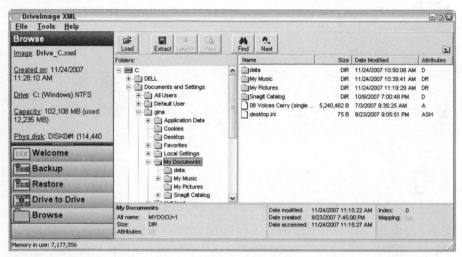

Figure 10-27 Browse the contents of your drive image using the .xml file.

You can also right-click an entire folder — such as My Documents — and choose Extract (or press Ctrl+S) to copy it to your current PC setup.

Perform a Complete System Restore (Advanced)

If your computer's hard drive crashes entirely, you can restore it to its past state using the DiX image you created. Restoring an image to a target disk will delete everything on the disk and copy the contents of the image to it. That means you *cannot* restore an image to a drive you're already using (because you can't delete the contents of a disk already in use). So if you booted up your computer on your c: drive, you can't restore an image to your c: drive. You need access to the target drive as a secondary disk. There are a few ways to do this. You can install the target drive in a PC in addition to its primary boot drive, or you can buy a hard-drive enclosure and connect the target as an external drive.

Either way, to restore a disk image to a drive you intend to boot from, you need the following:

- A PC running DriveImage XML
- The saved disk image files, whether they're on CD, DVD, the host PC, or an external drive
- A target drive with a partition at least the size of the drive image files

To start the restore process, in DriveImage XML, click the Restore button and then click the Next button, which will launch the drive restore wizard. From there, select the .xml file associated with the image and then select the target drive. (Remember, the target drive must be an existing partition that's the same size or larger than the image, and it must not be the active system drive.) *All files will be deleted from the target drive on restore*, so be doubly sure nothing is there that you need to save. As with the image-creation process, DiX will display a progress bar and estimated time left as it restores the image to the drive.

NOTE You can format and repartition the target drive using the Windows built-in Disk Management console or any partitioning software of your choice. To use the built-in disk manager, from the Start menu, choose Run, type compmgmt.msc, and hit Enter. In the console tree, choose Disk Management. Read more on how to create and edit partitions with the Disk Management console at http://support.microsoft.com/kb/309000.

After the image has been copied and restored to the target drive, you have to make that drive the active, boot partition for your PC to start using it. Either install the disk back into your PC or use the Disk Management console to set the target partition as Active and reboot your PC.

TIP See a video tutorial on using DriveImage XML on YouTube at http://youtube.com/watch?v=PTEnKA7tOXM.

Hack 108: Recover Files from an Unbootable PC

Level. . . . . . . **Advanced**
Platform. . . . **Windows**
Cost. . . . . **Free**

Few moments in computing are as heartbreaking as when you turn on your trusty PC only to receive that bone-chilling message:

```
Boot sector corrupt. Config.sys missing. Disk cannot be read.
```

In other words, you're dead in the water.

Or are you? Just because your computer can't boot up Windows from your hard drive doesn't mean you can't boot it up with another operating system on another disk just long enough to rescue your important files. This hack uses the completely free KNOPPIX Linux Live boot disk (http://knopper.net/knoppix/index-en.html) to safely move your files from a failing hard drive to a healthy USB drive — no Windows required.

> **NOTE** There are lots of flavors of bootable CDs and DVDs that you can use to get your computer running long enough to grab your files. Some of them require your original Windows installation disk to build, though. KNOPPIX is for users who have lost or no longer have access to their original Windows disks, don't want to build a boot disk, and who aren't afraid of a different-looking operating system.

What You Need

For the latest version (as of this writing, 5.01) of KNOPPIX to run, you need the following:

- Intel-compatible CPU (i486 or better)
- At least 82MB for graphic mode (which is what you want)
- A bootable CD-ROM/DVD drive (IDE/ATAPI, FireWire, USB, or SCSI)
- A standard SVGA-compatible graphics card
- A standard serial or PS/2 mouse, or IMPS/2-compatible USB mouse

If you use a USB mouse and keyboard, they may work with KNOPPIX, but it's smart to have a PS/2 option available just in case. Be sure to check the KNOPPIX site (`http://knopper.net/knoppix-info/index-en.html`) for updated system requirements for new versions.

Ready to turn your machine into a Linux-CD-booted powerhouse?

Prepare Your KNOPPIX Disk

You have two options for getting the Knoppix bootable disk: download and burn one yourself, or order one by mail.

Do-it-yourselfers in a hurry can use another computer to download a `.iso` file (`http://knopper.net/knoppix-mirrors/index-en.html`) and burn it to their own CD or DVD. (This, naturally, requires a CD or DVD burner and burning software.) If you opt to go this route, make sure you choose the most recent `.iso` file available (currently `KNOPPIX_V5.0.1CD-2006-06-01-EN.iso`). The DVD files are available from the `knoppixdvd` folder on the download server.

Alternatively, if you have time (or no friend with an available burner), order a KNOPPIX CD via mail for anywhere from $1.50 to $5.00 from a vendor listed at `http://knopper.net/knoppix-vendors/index-en.php`.

Set Your Computer to Boot from the CD or DVD Drive

Here things get as tricky as they're going to get. When your computer starts up, it boots itself on disks in a particular order (usually the floppy `A:` drive, then the `C:` drive) as set in the computer's base configuration (called the BIOS). To boot from CD or DVD, you have to edit the disk order to make your computer go to the CD or DVD *first*. How you do so will differ from machine to machine. For example, when my Dell first starts up, it has a message saying `Press F2 to enter setup`. That's what you want.

So here's what to do:

1. Insert the KNOPPIX CD into your CD/DVD drive.

2. Shut down your computer.

3. Disconnect any peripherals you don't need to grab your files (printer, Wi-Fi adapter, remote-control IR device — anything unnecessary).

4. Connect the drive to which you want to move your files — such as a USB drive or external hard drive.

5. Start up your computer and watch carefully for the message on how to enter your BIOS settings (such as the F2 message) and then press the correct key.

6. When you're in the BIOS settings, find the Boot Sequence option. Go into it and select the CD drive as the first bootable option.

WARNING One false move inside your BIOS can seriously affect your computer's operation. Be careful, and edit only the boot-sequence settings.

7. When your PC is set to boot from CD first, save and quit the BIOS.

Start KNOPPIX

The CD is in the drive and your computer is set to boot from it; you're golden. When you restart, you'll hear the KNOPPIX CD or DVD spinning right away. Your computer will bypass your crippled hard drive and begin booting up Linux. The first things you'll see are the Linux Penguin and progress messages as KNOPPIX gets itself started. It will take some time to detect your devices, but eventually you'll get a message to press Enter to continue with the Linux boot.

Press Enter and eventually you'll get to the full-on KNOPPIX desktop, as shown in Figure 10-28.

NOTE My first time out with KNOPPIX, I had to reboot three times before it ran successfully. The first time, the boot sequence got stuck in the Auto-Detecting Devices process. After 20 minutes, I restarted and tried again. The second time, I got to the desktop but was told the computer didn't have enough memory for graphical mode (but it most certainly does). The third try was a charm — startup happened in a minute and a half with all my disk drives mounted and the full KNOPPIX desktop. Moral of the story: if bootup ain't going well, try, try again.

Rescue Your Data

If you have no Linux experience, KNOPPIX may look odd and scary, but it isn't. See the hard-drive icons on the desktop? Click one to browse its contents — your Windows files. To copy your important documents, just open your USB drive (click its icon) and simply drag and drop files onto it.

When you attempt the copy, you may receive a message saying, "You cannot drop any items in a directory in which you do not have write permission." If you receive this message, change the permissions by right-clicking the USB drive and choosing Change Read/Write Mode, as shown in Figure 10-29.

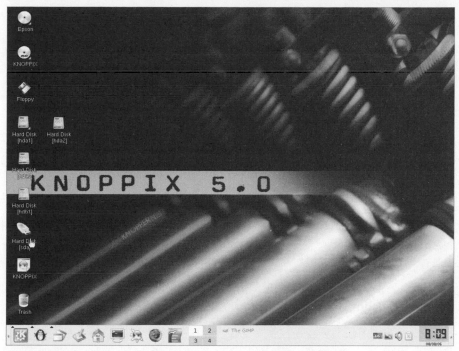

Figure 10-28 The KNOPPIX desktop booted from CD or DVD.

Figure 10-29 Change the permissions to write to your external drive in KNOPPIX.

Then, you can simply drag and drop files from your hard drive to your USB drive. When you're finished, you can shut down, reset your boot order to where it should be, and rebuild or repair your PC, knowing that your data is safe and sound.

A Linux boot CD or DVD such as KNOPPIX is also a low-overhead way for the curious to try Linux without having to install it. Just pop in the CD, reset your boot order, and go.

TIP Another popular bootable Linux distribution, Damn Small Linux (`http://damnsmalllinux.org`), can run within Windows from a USB drive or can boot from CD or DVD.

Reference

1. "Mac OS X 10.5 Leopard: About the Application Firewall," Apple.com, available at `http://docs.info.apple.com/ article.html?artnum=306938`.

CHAPTER 11

Manage Multiple Computers

You use more computers on a regular basis than any previous generation did. You've got your computer at work, your PC at home, your spouse's laptop, and the family Mac to take care of, and getting simple tasks done between them can be tedious. If you tend to work between several computers, you should know about several utilities already built into your operating system or available for free that can make sharing information and resources easy.

Using multiple computers lets you get online and work on files from lots of different locations, but with that capability come complications — such as your work getting out of sync. If you bookmark a web site at the office, it won't be there when you get to your home computer. If you bring work home from the office and you forget your updated files there, you're up a creek. If your spouse downloads photos from the digital camera onto her laptop, you don't get to see them — unless you've got the right setup.

Personal computers once amounted to giant, stand-alone calculators until someone came up with the idea of connecting them to exchange information. All the computers in your life are connected in some way, whether on your home network or over the Internet, and that means you can do a lot more with them, such as share disks and devices and even automatically sync files between them. This chapter covers several techniques for synchronizing files and bookmarks between computers over the Internet and on the same network.

If you have several computers on your home network — such as your teenager's laptop and your spouse's PC — see Hacks 109 and 110 to find out how to set up shared folders for you all to open and save files to a single place, whether you're working in Windows or Mac OS X. If you have many computers but just one printer, see Hack 113 for how to share that printer so that any computer can print documents to it. If you're thinking about switching to the Mac but don't want to give up Windows, you can roll two computers into one by running Windows on your new Mac, and Hack 114 tells you how. If you have dual monitors or a laptop hooked up to an external monitor, see Hack 115 to find out how to get the most out of the extended screen real estate. Finally, if you have two computers at one desk, you can control them both with a single mouse and keyboard; Hack 116 covers how.

Multiples can complicate things, but they don't have to. Whether you're sharing information between local computers, between operating systems, or over the Internet, this chapter shows you how to get all the computers in your life under control and sharing common resources.

Hack 109: Share Windows Files

Level. . . . . . . **Medium**
Platform. . . . **Windows and Mac OS X**
Cost. . . . . **Free**

If you have several computers at home, you want to easily transfer files between them without manually copying them to disk and walking it across the room (so-called "sneaker net"). All versions of Windows come with built-in support for sharing folders and opening and saving files to them from other computers on the network. This hack shows you how to share a Windows folder of family photos to all the other computers in the house, whether they're also PCs or whether they're Macs.

NOTE The screenshots in this hack are from Windows XP, but the instructions mostly work for Windows Vista as well; Vista-specific notes are included inline.

Share a Folder

To share a folder of photos from a central PC to other computers in the house, browse to that folder in Windows Explorer, right-click it, and choose Properties. On the Sharing tab, enter a share name, as shown in Figure 11-1.

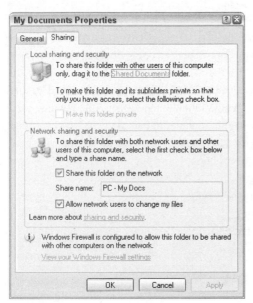

Figure 11-1 Share a folder in the folder's Properties dialog box, under the Sharing tab.

The name you set here is what other computers will see. This name can be different from the folder name itself. If you try to use a name more than 12 characters long, Windows will warn you about a possible incompatibility with some operating systems. To be safe, stick with a name that has fewer than 12 characters. In Figure 11-1, I'm sharing the My Documents folder as PC - My Docs. Also, select Allow Network Users To Change My Files if you want to save files to this shared folder from other computers.

NOTE If your computer is not set up for sharing files, you'll see a message to that effect with a link to run the Network Setup Wizard in the Sharing tab. Run the wizard to enable file and printer sharing on your computer first. Then you'll be able to name your shared folder.

Windows Vista users, be sure to click the Advanced Sharing button from the Sharing tab of your folder's Properties dialog box. There you can set the shared folder name and make the folder writable by other computers using the Permissions button.

Determine Your Computer Name

For other computers to connect to your shared folder, it's helpful to know your PC's network name. Most likely, you chose your computer's name when you first set it up (or maybe its manufacturer or previous owner did) and you've since forgotten it. To determine your PC's name, from Control Panel, click System. (Some users may have to go to the Performance And Maintenance category first; Vista users should use the System And Maintenance link.) From the System Properties dialog box, choose the Computer Name tab and write down the name listed next to Full Computer Name, as shown in Figure 11-2.

Figure 11-2 The System Properties dialog box displays your computer's network name, which other computers will use to browse to it.

In Figure 11-2, you can see I've named my PC Scully (that's right, *X-Files* fans!). Take note of your computer's name, which is what other computers on the network will see and access. (If you want to change your PC's name, click the Change button. To save the new name, you'll have to restart your computer.)

Vista users, your System Properties area will look different from Figure 11-2, but it will also list the name next to Full Computer Name.

Access the Shared Folder from Another PC

Now that your shared folder is all set up, you're ready to access it from another PC. This is the fun part: from any other Windows XP or Vista PC on the same network as the computer with the shared folder, from the Start menu, type two backslashes and the computer's name that you just wrote down. For example, from another PC, I typed **\\scully** into the Run box to browse the PC named Scully in Windows Explorer. There you can see all the shared items available on the host PC. In Figure 11-3, you see the PC - My Docs shared folder.

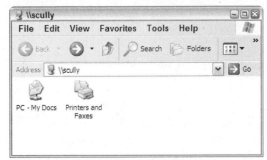

Figure 11-3 Browse to the computer with shared files or printers by prefixing its name with backslashes in Windows Explorer.

TIP You can access shared folders between PCs on a local network only *unless* you're running a VPN (virtual private network) as described in Hack 73. Using a VPN, you can access shared folders from your PC over the Internet — your home PC from the office, for example.

Access the Shared Folder from a Mac

After you've set up a shared folder on your PC, a Mac on the same local network can view, open, and save files there as well. If you're using Mac OS X 10.5, under the Shared header in Finder's sidebar, you'll see the PC sharing files listed automatically. From there, you can browse its available shared folders, as shown in Figure 11-4.

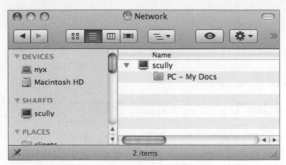

Figure 11-4 Browse to the PC hosting a shared folder by using the Shared header in Finder's sidebar.

TIP You can add a shared folder to Finder's sidebar for quick access. To do so, select the shared folder, and from Finder's File menu, choose Add To Sidebar.

Troubleshooting Tips

If you have difficulty connecting to your PC's shared folder, make sure of the following:

- **The computers are on the same local network.** If the computers are connected to the same wireless router, for example, they're on the same local network, which means they have similar IP addresses. To check whether the computers can communicate with one another, you can try pinging one from the other. From the command line on the host PC, type **ipconfig** to determine the computer's local IP address. Then, from the command line of the computer that's trying to connect, type **ping 123.56.7.8** (where 123.56.7.8 is the host PC's IP address). If the ping program gets a response from the host PC, the two machines can talk to one another.

- **The PC's firewall must allow file sharing.** Make sure the firewall running on the host PC allows for incoming connections to its shared folders. If you're using the Windows built-in firewall and you enable sharing, file sharing is automatically added to the firewall's Exceptions list. However, you may have to manually let file-sharing connections through on third-party firewalls.

Hack 110: Share Mac Files

Level. . . . . . . **Medium**
Platform. . . . **Mac OS X 10.5 and Windows**
Cost. . . . . **Free**

Just as you can share folders from Windows, Mac OS X also has built-in sharing that works with other Macs as well as PCs. Here's how to share a folder from your Mac and access it from other computers in your home or on any local network.

Share a Folder

To make a folder available to other computers on the network, go to your Mac's System Preferences' Sharing pane. Here you'll see a list of all the ways other computers can access your Mac. Select File Sharing and then click the + button under the Shared Folders column to add the folder you want to share, as shown in Figure 11-5.

Figure 11-5 In the Sharing pane of System Preferences, manage your Mac's shared folders list and set access permissions for each shared folder.

In this area, you can see what users and groups have what access permissions to those folders. Add and remove folders in the list by clicking the + and – buttons below the Shared Folders list. For a given folder, you can share using AFP (Apple Filing Protocol) to share the folder with other Macs, SMB (Server Message Block) to share the folder with PCs, and FTP to access the folder from any device that has an FTP client (see Figure 11-6). You can turn on all or any subset of those options for a given folder.

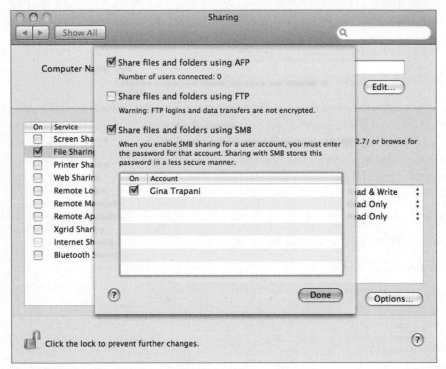

Figure 11-6 Click the Options button to select which protocols your Mac should use to share the selected folders.

To share your Mac's files only with other Macs, select Share Files And Folders Using AFP. To share your Mac's files with Windows PCs, select Share Files And Folders Using SMB. Then, select the user account for SMB sharing and, when prompted, enter your password. (Warning: sharing with Windows PCs will not work if no user account is set to On.)

Access the Shared Folder from Another Mac

After you've shared a Mac's folder using AFP, all the other Macs on the network will be able to see and connect to the share immediately. Macs running OS X 10.5 (Leopard) will list the other Mac's name under the Shared heading in Finder's sidebar. For example, if the Mac sharing a folder's name is `nyx`, on other Macs it will appear in Finder as shown in Figure 11-7.

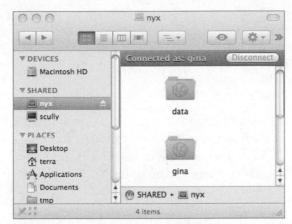

Figure 11-7 Networked Macs that are sharing files automatically show up under Shared in Finder's sidebar.

Click the Mac's name to browse its list of shared folders. If you can't see the shared folder that you know is there, click the Connect As button on the top right (under Finder's search box) and type in the username and password that has share access rights. After you're connected as an authorized user, you can open and save files there (depending on your access permissions).

Access the Shared Folder from a PC

When you turn on SMB (or Windows sharing) for a folder, Mac OS X gives you a message that reads something like

```
Windows users can access your computer at smb://xxx.xxx.x.x
```

where the xs are your Mac's IP address. You can indeed use that address, or you can simply use your Mac's name instead to access a shared Mac.

Either way, from your PC's Start menu, choose Run (Vista users, simply use the Search box) and type in your Mac's address prefixed by two backslashes, as shown in Figure 11-8.

Figure 11-8 Type your Mac's name prefixed
by two backslashes in Windows XP's Run box to
browse the Mac's shared folders in Windows Explorer.

In this example, because my Mac's name is nyx, typing \\nyx into the
Run box launches a Windows Explorer window that browses the Mac's
shared folders. From that window, you can open, copy, edit, and save
files from the shared folder over the network from your PC.

Hack 111: Synchronize Folders Between Computers

Level. . . . . . . **Medium**
Platform. . . . **Windows and Mac OS X**
Cost. . . . . **Free**

When you want two computers to always have the most updated version
of a set of files, you can waste time manually copying changes as you
make them between machines, or you can automatically sync your files
across computers using free software. Say you want the family-room PC
to store a copy of the latest batch of digital photos your spouse downloaded onto the computer in the den. Or maybe you'd like job files you
edit at home to automatically sync to your PC at the office without your
toting a disk back and forth yourself. Two free services allow you to sync
folders between computers on the same network, and synchronize files
between remote computers over the Internet.

Sync Files Between PCs on a Local Network with SyncToy

Free Windows utility SyncToy is a simple utility that synchronizes files
between two folders (located on the same PC or on different ones). Download SyncToy from http://lifehackerbook.com/links/synctoy (as of

this writing, version 2.0 is available in beta) and install it one PC that will be syncing with another. Start up SyncToy and click Create New Folder Pair to define a Left Folder and a Right Folder. Files will initially sync from left to right, so choose the folder with the source files on the left and the destination on the right. If you're syncing to another computer entirely, you will need to share the folder so that your computer can open and save files to it. See the preceding hacks — 109 and 110 — for how to share files from a PC or a Mac to another PC.

After you've chosen the Right Folder on the other PC, click the Next button. Select Synchronize as the Folder Pair action, and click Next to name your pair something descriptive, such as family room photo sync. Click the Finish button.

From here, you can configure, test, or run your new folder-pair action, as shown in Figure 11-9.

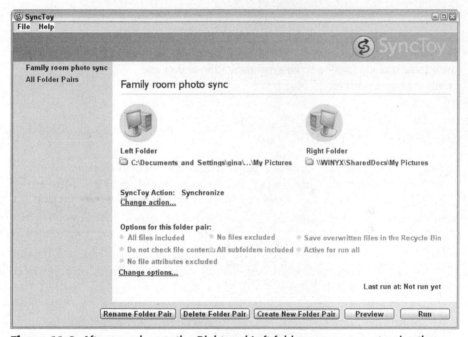

Figure 11-9 After you choose the Right and Left folders, you can customize the folder pair synchronization further in SyncToy.

Set SyncToy Action Options

To exclude any files from the synchronization action (such as system files, or maybe non-image files), click the Change Options link. There you can exclude files by name, extension, or subfolder; exclude hidden or system files; save overwritten files in the Recycle Bin; and choose other settings for your pair, as shown in Figure 11-10.

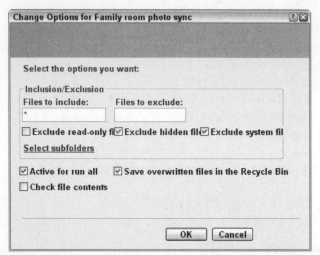

Figure 11-10 In the Change Options dialog box, you can include or exclude files from the synchronization action and configure other settings.

Dry-Run Your SyncToy Action

When you're satisfied with the synchronization action options, it's time to try the synchronization. Because you'll be copying large numbers of files and you don't want to accidentally overwrite anything important, you can preview the results of the sync without actually running it. Click the Preview button to see what files will be copied from where and to where, given your action specs. Adjust your action as needed. If you don't want to synchronize folders, you can also contribute or echo from the Left Folder to the Right Folder to perpetuate actions on the Left Folder to the Right without mirroring the contents exactly. See SyncToy's help menu for details on what the Echo and Contribute actions do.

When you're happy with the results of your SyncToy action's Preview, it's time to give it a try. Click the Run button to perform the sync between folders. You can set up any number of folder-pair actions in SyncToy to copy any number of folders to any number of other computers. The other computer doesn't have to be a Windows PC; Windows just needs to be able to browse to it to select it as the Right or Left Folder in SyncToy.

After you've set up SyncToy, each time you work on files in one place, you don't have to copy them manually but instead can just run your SyncToy action to update the folders elsewhere. That is, on either the family-room or den PC, you can run a SyncToy action that copies the latest digital-camera photos with one click.

Sync Files Between Macs and PCs over the Internet with FolderShare

If the two computers you're working with aren't on the same local network and aren't both Windows machines — such as your home Mac and your office PC — you can still sync files between them over the Internet using a free service called FolderShare (http://foldershare.com). Here's how to set up FolderShare:

1. On the first computer, go to http://foldershare.com and click Download. Download the appropriate FolderShare software for your system (either for Mac OS X or Windows) and install it. If you don't already have a FolderShare account, set one up using the installation wizard; you just need an email address and a password (that has at least one letter and one number in it.) You will also assign your computer a name that FolderShare will use to refer to it (make it something descriptive, such as Work PC or Home Mac).

2. If you're running firewall software such as Windows Firewall, when you complete the FolderShare installation, you may get a message asking whether the firewall should allow or block connections to and from FolderShare. For FolderShare synchronization to work, you must allow FolderShare traffic through your firewall.

3. On the second computer, repeat the same process. But when it comes time to set up or enter an existing account, choose I've Already Created An Account and enter the email address and password you set up in Step 1. If your second computer's firewall also asks, you will have to allow FolderShare through its firewall like you did on the first.

After FolderShare is set up on two computers, you're ready to start syncing folders between them. In Windows, click the FolderShare icon on the system tray and choose My FolderShare from the menu. The FolderShare web site will launch. Log in and click the Sync My Folders button, as shown in Figure 11-11.

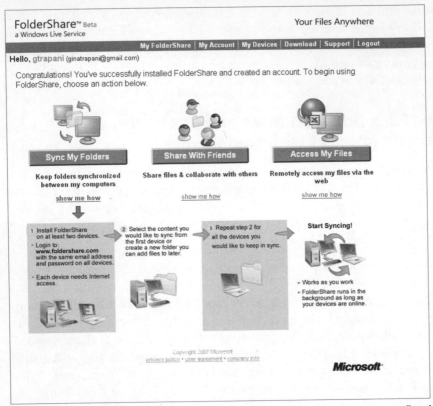

Figure 11-11 Click the Sync My Folders button in FolderShare to start configuring how it will synchronize your files between computers.

From here, you can choose a custom folder path or choose from commonly used folders, such as My Documents, My Pictures, or My Music. After you choose a folder, select a computer that the folder should sync to and a destination on that computer. After you've selected both devices and folders, FolderShare will create what it calls a library that you can name and set to automatically sync. For example, the two computers I have FolderShare installed on are named Desktop PC and Mac Laptop. I created a Work_files folder on the PC's desktop, which syncs to the laptop, as shown in Figure 11-12.

Click Complete Setup and Start Syncing to let FolderShare begin doing its thing. Any time you copy a file to a FolderShare folder on one computer, automatically in the background it will copy that file to the mirror folder on the remote computer. In my example, work files modified on the desktop or laptop will always stay in sync, regardless of location. As long as FolderShare is running and the computer is connected to the Internet, the files will update.

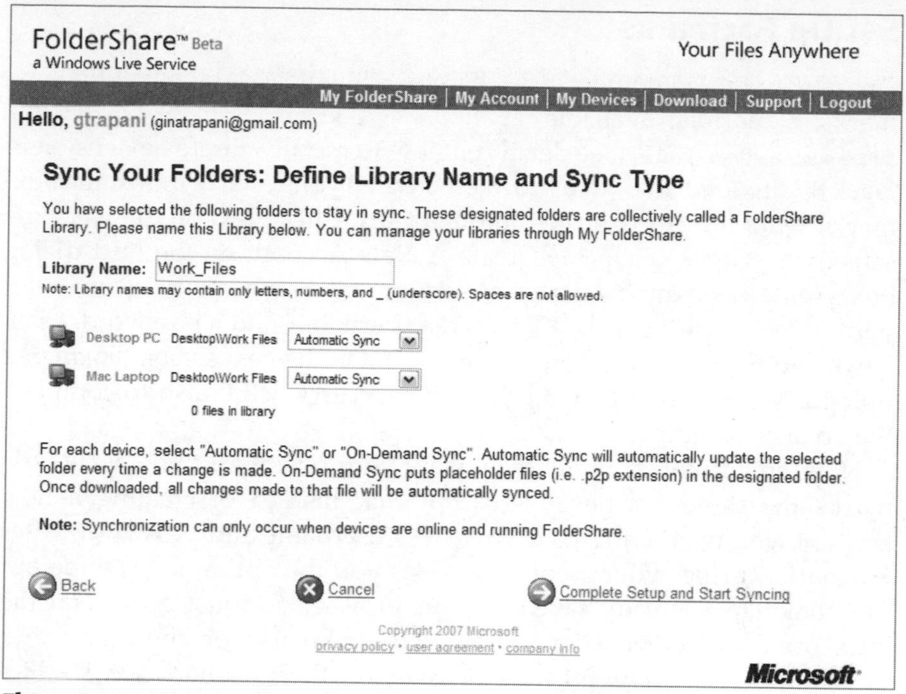

FolderShare™ Beta
a Windows Live Service

Your Files Anywhere

My FolderShare | My Account | My Devices | Download | Support | Logout

Hello, gtrapani (ginatrapani@gmail.com)

Sync Your Folders: Define Library Name and Sync Type

You have selected the following folders to stay in sync. These designated folders are collectively called a FolderShare Library. Please name this Library below. You can manage your libraries through My FolderShare.

Library Name: Work_Files

Note: Library names may contain only letters, numbers, and _ (underscore). Spaces are not allowed.

Desktop PC   Desktop\Work Files   Automatic Sync ▾

Mac Laptop   Desktop\Work Files   Automatic Sync ▾

0 files in library

For each device, select "Automatic Sync" or "On-Demand Sync". Automatic Sync will automatically update the selected folder every time a change is made. On-Demand Sync puts placeholder files (i.e. .p2p extension) in the designated folder. Once downloaded, all changes made to that file will be automatically synced.

Note: Synchronization can only occur when devices are online and running FolderShare.

◀ Back   ✖ Cancel   ➡ Complete Setup and Start Syncing

Copyright 2007 Microsoft
privacy policy • user agreement • company info

Microsoft

Figure 11-12 Set up a library in FolderShare that consists of two computers and a folder that syncs between them.

Hack 112: Synchronize Your Browser Bookmarks Between Computers

Level. . . . . . . **Medium**
Platform. . . . **All operating systems with Firefox**
Cost. . . . . **Free**

You've worked hard to perfect your browser bookmark list. You've organized all the sites and bookmarklets you use regularly into folders and on your bookmarks toolbar on your primary computer, and you want those same links available to you at work, at home, and on your laptop. Instead of exporting your bookmarks and manually importing them onto every computer you use — only to let them get out of sync again when you edit them on one computer — you can automatically sync your Firefox bookmarks using the free Foxmarks Firefox extension. Here's how.

Set Up Foxmarks

On one of your computers, using Firefox, download and install the Foxmarks extension, available at `https://addons.mozilla.org/en-US/firefox/addon/2410`. (See details on how to install a Firefox extension in Hack 85, "Extend Your Web Browser.") When you restart Firefox, the Foxmarks setup wizard launches automatically. Click Next on the welcome screen and choose Help Me Create A New Account on the next dialog box. Agree to Foxmarks' terms of service, and on the next screen, enter your name, email address, a Foxmarks username, and a password. Click Next, and Foxmarks creates your account. On the next screen, Foxmarks uploads your current bookmarks to its server. Click Finish to complete the Foxmarks setup.

Now, on any computer that you want your bookmarks on, install Foxmarks the same exact way — except that instead of creating a new account, you're entering your Foxmarks username and password. After Foxmarks verifies your account, it gives you the option to (1) wipe out the bookmarks already saved in your browser and just download the ones from the server; (2) wipe out the bookmarks on the server and upload the ones in your browser; or (3) merge the bookmark sets (see Figure 11-13).

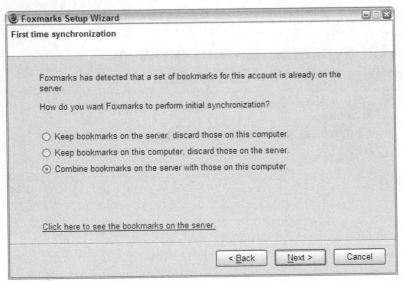

Figure 11-13 The first time you log into your Foxmarks account on a computer, you can download, upload, or merge your bookmarks.

Select the option you want for your setup, click Next, and Foxmarks will synchronize your bookmarks for the first time. When that process is complete, the computers with Foxmarks installed and logged in with your username will automatically synchronize in the background. As you make changes to your bookmarks on any computer, they will update across all the Foxmarks-enabled copies of Firefox you use — even if both computers are running Firefox at the same time.

NOTE Google offers a product similar to Foxmarks, a Firefox extension called **Google Browser Sync** (http://www.google.com/tools/firefox/ browsersync). **Although Google Browser Sync synchronizes more than just bookmarks (it also handles the browser's saved passwords, history, and session information), it doesn't work if you're running it in more than one browser at the same time. So if you leave your web browser up at home, you can't use Google Browser Sync at the office.**

To manually sync your bookmarks with Foxmarks or change other Foxmarks settings, from Firefox's Bookmarks menu, choose Foxmarks ➪ Settings. From the Foxmarks Settings dialog box, you can see the last time synchronization occurred, manually sync by clicking the Synchronize Now button, or change the account you're logged in with, as shown in Figure 11-14.

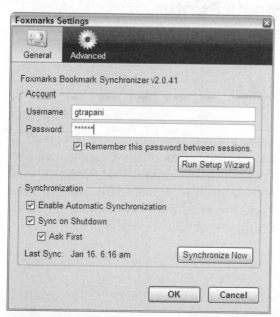

Figure 11-14 From the Foxmarks Settings dialog box, you can manually sync, switch accounts, or, using the Advanced tab, even configure your own server to store your bookmarks.

TIP If you don't want to store your Foxmarks bookmarks on the Foxmarks servers and you have access to your own FTP server, visit the Advanced tab in the Foxmarks Settings dialog box to save your bookmarks to your own remote server. Keep in mind, however, that doing this will keep your bookmarks from being available on the Web as detailed next.

Access Your Foxmarks Bookmarks on the Web

There may be times when you need to get to your bookmarks from a computer that doesn't have Firefox or Foxmarks installed, such as at an Internet café or from your in-laws' computer over the holidays. In those cases, you can get your bookmarks list on Foxmarks' web site at `http://my.foxmarks.com`. Log in with your Foxmarks username and password to view your bookmarks list on a web page. Bookmarklets — which by nature function only when saved in the browser itself — won't work from My Foxmarks, but regular web page links do. You can search, preview, edit, and rearrange your bookmarks while you're logged into My Foxmarks on the web as well.

Hack 113: Share a Single Printer Between Computers

Level. . . . . . . **Medium**
Platform. . . . **Windows and Mac OS X**
Cost. . . . . **Free**

You're typing a letter on the laptop in the living room and you want to print it — except that the printer's in the bedroom. Sharing a printer connected to a PC on your home network and printing to it from any other computer, even over a wireless connection, is a breeze. Whether you want to print from a Mac or another PC, here's how to share a single printer for use by any computer on your home network.

Share the Printer

First, you have to make the printer connected to the computer available for other computers to use. Here's how:

1. On the PC where the printer is connected, powered on, and working correctly, browse to your printer list (select Start ➪ Settings ➪

Printers and Faxes), right-click the printer's icon, and choose Sharing from the context menu.

NOTE If you don't have it turned on already, using the Network Setup Wizard, you must enable file and printer sharing on the PC to which the printer is connected to share it. Name the computer and the Windows network workgroup where it will live. By default, the workgroup name is MSHOME. After the Network Setup wizard is completed, restart the PC to save its settings.

2. On the Sharing tab of the printer's Properties dialog box, set your shared printer's name. Some older versions of Windows and other operating systems (such as Mac OS X) have trouble detecting printer names with spaces in them, so name your shared printer something that's all one word, such as EPSON_SHARE, as shown in Figure 11-15.

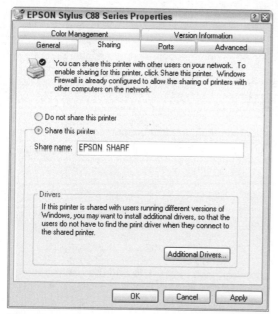

Figure 11-15 Name your shared printer on the Sharing tab of the printer's Properties dialog box.

Now your printer is ready for other computers on the same network to use it.

Connect to the Shared Printer from Windows

Your client PC (that is, the PC without the printer connected directly to it) must be a member of the same Windows workgroup that the server is to print to its printer. If it isn't a member already, run the Network Wizard to set the computer name and workgroup name (in this example, MSHOME.) You may have to restart to save those settings. (Note: You don't have to enable file and printer sharing on the client as you did on the printer server.)

Then, follow these steps:

1. After the client is in the same workgroup as the shared printer, in Printers, click Add Printer to start the wizard, and select the network printer option.

2. In the next screen of the Add Printer Wizard, browse the Windows network down through the workgroup to the shared printer (see Figure 11-16), and click Next to connect.

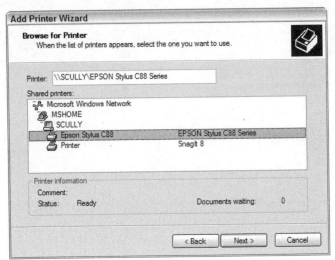

Figure 11-16 Browse the Windows network to find the computer with the shared printer attached to it.

You're done! Your PC's shared printer is available for use from the other PC on your home network.

Connect to the Shared Printer from a Mac

You can print documents to your shared Windows printer from a Mac as well. To set it up in OS X 10.5 (Leopard), first you must set the Windows workgroup that the printer lives in. In System Preferences, go to Network. In the leftmost column, select the connection to the network where your PC lives (for example, AirPort) and click the Advanced button. On the WINS tab, select the MSHOME workgroup and click OK. Then click Apply to save your setting.

Now, while still in System Preferences, choose Print & Fax. Click the + button to add a new printer, and choose Windows on the toolbar. In the leftmost column, select the Windows workgroup where the printer is located (in this example, MSHOME) and select the printer.

From the Print Using drop-down list, choose Select A Driver To Use and type in your printer name, which, if all goes well, will appear on the available driver list, as shown in Figure 11-17.

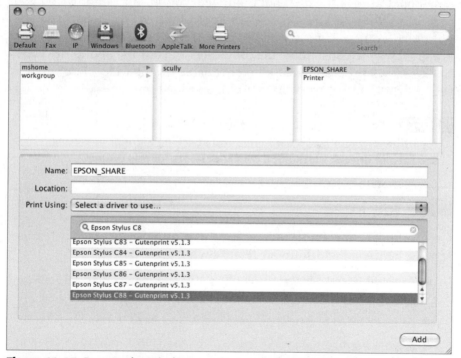

Figure 11-17 Browse the Windows workgroup to find the shared printer in the Mac OS X Add Printer box.

> **NOTE** If your printer driver isn't listed, try installing the Mac driver from the disk that came with your printer.

Click the Add button to put the shared printer on your printer list. Now, from any application on your Mac, you can print to the shared printer on the PC.

Hack 114: Have Your Mac and Windows, Too, with Boot Camp

Level....... **Advanced**
Platform. ... **An Intel-based Macintosh**
Cost........ **Free (plus the cost of the Windows operating system)**

You can have both a Mac *and* a PC on a single computer, using Apple's new Boot Camp software. Boot Camp lets you install Windows on your Mac in addition to Mac OS X. With Boot Camp set up, when you start your Mac, you can choose whether to use OS X or Windows. Boot Camp is a great way to consolidate the computers in your life and to run essential Windows programs that aren't available on the Mac. Here's how to set up Boot Camp to get a Mac and PC all rolled into one.

> **NOTE** Setting up Boot Camp is not a trivial task because it involves repartitioning your Mac's hard drive and installing another operating system and drivers. Block out a couple of hours for this project.

What You Need

Getting Boot Camp and Windows up and running on your Mac requires specific hardware and software. Here's what you need:

- An Intel-based Mac running OS X 10.5 (Leopard) with all software updates installed.
- At least 10GB of free space on your Mac's hard drive.
- A working printer connected to your Mac (with plenty of ink and paper!).
- A genuine Windows XP installation disk, which includes Service Pack 2. (Important: You cannot install XP using a disk that does not include SP2 and expect to download it after the fact. If you

have an old XP CD without SP2, see `http://lifehackerbook` `.com/links/slipstream` for more on how to add SP2 to your older Windows XP installation disk.)

Or

▪ A genuine Windows Vista Home Basic, Home Premium, Business, or Ultimate installation disk (32-bit version only).

Set Up Boot Camp

Before you get started, free up as much space on your Mac's hard drive as possible. (See Hack 105, "Free Up Hard-Drive Space," for more on how to visualize and cut back disk-space hogs.) Then back up all your important data, just in case. Do not skip this step! Finally, log on to your Mac as an administrative user (and log off any other users), quit all running applications, and if you're using a portable Mac, make sure it's plugged into a power source. Got all that? Great. Now it's time to get Boot Camp going.

Step 1: Launch the Boot Camp Assistant

The Boot Camp Assistant is a step-by-step wizard, located in `/Applications/` `Utilities/`, but it can help you only as long as you're in Mac OS X, which you are not throughout this entire process. So the first thing the Assistant does is prompt you to print the 26-page user guide. Yes, I groaned and balked at the waste of paper and ink this appears to be, too. But because you'll be rebooting your system and making major changes, a paper copy of the guide is a comforting help along the way when the onscreen Assistant isn't available.

In fact, Apple's user guide printout is more complete than any instructions I could include in this book, so rather than repeat the instructions it already contains, I offer additional information not included in the official instructions.

Step 2: Partition Your Mac's Hard Drive

After you've told the Boot Camp Assistant that you want to set up Windows on your Mac, you come to the scary (and fun!) part: splitting your Mac's hard drive into pieces and setting Windows to install on one of those partitions. The Assistant will show you a map of your Mac's hard drive. Click the divider to drag it and set the size of your Windows partition (which will take space away from the Mac partition). Alternatively, using the buttons, you can split the drive equally or use exactly 32GB for Windows, as shown in Figure 11-18.

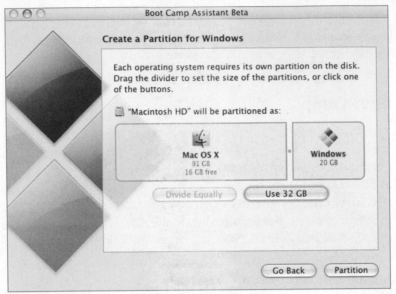

Figure 11-18 Using the Boot Camp Assistant, set the size of the Windows partition.

What size should your Windows partition be? Good question. This decision is difficult to undo later, so do consider a couple of questions before you decide:

- What will you use Windows to do and how much how much hard-drive space will that take up?

  If you're using Windows just to play PC games, for example, you won't need much space (10–20GB will do.) But if you want to manage your photo library in Windows (which I do, with Picasa, because I prefer it over iPhoto), you'll need enough space to accommodate all your photos. It's impossible to know in advance exactly how much space you'll need, but guesstimate as best as you can. Also, keep in mind that you can attach external drives to add space in Windows. But remember: files stored in the Mac OS *cannot* be accessed from within Windows, so make sure you have enough space for all the programs and files you'll want in Windows.

- What format will the Windows partition be, FAT or NTFS?

If your Windows partition is larger than 32GB, you will have to format it as NTFS, not FAT. Mac OS X cannot write to NTFS-formatted drives, but it can write to FAT drives. That means that a Windows partition greater than 32GB will be read-only in Mac OS. In general, FAT is considered less reliable than NTFS. (Windows Vista uses *only* NTFS, so the 32GB threshold isn't a factor if you're installing Vista.)

After you've chosen how to split your hard drive between Mac and Windows, click the Partition button.

Step 3: Start the Windows Installation

With your partition created, insert your Windows installation disk and click the Start Installation button in the Boot Camp Assistant. Your Mac will reboot from the Windows installation disk and begin working. Two things to know when you're installing Windows:

- When it comes time to select the partition to format, be absolutely sure to choose the partition labeled C:Partition3 <BOOTCAMP>. Vista will list it as Disk 0 Partition 3 BOOTCAMP. One false move here and you could wipe out your entire Mac, so choose carefully.

- If your partition is less than 32GB and you're installing Windows XP, you'll have a choice between the NTFS or FAT Windows format. NTFS is recommended, although FAT is okay, too. Whatever you do, don't select Leave The Current File System Intact — make sure you format the partition to NTFS or FAT.

Complete the rest of the Windows XP installation per the installation disk's instructions.

Step 4. Install the Windows Drivers for Your Mac's Hardware

After you're completely booted into your new Windows installation, eject the installation disk and insert your Mac OS X 10.5 installation CD. Let Autorun launch setup.exe, and follow the onscreen instructions. When the drivers are installed, Windows will recognize your Mac's devices (such as the Bluetooth receiver, video adapter, iSight camera, and wireless receiver). If you receive a message saying that the software hasn't passed Windows testing, click the Continue Anyway button. You'll have to reboot to finish this installation. Then you're done!

You Choose

Now you have the choice to start either Mac OS X or Windows on your Mac. To make that choice when you turn on your computer, hold down the Option key and you'll see the two partitions you set up, as shown in Figure 11-19. Click the one that has the operating system you want to use.

Figure 11-19 Hold down the Option key when you start your Mac to choose which operating system to boot into.

Alternatively, if the computer is already running, use the Boot Camp software to restart in a particular operating system. In Windows XP, click the Boot Camp icon in the system tray, and in the Startup Disk tab, select Macintosh HD or Windows and click the Restart button to move into that operating system, as shown in Figure 11-20.

Figure 11-20 Use the Boot Camp control panel in Windows (located in the System Tray) to restart your Mac in OS X or Windows.

While you're in OS X, you can do the same thing by going into System Preferences and choosing Startup Disk.

Using a Mac Keyboard in Windows

When you first start using Windows on your Mac, one of the first things you'll notice is that the Mac keyboard is different from Windows keyboards. It has a Command key but no Windows key; on MacBooks and iBooks, the keyboard has a Delete key but no Backspace key; it also has no Print Screen key. The Boot Camp user guide you printed includes a complete table of Mac keyboard Windows action mappings, but the most important ones to know are the following:

- The Option key is the Windows Alt key.
- The Command key is the Windows key.
- The Delete key is the equivalent of Backspace. To forward-delete with it on built-in Apple keyboards (on your Mac notebook), use Fn+Delete. (External Apple keyboards have a forward-delete key.)
- The Windows Print Screen key is F14 on an external Apple keyboard.

Your best bet is to bookmark the Boot Camp key-mapping reference in Windows for easy reference the next time you need to use Print Screen or Delete. It's located at `http://docs.info.apple.com/article.html?artnum=304270`.

> **TIP** For more documentation, user discussions, troubleshooting, and frequently asked questions about Boot Camp, see Apple's support section for it at `http://www.apple.com/support/bootcamp`.

Hack 115: Optimize Your Dual Monitors

Level. . . . . . . **Advanced**
Platform. . . . **Windows**
Cost. . . . . **Free**

Studies show that multiple monitors increase computer users' productivity.[1] Now that you've added another monitor to your computer setup, you've got double the screen real estate to get things done — but are you putting all that space to good use? Whether you want to stretch your desktop wallpaper or taskbar across two screens or perfectly snap all your windows into place every time, a few utilities are available that can help you make the most of every last pixel of your dual monitors. Read on to take a look.

The Basics

If you haven't taken the plunge into doubling up on monitors, you have a few options for doing so. You can install a second video card inside your computer or replace your current video card with one that supports two monitors. Alternatively (and most easily), you can just plug an external display into your laptop and use your laptop's flip-up screen as your second monitor. For more information on upgrading your computer to dual monitors, see http://lifehackerbook.com/links/dualmonitors.

When you have your dual screens hooked up, go to your system's display settings to configure their arrangement. One of the screens will be your primary monitor (numbered 1) and the other will be the secondary. Click the Identify button to throw numbers up on each screen, letting you know which is which. If one of your monitors is smaller than the other, drag and drop it to align to the top or bottom of its comrade in the same way the screens are physically aligned on your desk, to ensure the smoothest window and mouse movement between the two. In my case, my MacBook Pro (Boot Camping Windows, that is) is the primary monitor to the bottom right of my widescreen, as shown in Figure 11-21.

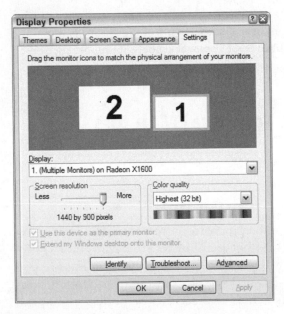

Figure 11-21 Identify and arrange your dual monitors in the Windows Display Properties dialog box.

Get Your Dual-Monitor Wallpaper On

Out of the box, Mac OS X handles dual monitors better than Windows: You can set screen-specific wallpaper images by default without any extra software. Just choose Set Desktop Background, and a panel appears on each screen to configure them separately.

Windows can't set different wallpaper images on a per-screen basis by default; when you choose your wallpaper, it appears on both screens. That wouldn't be so bad except for Windows' inability to deal with different-sized monitors. If you choose the "stretch" option and you have two monitors of different sizes, Windows XP can't stretch the image properly to fill in each screen. If you've installed a dual monitor video card, its drivers may give you the capability to configure each screen individually, but that leaves the laptop-with-second-monitor types out of luck — without the right software, that is.

One free utility, DisplayFusion, sets per-monitor wallpaper *or* stretches one panoramic image across two screens, as shown in Figure 11-22. Download DisplayFusion from `http://binaryfortress.com/displayfusion`.

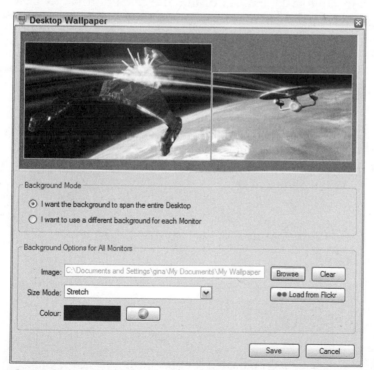

Figure 11-22 Stretch panoramic wallpaper across two monitors using DisplayFusion.

DisplayFusion offers a nice perk: the capability to search the popular photo-sharing site Flickr.com for wallpaper images built right in. DisplayFusion requires the free .NET runtime program, and it works on both XP and Vista.

Extend Your Taskbar Across Monitors

It's easy to move your Windows taskbar from one monitor to the other. Make sure it's not locked (right-click and deselect Lock The Taskbar) and then just click and drag it to any side of either monitor to make it stick. The problem is, you don't want to have to scoot your mouse over to the place where the taskbar lives every time you need it (especially now that your mouse has all that way to travel). Instead, a couple of utilities can extend the taskbar across your two screens.

From the free downloads department, you can grab the MultiMon Taskbar program, available at `http://www.mediachance.com/free/multimon.htm`. This little utility adds a taskbar to your secondary monitor (including a clock) and lists only the programs that are open on each screen in their respective taskbars. MultiMon also adds buttons to each window near the Minimize button to move windows between monitors, and handy keyboard shortcuts that do the same. (Try it: Ctrl+Alt+Right Arrow and Ctrl+Alt+Left Arrow.) The taskbar that MultiMon adds doesn't necessarily match your Windows theme, so it can look out of place; I also had trouble with its taskbar floating above the bottom of my screen instead of sitting flush. MultiMon gets the job done, but a better taskbar extension is offered in UltraMon, a $40 software application that also handles wallpaper and screensavers. Take a look at the smooth taskbar extension across two screens with UltraMon in Figure 11-23.

Figure 11-23 Multimonitor manager UltraMon stretches the taskbar across your second monitor and shows on each taskbar only the programs that appear on each taskbar's screen.

If you're willing to plunk down some cash for superior multiple monitor management — with extended taskbars, per-monitor screensavers, and lots more dual-monitor control — you want UltraMon. A single license will set you back $39.95, but UltraMon includes all the multimonitor features you want in one package. A free trial is available for download at `http://www.realtimesoft.com/ultramon`.

Managing Windows

Now that you have your wallpaper and taskbar sussed out, it's time to start taking advantage of all that screen real estate with the apps you're actually using all day. The biggest benefit of multiple monitors is having fewer overlapping windows. You can have several documents and programs open and visible without obscuring the others — which means you can multitask without having to switch between windows by clicking your taskbar or pressing Alt+Tab.

On Windows, you can tile windows without any extra software. Just select as many open windows as you want by Ctrl+clicking them on the taskbar, right-clicking, and choosing Tile Vertically (or Tile Horizontally), as shown in Figure 11-24.

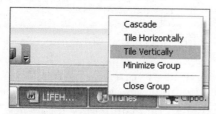

Figure 11-24 Ctrl+click multiple taskbar windows and choose Tile Vertically to make them visible but fill the entire screen width and height.

If Windows built-in tiling doesn't do enough for you, there are a few utilities that do more. Easily resize and move windows into screen halves or quadrants with freeware WinSplit Revolution, available at `http://reptils.free.fr`. WinSplit Revolution offers handy hot keys for moving windows between screens as well as to quadrants of the current monitor. Figure 11-25 is an example of how WinSplit can arrange three windows in a grid for easy multitasking.

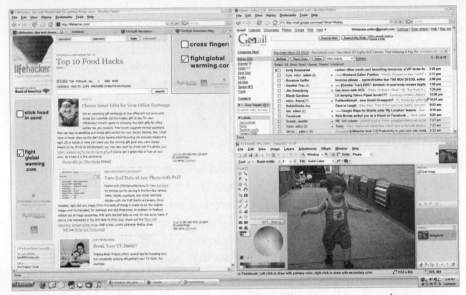

Figure 11-25 WinSplit Revolution can arrange windows in screen quadrants, halves, or a combination of these across multiple monitors.

Desktop Pinups and Overlays

Of course, you don't have to fill your entire desktop with active windows. Multiple monitors are also a nice way to keep "ambient" information in your visual field without its being right in your face all day. My laptop monitor is off to the side so that I use it for secondary applications (such as IM, email, a music player), but it also comes in handy for to-do lists, system-monitoring graphs, and even a calendar. My favorite desktop overlay utilities are Samurize for Windows (http://samurize.com) and GeekTool for Mac (http://projects.tynsoe.org/en/geektool). I use both to embed my to-do list and calendar on my desktop; both also can embed images such as web site traffic graphs. You can also embed a Microsoft Outlook calendar on your secondary monitor and even use Windows Active Desktop to embed your Google Calendar. For more information on overlaying or embedding information on your desktop, see http://lifehackerbook.com/ch11.

Hack 116: Control Multiple Computers with a Single Keyboard and Mouse

Level. . . . . . . **Advanced**
Platform. . . . **Windows**
Cost. . . . . **Free**

If you have two or more computers at one desk, you don't want two or more sets of keyboards and mice cluttering up the tabletop, too. You can buy a hardware gadget that lets you share a single keyboard and mouse with several computers (which involves a mess of tangled wires), or you could use a free software solution called Synergy. The Synergy application runs on all the computers you're using — the one that has the keyboard and mouse connected and the one(s) that do not — and lets you control all of them from that keyboard and mouse. That means you can move your mouse off one computer's screen and it will appear on the other, where you can type and work as well. Synergy also lets you share Clipboard contents between computers. If you copy information to the Clipboard on one computer and move your mouse to the other, you can paste it there, even though they're two different systems. Sound too good to be true? It's not!

Synergy works between any number of PC, Mac, and Linux desktops. For simplicity's sake, this hack sets up two PCs to share a single keyboard and mouse using Synergy.

Before you get started, you need to know two terms — *server PC* and *client PC*. When you set up Synergy, you'll have one "server": this is the computer that has the keyboard and mouse physically connected to it. The rest of the computers will be "clients." First, set up the server.

Set Up the Synergy Server

Download Synergy for Windows for free from `https://sourceforge` `.net/project/showfiles.php?group_id=59275&release_id=406637` and install it on your PC. As of this writing, the most current version available for Windows is the `SynergyInstaller-1.3.1.exe` file. Run Synergy and select Share This Computer's Keyboard And Mouse (Server), as shown in Figure 11-26.

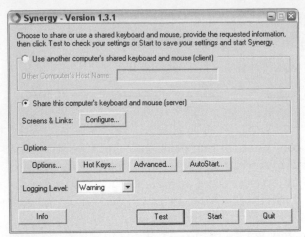

Figure 11-26 Enable the Synergy server by selecting the Share This Computer's Keyboard And Mouse option.

> **NOTE** Mac users should check out the graphical Mac Synergy client/server application, available as a free download from `http://software.landryhetu.com/synergy`.

Then click the Configure button to open a Screens And Links dialog box, where you'll add all the computers that will be controlled by the server's keyboard and mouse and their position in relation to each other.

Configure Multiple Synergy Screens

In the Screens And Links dialog box, under Screens, click the + button to add a screen. First you must add the server's computer name itself, and it should match the computer's network name. To find that name, right-click My Computer, choose Properties, and go to the Computer Name tab. My server computer name is Scully, so that's what the first Synergy screen name is, as shown in Figure 11-27.

Now, to add the other computer to Synergy, you need to know its name as well (mine is Mulder). Click the + button again to add it.

Link the Screens

After you've added to the list all the computers that the Synergy server will control, set what position they are in relation to one another. That's the only way Synergy will know where to put the mouse pointer when you, say, move it off to the side of one of your screens. Using the drop-down lists under Links, for each screen, list what's to the left or right of it, as shown in Figure 11-28.

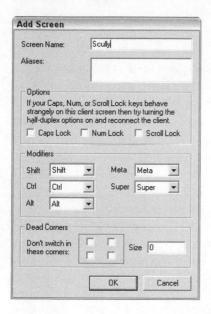

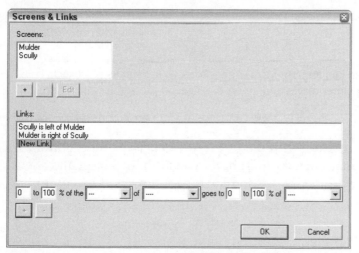

Figure 11-27 Add the server's name to Synergy's list of controlled screens.

Figure 11-28 In the Screens & Links dialog box, define where each screen is positioned in relation to the other.

If you have a particularly wild screen position (a checkerboard of flat-screens, perhaps?), you can even set up screens on top of and below each other here.

Set Up the Synergy Client

Download and install Synergy on the client computer (the one without the keyboard and mouse connected) exactly the same way as you did on the server, except choose Use Another Computer's Shared Keyboard And Mouse. Enter the name of the server computer. To try the connection, click the Test button: first on the server and then on the client PC. Try moving the mouse off the server screen. If all goes well, it will land on the client screen safely! During the test, both the client and server will display Synergy's log, which will show you a history of Synergy-related activity, as shown in Figure 11-29.

```
Synergy 1.3.1 Server                                                    _ □ ⊠
INFO: Synergy server 1.3.1 on Microsoft Windows Server XP
NOTE: started server
INFO: screen "Scully" shape changed
NOTE: accepted client connection
NOTE: client "Mulder" has connected
INFO: switch from "Scully" to "Mulder" at 0,367
INFO: leaving screen
INFO: screen "Scully" updated clipboard 0
INFO: screen "Scully" updated clipboard 1
INFO: switch from "Mulder" to "Scully" at 1902,450
INFO: entering screen
INFO: switch from "Scully" to "Mulder" at 0,508
INFO: leaving screen
INFO: switch from "Mulder" to "Scully" at 1910,381
INFO: entering screen
```

Figure 11-29 When you test Synergy's connections, its log shows you exactly where the mouse pointer leaves and enters the screens you set up, and when the Clipboard contents change.

When you're satisfied with the test results, click the Stop button. To run Synergy for real, click the Start button on both the server and client. Now you're sharing the mouse and keyboard between two computers simultaneously.

Reference

1. Ivan Berger, "The Virtues of a Second Screen," *The New York Times*, April 20, 2006 (http://nytimes.com/2006/04/20/technology/20basics.html).

Index

427